KU-236-667

Excusing Crime

Jeremy Horder

OXFORD
UNIVERSITY PRESS

UNIVERSITY OF WINCHESTER

OXFORD

UNIVERSITY PRESS

Great Clarendon Street, Oxford OX2 6DP

Oxford University Press is a department of the University of Oxford.
It furthers the University's objective of excellence in research, scholarship,
and education by publishing worldwide in

Oxford New York

Auckland Cape Town Dar es Salaam Hong Kong Karachi
Kuala Lumpur Madrid Melbourne Mexico City Nairobi
New Delhi Shanghai Taipei Toronto

With offices in

Argentina Austria Brazil Chile Czech Republic France Greece
Guatemala Hungary Italy Japan Poland Portugal Singapore
South Korea Switzerland Thailand Turkey Ukraine Vietnam

Oxford is a registered trade mark of Oxford University Press
in the UK and in certain other countries

Published in the United States
by Oxford University Press Inc., New York

© J Horder 2004

The moral rights of the author have been asserted

Crown copyright material is reproduced under Class Licence
Number C01P0000148 with the permission of OPSI
and the Queen's Printer for Scotland

Database right Oxford University Press (maker)

First published 2004
First published in paperback 2007

All rights reserved. No part of this publication may be reproduced,
stored in a retrieval system, or transmitted, in any form or by any means,
without the prior permission in writing of Oxford University Press,
or as expressly permitted by law, or under terms agreed with the appropriate
reprographics rights organization. Enquiries concerning reproduction
outside the scope of the above should be sent to the Rights Department,
Oxford University Press, at the address above

You must not circulate this book in any other binding or cover
and you must impose the same condition on any acquirer

British Library Cataloguing in Publication Data

Data available

Library of Congress Cataloging in Publication Data

Data available

Typeset by Newgen Imaging Systems (P) Ltd., Chennai, India
Printed in Great Britain
on acid-free paper by
Antony Rowe Ltd., Chippenham, Wiltshire

ISBN 978-0-19-826482-8 (Hbk.)
ISBN 978-0-19-922578-1 (Pbk.)

1 3 5 7 9 10 8 6 4 2

UNIVERSITY OF WINCHESTER

03202992 | 345/HOR
0 A

EXCUSING CRIME

2

THE LIBRARY

UNIVERSITY OF
WINCHESTER

KA 0320299 2

UNIVERSITY OF
WINCHESTER

For Joanne, Alice, John,
Sylvia, and Jane

General Editor's Introduction

This monograph stands out as an original and sustained contribution to the development of coherent criteria for the recognition of excuses for otherwise criminal conduct. Despite uncertainties in English law about the scope of the courts' freedom to create new forms of excuse, the subject has a continuing vitality on several levels. The kind of scholarly exploration of the issues found in this volume is not only important in intellectual terms as a refinement of the doctrinal foundations of the criminal law, but it is also capable of stimulating (directly or by indirect means) initiatives by law reformers, appellate courts, and even judges and lawyers at trial level. Jeremy Horder raises a whole range of issues about the social and political significance of recognizing excuses, and about the preferred analysis of the conditions giving rise to excuses. The book assesses an array of particular excuses, from mercy killing to mistake of law, from duress to due diligence, in the context of an analysis that draws on philosophical argument and much more. This is a fine study that will provide a new point of departure for debates about criminal liability.

Andrew Ashworth

Preface

I hope not too much justification is really needed for writing a book concerned with when and why the law should excuse those who admit having committed wrongdoing intentionally or knowingly. Plenty has been written about justification *and* excuse (some more will be said here, in chapter 3.1); but in discharging the burden of explaining the basis of the vital distinction between those two concepts, it is all too easy to lose sight both of the broad sweep of background explanation for excusing in general, and of the theoretical detail required to explain individual excuses themselves. In seeking to provide both that background justification, and the theoretical detail, this book can be thought of as a companion volume to R. D. Mackay's study of what I would—but he might well not—call (partial) denials of responsibility: insanity, automatism, diminished responsibility and unfitness to plead, in his work entitled *Mental Condition Defences in the Criminal Law* (Oxford: Clarendon Press, 1995).

Very long monographs are nowadays destined to remain unread, and it is inexcusable to do nothing more in a book than simply repeat or refine what one has already made tolerably clear in articles elsewhere. So, I have tried to stay reasonably brief in what I have to say (within the constraints imposed by the need to take others' arguments with the seriousness they deserve), and relatively fresh in my thinking. No doubt, in both respects, the book could have been very considerably improved. In the writing of the book, I have tried not to trespass too much on the valuable time of colleagues; but I have learned a great deal from comments on previous drafts of particular chapters that I have received from Andrew Ashworth and Victor Tadros, and in discussions on particular aspects with Antony Duff, Stephen Shute, Grant Lamond, and William Wilson. I should mark out Andrew Ashworth for special thanks, for his unfailing tolerance of the less well-directed of my theoretical enthusiasms, over what has now been nearly twenty years. I also benefited very considerably from the chance to present earlier drafts of chapters at staff seminars at the universities of Birmingham and Nottingham, at the kind invitation of Stephen Shute and Andrew Simester, respectively. I hope they will feel that the profound impact that their own comments had on the direction my work is evident now. Most of all, I am grateful for the impact on my thinking of the work on excuses, and on the theory of criminal law more generally, already done by friends and colleagues—work that sometimes comes in for close and critical scrutiny in this book. Along with those mentioned above, these include: Alan Brudner, John Finnis, John Gardner, Timothy Macklem, Michael Moore, Alan Norrie, Joseph Raz, and Bob Sullivan. Without the guidance of all those who have ventured down similar theoretical paths before me, there would hardly have been a book worth writing. I am also delighted to thank Falcon Chambers, Falcon Court, London, for the opportunity to do so much of the work towards this book whilst accommodated in their premises off Fleet Street. It was a privilege to work in such distinguished legal company. Finally, thanks to John Louth, and Gwen Booth (both of OUP), and to Sara Smith, Worcester College, Oxford, for her help in the preparation of the final manuscript (with apologies for mis-pronouncing her name on degree day!).

Jeremy Horder
St Benedict's Day, 2003

Preface to the paperback edition

Since the first publication of this book in 2004, courts and commentators have not been idle. The doctrine of provocation has been restored to the state in which it was left by *DPP v Camplin* [1978] AC 705, by the decision of the Privy Council in *A-G for Jersey v Holley* [2005] UKPC 23. I have noted this crucial development where possible, within the severe limits imposed by the need to avoid re-paginating. However, the original extensive discussion of the ill-fated decision of the House of Lords in *R v (Morgan) Smith* [2001] 1 AC 14 is still warranted because it represents not just a difference of judicial opinion, but a key difference in theoretical approach. The House of Lords has also (rightly) affirmed the importance of taking an 'evaluative' approach to cases where the circumstances of duress have been mistaken: *R v Z* [2005] UKHL 22. I also take comfort from what seems to me to have been the development of a theoretical approach to defences supportive of my own, by William Wilson, 'The Structure of Defences' [2005] *Crim LR* 108.

Jeremy Horder
St Sylvester's Day, 2007

Contents

Table of Cases

Table of Legislation

Statutory Instruments

European Conventions

Introduction

In what circumstances should people be excused when they have, perhaps intentionally or knowingly, committed criminal wrongdoing?[1] In seeking to answer this question, I will be exploring in depth the theoretical underpinning of existing excuses, and through such exploration calling into question the rationale for the restricted range of such excuses in most legal systems. I will not, though, be providing very detailed explanation of the existing law in any given legal system. The excellence of the treatment of excuses to be found in modern criminal law textbooks,[2] means that the writer of a monograph on this subject has to a large extent now been freed from the obligation to perform this task, and can concentrate more fully than a textbook writer could realistically hope to do on why things are as they are, and on how they should be. In what respects, then, can this work claim to have something new to say about excuses for criminal wrongdoing? As we will see, in chapters 4–6, I argue in favour of three excuses that currently have, at best, only limited or partial recognition in criminal law: 'diminished capacity', 'due diligence' and 'demands of conscience' excuses. Important though they are to this work, however, it is not in respecting the detail of these excuses that any special claim to originality will be made. I hope that a different way of thinking about excuses emerges from three arguments or approaches that are made or adopted in chapters 1–3, and at the beginning of chapters 4 and 5.

First, there is the argument in chapter 1 in favour of a distinction between the necessary conditions for a claim to be classified in theory as genuinely excusatory (conditions which are relatively easily met), and the sufficient conditions that must be met if such an excusatory claim is to be treated as one that ought to be recognized in law (conditions which are much harder to meet). In a way that has not been properly brought out in other examinations of excuses, I suggest that the sufficiency conditions are shaped

---

[1] My main focus will be cases in which the claim to excuse is for wrongdoing that may have been quite intentionally or knowingly committed, because it is cases of this kind that pose the most difficult moral questions. I will not focus *specifically* on actual or potential excuses for unintentional wrongdoing, as by mistake or clumsiness, although a good deal will be said along the way about such instances of claims to excuse.

[2] See, for example, Andrew Ashworth, *Principles of Criminal Law* (Oxford: Oxford University Press, 1995), 3rd edn., chapter 6; William Wilson, *Criminal Law: Doctrine and Theory* (Harlow: Longman, 2003), 2nd edn., chapter 9; A. P. Simester and G. R. Sullivan, *Criminal Law: Theory and Doctrine* (Oxford: Hart Publishing, 2000), 1st edn., chapters 16–19 and 21.

and determined by strategic concerns or 'common goods' that connect the recognition of an excusing condition in law with the maintenance and enhancement of moral respect for the role played by the criminal law within the legal system as a whole. It is a mistake to suppose that only the creation of *offences* represents criminal law's contribution to society's commitment to the common good of upholding respect for the individual and general interests of persons, whereas the creation of defences—and excuses, in particular—represents no more than a concession to the individual weaknesses that may lead people into wrongdoing that conflicts with that common good. On the contrary, the way in which excuses—and defences, more generally—are defined and restricted, through the sufficiency conditions examined in chapter 1, is shaped by considerations of the common good every bit as much as the definition and scope of offences. In that regard, though, it would also be a mistake to see in the distinction between the necessary and the sufficient conditions of excuse a distinction between matters of (intrinsically valuable) 'principle', and matters of (only instrumentally valuable) 'policy'. The sufficiency conditions that excuse claims must satisfy to be worthy of legal recognition are partly *constitutive* of a morally sound and flourishing criminal law, and can thus themselves have intrinsic value. They are not, as libertarian and critical legal scholars are alike wont to suppose, simply authoritarian or (in some other way) 'politically' motivated restrictions on how far one can accommodate in law what are perceived to be morally sound claims to excuse, restrictions which, it is more or less openly admitted, are kept in place simply to ensure that the governing capacity of the criminal law is not unduly weakened.

Secondly, in chapter 2, there is something different to be found in the employment of concepts from the philosophy of practical reason to the analysis of excusing conditions. So, for example, we will see that most duress and provocation cases are focused principally on the 'operative' (desire-based) reason for someone's action, whereas mistake cases are focused principally on the 'auxiliary' (belief-based) reason for someone's action. Further, all these excuses are analysed in terms of three different dimensions to excusatory claims that are distinguished in chapter 2. First, there is the distinction between 'explanatory' and 'adopted' reasons for acting wrongly, a distinction that—in one way—challenges the claim to moral primacy of the distinction between intentional and unintentional wrongdoing. Then there is the distinction between 'actively justificatory' and 'capacity-focused' claims to excuse, and the distinction between predominantly normative and predominantly ascriptive claims to excuse, distinctions all too commonly run together in accounts of excusing conditions. A claim to excuse can be actively justificatory, such as a mistake ('I *thought* I was doing something permissible'), but predominantly ascriptive ('I should not be blamed, although what I did was plainly wrong'). But an excusatory claim can also, like some duress cases, be capacity-focused ('although I knew I was doing wrong, no one could reasonably have been expected to contain their fear for their own safety'), whilst also being predominantly normative ('I did not *by much* exceed what would have been a permissible choice of evils'). Linking all these cases together as recognized claims to excuse, however, is the fact that they can be explained by what can be called the 'classical' view of excusing conditions. This is a view with a long intellectual and legal heritage, according to which what marks out the necessary conditions for an excuse is that there is some rational defect in a moving force—be it predominantly operative reason, or predominantly auxiliary reason—behind the action. An action can be rationally defective, *inter alia*, because the sheer phenomenological strength of a desire (to escape a threat; to retaliate in anger) prevents or severely inhibits the rational direction of conduct by an agent, or because ignorance of crucial guiding reasons means that the action will not adequately reflect the balance of reasons and will hence not take a rational direction.[3] In the classical view of excusing conditions, when an action has a rational defect of such a kind in its moving force, there is case for excuse if and when it is judged that even someone well-equipped with rational powers (of self-control, of foresight, and so forth) might well also have acted in that—rationally defective—way, in the circumstances.

The third and final claim to originality in this work will be the way in which it is suggested that we must move beyond the classical account of excusing conditions. As we will see at the start of chapter 5, some left-wing thinkers have associated the classical view of excusing conditions with a supposedly 'liberal' outlook on the scope of excuses, attacking the limited vision of the classical view in order to bolster their critique of liberalism as a moral, political and legal philosophy; but it will be argued that this association is a mistaken one. On the contrary, the narrow scope of excusing conditions endorsed by the classical view is just as at home—and perhaps more at home—in authoritarian legal regimes than in liberal ones. A truly liberal view of excusing conditions will go well beyond the limits of rational defects in the moving force behind conduct, and hence beyond the classical view of excuses. I try to give new impetus to the development of excuses by formulating a truly liberal vision of their scope, a vision that—as will be claimed in chapter 1 and chapter 6—it is not beyond the jurisprudential competence of the courts, in common law jurisdictions, to do at least something to turn into a reality. The liberal credentials of the theory stem from its foundation in two well-known but under-employed injunctions, held to

---

[3] Some, otherwise highly classical, thinkers, like H. L. A. Hart, include mental disorder amongst those causes of a rational defect in the motive force behind an action that can have an excusatory effect; but the more purely classical view of excuses treats such instances of rational defect as denials of responsibility rather than as excuses, because in such cases there are usually no moral benchmarks by which to judge whether rationally defective actions were more or less understandable, in the circumstances: see the discussion of Hart's views, and the contrast with Aristotle's views, in chapter 1, and the brief discussion in chapter 3.1.

be binding on the liberal state by Ronald Dworkin: the obligation to treat
people with 'concern', as capable of suffering and frustration, and also with
'respect', as people capable of forming and acting on intelligent, active conceptions of what is worthwhile.[4] The obligation to treat people with concern
generates the need to recognize, as genuinely excusatory, some claims to at
least partial excuse for wrongdoing, by those with mental deficiencies falling
short of insanity or diminished responsibility (as these are currently understood). The nature of these claims is explored in chapter 4. In the classical
view of excuses, instances in which the cause of a rational defect in the motivating force behind an action is mental disorder or deficiency, are to be
sharply distinguished from truly excusatory claims focused on such defects.
The former are to be treated instead as purported denials of responsibility,
because it makes no ethical sense morally to *judge* rational failings attributable to mental disorder. So, the standards of conduct that would have been
observed, in the circumstances, by someone adequately equipped with
rational powers, judgmental standards central to the very idea of an excuse
for wrongdoing (as we will see in chapter 1), are quite irrelevant. In the classical view, there is no *tertium quid*. In a liberal account of excuses, however,
subject to important restrictions dictated by 'common good' considerations,
it ought sometimes to be possible to make a genuine claim to partial excuse,
even though the wrongdoing in question is to some extent attributable to
a mental deficiency insufficient to amount to a denial of responsibility. This
can be done if and when someone fell prey to the effect of the disorder or deficiency only because of the effect of circumstantial pressure (such as provocation or duress), a response to which *can* be judged by the moral standards of
people well-equipped with rational powers. More generally, these arguments
are developed in the light of an examination of sentencing policy in cases
where someone is partially excused. For reasons that will become clear, it is
proposed that the normal sentence when someone is acquitted of a 'first-
degree offence', and convicted only of what will be called a 'second-degree
offence', should be a non-custodial sentence, even in provocation cases where
the victim was intentionally killed. By way of contrast, it is the obligation to
treat people with respect that generates the need to develop the 'demands-of-
conscience' excuse, and the 'due diligence' excuse, discussed in chapters 5 and 6
respectively. In both these cases, people may be in a position to give fully
rational assent to their conduct at the time of acting, taking their claims outside the scope of the classical view of excuses. It is the moral force behind the
claim—the claim that someone reasonably regarded him- or herself as not free
to abandon his or her beliefs in order to remain law-abiding, or that someone
had done everything humanly possible to avoid wrongdoing—that drives
the liberal imperative to create the excusatory space in question, in each
case. As we will see, at least some such claims must be set apart from other
potential claims to excuse which appear to be of a broadly similar kind, as

[4] Ronald Dworkin, *Taking Rights Seriously* (London: Duckworth, 1977), 272.

when someone appeals to the sense of injustice that, as they see it, compelled them to steal from the rich to give to the poor. What divides the two kinds of case is the role that considerations of the common good—the sufficiency conditions—play in dictating how limited the excusatory space (if any) is to be in each case. Whilst, in 'demands-of-conscience' and 'due diligence' cases, such considerations or conditions permit, but carefully delimit, such space, in what one might call the 'Robin Hood' case, the same considerations or conditions eliminate the case for an excuse altogether.

Putting aside the suggestions for sentencing policy in partial excuse cases, the arguments offered here will be all too familiar in one respect. They are firmly within the tradition of so-called 'analytical', or—more correctly— 'applied ethical' thinking about law, and they are in that respect aimed at judges in the higher courts, and at other law reforming bodies, as well as at law students. In that regard, Lindsay Farmer has recently argued that such an approach to the criminal law is largely an irrelevance. Farmer says, 'most judges are probably too busy to read or engage with [such] arguments,' and that the arguments will be '[t]oo abstract for the policy maker and too difficult for the average undergraduate law student', leaving them to be read only by other criminal law theorists.[5] I hope it will not be thought to detract from the high regard in which I hold his work in general if I suggest that Farmer's criticisms fall very wide of the mark. Undergraduate law students are at least as intelligent and well-qualified, at the point of entry to university, as undergraduate philosophy students, the latter being asked straight away to get to grips with material considerably more abstract and more philosophically (if not intellectually) demanding than that found in the writings of criminal law theorists. What really distinguishes each body of students is, of course, the expectations each has of what their respective courses will involve reading; but in university study—as in recommendations academics think it right to make to policy makers—the audience's expectations are sometimes to be confounded, not simply met. When it comes to the question whether judges are 'too busy' to engage with criminal law theory, that they are not too busy for this is amply illustrated by the case law itself.

Let me give just one example (there are others[6]) of an instance in which, far from simply relying on an argument already made by a criminal law theorist—these are too numerous to be worth listing here—a court went *beyond* any existing legal—theoretical writing in search of the illumination that can be provided by a philosophical perspective on practical problems. In *Re A (Children) (conjoined twins: surgical separation)*,[7] the Court of Appeal was faced with the question whether it should sanction an operation

---

[5] Farmer, Lindsay, reviewing Stephen Shute and A. P. Simester (eds.), *Criminal Law Theory: Doctrines of the General Part* (Oxford: Oxford University Press, 2002), (2003) 23 *Legal Studies* 369.

[6] See, for example, the use of Cartesian philosophy to analyse the doctrine of provocation in the speech of Lord Hoffmann in *R v (Morgan) Smith* [2001] 1 AC 146, 160–61.

[7] [2000] 4 All ER 961 (CA).

to separate conjoined twins that would inevitably result in the swift death of one (weaker) twin whilst being very likely to save the life of the other (stronger) twin in the longer term, in circumstances where both would die soon without the operation. One important question for the court was whether it would, in effect, be judicially approved murder to order that the weaker twin be separated from her stronger sister, and hence whether the weaker twin was a 'reasonable creature' protected by the law of murder according to Lord Coke's famous understanding of who can be a victim of murder (3 *Co Inst* 50). Brooke LJ said, of this possibility:

Spurred on by this suggestion . . . we explored with counsel some of the thinking of seventeenth century English philosophers in an effort to ascertain what Coke may have meant when he used the term 'any reasonable creature' as part of his definition. We had in mind their absorbing interest in the nature of 'strange and deformed births' and 'monstrous births' (see Thomas Hobbes, *Elements of Law* (1640, part II, ch. 10, section 8)), and John Locke, *An Essay Concerning Human Understanding* (1690, Book III, ch. III, section 17, Book III, ch. VI, section 15 and 26 and Book III, ch. XI, section 20).[8]

Philosophical argument cannot tell people what values they should believe in, any more than sociological research can; but, like sociological research, it can unseat or shake the assumptions on which such value-related beliefs may be based. When it is the assumptions lying behind the values embodied in law that are in issue, legal academics simply fail in one of their duties if they do not seek to subject these assumptions to scrutiny, and philosophical analysis can be as crucial in this task as any other form of analysis. *Excusing Crime* seeks to make a modest contribution along just such lines.

[8] [2000] 4 All ER 961 1025.

1

The Domain of Excuses: A Theoretical Overview

1. THE NECESSARY CONDITIONS OF EXCUSE

No criminal lawyer seriously entertains the proposition that a criminal law code should avoid making any space for excuses, whilst providing for justifications. One reason for this is that any attempt to shut out excusatory claims, whilst permitting claims of justification, would involve sheer arbitrariness. By way of example, in a case where conduct falls on the boundary between the outer limits of (justifiable) reasonable defensive force and the beginning of (more or less, excusable) excessive force, it is hard to tell just when a genuinely justificatory claim ends and an essentially excusatory one begins.[1] Moreover, in some instances,[2] such as possession of an offensive weapon or obstruction of the highway, so long as D's[3] explanation respectively for the possession or for the obstruction is sound enough to make criminal conviction morally inappropriate, it may make little or no difference whether that explanation is rightly categorized as a good excuse or as an adequate justification. Either should amount to a sufficient case for an acquittal.[4] More broadly, in principle, it ought to be recognized that to any criminal charge there may be an answer or explanation that would make it morally repugnant to convict in the circumstances, even if the elements of the offence are made out, and even if there were understandable reasons

---

[1] By way of contrast with a number of other common law jurisdictions, 'excessive defence' is not, as such, an excuse or partial excuse in English law, even in murder cases: *R v Clegg* [1995] 1 AC 482. As we will see, English law overcomes this problem by somewhat artificially stretching its understanding of the limits of conduct justified in self-defence: see the discussion in chapter 2.4 below. In itself, this may be no bad thing, but the artificiality involved ought more openly to be recognized. The issues have recently been addressed by the Law Commission for England and Wales, *Partial Defences to Murder*, Law Commission Consultation Paper No 173 (HMSO, 2003), part 9.

[2] Principally, those where even the *prima facie* wrongfulness of D's conduct may depend on the reasons he or she gives for the conduct in question.

[3] In spite of the slight awkwardness, I shall use the short forms 'D' and 'V' throughout, as is now quite common practice, rather than the full forms 'defendant' and 'victim' respectively.

[4] So, for example, section 139(4) of the Criminal Justice Act 1988 provides that it is a defence—in relation to a charge of possessing an offensive weapon in a public place—'for a person . . . to prove that he had *good reason or lawful authority* for having the article with him in a public place' (my emphasis). No distinction is drawn, here, between the justificatory case ('lawful authority'), and the potentially excusatory one ('good reason').

why a prosecution was brought in the first place. In practice, such cases will stretch well beyond those involving circumstances of justification. For these reasons, although excuses may vary in nature and extent from one jurisdiction to the next, they have found a place even in the most unforgiving of criminal codes.[5]

So, what is an excuse? There are different ways of seeking to answer this question. It would be possible to concentrate solely on the development of excuses in the courts. Alternatively, one could seek to elaborate on the extensive discussion of how excuses are to be distinguished from justifications, and on whether excuses should be distinguished from denials of responsibility such as insanity or infancy.[6] Although these important demarcation disputes will inevitably be confronted from time to time, by and large an attempt is made to plot a different course in this work. Putting on one side detailed consideration of the tangled web of authority that now purports to govern excuses in English law, I ask what kind of claim an excusatory claim is (chapter 1), what is the best way to understand the theoretical foundation of excuses (chapters 2 and 3) what kind of excuses there could and should be (chapters 4, 5 and 6), and what the consequences of successful excusatory pleas should be (chapter 4). In other words, I try to keep the focus on the kinds of claim that ought to excuse, in whole or in part, rather than solely on the way in which excuses take their place within the hierarchy of defences.[7] In that regard, to return to the question posed at the beginning of the paragraph, I shall be adopting a broad definition of the kind of claims that can count as genuine candidates for excuse, in general terms; but I shall also be adopting a relatively narrow or restrictive understanding of the circumstances in which, as it were, candidature should be successful. The law should set stiff conditions to be met if an excuse (broadly defined) is to be formally recognized within a criminal code. We can think of the difference between the considerations that make a claim a candidate for excuse, and the conditions that must be satisfied if the candidature is to be successful, as a difference between the necessary and the sufficient conditions for an excusing condition to be recognizable in law.

To be recognizable as such, it is a necessary condition of any claim to excuse that it is an explanation for engagement in wrongdoing (an explanation not best understood as a justification, as a simple claim of involuntariness, or as an out-and-out denial of responsibility) that sheds such a favourable moral

---

[5] Mistake, for example, finds a place, in the guise of the denial of intention in homicide cases, under shari'a law: see G. D. Baroody, *Crime and Punishment under Islamic Law*, 2nd edn. (London: Regency Press, 1979), 10–11.

[6] For recent discussion of the former issue, see M. L. Corrado (ed.), *Justification and Excuse in the Criminal Law* (New York: Garland, 1994). For some recent discussion of the latter issue, see John Gardner, 'The Gist of Excuses' (1998) 1 *Buffalo Criminal Law Review* 575; Jeremy Horder, 'Criminal Law: Between Determinism, Liberalism and Criminal Justice' (1996) 49 *Current Legal Problems* 159.

[7] For a defence of the view that there is, morally speaking, a theoretical 'hierarchy' of defences, see chapter 3.1 below.

light on D's conduct that it seems entirely wrong to convict, at least for the full offence.[8] So defined, claims that are candidates for excuse overlap to some extent with claims treated as claims for mitigation of sentence; but claims that meet the necessary conditions for excuse are by no means just the most pressing of the claims for mitigation of sentence that D might plausibly make. Excuses are morally as well as legally distinctive in character. Excuses excuse the act or omission amounting to wrongdoing, by shedding favourable moral light on what D did through a focus on the reasons that D committed that wrongdoing, where those reasons played a morally 'active' role in D's conduct (meaning that what D did or what happened to D can be subject to critical moral evaluation).[9] So long as those reasons did play a morally active role in D's conduct, it can still be appropriate to speak of the case for 'excusing' D, even when D combines a factor (duress, say, or provocation) with respect to which he or she was morally active, with a factor (mental disorder, say, or involuntariness), with respect to which he or she was morally 'passive'.[10] The existence of a morally active dimension to what happened to D or to what D did, means that the event stands to be evaluated in the light of underlying 'guiding' reasons, reasons that dictate how D *ought* (not) to have behaved, in failing to control his or her nerves, or in losing his or her temper, as well as in striking someone, and so forth.[11] The applicability of guiding reasons gives rise to the critical, judgmental or evaluative element in a claim, making it to at least some extent excusatory, even if its potential for success must sometimes turn in part on the influence of some morally passive physical or mental weakness or deficiency, on which guiding reasons can have no bearing. I will say more about the excusatory character and potential of reasons with respect to which D is morally active in a moment. It follows, though, that excuses ought to be distinguished from out-and-out denials of responsibility, of the kind constituted by a claim to acquittal focused solely

[8] The phraseology of 'favourable light' is taken from John Gardner, 'The Gist of Excuses', 578, where he contrasts the possibility that wrongful conduct will be shown up in a favourable light with the possibility that conduct could be shown up in a not unfavourable light, or an indifferent light. I do not want to make more of these additional distinctions, although they can clearly be made to serve a theoretical purpose, in that the amount of favourable moral light shed on one's conduct is a matter of degree.

[9] On the morally active side to our natures, see chapter 2.7–2.9 below. In spite of the apparent focus exclusively on human individuals in this work, corporate Ds are not beyond its compass in any significant way. Their actions always stand to be evaluated in the light of guiding reasons, because their decisions, customs, practices, and so forth ought to have a rational justification and to be subject to rational scrutiny. Even so, the analysis in chapter 6 below is perhaps of the greatest relevance to corporate Ds.

[10] Chapter 4 below is devoted to discussion of the case for excusing when D seeks to combine evidence of mental disorder with a factor such as duress or provocation.

[11] See Joseph Raz, *Practical Reason and Norms* (Oxford: Oxford University Press, 1990), 15–19, for an explanation of 'guiding' reasons. See John Gardner, 'Justifications and Reasons', in A. P. Simester and A. T. H. Smith (eds.), *Harm and Culpability* (Oxford: Clarendon Press, 1996), 103, for an explanation of the distinction between explanatory and guiding reasons. I shall be dividing the notion of explanatory reasons into 'adopted' and 'explanatory' reasons. For detailed consideration, see chapter 2.2 below.

on the effects of a severe mental disorder or deficiency (such as insanity). For, in such cases, guiding reasons—reasons concerned with how D ought to have behaved—have no moral significance, and we cannot judge D's conduct objectively in the light of an applicable moral standard.[12]

Excusatory reasons, with respect to which one is morally active, can be divided into two general kinds, 'explanatory' reasons and 'adopted' reasons.[13] Adopted reasons are reasons that (even in the blink of an eye) one positively chooses to or makes one's mind up to act on, whereas explanatory reasons are not. An explanatory reason is a reason why something happened to one or why one acted in a certain way, whether accidentally (as in the case of clumsiness) *or* intentionally, without choice or decision, but where there was still a morally active dimension to what happened or to what was done.[14] If a dancer accidentally trips, and in so doing, treads on his or her partner's toes, the accident may be treated as a straightforward denial of voluntariness, on the basis that what happened was a freak accident that could have happened to anyone. There is, though, the potential for an excusatory issue to emerge from behind this categorization of what happens to the dancer. Guiding reasons—in the form of reasons not to tread on someone's toes—clearly have a particular moral salience when one is dancing with a partner; and one can seek to guard against accidents. So, there will always potentially be an issue about whether the dancer could reasonably and should have done more to avoid tripping, bearing in mind the need, in context, to keep his or her dance movements fluid, spontaneous and well timed, etc. This is a classic capacity-focused, excusatory issue, where the dancer's plea, 'I could not, in the circumstances, reasonably have been expected to do more to avoid tripping and hence treading on my partner's toes', is an explanatory (excusatory) reason.[15] We should note, further, that the dancer's claim remains in some sense excusatory in character, even if he or she puts

[12] On the importance of this, as a distinguishing mark of claims to acquittal that are truly excusatory, see chapter 3.2 below. See also Jeremy Horder, 'Criminal Law: Between Determinism, Liberalism and Criminal Justice'; John Gardner, 'The Gist of Excuses'. As we shall see in chapter 3 below, my account of excusatory claims parts company with Gardner's at the point where pleas are not 'out-and-out' denials of responsibility, but are mixed with an excusatory element that can be evaluated in the light of an applicable standard. For me, but not for him, such claims (the most well known are some pleas falling just within the outer limits of diminished responsibility) can be treated as excusatory ones.

[13] A distinction examined in more depth in chapter 2.2 below. In Gardner's usage, what I am treating as separate kinds of reason—explanatory and adopted—are treated simply as explanatory reasons: see John Gardner, 'Justifications and Reasons'.

[14] So, the distinction I am drawing, being one that can include a contrast between two forms of action that are both intentional under some description, cuts across Aristotle's much more familiar distinction between 'doing wrong' (*adikein*), and doing something that is merely in fact wrong (*per accidens*): see further, J. L. Ackrill, *Essays on Plato and Aristotle* (Oxford: Clarendon Press, 1997), 215. The case for not setting great theoretical store only by the distinction between intentional and unintentional conduct, when explanatory—as opposed to adopted—reasons are in issue, is made in chapter 2.2 below.

[15] For a discussion of the capacity basis of excuses, see chapter 3 below. Of course, that a claim by someone such as the dancer can, morally speaking, be regarded as excusatory in

the whole episode down to his or her clumsiness. In such a case, the dancer gives a reason why the accident occurred that relates to an individual condition or disposition (the clumsiness), with respect to which he or she should be regarded as to a degree morally active, and hence for the manifestation of which he or she must thus accept some moral responsibility. Even though the clumsy dancer's claim resembles a claim of simple involuntariness, clumsy people can usually try with some prospect of success to be less clumsy, if they absolutely have to (this is the morally active dimension to what the dancer did). So, the issue is whether the dancer could and should have done more to keep his or her tendencies to clumsiness under control, given the need also to keep his or her dance movements fluid, well timed, and so on. As in the initial example where the dancer simply trips, this issue involves a capacity-focused question of excuse, even though there is now a more 'individualized' character to that question than there is to the question how much, in general, competent dancers should do to avoid treading on their partner's toes. In that regard, the question how much care we can reasonably expect *D him-* or *herself* to take is an excusatory question, albeit not the same excusatory question as the question how much care we can expect of competent dancers in general. The distinction between subjective and objective versions of the capacity theory of excuses that this example exploits will be examined in more detail in chapter 3.6 below.

In the case of intentional conduct, when one seeks excuse by putting a killing down to an instantaneous loss of self-control (provocation), or ascribing to the impact of sheer terror an 'instinctive' defensive response that is too heavy-handed (excessive defence), one may also be giving an explanatory reason for the action. In such cases, the phenomenological strength of the desire at the heart of the emotion (the urge to kill; the desire to ensure the attack is thwarted) spontaneously eclipses or bypasses the restraining or moderating power of reason. So the actions taken, albeit intentional, are not chosen: they are not based on 'adopted' reasons.[16] Indeed, in the kind of

---

character does not mean that that character will be what gives it a legal significance. In law, the question is always, 'what effect does D's claim have, if any, on the specific legal wrong in issue?' It will sometimes be the case that the mere fact that someone tripped gives him or her grounds to deny the fault element (intention; foresight) in that wrong. This being so, in law, one need not probe deeper to explore the potentially excusatory factors at play behind the fact that the person in question tripped. In law, someone can perfectly well say, 'there was no excuse (morally) for tripping, but the brute fact is that, in tripping, I did at that moment not realize I would end up making painful contact with V'. Even so, the excusatory issues are liable to come to the surface when, say, it is D's own fault that he did not have the relevant mental element, as when D is voluntarily intoxicated: see Simon Gardner, 'The Importance of *Majewski*' (1994) 14 *Oxford Journal of Legal Studies* 279, and Jeremy Horder, 'Sobering Up? The Law Commission on Criminal Intoxication' (1995) 58 *Modern Law Review* 534.

[16] Which is not to say that, when one gives an explanatory reason for engaging in intentional conduct, one is of necessity conceding that what was done was irrational. There is nothing necessarily inherently more rational about conduct whose motive force is an adopted reason, as opposed to an explanatory reason: see chapter 2.8 below.

cases I have in mind, the actions bear some family resemblances to conduct
that is involuntary, as in the case, say, of clumsy actions. Nonetheless, there
is clearly still an evaluative dimension to what D does. As we will see in
chapter 2.8–2.9 below, we can still ask whether D should have let his or her
temper, or terror, get the better of him or her to the extent that it did. As Derek
Parfit puts it, conduct that is, 'not deserving the extreme charge "irrational"
[may, nonetheless, be] open to rational criticism'.[17] One must, however, take
care with examples of this kind, in general (angry or fearful actions). People
who are provoked to anger, or fearful of threats, can sometimes still remain in
evaluative control of their consequent conduct throughout, and can hence
make genuine—reasoned—choices, even if they are not the choices they
would have made in a calm frame of mind.[18] How do all such actions, actions
based on an *adopted* reason (a reason D chose to act on) come to be excused,
whether or not they are grounded in an emotional reaction?

There are different routes to excuse for such actions, actions based on
adopted reasons, which is why it is important to have a broad understanding
of the necessary conditions of excuse. Finding an understandable 'rational
defect' in a morally salient motivating force or factor behind an action is perhaps the most commonly encountered route to excuse, particularly but not
solely where the action is grounded in a strong emotional reaction.[19] In a case
of angry or fearful action, D might claim that the phenomenological strength of
an understandable emotion (D's 'operating' reason)[20] so diminished in significance any countervailing evaluative considerations that the wrongful
course seemed overwhelmingly attractive or proper, in a way it could and
should never rationally have done. By way of contrast with the examples discussed in the preceding paragraph, however, in such cases it is still correct to
say that D chooses his or her action from the balance of applicable reasons.[21]

---

[17] Derek Parfit, *Reasons and Persons* (Oxford: Oxford University Press, 1984), 119, cited in
this form by John Gardner and Timothy Macklem, 'Reasons', in J. Coleman and S. Shapiro
(eds.), *The Oxford Handbook of Jurisprudence and Philosophy of Law* (Oxford: Oxford
University Press, 2002), 444 n. 4.

[18] See e.g. the discussion in Jeremy Horder, *Provocation and Responsibility* (Oxford: Oxford
University Press, 1992) chapter 5. As we will see, it can be controversial whether a plea should
excuse if the action was founded on an adopted reason, whatever the influence of the additional
element of human weakness or deficiency. Provocation cases are like this. The case for excusing serious violence in such cases is much weaker where D *decides to* make his or her anger
grounds for retaliation (where retaliation is his or her adopted reason for action), as compared
with the case where a loss of self-control is merely the explanatory reason for the retaliatory
conduct: see chapter 2.12 below.

[19] See Michael S. Moore, *Placing Blame* (Oxford: Clarendon Press, 1998), 538, '[M]oral
excuses, like legal excuses, are not based on causation, but on interference with practical
reasoning'. This builds on his analysis, in similar terms, in Michael S. Moore, *Law and
Psychiatry: Rethinking the Relationship* (Cambridge: Cambridge University Press, 1984).

[20] For the distinction between operating and auxiliary reasons, see chapter 2.7 below.

[21] I do not mean that D spends time weighing up competing considerations before coming
to a decision, although that is possible. D simply chooses to act for the reason that seems
best, something that can happen quickly and spontaneously but does not involve a 'loss of

D's choice hence has some of the hallmarks of a rational choice, but is a defective example of such a choice, for the reasons just given. So, for example, in an excessive defence case, the fulfilment of the necessary conditions for excuse could hinge on a finding that the sheer strength of D's fear made the choice of a heavy-handed course of action as a means of thwarting an attack *seem* entirely rational and proper, but only because of the mental domination achieved by the desire to ensure that the attack is thwarted. To give a different kind of example, a morally salient rational defect in a motivating factor behind the action also underpins the excusatory element in many factual mistake cases where, as things turn out, the mistake leads D into wrongdoing.[22] In such cases, D commonly acts for an adopted reason, deciding on or choosing a course of action in a normal way. So, D's choice appears to have some of the hallmarks of a rational choice. D chooses that course of action, though, in the more-or-less understandably mistaken belief that a state of affairs exists (D's 'auxiliary' reason)[23] that makes a crucial—morally salient— difference to the rational justification for that course of action, when no such state of affairs really exists. So, there is a rational defect lying behind D's choice. These different kinds of rational defects in morally salient motivating forces or factors behind actions can, of course, combine. So, one might be mistaken about the existence or nature of provocation (one kind of rational defect) that then led one into precipitate action following a loss of self-control (another sort of rational defect).[24]

These kinds of mistake cases, in which the existence of a rational defect in a morally salient motivating force or factor behind D's choice does important excusatory work,[25] are very different from cases where the adopted reason for which D commits the wrongdoing reflects a salient *moral* mistake. This happens where, for example, D decides (adopted reason) to abide by the demands of his or her religion as a matter of conscience, even though to do

---

self-control', or being overwhelmed by some other emotion: see J. L. Austin, 'A Plea for Excuses', reprinted in M. L. Corrado (ed.), *Justification and Excuse in the Criminal Law*. A choice can be rational when it has this character. As administrative lawyers are all-too-well aware, however, a choice can be rational but unjustified. That D, in an excessive defence case, took the defensive steps that seemed to him or her best at the time, does not—very obviously—guarantee that that course of action will be justified. A choice is normally only justified when it reflects a reason that is one of those that—either by itself or with the support of other reasons—is on the 'winning' side in the balance, objectively judged: see John Gardner, 'Justifications and Reasons'.

[22] On mistakes as denials of the mental element, in law, as opposed to the foundation of an excusatory claim, see n. 15 above.

[23] For the distinction between operating and auxiliary reasons, see chapter 2.7 below.

[24] This possibility is anticipated in *R v Graham* [1982] 74 Cr App Rep 235, 241, on which see chapter 2.9 below.

[25] Naturally, the question whether or not D's mistake was reasonable may also be made to do excusatory work: see further, chapter 2.9 and 2.10 below. When D had reasonable grounds for thinking he or she was entitled to proceed as he or she did, when what D did was in fact wrong, Heidi Hurd says that D was epistemically justified, but not morally justified, in so acting: Heidi Hurd, 'Justification and Excuse, Wrongdoing and Culpability' (1999) 54 *Notre Dame Law Review* 1551, 1564. This distinction is briefly criticized in chapter 2 below.

so means D will perform acts regarded as wrong in law, a case discussed in chapter 5 below. The defect in the motivation for D's choice here is not rational, but moral: he or she simply gets the balance of reasons wrong by sticking to what conscience demands. D (*ex hypothesi*) understands the demands of his or her religion well enough to know how believers mean them to influence the balance of reasons. So, the excusatory work is now being done by a sense that it is understandable, albeit morally mistaken, to get the balance of reasons wrong by putting conscience-based compliance with religious demands ahead of avoiding legal wrongdoing.[26] Even so, as in all the examples discussed to date, what matters in this category of cases is a capacity-focused question examined in chapter 3.6 below: could and should more have been expected of D, rationally or morally (as the case may be)? This category of case shares something else with those discussed earlier. It is as true of this category of cases as of all the 'adopted reason' cases briefly discussed so far, that the importance to the excuse of the rational or moral defect in a motivating force or factor behind the choice is that the adopted reason is given for doing the very thing that is, in fact, prohibited by law. In other cases, discussed in chapter 6 below, the excusatory focus is on reasons for action D adopted to *avoid* committing wrongdoing, in spite of which the wrongdoing occurred. This is so, for example, when D says he or she should be excused on a 'due diligence' basis (normally, in regulatory cases), because no more could reasonably have been expected than that he or she put in the effort he or she did put in, taking the steps he or she chose to take, to try to ensure that wrongdoing would be avoided. Given that the adopted reasons— the compliance strategy, in effect—bear on steps taken to avoid wrong-doing, rather than being reasons to commit the act involving wrongdoing itself, there is no need for them to manifest some rational or moral defect. Indeed, as we will see in chapter 6 below, it may be that we would not excuse, on a 'due diligence' basis, unless we could find no rational (and still less, moral) fault whatsoever with the compliance strategy D adopted.

Whilst mitigating circumstances can clearly bear on the explanatory or adopted reasons for the act or omission amounting to criminal wrongdoing, there is no necessary conceptual connection between them. It could be right to mitigate a sentence in response to developments after the commission of the act, such as V's forgiveness, or D's co-operation with the authorities. It could also be right to mitigate the sentence in response to, morally, purely passive factors underlying the crime's commission not amounting, as such, to a denial of responsibility, like D's deprived upbringing.[27] Some factors can be mitigating in a non-excusatory way, or can be dealt with as excusatory claims, depending on what it is that 'counts' about them in context. For

---

[26] If it is *not* morally mistaken to take this course of action, of course, D ought to be regarded as fully justified, and should not need to rely on an excuse: see chapter 5.3 below.

[27] For a general discussion, see Andrew Ashworth, *Sentencing and Criminal Justice* (London: Butterworths, 1995), 2nd edn., 133–149.

example, following the definition of the necessary conditions of excuse just given, youth can only be pleaded in an excusatory way if it is tendered as an argument (say) about the understandable nature of the impulsiveness or lack of adequate foresight (i.e. the rational defect in a morally salient motivating force or factor) that lay behind the act itself. Youth can also, though, be relevant to mitigation in a non-excusatory way, i.e. even if it did nothing to shed light on the reasons why D did as he or she did. This would be the case if the court believes that it would be wrong to sentence D for as long a period in prison as someone older, for the same offence, because the impact of the same period of experiencing imprisonment would be disproportionately harsh on a younger person. The example of youth shows, though, that even if a factor can be pleaded in a genuinely excusatory way (in that it meets the necessary conditions for excuse), this obviously does not mean that it ought to gain recognition as a formal excusing condition, rather than being left as a matter for mitigation of sentence. Whether a plea ought to gain recognition as a formal excuse must turn on how significant the sufficiency conditions for an excuse are, in a given kind of case.

2. THE SUFFICIENT CONDITIONS FOR AN EXCUSE

Even armed with an excusatory explanation for wrongdoing of a morally forceful kind, Ds will not meet the sufficiency conditions for the provision of a formal excuse in law for their wrongdoing, unless the case for excuse still seems compelling when the law's 'strategic' or 'common good' concerns have been addressed. In very general terms, a strategic concern is a concern about the need to maintain the integrity and flourishing of a common good that is supported (and perhaps, in part, defined) by law.[28] The moral demands of a legally supported common good should take precedence over lesser moral or non-moral concerns, such as (where citizens are concerned) matters of individual convenience, and purely partisan pleading of special interests, or (where officials are concerned) the temptation to shield from justice those whose understandable but culpable moral failings have led them to act against the common good.[29] In that regard, as John Finnis puts it:

[T]he reasons that justify the vast legal effort to render the law . . . relatively impervious to discretionary assessments of competing values and conveniences are reasons

---

[28] In *Ethics in the Public Domain* (Oxford: Clarendon Press, 1994), 52, Joseph Raz defines a common good as a good that 'refers not to the sum of the good of individuals but to those goods which, in a certain community, serve the interests of people generally in a conflict-free, non-exclusive, and non-excludable way'. He relies on the seminal discussion in J. M. Finnis, *Natural Law and Natural Rights* (Oxford: Clarendon Press, 1980), chapter 6.

[29] Naturally, the demands of the common good shape offences as much as they do defences. It is often claimed, for example, that the law's insistence that people wear seatbelts whilst driving, or helmets whilst motorcycling, is a 'paternalistic' concern; but that would only be true in such cases if an intelligent conception of the good, rather than a matter of simple convenience, was being overridden in the interests of reducing the incidence of costly and harmful accidents.

that . . . relate particularly to the extent, complexity and depth of the social inter-
dependencies which the law . . . attempts to regulate. Such an ambitious attempt as
the law's can only succeed in creating and maintaining order, and a fair order, inasmuch as individuals drastically reduce the occasions on which they trade off their
legal obligations against their individual convenience or conceptions of social
good.[30]

So far as justifications are concerned (although the argument applies with as
much force to excuses), this argument has found legal support in, for example,
the judgment of Dickson J in the decision of the Supreme Court of Canada
in *Perka et al. v R*,[31] in which he said, 'no system of positive law can recognize any principle which would entitle a person to violate the law because
on his view the law conflicted with some higher social value'.[32] So, what are
the strategic legal concerns, or common goods, to which individual convenience, idiosyncratic conceptions of the good, instances of special pleading,
and so forth, are to be subordinated, in the shaping of excusing conditions?[33] In no particular order of importance, at least some could be described
as follows:

(i)   *Maintaining a close match between how a defence—and the prohibitions
      to which it applies—ought morally to be regarded by those whom it gov-
      erns, and by those who must interpret and develop it, and how it is
      regarded.*[34]
(ii) *Preventing the development of defences perverting or distorting,
      amongst citizens and officials alike, a proper understanding of the
      importance (absolute and relative) of personal and proprietary inter-
      ests, along with public or common goods.*

As it happens, when the common good of accident reduction does come into conflict with
a refusal (say) to wear a helmet that is genuinely based on a conception of the good, such as the
religious demand that turbans be worn instead of helmets, the law yields to the moral force of
this conception for the individuals or groups in question: see the Motor-Cycle Crash Helmets
(Religious Exemption) Act 1976. More generally, though, by enforcing these prohibitions the
law is rightly emphasizing the moral significance of the common good in question over what is
(for the vast majority) a matter of simple non-moral convenience, rather than a matter bearing
on their conception of the good.

[30] J. M. Finnis, *Natural Law and Natural Rights*, 319.   [31] (1985) 13 DLR (4th) 1.

[32] Ibid., 14 (my emphasis). Note, however, that Dickson J speaks of individuals purporting
to act for the sake of 'higher value' rather than, as Finnis does, speaking of acting for the sake
of 'individual convenience'. This distinction can matter, in some instances, as we will see in
chapter 5 below in the discussion of the demands of conscience.

[33] Sufficiency conditions for excuse overlap to a substantial degree with those that help to
shape justifications in criminal law, such as consent and necessity, and in the discussion of such
conditions in ensuing sections, both instances of excuse and justification will be a source of
examples. For general discussion, see Jeremy Horder, 'On the Irrelevance of Motive in Criminal
Law', in Jeremy Horder (ed.), *Oxford Essays in Jurisprudence*, 4th Series (Oxford: Oxford
University Press, 2000), 177–184; A. P. Simester and G. R. Sullivan, *Criminal Law: Theory and
Doctrine*, 1st edn. (Oxford: Hart Publishing, 2000), 640–642.

[34] (i) looks in some sense like an overarching concern, only in relation to which do the other
concerns gain moral significance; but I do not want to argue this point here.

(iii) *Ensuring that the availability of defences does not undermine the promotion of a culture of compliance and law-abidingness, in relation to the State's good faith attempts to promote the common good through regulation.*

(iv) *Maintaining, through the provision of appropriate defences, a sense of reciprocity in criminal proceedings, whereby there are, in point of fault, always one or more morally significant answers to the charge that Ds could make, however restricted the circumstances in which such answers can be made.*

(v) *Discouraging the emergence of a 'defence industry' fostered by experts and professional advisers, in relation to particular kinds of claim, of a kind likely to result in the success of too many unmeritorious claims.*

(vi) *The need to encourage citizens to seek redress through political or bureaucratic processes rather than resorting to 'self-help', especially where the latter entails the use of force.*

(vii) *Ensuring that the circumstances in which a defence may be pleaded do not entail intractable problems of proof for either or both of the prosecution and the defence, meaning that they are likely to be unable to discharge their legal, evidential or tactical burdens in relation to crucial issues.*

(viii) *Maintaining a relationship between the legislature and the courts in which it is understood on both sides that the former must take responsibility for the resolution of morally complex issues raised by an excusatory (or justificatory) claim that it is beyond the competence of an adversarial process to resolve in a definitive and satisfactory way.*

These strategic concerns overlap and are usually inter-related. For example, in relation to (i), the close match in question could be lost if an excuse is, in pursuit of an understandable wish to be as generous as possible to the accused, defined in such a way that it in effect permits exploitation of its terms by those seeking to, but not meant to, benefit from it. Such exploitation—at the heart of the concern in (v), and (vii)—may undermine respect for the law's claim to value the interests protected by the offences to which the excuse applies, in so far as its breadth entails that unmeritorious claims might foreseeably succeed, thus bringing into play the concerns in (ii) and in (iii).[35] Moreover, such exploitation may also undermine moral respect for the excuse itself, in so far as its ethical currency will rightly be perceived to stand persistently to be devalued by the success of unmeritorious claims.[36]

[35] It should not be supposed, however, that strategic concerns are focused solely on occasions for limiting the scope of excuses. It could be that respect for the law would be undermined by the failure to develop or extend some kinds of excuse or justification: see chapter 6 below.

[36] This seems to be part of John Gardner and Timothy Macklem's argument against the dramatic extension of the provocation excuse in *R v (Morgan) Smith* [2001] 1 AC 146: see John Gardner and Timothy Macklem, 'Compassion Without Respect: Nine Fallacies in *R v Smith*' (2001) *Criminal Law Review* 623.

Even a mere chance that such an undermining of respect may be the result of developing or extending an excuse (or justification) could be enough to justify refusing to take such a step, perhaps particularly where it is crimes involving *mala in se* to which the defence is to apply. It is, moreover, important to stress that the sufficiency conditions for excuse, strategic legal concerns of the kind just mentioned, are genuinely moral concerns. They are not simply trumped-up so-called 'policy' arguments used to override the moral claims to excuse of Ds who have satisfied the necessary conditions for an excuse. Even some theorists willing to grant an important role to such concerns within the criminal law sometimes mistakenly deny this. For example, in his discussion of voluntary euthanasia, Joel Feinberg claims that if a blanket ban on the practice is to continue to be justified, it can only be, 'in terms of "pragmatic" policy considerations, such as the need to provide safeguards against mistake and abuse'.[37] In what way, though, could a concern for mistake or abuse in the committing of euthanasia, a concern for what Feinberg himself describes as 'the inadvertent or contrived deaths of nonconsenting patients',[38] come to be seen as a purely *pragmatic* rather than as a genuinely moral concern? The only way in which this could begin to make sense is if moral concerns are strictly confined—as, indeed, Feinberg confines them—to the realm (highly restrictively understood) of individual interests; but modern liberal theory rejects this idea outright, recognizing that common goods have weighty intrinsic moral value.[39]

So, to take strategic legal concerns seriously, as a lawyer or theorist, is to show that one has grasped how individual claims to excuse must be capable of being accommodated within the much broader and highly complex political task of establishing and maintaining a (morally) sound legal order, one that sustains relevant common goods.[40] Now, to be sure, whilst judges often rely on strategic considerations when refusing to develop a defence, they also often exaggerate the likelihood that granting a defence will have the kind of adverse consequences that raise a strategic concern, or (even worse) they misunderstand the kinds of adverse consequences that raise a genuine strategic concern. Further, judges sometimes make decisions hinge on strategic concerns when they are not in as good a position as Parliament to gauge whether the concern should exercise a decisive influence in the (kind of) case being considered.[41]

---

[37] Joel Feinberg, *Harm to Self* (New York: Oxford University Press, 1986), 374 (his quotation marks around 'pragmatic'). [38] Ibid.

[39] See n. 28 above, and Joseph Raz, 'Right-Based Moralities', in Jeremy Waldron (ed.), *Theories of Rights* (Oxford: Oxford University Press, 1984), chapter 11.

[40] See J. M. Finnis, *Natural Law and Natural Rights*, chapter 6, and passage cited just after the start of this section.

[41] All of these claims about the misuse of 'strategic concern' arguments could be sustained, for example, about the decision of the majority, and of the speech of Lord Jauncey in particular, in *R v Brown* [1994] 1 AC 212. In that case, the House of Lords refused to permit consent to be a defence to a charge of assault occasioning actual bodily harm, when the 'assault' occurred during the course of consensual sado-masochistic activity. For a more measured understanding of the limits of the adversarial process to account properly for strategic concerns, see Lord

It should not be supposed, however, that the tension this kind of mismanagement of cases can create in a system of criminal law, between the pressure to develop excuses and strategic legal concerns, stems from a natural opposition between individual rights and common goods. When a formal excuse is created in law, upon the satisfaction of certain factual and evaluative criteria (of different kinds, depending on the nature of the excuse), Ds may have a right to be excused under that heading. As with all rights, the right depends in part for its justification on the strong interest that Ds themselves have in avoiding, in whole or in part, official censure through conviction when the necessary conditions for excusing have been met. As with all rights, though, Ds' own interests, however pressing, are not in themselves sufficient reason to create a right unless to create such a right would *itself* serve or further a common good.[42] Providing an excuse will serve a common good, if (other things being equal), for example, to have no excuse will bring the law into disrepute amongst officials and citizens alike by, say, confounding reasonable expectations, by encouraging widespread unauthorized bending of the rules elsewhere in the system to accommodate defendants with the relevant claim, and so forth.[43] Appearances to the contrary notwithstanding, in that regard, the role of strategic considerations in shaping defences need never be purely a restrictive one. The almost inevitable unpredictability of the circumstances in which the necessary conditions for excuse (or justification) may be fulfilled, means that it also serves a common good to keep the list of possible excuses or justifications open. Moral respect for the law's demands, and a culture of compliance and law-abidingness (common good (iii) above), may actually be undermined by a restrictive or rigid approach to the development of defences to some crimes, if such an approach means Ds stand to be convicted when they are entirely blameless. Moreover, the fact that defences do not by and large exist to guide citizens but to provide for their exculpation,[44] means that the continuing exercise by judges of an active discretion to expand existing or to develop new excuses can be tolerated (and perhaps encouraged), even when the legislation has itself already provided for some of the circumstances in which D may be excused.[45]

As we will see in the next two sections, some theorists who discuss the scope of excuses have erred by concentrating too narrowly on the necessary conditions for excusing, overlooking the sufficiency conditions. They end up with

---

Wilberforce's comments on the development of defences, cited in the text in section 7 below.

[42] Joseph Raz, *Ethics in the Public Domain*, 52–55.

[43] Both these ways in which the law could be brought into disrepute, if there is no excuse, reflect 'rule of law' concerns of a very broad kind.

[44] This generalization should not be taken too literally: see Jeremy Horder, 'On the Irrelevance of Motive in the Criminal Law', 183. See also the discussion in section 4 below.

[45] A. T. H. Smith, 'Judicial Law-Making in the Criminal Law' (1984) 100 *Law Quarterly Review* 46, 63–67, discussed in A. P. Simester and G. R. Sullivan, *Criminal Law: Theory and Doctrine*, 1st edn., 649–650. See further section 7 below.

UNIVERSITY OF WINCHESTER

an over-broad understanding of excuse. Other theorists, by way of contrast, focus exclusively on excuses that already pass the tests for the necessary conditions for excusing because they have certain effects (such as obstructing the rationality of choice). This leads them to overlook the possibility that there may be other excuses satisfying the necessary conditions (and also the sufficiency conditions), but in different ways, i.e. other than through interfering with the rationality of choice. They end up, thus, with an over-narrow understanding of excuse. In sections 3, 4, and 6, I will give an example of each.

3. OVER-BROAD CONCEPTIONS OF EXCUSE: H. L. A. HART'S ACCOUNT[46]

In his attempt to rebut arguments for the relentless application of unrestrained utilitarian thinking to criminal law and punishment, Hart highlighted the importance of justification and excuse within the criminal law, as an example of the need for a focus on the deserts of the offender, as well as on the efficient achievement of what he took to be the (happiness-maximizing, crime-reducing) general aims of criminal law and punishment.[47] In doing this, Hart perhaps initiated what has now become the regrettable standard practice (a practice, ironically, avoided by Bentham, Hart's main target) of regarding the rationale for excuses as detached from a theory of the general aims—or common goods—the criminal law is meant to achieve or sustain. Hart claimed that we should look at the existence of excusing conditions as 'something that *protects* the individual against the claims of the rest of society', as 'a requirement of fairness or of justice to individuals independent of whatever the General Aim of punishment is . . .'[48] Such a view prioritizes the necessary conditions for excusing over the sufficient conditions. Indeed, it is hard to see, on this view, how the sufficient conditions could have any relevance to an excuse at all. Such an individualistic view of the place of excuses within the criminal law can be challenged, simply by pointing out that what Hart calls the 'claims of the rest society' can actually include common goods—such as common good (i), a broad match between the shape of the law and people's reasonable moral expectations—capable of incorporating a right to be regarded as excused (or justified) in certain circumstances.

Significantly, at the cost of some apparent inconsistency with his very broad understanding of excuses, Hart did in at least one instance suppose that the character of excuses was to be shaped by the 'claims of the rest of society', rather than being limited to the protection of the individual from such claims.

---

[46] A sympathetic reading of Hart's theory is to be found in Michael S. Moore, *Placing Blame*, 549–562.

[47] H. L. A. Hart, *Punishment and Responsibility* (Oxford: Clarendon Press, 1968), 14–17.

[48] Ibid., 44, and 14, respectively (Hart's emphasis on 'protects').

That was when questions of proof might prove intractable for the prosecution, as in cases when subjective mental states (like loss of self-control) were in issue, where he thought one might become dangerously reliant on D's own version of events.[49] In spite of this acknowledgement of the force that strategic concerns, such as (vii) above, can have in circumscribing excuses, Hart's basic instinct was to suppose that excuses should be explained in an individualistic way, that is, detached from a concern with common goods. This view has proved to be highly influential, even in the most unlikely of places.

4. Over-broad Conceptions of Excuse: Alan Norrie's Account

Amongst influential contemporary commentators, Alan Norrie is one whose concern in discussing excuses is largely with the necessary conditions, to the exclusion of the sufficient conditions. He argues that the law adopts a narrow view of the meaning of intention in order to confine 'broader issues of normative judgment'[50] to excuses (alongside justifications):

[I]n relation to intentionality we see the way in which matters of normative justification and judgment are suppressed within the law's base categories. Once that is done, and these categories have been 'secured' against moral infection, issues of justification and excuse are permitted as 'subsidiary' categories within the law's architechtonic. These are subsidiary issues because the law has made them so, driving a wedge between legal and *genuinely moral* judgment.[51]

When seeking to highlight a contrast with the law's allegedly restrictive understanding of intention, Norrie presents justifying and excusing conditions (matters of 'genuinely moral judgment') in terms solely of the fulfilment of what I have called the necessary conditions for excusing. Small wonder, then, that when he turns his attention specifically to the way in which the law in fact shapes justifications and excuses, he feels bound to accuse it of moral betrayal when it refuses to regard conduct as justified or excused in some cases in which the necessary conditions for excusing appear to have been fulfilled.[52]

Consider the 'justification' case of *London Borough of Southwalk v Williams*.[53] A homeless family with young children, disappointed by the

---

[49] Ibid., 32–33. Hart does not allude to the possibility that these supposed problems of proof can be met, at least in some cases, not only by using the 'reasonable man' concept as a heuristic guide, but also by evidentiary devices such as corroboration warnings or shifting the burden of proof. Even so, he is surely right to identify problems of proof as a strategic concern, with a common good—(vii) above—at stake.

[50] A. Norrie, '"Simulacra of Morality"? Beyond the Ideal/Actual Antimonies of Criminal Justice', in R. A. Duff (ed.), *Philosophy and the Criminal Law: Principle and Critique* (Cambridge: Cambridge University Press, 1998), 126.   [51] Ibid., 128 (my emphasis).

[52] His argument, in that regard, is further considered in chapter 5.6 below.

[53] [1971] 2 All ER 175. Although the case is really one about justification, rather than excuse, the issues raised have an important bearing on the discussion that follows.

failure of their local authority to find housing for them, breaks into vacant local authority property and makes their home there. Should the family be regarded as justified in committing a trespass?[54] The court held that there was no justification for the trespass. In justifying the decision, Lord Denning said this:

If homelessness were once admitted as a defence to trespass, no-one's house could be safe. Necessity would open a door which no man could shut . . . The plea would be an excuse for all sorts of wrongdoing. So the courts must for the sake of law and order take a stand. They must refuse to admit the plea of necessity to the hungry and the homeless; and trust that their distress will be relieved by the charitable and the good.[55]

In the bulk of this passage (with characteristic hyperbole), Lord Denning relies on a combination of two arguments relating to the sufficiency conditions for the creation or extension of a defence to cover particular circumstances, arguments that may perfectly defensibly be employed under certain conditions.[56] The first is a 'slippery slope' argument, the argument that if the necessity plea were permitted in this (*ex hypothesi*, deserving) case, the courts might have to permit it to be successfully employed in less-deserving cases.[57] The second argument relies for its force on a combination of the strategic concern or common good (vi), set out in section 2 above (discouraging the use of force as a form of 'self-help'),[58] and concern (i) (maintaining a close match between how defences ought to be regarded, and how they are regarded). The argument is that to permit the defence of necessity in this case would send out the wrong kind of moral (and hence, legal) message. Citizens who become aware of the decision might gain the impression that they are more or less free to decide for themselves what steps it is appropriate to take to resolve housing difficulties—and perhaps a broad range of other social problems—impinging on their individual lives, in the full expectation that if the courts sympathize with their plight, there will be no adverse legal consequences when they invade others' rights through their actions. Criminal justice (and other public) officials, labouring under a similar impression, might feel that they must adjust their policies towards law-breaking likewise.

---

[54] See Simon Gardner, 'Necessity's Newest Inventions' (1991) 11 *Oxford Journal of Legal Studies* 125.   [55] *London Borough of Southwalk v Williams* [1971] 2 All E R 175, 179.

[56] At the time *London Borough of Southwalk v Williams* was decided, there was some doubt whether the defence of necessity existed, as a formally recognized defence in English law: see Simon Gardner, 'Necessity's Newest Inventions'.

[57] The House of Lords has relied—somewhat implausibly—on such an argument, in justifying a refusal to allow the excuse of duress to apply in murder cases, for fear that the defence could become 'a charter for terrorists, gang-leaders and kidnappers' (the words of Lord Simon, for the minority in *DPP v Lynch* [1975] AC 653, 688. His argument found favour with the House of Lords in the later case of *R v Howe* [1987] 1 All ER 771). This argument really relates to strategic concerns or common goods (vi) and (viii), from section 2 above, although there are hints that (ii) and (v) also concerned the House of Lords.

[58] *London Borough of Southwalk v Williams* [1971] 2 All ER 175, 181, 'The law regards with the deepest suspicion any remedies of self-help, and permits these remedies to be resorted to only in very special circumstances' (per Edmund Davies LJ).

Whilst it is obviously fanciful to suppose that a single decision by the Court of Appeal could lead to the kind of widespread anarchy Lord Denning fears, his use of such arguments has a sound legal–philosophical basis, in the sufficiency conditions that must be met for an excuse to be created (or for it to have an application in particular circumstances).

For Norrie, however, as a matter of individual justice (what he calls, in the passage cited earlier, 'genuinely moral judgment'), there was 'a clear matter of necessity in play' in this case,[59] and the family should have been regarded as justified. Norrie regards the court's decision as founded on a judicially perceived need to 'partition . . . off broader questions of social justice' like the problem of homelessness, when developing defences, even if that means overlooking the demands of individual justice—and hence the necessary conditions for justifying or excusing—in a particular case.[60] For Norrie, when D is denied an excuse or justification, even though the individual circumstances suggest that it would be morally repugnant to convict (the necessary conditions for excusing), D is being sacrificed in order to maintain a façade of detachment within criminal law doctrines from questions of social justice, these questions being conveniently hived off by the court for resolution by the nearest bureaucratic agency or charity. The fact that, behind the façade, mitigation of sentence is then permitted to make some amends for the enforced sacrifice simply compounds this alleged anomaly.[61] For Norrie, if the individual circumstances in which D committed the wrongdoing exercise a strong moral 'pull' in favour of lenient treatment, then what reason could there be to confine their relevance solely to mitigation of sentence?

It is, though, only in the final few words of the last sentence of the passage cited from *Williams* that Lord Denning employs a 'partitioning-off' argument of the kind that Norrie regards as central to the decision. For the most part, Lord Denning's arguments are taken up with the kind of sufficiency conditions that could perfectly legitimately count against extending the defence of necessity to the circumstances under consideration. Moreover, far from being a matter for criticism, for anyone who believes in the supremacy of the legislature over the courts when it comes to determining how social and economic policies are to be implemented, the court's use of a 'partitioning-off' argument in *Williams* is entirely appropriate. As Lord Hoffmann has more recently put it, 'in a field such as housing law, which is very much a matter for the allocation of resources in accordance with democratically determined procedures, the development of the common law should not get out of step with legislative policy'.[62] Indeed, even Norrie himself eventually has

---

[59] See his discussion of the case in Alan Norrie, 'From Criminal Law to Legal Theory: The Mysterious Case of the Reasonable Glue-Sniffer' (2002) 62 *Modern Law Review* 538, 543–544.　　　　　　　　　　　　　　　　　　　　　　　　　　　　　　[60] Ibid., 544.

[61] See his discussion of the defence of necessity in Alan Norrie, *Crime, Reason and History*, 2nd edn. (London: Butterworths, 2001), 156–161.

[62] *London Borough of Southwalk v Mills* [2001] AC 1, 10.

to concede (although the concession is tucked away in a footnote), that it is hard to see on what grounds the Court of Appeal might genuinely be justi-fied in using the law of trespass, in individual cases, to dictate what might have to be a change in general policies adopted by housing and welfare agencies which are employed to use a knowledge and expertise in allocating scarce resources that the Court of Appeal cannot hope to match.[63]

Surely, it might be said, sensitivity to the law's legitimate strategic con-cerns cannot undermine the view that, in a case like *Williams*, judges should not themselves seek to determine as a matter of law what counts, or does not count, as action justified under conditions of necessity? The entire mat-ter should perhaps be left to the fact-finder (magistrate or jury) to deter-mine, evaluation of claims being on a simple case-by-case basis. Such an open-ended approach, whether it is justifications or excuses that are in issue, holds out the tantalizing prospect of acquittal to almost anyone with a plaus-ible claim that their wrongdoing can be viewed in a favourable light; but we should have confidence, so the argument runs, that fact-finding judges and juries can distinguish from amongst such claims those that truly merit excuse or justification. We can call this kind of argument an argument for wholly facilitative ('fact-finder empowering') rules governing defences. Wholly facilitative rules hand to the fact-finder the task of deciding, for example, not only when (in fact) a D acted under conditions of justification or excuse, but also what are (in an evaluative sense) to count as the condi-tions of justification and excuse themselves. The adoption of wholly facilit-ative rules may in some circumstances be appropriate, as when it would be best to leave entirely to the fact-finder the task of deciding what counts as a 'reasonable excuse' for committing some preparatory or regulatory crime. A proposal to adopt more or less wholly facilitative rules can nonetheless

[63] Alan Norrie, 'From Criminal Law to Legal Theory: The Mysterious Case of the Reasonable Glue-Sniffer', 544 n. 29. Norrie thinks that the argument for the Court of Appeal leaving the matter to housing and welfare agencies would only work if it could be shown (to the Court of Appeal's satisfaction?) that 'the social problem was or could be effectively dealt with by the other agency' (ibid.). The key word here, of course, is 'effectively'. Would Norrie's test only be satisfied if every applicant for housing support was successful? Would his test be satisfied if every 'deserving' case was successful (and is the Court of Appeal to determine what counts as a relevant desert-based consideration?)? More broadly, how plausibly can it simply be assumed that the Court of Appeal is justified in using defences to civil and criminal liability to shame government agencies for problems that may not be of their own making, when it seems equally plausible to argue that it is to Parliament that such agencies should be accountable, and that it is Parliament's responsibility to ensure that such agencies can function 'effectively'? Ironically, then, like thorough-going liberal theorist Ronald Dworkin, Norrie seems to hold an over-optimistic view of the value of encouraging people to resolve legal uncer-tainty through litigation, hence risking the legal equivalent of martyrdom if the courts resolve the uncertainty against them. Dworkin's way of putting it, in *Taking Rights Seriously*, 217, was, 'Our legal system pursues these goals ["the development and testing of the law through experimentation by citizens and through the adversary process", ibid., 216–217] by inviting citizens to decide the strengths and weaknesses of legal arguments for themselves, or through their own counsel, and to act on these judgments, although that permission is qualified by the limited threat that they may suffer if the courts do not agree.'

also bring us up against a number of the law's strategic concerns, as described in section 2 above.

Underpinning Lord Denning's reasoning in *Williams* is the thought that there can sometimes be overriding strategic value in structuring or shaping facilitative ('fact-finder empowering') rules by reference to 'determinative' rules. Determinative rules may shape the operation of facilitative rules in different ways. They may simply specify limits to what may count as, say, a 'reasonable' excuse, in a particular context (not drunkenness, perhaps), or they may impose a more general theoretical constraint on the scope of mitigation (such as the need to show that there was a loss of self-control, in provocation cases). In that regard, it is significant that when judges have drawn up rules for defences, they have eschewed a *wholly* facilitative structure for such rules, in favour of a partially facilitative structure. The law determines the criteria according to which conduct is to be evaluated (such as some version of the reasonable person test), and the fact-finder's facilitative role is confined to deciding whether those criteria have been met in any given case.[64] The aim of determinative rules is in part to support strategic concerns or common goods (i) and (v) (see section 2, above), reducing the likelihood that courts and juries will constantly have to confront speculative or unmeritorious individual cases, even if judges and juries could in all probability be trusted successfully to distinguish between these when they confront them. The value in this does not lie, or lie solely, in the inconvenience the criminal courts may experience in having to deal with unmeritorious cases. A legal system whose defences were comprised of wholly facilitative rules would have too much potential not only for V's rights wrongly but mistakenly to be invaded, but also for Ds needlessly to be subjected to the harsh treatment constituted by the prosecution process, when it may have been the Ds' misunderstanding of the likely outcome that led to the need for the process to be undertaken. Justice can be served, thus, if such misunderstandings—and hence the needless risk of a prosecution for a rights

[64] Almost needless to say, there is more a difference of degree than of kind between defences that could be described as wholly facilitative, and those that are best described as partially facilitative, a difference understandably sometimes overlooked by judges. In the provocation case of *R v (Morgan) Smith* [2001] 1 AC 146, the development of the doctrine of provocation in that case ought best to be described as the reduction of the determinative element in what nonetheless remains a partly—rather than wholly—facilitative set of rules for mitigation (the law, after all, continues to set the standard for evaluation, and to rule out consideration of factors like self-induced intoxication); but the development of the doctrine was (mis)understood as the adoption of a wholly facilitative set of rules for mitigation: see the argument of Lord Hoffman in *R v (Morgan) Smith* [2001] 1 AC 146, 163, where, speaking of the effect of section 3 of the Homicide Act 1957, he says, 'the jury was given a normative as well as a fact-finding function. They were to determine not merely whether the behaviour of the accused complied with some legal standard, but could determine for themselves what the standard in the particular case is'. That this understanding of the objective condition in provocation cases is not really thought by Lord Hoffmann to be as wholly facilitative as it is presented as being, is evidenced by the fact that he himself would have the jury told that they must rule out from consideration the effects, for example, of possessiveness or jealousy: see *R v (Morgan) Smith* [2001] 1 AC 146, 169, and the discussion in chapter 4.5 and 4.8 below; but see now *A-G for Jersey v Holley* [2005] UKPC 23.

invasion—are avoided by the use of determinative rules, which are designed to do as much as possible to discourage more or less understandably speculative or misconceived claims, rather than by leaving the law so open-ended that the resolution of uncertainty must come through a criminal trial.[65]

The way in which this claim for the importance of strategic considerations in the construction of defences has been made, may give the impression that such considerations only really have 'bite' when the ability of the law to guide conduct *ex ante* is in issue, and that will only be so when justifications, rather than excuses, are in play.[66] Not so. Far from all justifications involve the *ex ante* guidance of conduct.[67] Certainly, some justifications, such as the justification given by a police officer for a search of property authorized by a search warrant, are indeed wholly *ex ante* in character.[68] Other justifications, however, such as pleas of self-defence or necessity by private citizens, are more in the nature of a plea for *ex post facto* vindication of the action taken in the circumstances, on the basis of moral considerations (such as the necessity and proportionality of self-defensive force) it is now claimed that the law should regard as having provided for that action an adequate (justificatory) basis. This feature gives such justificatory pleas something in common (as well as a claim of *ex post facto vindication*) with excusatory claims such as reasonable mistake or due diligence. For, contrariwise, such excusatory claims can have a conduct-guiding dimension to them. If it were a defence to a regulatory offence that one could have done no more than one did to avoid committing it (a 'best endeavours' defence), that would certainly be an excusatory rather than a justificatory defence; but it would also be a defence with some conduct-guiding implications, if one wished to put oneself in a position to plead it successfully. In any event, strategic considerations are not confined in their focus to the likely direct effects on how citizens will think and behave. As strategic consideration (v) above implies, it can be important to seek to influence for the good the way in which legal advisers and other experts analyse, categorize, and advise on the plausibility of running particular pleas, as the following examples illustrate.

Strategic concerns of the kind just raised can also be important when considering the nature and scope of excusatory claims based on 'explanatory',

[65] See the remarks at n. 63 above.

[66] Because only when a justificatory rule is in play could D misunderstand its function and unwittingly but wrongly use it as a basis for invading another's rights. For such an argument, see Paul H. Robinson, *Structure and Function in Criminal Law* (Oxford: Clarendon Press, 1997), chapter 5C. These issues are also discussed in some detail in Peter Alldridge, 'Rules for Courts and Rules for Citizens' (1990) 10 *Oxford Journal of Legal Studies* 487, and in Meir Dan-Cohen, 'Decision Rules and Conduct Rules: On Acoustic Separation in Criminal Law' (1994) 97 *Harvard Law Review* 625.

[67] See Jeremy Horder, 'On the Irrelevance of Motive in Criminal Law', 189.

[68] *Ex ante* guidance plays a crucial role for those acting in a public or semi-public capacity, such as law enforcement officials or doctors: see Jonathan Rogers, 'Justifying the Use of Firearms by Policemen and Soldiers: a Response to the Home Office's Review of the Law on the Use of Lethal Force' (1998) 18 *Legal Studies* 486.

rather than 'adopted', reasons for action, or when dealing with partially excusatory claims in which mental disorder or deficiency is an important aspect of D's claim. The important message that it is essential to restrain violent urges even in the face of grave provocation, is lost or distorted if the test for excusing provoked violence becomes so diluted as to invite, as Gardner and Macklem put it, 'an evaluative free-for-all in which anything that induces sympathy by the same token helps to excuse'.[69] Similarly, the message that self-restraint must be exercised becomes corrupted if the law's definition of mental disorder is too easily satisfied by, for example, claims of prior 'victimization'. As Jill Peay suggests, offenders can be only too willing to be persuaded to see their behaviour as the uncontrollable product of disorder if there is an anticipated benefit in so doing; and hence, 'The scene is set: . . . victimisation in one form or another is a common, if not universal, experience; psychiatrists are peculiarly reliant on what their clients tell them; offending is widespread. All of the ingredients are present to permit a re-structuring of experiences as explanations or excuses'.[70] There is an irony here. In both provocation and diminished responsibility cases, professional advisers are under an obligation not unduly to influence the self-perception of a D in order to make it 'fit' the legal doctrines; but sweeping away determinative rules would effectively side-line this obligation, because there would no longer be any restrictive legal doctrines D's self-perception would be required to fit. The price paid for this, however, is that, in the shadow of facilitative rules, the integrity of the defences can be undermined by the very fact that purely solipsistic narrative has acquired as much potential excusatory significance as the best grounded moral claim. Strategic concerns of the kind at issue in (v) above then re-emerge, with the prospect that legal advisers will have even greater incentives to encourage D to rely on untestable and uncorroborated assertions about him- or herself, as well as about his or her treatment at the hands of V, (backed, wherever possible, by medical evidence providing such assertions with a veneer of scientific objectivity).[71] Such a development would, of course, simply highlight further existing anomalies about the way in which expert evidence tendered by the defence can find its way into court. As John Spencer most memorably put it:

[E]ither or both of the parties [can be] palming off upon the court someone who, though not bogus . . . is cranky, senile, or generally ill-thought of within the profession. Matters are made worse by . . . the fact that the defence (although not the prosecution) is free to

[69] John Gardner and Timothy Macklem, 'Compassion without Respect? Nine Fallacies in *R v Smith*', 635.

[70] J. Peay, 'Mentally Disordered Offenders, Mental Health and Crime', in Mike Maguire, Rod Morgan, and Robert Reiner, *The Oxford Handbook of Criminology*, 3rd edn. (Oxford: Oxford University Press, 2002), 775. See further, chapter 4.6 below.

[71] By making evidence of mental disorder relevant to provocation cases, *R v (Morgan) Smith* [2001] 1 AC 146 simply encouraged this kind of practice, disregarding (amongst other strategic concerns) the concerns in (v) above. See now, *A-G for Jersey v Holley* [2005] UKPC 23.

shop around, tearing up one 'unhelpful' expert report after another, until at last it finds the man or woman who is ready to say what it wants the court to hear.[72]

5. STRATEGIC CONSIDERATIONS AND 'OBJECTIVISM' IN EXCUSES

Does it necessarily follow that adequate sensitivity to strategic considerations or common goods entails that one must be an unashamed 'objectivist' about standards for judgment in excuse cases, insisting that in all cases it is agent-neutral standards that provide the benchmark against which the adequacy of D's excusatory claim is tested, and never simply the standards D him- or herself was capable of reaching? I doubt it. A modified form of objective assessment is defended later in chapter 3.6 below, but that defence does not have to (even if it might) follow from the need to reflect in the conditions for excuse the kinds of strategic considerations currently at issue. It could be that a rigorous application of the test of 'each according to his or her abilities', the kind of test briefly endorsed by the House of Lords as the appropriate test for judging whether control of the urge to kill could reasonably have been retained in the face of provocation,[73] would do enough to avoid the spectre of Gardner and Macklem's 'evaluative free-for-all'. Certainly, in Lord Hoffmann's view, the need for the adoption of a more (but still not wholly) facilitative approach in provocation cases comes from his understanding that in the historical development of determinative rules to govern such cases, 'what has been rendered unworkable is not the principle of objectivity, but the particular way of explaining it'.[74] Whether or not one agrees with the decision in which this view was expressed, *R v (Morgan) Smith*,[75] his point reveals a more fundamental truth. Objective standards, in one form or another, are best understood as part of the necessary conditions, rather than as part of the sufficient conditions, for excuse. To show that someone well-equipped with powers of self-control might have done as one did, or—the weaker standard—that one did as much as could reasonably have been expected of one, is arguably to do no more than show one's action in the kind of favourable light that can make an explanation for it in principle excusatory (the necessary condition). So, such objective standards—be they strong or weak—should not be given explanations or rationalizations that falsely suggest that they are restrictions on what would otherwise be plausibly excusatory explanations for one's conduct

---

[72] J. R. Spencer, 'The Neutral Expert: an Implausible Bogey' (1991) *Criminal Law Review* 106. Spencer adds that fear of cross-examination amongst less-articulate experts may simply leave the field open to 'the usual cabal of log-rollers, time-servers, self-publicists and people with friends', citing M. N. Howard, 'The Neutral Expert: a Plausible Threat to Justice' (1991) *Criminal Law Review* 98.

[73] See *R v (Morgan) Smith* [2001] 1 AC 146 now effectively overruled by *A-G for Jersey v Holley* [2005] UKPC 23.   [74] See ibid., 173.

[75] *R v (Morgan) Smith* [2001] 1 AC 146.

(the sufficiency conditions), like the rule requiring the fact-finder to ignore evidence of self-induced intoxication,[76] even if there are strategic considerations or common goods that stand to be compromised if weaker objective standards are preferred to stronger ones in the setting of the necessary conditions for excuse.

When it comes to choosing between stronger (less individualized) or weaker (more individualized) standards, though, in his ruthless exposure of judicial vacillation over the correct tests to apply for the satisfaction of justifications and excuses, Norrie suggests that judges are caught up in a dilemma characteristic of philosophical and legal argument in conditions of modernity, at least since the time of Kant and Hegel. He says:

They [judges] . . . see justice as a matter of universal principle based upon individual freedom and reason . . . [but] there is a crisis of justice resulting from social conditions. The universalised abstract individual has to be counterposed to individual particularity under contemporary moral and social conditions.[77]

Whether or not English law has ever worked with a conception of universality anything like that made famous by Kant may be doubted.[78] More significantly, as the foregoing analysis suggests, the law need not find itself confronting the horns of a dilemma, having to make an impossible choice between judgment by reference to an absurdly abstract conception of the 'reasonable person', or judgment by reference to the D's own values and standards, however inadequate, misconceived or debased. There is more than one choice lying between these two extremes; and these choices, such as judgment in accordance with what D him- or herself was reasonably capable of achieving, might—at least, on some views—both satisfy the necessary conditions for an excuse, and pose no serious threat to common goods.[79]

---

[76] One can, of course, imagine an argument for saying that the irrelevance of self-induced intoxication is an irrelevance that comes from the need to meet the necessary conditions for excuse. The argument would be that someone whose provoked or fearful reaction is influenced by self-induced intoxication simply fails to show up their reaction in a favourable light. One should resist this line of argument, because the necessary conditions for excuse are not hard to meet, and rarely, if ever, defeated by matters of detail (however important) of this kind. Someone who has been drinking at home, and hence kills when enraged by the persistence of a door-to-door sales representative who has called unexpectedly, can—for the purposes of the necessary conditions of excuse—show up their reaction in a favourable light even if they would never have reacted so disproportionately when sober. However, more generally (so the theory goes), to take the fact the D acts in a drunken rage into account would, *inter alia*, threaten common goods (i) and (ii). So, it is for strategic reasons, for better or worse, that we have the 'exclusionary' rule: see *R v Majewski* [1977] AC 443.

[77] Alan Norrie, 'From Criminal Law to Legal Theory: The Mysterious Case of the Reasonable Glue-Sniffer', 546.

[78] See M. Dubber, review of A. Norrie, 'Punishment, Responsibility and Justice: A Relational Critique', (2002) 65 *Modern Law Review* 311.

[79] For a defence of such a test, in relation to a 'diminished capacity' excuse, see chapter 3.6–3.7 and chapter 4.6–4.10 below. Hart himself, of course, gave theoretical prominence to the idea that the 'reasonable person' standard need not and should not be a purely abstract standard, through his thesis (considered in section 6 below) that each D should have had a fair opportunity to avoid wrongdoing. See the discussion in A. P. Simester, 'Can Negligence be Culpable?', in Jeremy Horder (ed.), *Oxford Essays in Jurisprudence*, 4th Series, chapter 5.

6. OVER-NARROW CONCEPTIONS OF EXCUSE: BEYOND 'CHOICE' THEORY

As we will come to understand more fully in chapters 5 and 6 below, the common law has always worked with a narrow conception of excuses. This conception can be called the 'classical' conception or theory of excuses. The common law or classical conception of excuse (as distinct from its conception of justification, sheer involuntariness or of mental disorder) more or less self-consciously tracks closely Aristotle's account of, first, a distinction between voluntary and involuntary conduct, and, secondly, of what is rationally chosen conduct, both considered below.[80] Excuses fashioned through common law development have always been largely restricted to claims of mistake, duress, and provocation, regarded by Aristotle (for reasons outlined below) as having an impact either on the absolute voluntariness of conduct, or on whether or not it can be regarded as 'reasoned through' or rationally chosen. Before the emergence of the regulatory state, the narrowness of the classical approach could perhaps be justified as having the effect of confining judicial creativity, in relation to defences that excuse crimes *mala in se*, to legal conceptualization of moral issues arising on 'one-off' occasions or in emergencies.[81] These are moral issues that—whilst controversial—had sufficient clarity and determinacy to make them suitable for resolution through the adversarial process (and through exegesis in the influential work of judge-writers from the seventeenth to the nineteenth centuries). As we will see in chapter 6 below, in the regulatory state, even though Parliament itself has a responsibility for developing excuses, that justification for keeping judicial activity within the confines of such a narrow approach no longer looks adequate.

On Aristotle's (confusingly broad) view, conduct undertaken in ignorance of salient facts is to be regarded as 'involuntary' (*akousion*);[82] and so

---

[80] The account forms part of Aristotle's discussion of the nature of moral goodness, in Aristotle, *Nichomachean Ethics*, Thomson, J. A. K. (trans.) (London: Penguin, 1955). There is some evidence that, perhaps through the benefit of a classical education, judges were directly influenced by the account of involuntariness in Book 3 of Aristotle's *Nichomachean Ethics*: see *Renigger v Fogossa* [1552] 1 Plowd 1. The idea of something decided '*kata ton orthon logon*', according to 'right reason', or as I am putting it 'reasoned through', is notoriously difficult to pin down. For a recent examination of the proposition that the idea of *logos* is linked to the idea of argument, in both moral and political philosophy, see John Gardner, 'The Mark of Responsibility' (2003) 23 *Oxford Journal of Legal Studies* 157, 163–164.

[81] For further discussion of this point, see Jeremy Horder, 'On the Irrelevance of Motive in Criminal Law'.

[82] As far as ignorance is concerned, Aristotle equates involuntariness with a mere lack of intention to act under the salient description. So, for him, sexual intercourse without consent, where the perpetrator was unaware that V was not consenting, would be 'involuntary'. By this usage, Aristotle seems to have in mind what is sometimes known as 'moral' involuntariness. For further discussion, see W. F. R. Hardie, *Aristotle's Ethical Theory*, 2nd edn. (Oxford: Clarendon Press, 1980), 156–157; C. Finkelstein, 'Duress: A Philosophical Account of the Defence in Law' (1995) 37 *Arizona Law Review* 251, 275–278. The very early common law is

are some kinds of conduct intentionally engaged in under coercion. As far as the relationship between coercion and involuntariness is concerned, Aristotle draws a distinction between two kinds of coerced conduct. First, conduct can be involuntary when for the agent it is 'compulsory without qualification [namely] when the cause is external and the agent contributes nothing to it'.[83] Secondly, pieces of conduct can be involuntary 'in themselves' or 'absolutely', but nonetheless voluntary 'at the given time and cost' (actions *intentionally* engaged in under coercion).[84] Confusing though it can be, the framework for discussion he sets up has been highly influential. So, it is worth briefly trying to reconstruct his argument even though the argument is not really directed at providing a 'theory of excuses' as such.[85] In rather too brief a discussion, Aristotle's observations on what would now be called the theory of excuses are to be found at the start of book (iii) of the *Nichomachean Ethics*. He begins by claiming that actions are involuntary when performed under compulsion or through ignorance, because then the originating cause of the action 'has an external origin of such a kind that the agent or patient contributes nothing to it'.[86] As far as compulsion is concerned, this claim very obviously requires immediate qualification, as Aristotle recognizes, because action taken under compulsion can involve a decision to do something to avoid a threat (and can hence involve something contributed by the agent 'from the inside'), and is not the same as when 'a voyager [is] conveyed somewhere [unexpected?] by the wind'.[87] So, his claim that actions intentionally undertaken to avoid dire consequences are involuntary must immediately be modified, becoming a claim that such actions are only 'presumably' involuntary, and only then when considered 'absolutely', on the grounds that 'nobody would *choose* to do anything of this sort in itself'.[88] I shall come back to this point about choice in a moment. Having apparently thus nailed his flag to the mast, making absence of choice the key to 'involuntariness' through compulsion, Aristotle then modifies this claim straightaway as well.

What matters, it seems, when D intentionally acts to avoid certain consequences, is not so much the subjective *experience* of lack of choice, but

---

uncertain on the point: see Samuel E. Thorne, and J. H. Baker (eds.), *Readings and Moots at the Inns of Court in the Fifteenth Century* (London: Selden Society, 1990), ii, 74 and 274. Hale, however, employs the Aristotelian understanding: see Sir M. Hale, *Pleas of the Crown*, I, 42: '*Ignorantia facti* . . . in many cases makes the act morally involuntary'.

[83] *Nichomachean Ethics*, iii, 1110a17-b7.

[84] Ibid. Some modern courts and commentators have picked up this way of looking at action under coercion or conditions of necessity, describing it as 'normatively' involuntary: see e.g. *Perka v R* (1984) 13 DLR (4th) 1, drawing on George P. Fletcher, *Rethinking Criminal Law* (Boston, Mass.: Little, Brown, 1978), 803.

[85] It is one small aspect of Aristotle's theory of moral goodness.

[86] *Nichomachean Ethics*, iii, 1109b30-1110a16.   [87] Ibid.

[88] Ibid., 1110a17-b7 (my emphasis).

how well or badly, ethically speaking, D can be said to have done in so acting:

> Sometimes people are actually praised for such actions [under duress] when they endure some disgrace or suffering as the price of great and splendid results; but if the case is the other way round, they are blamed, because to endure the utmost humiliation to serve no fine or even respectable end is the mark of a depraved nature. In some cases, however, the action, though not commended, is pardoned: *viz* when a man acts wrongly because the alternative is too much for human nature, and nobody could endure it.[89]

This passage endorses a more familiar three-fold distinction between justi-fied conduct, conduct that is both unjustified and inexcusable, and excused conduct. In that regard, in the final words of the passage, Aristotle hints that what matters to excuse is not simply whether D him- or herself found the threat too much to endure (and hence, subjectively, experienced an absence of choice), but how well D's choice to do wrong stands up, ethically, against a standard of what we can expect a mentally well-equipped adult to endure before making such a choice. I shall have more to say about this— 'standards'—view of excusing conditions in due course.[90]

A somewhat clearer basis for regarding actions as excusable, as distinct from conditions that render conduct involuntary, emerges from Aristotle's discussion of action in anger. As indicated above, for him, an act is voluntary when its originating cause is internal to the agent him- or herself;[91] but a vol-untary act is, for Aristotle, only truly chosen when it is has been reasoned through, and is hence based on something like (the balance of) rational prin-ciple.[92] Now, Aristotle tells us that actions due to temper are voluntary, but not rationally chosen. In his view, such actions are voluntary, because 'irra-tional feelings are considered to be no less part of human nature that our considered judgements';[93] but such acts are not chosen, because 'still less is choice to be identified with temper; for acts due to temper are thought to involve choice less than any others'.[94] Not for the first time, thus, the concept

---

[89] *Nichomachean Ethics*, iii, 1110a17-b7.

[90] See chapter 3.6 below. There is also a good deal in Aristotle's discussion of conduct made involuntary through ignorance, however, to give succour to those who would like to claim Aristotle's theory of excuses was based on a '(good) character' theory of excuses, rather than on a 'capacity' or 'standards' theory. He claims, for example, that if it turns out that you are indifferent to the hurt you caused by accident, the accident should not be regarded as truly involuntary: *Nichomachean Ethics*, iii, 1110b7-31, because (*ex ante*) you obviously cared too little about causing such accidents. See the interpretation of the relevant passages in J. O. Urmson, *Aristotle's Ethics* (Oxford: Basil Blackwell, 1988), 46, and for a modern version of the argument, see Jean Hampton, 'Mens Rea' (1990) 7 *Social Policy and Philosophy* 1, 27, '[I]gnorance is a function of faulty character . . . so we locate the defiance not at the time of the [unintentional] act, but earlier, during the process of character formation . . .'

[91] *Nichomachean Ethics*, iii, 1110a17-b7; 1111a18-b5.   [92] Ibid., 1111b31-1112a17.

[93] Ibid., 1111a18-b5. The point being that if 'irrational' feelings are a part of ordinary human nature, then, considered as originating causes of conduct, they are internal, and hence issue in voluntary forms of conduct.

[94] Ibid., 1111b5-31. The point being that the unpremeditated and spontaneous overwhelm-ing of reason by anger, whilst sometimes praiseworthy (and, more generally, open to evaluation), cannot be said to issue in conduct motivated by rational principle.

of voluntariness employed by Aristotle threatens to cloud the analysis. However naturally 'human' it may be, provoked anger has at least some part of its originating cause lying outside the agent, in the provoking conduct of the person who generated the anger.[95] So, on the view of involuntariness he outlined when discussing coercion, there is something to be said for regarding provoked anger as involuntary; but that looks counterintuitive, and inconsistent with what he is now saying, which is that angry actions are voluntary because they are all-too-human. It is, then, best to put the 'external cause' element in Aristotle's account of voluntariness on one side, and agree with him that in mentally well-equipped people, angry actions are rightly regarded as voluntary; but they are not truly chosen, because they are not reasoned through.[96] In such cases, what Aristotle calls the 'desiderative' or 'appetitive' part of the soul (passion) gets the better of reason, short-circuiting the process of reasoning through, in practical deliberation. Although he does not make the point explicitly, we can further assume that—by way of analogy with his discussion of coercion—Aristotle would not regard as excusable action in anger that is too disproportionate to provocation received. For, it is not, or not only, the subjective experience of lack of choice in one's actions that is crucial for excusatory purposes, when anger overwhelms us, but the objective judgment that the provocation might have made almost anyone give in to his or her feelings and commit the wrong.[97] In retrospect, this is also the best explanation of Aristotle's analysis of conduct intentionally engaged in under coercion that falls to be excused (as opposed to justified).[98] Putting aside the issue of 'external cause', such conduct ought to be regarded as voluntary, fearful action being only too human in nature. One would not have done as one did, however, if one had had a proper chance to guide one's actions by reasoning them through, rather than being led by one's fear of an imminent threat. One's fear just more or less understandably dictated one's conduct in committing the wrong.[99]

This Aristotelian theme, as a basis for explaining the theoretical foundations of the traditional excuses, is pursued further in due course. It would not be right, however, to regard the foregoing discussion as an attempt to

---

[95] A point perhaps most famously made by J. L. Austin, 'A Plea for Excuses'. For further discussion, see Andrew Ashworth, 'The Doctrine of Provocation' (1976) 35 *Cambridge Law Journal* 292.

[96] For further philosophical analysis of both these ideas, see chapter 2.10 and 2.11 below.

[97] For more detailed discussion, see Jeremy Horder, *Provocation and Responsibility*, chapter 8.

[98] It may be that Aristotle did not explain intentional action under coercion in this way, as compared with angry action, because it seems obvious that one chooses between evils in a case of coercion, whereas one seems to act more spontaneously and without choosing between alternatives in cases in which one is provoked into a response in anger; but if this is the reason, then that just shows Aristotle did not think hard enough about the range of responses there can be to fear and anger: see chapter 2.10–2.12 below.

[99] For more detailed philosophical discussion, see chapter 2.10–2.12 below.

elaborate on Aristotle's 'theory' of excuses, because he did not really have such a theory. Although he says that his observations may be 'useful also for legislators with a view to prescribing honours and punishments',[100] his discussion of involuntariness, coercion and action in anger are really intended merely as a prelude to a broader investigation of moral goodness, in the guise of authentic and informed reasoning towards, and choice of, what is truly good (the mark of the person of good character).[101] Even so, some of the structure (re)constructed above has become highly influential in shaping some judges' understanding, as well as the understanding of some theorists, of the nature and limits of excuses, and the Aristotelian character of this influence explains why I term it the 'classical' conception of excuses. As regards the development of excuses at common law, for example, Hart says that the excuses of 'Mistake, Accident, Provocation, Duress and Insanity',[102] were rightly developed and applied by courts to what he regards as the most serious crimes (murder is his favourite example) because, even where serious crimes are in issue:

[E]xcusing conditions . . . are regarded as of moral importance because they provide for all individuals alike the satisfactions of a choosing system. Recognition of excusing conditions is therefore seen as a matter of protection of the individual against the claims of society for the highest measure of protection from crime that can be obtained from a system of threats. In this way the criminal law respects the claims of the individual as such, or at least as a *choosing being* . . .[103]

In this passage, Hart himself appears to share with common lawyers the view that the narrow, classical Aristotelian framework for understanding the

---

[100] *Nichomachean Ethics*, iii, 1109b30. See also ibid., 1113b21-1114a8, '[Legislators] impose punishments and penalties upon malefactors (except where the offence is committed under duress or in unavoidable ignorance) . . .'   [101] Ibid., 1113a12–34.

[102] H. L. A. Hart, *Punishment and Responsibility*, 31. Mistakenly, Hart includes insanity amongst the excusing conditions, when—as Aristotle himself recognized—insanity is a threshold condition of responsibility, and not a case in which D is genuinely claiming excuse on the grounds (say) that, ordinary human nature being what it is, no one could reasonably have been expected to do better: see e.g. *Nichomachean Ethics*, iii, 1148b20-1149a11. A modern defence of the Aristotelian view is to be found in John Gardner, 'The Gist of Excuses'. It should be noted, though, that some see the inclusion of insanity amongst excusing conditions as a positive theoretical virtue: see K. J. M. Smith and William Wilson, 'Impaired Voluntariness and Criminal Responsibility: Reworking Hart's Theory of Excuses—The English Judicial Response' (1993) 13 *Oxford Journal of Legal Studies* 69.

[103] H. L. A. Hart, *Punishment and Responsibility*, 49 (Hart's emphasis). The theory, touched on in this passage, that excuses are rightly regarded as individual claims 'against' the claims of society was criticized in section 3 above. Hart makes the claim in a more unconditional way, in H. L. A. Hart, *Punishment and Responsibility*, 44, 'it is clear that we look on excusing conditions as something that *protects* the individual against the claims of the rest of society' (Hart's emphasis). To be fair to Hart, it might be perhaps that a defence of excuses would take on that appearance if it were proposed to abolish them in pursuit of 'the highest measure of protection' against crime; but in practice, states worldwide have found plenty of means by which to pursue (or to give the impression of pursuing) such a measure of protection without abolishing all trace of excusing conditions.

necessary conditions for excuse, in terms of an absence of choice, is the right framework when crimes *mala in se* are in issue. In that regard, it is not only the common law that has been shaped by its Aristotelian inheritance. Given a more modern-looking, neo-Kantian gloss, the 'choice' theory of excuses continues to be influential in academic thinking about excuses today.[104]

Hart was also, however, perhaps one of the first to see that a theory of excuses does not have to relate to conditions that interfere with a *choice* to do wrong. The necessary conditions for excuse do not have to be restricted in that way. At common law, Hart suggests, it is on responsibility for 'serious' crimes (crimes to conviction for which stigma attaches) that excuses have historically had a morally significant bearing, in virtue of what he calls 'the doctrine that a "subjective element", or "*mens rea*", is required for criminal responsibility'.[105] The bearing the one is supposed to have on the other is moral, in that if liability for serious crimes depends on the subjective element of free 'choice' (understood to include subjective recklessness alongside intention), then what makes excuses such as mistake, provocation, and duress relevant to such crimes is that, as Aristotle suggested, they put in question whether or not the wrongdoing was freely chosen. As far as crimes of strict liability are concerned, where the doctrine of subjective *mens rea* is not applied at common law, Hart goes on to say that the theory (to which he is not wholly unsympathetic) is that, 'the law, like every other human institution, has to compromise with other values besides whatever values are incorporated in the recognition of some conditions as excusing'.[106] In that regard, he thought, it might be considered to be the triumph of the value of a concern for 'social welfare' that has precluded the application of excusing conditions to crimes of strict liability in the courts.[107] Hart points out, though, that how 'strict' liability turns out to be rests, in any individual case, on the attitude the courts take towards the interpretation of the crime in question,[108] and it may be that duress and insanity can through creative interpretation be given some application to crimes of so-called strict liability.[109]

Building on these observations, in spite of his obvious sympathy with the 'choice' account of excuses as they apply to crimes that are *mala in se*,

---

[104] See e.g. Andrew Ashworth, *Principles of Criminal Law*, 3rd edn., 99; Michael S. Moore, 'Choice, Character and Excuse' (1990) 7 *Social Policy and Philosophy* 29.

[105] H. L. A. Hart, *Punishment and Responsibility*, 31.

[106] Hart adds at this point that it may not always be clear what values are to be regarded as triumphing over the values that makes excusing conditions important. To be fair, Hart does make it clear at this point (as at several others) that crimes of strict liability have not escaped criticism, as 'an odious and useless departure from proper principles of liability'.

[107] H. L. A. Hart, *Punishment and Responsibility*, 33–34. In that regard, Hart suggests, 'the utilitarian argument that [strict liability] prevents evasion of the law by those who would be prepared to fabricate pleas of mistake or accident has some plausibility' (ibid., 179). This claim obviously combines elements of what I outlined as strategic concerns (iii) and (v) in section 2 above.

[108] H. L. A. Hart, *Punishment and Responsibility*, 112.

[109] Ibid., 242. See the discussion in A. P. Simester and G. R. Sullivan, *Criminal Law: Theory and Doctrine*, 1st edn., 167–168.

Hart himself advocates discarding the classical conception of excuses, with its narrow Aristotelian framework. He shifts his theory of excuses on to a different theoretical foundation to that unquestioningly employed by the common law. As a result, in Hart's theory, crimes of strict liability become as significant as any other crimes to a theory of excuses:

[A] primary vindication of the principle of responsibility could rest on the simple idea that unless a man has the capacity and a fair opportunity or chance to adjust his behaviour to the law its penalties ought not to be applied to him . . . Such a doctrine of fair opportunity would not only provide a rationale for most of the existing excuses which the law admits in its doctrine of mens rea but it could also function as a critical principle . . . That is, in its light we might . . . press further objections to strict liability.[110]

It has never been altogether clear how much of an improvement this theoretical move has turned out to be. Some have regarded a 'lack of capacity' as irrelevant to excuses, seeing it as having a bearing only on denials of responsibility,[111] an issue tackled (so far as the putative partial excuse of 'diminished capacity' is concerned) in chapter 4 below. Moreover, the idea of a lack of 'fair opportunity' has always been too loose or abstract to give much theoretical illumination. Too much hinges on the concrete theory of 'fairness' that must fill it out, for the idea to be capable of doing useful work in itself.[112] Even so, perhaps surprisingly, although there has been plenty of theoretical discussion of whether the traditional excuses (mistake; provocation; duress) can be explained by seeing them in terms of a lack of 'capacity' and/or of a lack of 'fair opportunity',[113] the suggestion that a lack of 'fair opportunity' doctrine might be developed in a more sophisticated way to provide a defence to crimes of strict liability has received significantly less attention. An effort to remedy this is made in chapter 6 below, although, when it comes to excusing the commission of regulatory offences, we will see the 'fair opportunity' doctrine does not escape the limitations of a common law perspective on excuses as well as does the alternative 'due diligence' defence. In essence, Hart sees a lack of 'fair opportunity' in terms of the unreasonableness of cognitive or emotional demands placed on D (along with the effects of mental disorder), the kinds of factors central to Aristotle's classical account of excusing conditions. By way of contrast, I will argue that the (extent of the) effort made by those subject to regulation to avoid committing offences has a special, 'liberal' excusatory significance, beyond that inherent in the idea that D lacked a 'fair opportunity'—understood in cognitive or emotional terms—to avoid committing the offence. It is thus necessary to break free from the confines of the traditional account of excuses, if one is to appreciate the true theoretical significance of a 'due diligence', as opposed to a 'no fair opportunity' excuse.

[110] H. L. A. Hart, *Punishment and Responsibility*, 181.
[111] See e.g. John Gardner, 'The Gist of Excuses'.
[112] In chapter 2 below, a much more elaborate set of theoretical foundations for the excuses is laid out.   [113] See e.g. Andrew Ashworth, *Principles of Criminal Law*, 3rd edn., 254.

7. WHOSE RESPONSIBILITY IS IT TO DEVELOP EXCUSES?

Few would dissent from the proposition that the courts should not create new criminal offences, even if it must also be accepted that the courts will inevitably—and perhaps should—on some occasions extend or restrict the reach of existing offences through the exercise of their power and duty to interpret the law, as well as simply to apply it.[114] Is the position the same where defences, and excuses in particular, are concerned? The answer is likely to vary from jurisdiction to jurisdiction, depending on how active a role remains for judges in making law. In England and Wales, where judges retain not insignificant powers of law creation, in discharging their role within the adversarial process, the traditional excuses and exemptions—duress, mistake, provocation, and insanity—have been, of course, wholly or mainly the product of the use of such powers of law creation.[115] Much doctrine now constituting and governing them, including rules concerned with whether excuses are to apply to particular offences, still remains legally binding in virtue of its status as common law, rather than through statutory embodiment. That inevitably means that the courts must take some responsibility for the restriction or expansion of these excuses, because it is they who are charged with maintenance of a common law that commands moral as well as legal authority.[116] What, though, of the creation of new excuses?

It seems hard to deny that there remains an inherent common law power to create new excuses, and to decide whether or not to apply them to particular crimes. Such a power has arguably been reinforced, under section 3 of the Human Rights Act 1998, by the modern duty on courts to 'give effect' to legislation, including criminal legislation, in a way that is compatible with the rights created under the European Convention on Human Rights.[117] To exercise such a power to create excuses would be to exercise precisely the same power that has been authoritatively (if sometimes controversially) used in relatively recent times, for example, to develop a broad-ranging excuse of

[114] For general discussion, see A. T. H. Smith, 'Judicial Law-Making in the Criminal Law'; Andrew Ashworth, 'Interpreting Criminal Statutes: A Crisis of Legality?' (1991) 107 *Law Quarterly Review* 419; Andrew Ashworth, *Principles of Criminal Law*, 3rd edn., chapter 3; Jeremy Horder, 'Criminal Law and Legal Positivism' (2002) 8 *Legal Theory* 221, 237–241.

[115] Historically, it may well be that an understanding that crimes *mala in se* are subject to such excuses stems from arguments to that effect emerging from medieval debates and moots in the Inns: see Samuel E. Thorne, and J. H. Baker, *Reading and Moots at the Inns of Court*, ii, introduction.

[116] Obviously, there are some large issues here that cannot be addressed in the present context. There is a wide-ranging and sensitive discussion in Andrew Ashworth, 'Interpreting Criminal Statutes: A Crisis of Legality?', 438–447. The passing of the Human Rights Act 1998 may also give fresh impetus to debates about the range of defences, given that judges are now under an obligation to take account of human rights jurisprudence in reaching judgment under adversarial process: see further, Ben Emmerson and Andrew Ashworth, *Human Rights and Criminal Justice* (London: Sweet & Maxwell, 2001), chapter 8.

[117] See, in particular, the discussion of the importance of the good of 'reciprocity' (strategic consideration (iv), in section 2 above) to a fair trial, in chapter 6.4 below.

mistake.[118] Parliament, however, has now begun to take more interest in carving out excuses to crimes it creates by statute, often tailoring those excuses in a very precise way to fit the particular context.[119] Should that entail that the courts leave the development of new excuses, and the question whether they are applicable to particular crimes, to Parliament? This seems unlikely. There can be little doubt that Parliament is well-placed, from an expert point of view, to develop very context-specific defences, when it creates new crimes (usually, but not solely, in a regulatory context). That is in itself a reason for the courts to refuse to seek to fashion such defences themselves, even if in theory they have the power to do so.[120] Nonetheless, so long as the issues at stake neither turn on expert knowledge and opinion the courts do not possess, nor involve highly open-ended, wide-ranging and controversial moral issues much better addressed through the legislative rather than through the more haphazard adversarial process,[121] the courts are legally and politically competent to create new general defences to statutory (or common law) crimes. This is significant, in that (as we will see in chapter 6 below) the fact that a crime has some context-specific defences that apply to it cannot rule out the possibility that, in all the circumstances, it may turn out to be right to apply to those crimes a more general excuse that it is within the courts' competence to create, such as the 'due diligence' excuse, even if such a defence found no place in the original statutory scheme. In summary, as Lord Simon has put it, speaking of the judicial development of excuses in the light of what I have called the strategic concerns at the heart of the sufficient conditions for excusing:

I am all for recognising frankly that judges do make law. And I am all for judges exercising this responsibility boldly at the proper time and place—that is, where they feel confident of having in mind, and correctly weighed, all the implications of their

[118] The development of a distinctive excuse of mistake in the modern era is traced in the excellent discussion to be found in Glanville Williams, *Criminal Law: The General Part* (London: Stevens, 1961), chapter 5. For the debate about Sir James Stephen's influential views on judicial creativity, in this regard, see A. T. H. Smith, 'Judicial Rule-Making in the Criminal Law', 63, and the references cited at n. 90. I speak of the 'modern era' because whilst it has been clear enough since medieval times that some kinds of mistake or ignorance would prevent the infliction of harm being regarded as felonious, this was probably simply because a claim of mistake was just one amongst a number of ways of rebutting the presumption of malice, and not because 'mistake' was regarded as a distinct excuse to some crimes but not to others.

[119] See e.g. the Education Act 1996, where a number of more or less context-specific excuses and justifications are set out that can be pleaded in response to a charge that a parent has criminally failed to ensure that their child attends regularly at school, an offence contrary to s.444(1) of that Act. See also the Food Safety Act 1990. For further discussion of this point, see the end of chapter 6.3 below.

[120] Further, even where the development or extension of a more general, common law defence is in issue, it could be right to leave the matter to Parliament if the moral issues at stake are especially wide-ranging and controversial in character. For such an argument, where the application of the excuse of duress to murder was in issue, see the speech of Lord Kilbrandon in *DPP v Lynch* [1975] AC 653, 700. For a closely related discussion, see George P. Fletcher, *Rethinking Criminal Law*, 792–798.

[121] In other words, so long as the considerations set out in strategic concern (viii), in section 2 above, are met. For discussion of this point, in relation to justifications, see Jeremy Horder, 'On the Irrelevance of Motive in Criminal Law', 189.

decision, and where matters of social policy are not involved which the collective wisdom of Parliament is better suited to resolve.[122]

The matter could be left there, but it is worth seeking to give the discussion a slightly deeper theoretical perspective, since both judges and theorists continue to express concern about judicial activism (as well as, sometimes, about judicial 'passivity'),[123] in relation to the development of excuses.[124] For legal positivists, a legal system is comprised (a) of binding standards (such as rules and principles) for, *inter alia*, guiding or judging behaviour as well as for determining how disputes are to be resolved, *and* (b) of more or less limited and structured discretionary powers to develop such standards and to resolve disputes ungoverned by existing standards.[125] Where (b) are concerned (the discretionary powers), whilst Parliament has a well settled power to change or develop *inter alia* the standards for guiding and judging behaviour, by rule-of-law convention, it does not employ that power to resolve individual disputes, leaving this—as appropriate—to the executive and to the judiciary.[126] In resolving individual disputes arising in a statutory context, judges are bound by whatever existing legal standards have a bearing on the case. In the absence of such standards (or where those standards do not make a decisive difference), however, judges may still be bound—politically, *qua* public officials— to resolve the dispute in accordance with moral or other evaluative standards, or at least to have regard to a sub-set of such standards, if the relevant interpretive convention so dictates.[127] In that regard, as Raz puts it:

Given that the courts are manned by people who will act only in ways they perceive to be valuable, principles of adjudication will not be viable, will not be followed by

---

[122] *DPP v Lynch* [1975] AC 653, 695, cited by A. T. H. Smith, 'Judicial Law-Making in the Criminal Law', 63 n. 81.

[123] See e.g. A. P. Simester and G. R. Sullivan, *Criminal Law: Theory and Doctrine*, 1st edn., chapter 6; Jeremy Horder, 'Strict Liability, Statutory Construction and the Spirit of Liberty' (2002) 118 *Law Quarterly Review* 458.

[124] See e.g. Paul H. Robinson, M. Cahill, and U. Mohammed, 'The Five Worst (and Five Best) American Criminal Codes' (2000) 94 *Northwestern University Law Review* 17, 'It is imperative . . . that a code include all appropriate defences and leave nothing to the whim of the judiciary'. And, for as strong a statement from a Law Lord, see Lord Kilbrandon's comments on the suggestion that the House of Lords should have a role in reforming the defence of duress, in *DPP v Lynch* [1975] AC 653, 700, 'It will not do to claim that judges have the duty—call it the privilege—of seeing to it that the common law expands and contracts to meet what judges conceive to be the requirements of modern society. Modern society rightly prefers to exercise that function for itself, and this it conveniently does through those who represent it in Parliament.'

[125] The classic modern statement of this view is to be found in Joseph Raz, *The Authority of Law* (Oxford: Clarendon Press, 1979), chapters 3 and 9, but Raz's view is in a way a development and elaboration of Hart's concept of a legal system.

[126] One ingenious way to get around the rule-of-law convention is for the government to persuade Parliament to empower one of the government's own ministers to develop standards and resolve individual disputes, as he or she goes along, in the name of upholding the aims of the statute in question: see e.g. the powers of the relevant minister under the Race Relations (Amendment) Act 2000. The rule-of-law propriety of such measures must be open to serious question.

[127] Joseph Raz, *The Authority of Law*, 96–97; Joseph Raz, *Ethics in the Public Domain*, chapter 14. When interpreting statutes, judges may also be bound to take account of, if not necessarily to follow, rules and standards developed at common law.

the courts, unless they can reasonably be thought to be morally acceptable, even though the thought may be misguided . . . quite commonly courts have the discretion to modify legal rules, or to make exceptions to their applications, and where they have such discretion they ought to resort to moral reasoning to decide whether to use it and how. It follows that legal expertise and moral understanding and sensitivity are thoroughly intermeshed in legal reasoning . . .[128]

One of the ways in which, as Raz puts it, legal expertise and moral understanding become 'intermeshed', is through the development of over-arching doctrines to guide judges in the exercise of their discretion to resolve disputes that turn on matters of interpretation under a great variety of statutes. One such doctrine is the so-called presumption that *mens rea* (which, broadly construed, may take the form of recognition of an excusatory plea) will be required before someone may be convicted of a criminal offence.[129] Doctrines of this kind, part of whose moral significance comes from the understanding that they are of general application, enable the courts to give substance to the claim that they are, in Lord Simon's words, 'a mediating influence between the executive and the legislature on the one hand, and the citizen on the other'.[130] So, in contexts as diverse as food safety,[131] licensing law,[132] anti-drug legislation,[133] and sexual or morals offences,[134] judges have sometimes been willing to 'read in' requirements of substantive *mens rea*, or defences of reasonable or of honest mistake, to the criminal offences created by the legislation.[135] The courts have on occasions been prepared to do this, in spite of what would undoubtedly in each case have been special pleading by prosecutors or experts called to give evidence that, in the particular context, strict criminal liability was more helpful and appropriate in promoting the aims of the legislation.[136]

Naturally enough, the duty to act—as one perceives it—morally (or in accordance with other binding non-legal standards, as appropriate) binds legislators and members of the executive as much as it binds judges. So, when creating criminal offences, the legislature is under a duty to give consideration to whether it would be morally appropriate to create excuses, even though the creation of such excuses might be perceived by some as detracting from the likelihood that the legislation in question will achieve

---

[128] Joseph Raz, *Ethics in the Public Domain*, 333–334 and 335.

[129] See e.g. the speech of Lord Reid, in *Sweet v Parsley* [1970] AC 132, 148, in which he claims (perhaps with a degree of hyperbole) that, 'there has for centuries been a presumption that Parliament did not intend to make criminals of persons who were in no way blameworthy in what they did.' For further discussion, see chapter 6.5 below.

[130] *Stock v Frank Jones (Tipton) Ltd.* [1978] ICR 347, 353.

[131] *Core v James* (1871) LR 7 QB 135.   [132] *Sherras v De Rutzen* [1895] 1 QB 918.

[133] *Sweet v Parsley* [1970] AC 132. For further discussion of this case, see chapter 6.1 below.

[134] *B (a minor) v DPP* [2000] 2 AC 438; *R v K* [2001] 3 WLR 471; *R v Tolson* (1889) 23 QBD 168.

[135] It is, of course, no part of my argument that judges have taken this approach with any degree of consistency, or with the courage of true conviction: see Jeremy Horder, 'Strict Liability, Statutory Construction and the Spirit of Liberty'.

[136] For a modern example in which expert evidence was given on this point, see *Barnfather v London Borough of Islington Education Authority* [2003] EWHC 418.

its aims. It may be, of course, that legislatures commonly neglect this duty. As Paul Robinson puts it, 'The very immediacy and import of criminal law render it all the more susceptible to mere politicking rather than deliberate craftsmanship',[137] a gloomy view of the way legislatures behave shared (on this side of the Atlantic) by Glanville Williams, for whom, 'Statutes, which are generally drafted by Government officials, often neglect juristic principles'.[138] Indeed, Lord Devlin has gone so far as to say that:

The fact is that Parliament has no intention whatever of troubling itself about *mens rea*. If it had, the thing would have been settled long ago . . . One is driven to the conclusion that the reason why Parliament has never done that is that it prefers to leave the point to judges and does not want to legislate about it.[139]

This passage misleads, however, in a number of respects.

First, historically, there was always at least some legislative interest in fault requirements during the years in which the establishment of a regulatory state in Britain gathered significant momentum.[140] Secondly, there is now far less evidence that legislatures still prefer to leave matters of fault and excuses solely for the courts to decide on, especially where specialized excuses tailored to the regulatory context are in issue.[141] Finally, even if legislatures always turned their attention to fault and the excuses at the time of enactment, that ought not to be regarded as settling the issue once and for all time. If D's claim is that justice demands that an excuse, such as 'due diligence', be applied to a statute to avoid a wholly wrongful conviction, it would be irresponsible for the courts to reason that, since Parliament was under an obligation to consider whether or not to introduce this excuse, and did so consider, D's claim can be dismissed on the grounds that the courts have been relieved of any obligation themselves to consider whether or not to introduce such an excuse, however long ago and however cursorily Parliament may have considered the matter. The question for the courts in relation to any individual D, just as much as for the legislature more generally,

---

[137] Paul Robinson, M. Cahill, and U. Mohammed, 'The Five Worst (and Five Best) American Criminal Codes', 64.

[138] Glanville Williams, *Textbook of Criminal Law*, 2nd edn. (London, Stevens, 1983), 18. I have criticized the notion that there might be an apolitical realm of 'juristic principles' and 'deliberate [legal] craftsmanship': see Jeremy Horder, 'Criminal Law', in Peter Cane and Mark Tushnet (eds.), *The Oxford Handbook of Criminal Law* (Oxford: Oxford University Press, 2003), 228–229.

[139] Patrick Devlin, *Samples of Lawmaking* (Oxford, Oxford University Press, 1962), 71.

[140] See chapter 6.2 below for fuller discussion. Under section 5 of the Sale of Food and Drugs Act 1875, D was not liable for a range of offences concerned with selling or preparing food unfit for consumption, 'if he shows to the satisfaction of the Justice of the court . . . that he did not know . . . and that he could not with reasonable diligence have obtained that knowledge [that the food might be injurious to health].' See also section 29 of the Public Health Act 1875, and Vaccination (Amendment) Act 1867, which says, 'Every parent . . . who shall neglect to take such child . . . to be vaccinated . . . and shall not render a reasonable excuse for his neglect shall be guilty of an offence'.

[141] See the discussion at the end of chapter 6.3 below; but see also Andrew Ashworth, 'Is the Criminal Law a Lost Cause?' (2000) 116 *Law Quarterly Review* 225.

is always, 'given that someone's claim fulfils the necessary conditions for excuse, does justice demand that (with whatever limitations are appropriate) such a claim be regarded as meeting the sufficient conditions for excuse as well?'.[142]

This point returns us to the 'common good' considerations we encountered in section 2 above. Just as people's respect for legal obligations, and for the moral integrity of the excuses applied to them, can be undermined if those excuses are too generous, so, *mutatis mutandis*, people's respect for legal obligations can be undermined if conduct deemed criminal is regarded as wholly inexcusable however much D may have done to avoid transgression (strategic consideration (iv) in section 2 above). As we will see in chapter 6.4 below, the maintenance of such respect for legal obligations, and more broadly for trial processes triggered by breach of these obligations, through an openness to excusatory arguments, is an aspect of the common good of 'reciprocity' within the criminal justice system, alongside procedural due process. This brings us back to the relevance to excuse-creation of what I have been calling strategic concerns.[143] It may be that it is well within the competence of a higher court to decide, whether the possible undermining of respect for legal obligations amongst citizens is a more real and weighty danger than the countervailing danger that creating a given excuse will encourage too many unmeritorious claims, thus undermining the prospects for successful prosecution of cases against offenders by an under-staffed and under-resourced regulatory agency. So, there should, on the part of the courts, be no shirking the responsibility for deciding whether or not justice demands the creation of an excuse, on the grounds that it is beyond the courts' competence to tackle such a question.

---

[142] This is, in effect, acknowledged by Lord Millett in *R v K* [2002] 1 AC 462, 480, where he claims that the courts may have the power to create a defence (in this case, of honest mistake) to a crime even when it is clear that Parliament has passed up the opportunity to create the defence itself, if, 'Parliament has signally failed to discharge its responsibility for keeping the criminal law in touch with the needs of society,' and there has been a 'persistent failure of Parliament to rationalise this branch of the law even to the extent of removing absurdities which the courts have identified'.

[143] A relevance acknowledged by Lord Simon in *DPP v Lynch* [1975] AC 653, 695, cited in the text at n. 122 above.

2

An Anatomy of Excuses

1. MOTIVATIONAL AND JUDGMENTAL ELEMENTS IN EXCUSES

In this chapter, I seek to provide an 'anatomy' of excuses, a close examination of the sometimes very different elements of which each is comprised. The anatomy is to be performed on the necessary conditions of excuse, set out in chapter 1 above.[1] These conditions exist if, *inter alia*, it is possible to shed sufficiently favourable moral light on an act or omission amounting to wrongdoing (with respect to which D remained morally active), by reference to the explanatory or to the adopted reasons that D committed that wrongdoing. The argument will not be easy going, because if one takes this broad view of what ought to excuse, there will be no simple answer to the question, 'what are the essential elements of an excusing condition?'. Matters will be complicated further still by the fact that, as when explaining the three dimensions of excusing conditions (set out below), I will seek to avoid taking the existing range of excuses, or the way in which they have been developed in particular jurisdictions, to exhaust the considerations at stake. Instead, the analysis will proceed as if other potential excuses, like excessive defence, diminished capacity (considered in chapter 4 below), or the demands-of-conscience (considered in chapter 5 below), already present themselves to be theoretically explained.

It is well-recognized that excuses can have both motivational and judgmental elements to them.[2] On Hart's view (chapter 1.3 and chapter 1.6 above), excusing conditions are focused in part on rational defects in any morally salient 'moving force' behind the act or omission, such as mental disorder, a mistake, a provoked loss of self-control, coercion, and so forth, and in part—at least where excuses other than insanity are concerned—on a judgment that D's action, on the basis of or in response to this moving force, was within the bounds of 'the reasonable'. This is in a way too narrow, and in a way too broad an understanding of excuses. On the one hand, it is too broad, in so far as it encompasses the view that conduct attributable solely to an irrationality brought about by mental disorder in the agent

---

[1] The sufficient conditions for excuse are examined in more detail in chapters 4 and 5 below.

[2] See, by way of example, Glanville Williams' distinction between the 'factual' and the 'evaluative' elements in a provocation plea: *Textbook of the Criminal Law*, 2nd edn., chapter 24.2 and 24.3.

him- or herself excuses.[3] Being an account of how D came to commit wrong-doing with respect to which he or she is morally passive, such an account is really an explanation of how he or she is denying responsibility for, rather than excusing, the wrongdoing. An excusatory account of wrongdoing pre-supposes that D was in some respect morally active with regard to the com-mission of the wrongdoing, connecting him or her to applicable guiding reasons. We will see what it means to be morally 'active' with regard to wrongdoing in sections 9, 10, and 11 below.[4] On the other hand, in its exclusive focus on rational defects in a morally salient moving force behind an action, Hart's understanding of excuses is too narrow. His understanding is theoretical prisoner to the limited range of excuses it purports to explain. It is, of course, important to understand how rational defects in a morally salient moving force behind an action come to excuse, and most of this chapter will be taken up with providing such an understanding. Wrong-doing can be excusable, however, even when there is no such defect. So, for example, if and when D seeks excuse on a demands-of-conscience basis (see chapter 5 below), or on a 'due diligence' basis (see chapter 6 below), D does not seek to rely on any rational defect in the moving force behind his or her action. It is accepted in such cases that D is the rational author of an action for which he or she could give a rational justification. In the demands-of-conscience case, D goes wrong, albeit perhaps understandably, in prioritiz-ing the demands of conscience over the particular demands of the law in question; but to have acted wrongly (in an unjustified way) is not necessarily to have acted irrationally. D's excuse is focused, then, on the claim that no more could reasonably have been expected of D than that he or she stick by his or her conscience (or, in the 'due diligence' case, that D make the kind of efforts he or she made to avoid the outcome), even though what was done was wrong.

When it comes to the judgmental element in excuses, moreover, it can be misleading or over-simplistic to say that one satisfies this element simply by showing that what one did fell within the bounds of 'the reasonable'. In some cases (like provocation), the partial excuse turns on how reasonable it was to have lost control of an overwhelming urge to kill, it being recognized that it was wholly unreasonable actually to have killed. In other cases (such as excessive defence or some duress cases) the complete excuse turns in part on an analogous finding that it was reasonable to have feared for one's safety, but it also turns on a finding that it was not too unreasonable actu-ally to inflict the harm that one did in order to make oneself safe. In other words, in some cases, what 'one did'—that which falls to be considered for excuse—is apt to cover one *or both* of one's emotional reaction (losing one's

---

[3] As we will see, in chapter 4 below, less-than-full rationality can be combined with an excusatory element to make a case for excuse. See also chapter 3.1 below, on the defence 'ladder'.

[4] See also, Jeremy Horder, 'Criminal Law: Between Determinism, Liberalism and Criminal Justice'; John Gardner, 'The Gist of Excuses'.

temper; fearing for one's life), and one's physical response to that reaction (lashing out; thwarting the attack; averting the threat by complying with certain demands). Indeed, it is arguable that whether one should only be partially excused, or should be completely excused, ought to turn on whether only one, or whether both, of these aspects of what one did falls within the bounds of 'the reasonable'.[5]

It is important not to lose sight of the distinction between the motivational and the judgmental elements to excuses. Even so, I want to make a fresh start by focusing on three different dimensions to excuses, in sections 2 to 6 below, without turning into an issue of critical importance the question whether they involve either motivational or judgmental elements. Against that background, I will then go on, in sections 7 to 13 below, to break down for the purposes of existing excusing conditions the meaning of a 'rational defect' in a morally salient moving force behind an action respecting which one remains morally active.

2. The First Dimension to Excuses

The first dimension to excuse does concern differences in the nature of the morally salient moving force or motivating element behind D's conduct. There are, of course, many different ways in which one could seek to analyse and distinguish forms of human motivation. E. J. Bond, for example, distinguishes four categories.[6] Category 1 involves acts done from 'simple inclination', as (say) when one whistles on the way to work. These are actions done for their own sake, requiring no foundation in true belief or an ulterior point to justify them.[7] Category 2 involves acts done from 'a certain emotion', as when I give as my explanation for an action the fact that 'I was afraid', or 'I was jealous'. In this category, beliefs—about which one can clearly be mistaken—play a role in the experience of the emotion. So, there can be third-person evaluation of D's explanation ('he or she had no reason to be angry, or to be as angry as he or she was') in any given case. Category 3 involves 'unwilled desires or aversions', such as hunger, that come upon us without our having to believe or think something to be the case. Here, my explanation for doing something—say, that 'I was hungry'—may in itself

---

[5] It is plausible to suppose, for example, that part of the explanation why duress is a complete excuse, whereas provocation is only a partial excuse, turns on this difference in the ways that what one did can fall within the bounds of 'the reasonable'. That would certainly do something to explain why there have been calls for duress to be only a partial—rather than a full—excuse in murder cases. In such cases, reasonable though it may have been to fear for one's life if one did not comply with the threatener's demand, *deliberately killing* another to avert the threat by complying with the demand falls wholly outside the bounds of what would have been reasonable.

[6] E. J. Bond, *Reason and Value* (Cambridge: Cambridge University Press, 1983), 16–18.

[7] See the point made about actions that need no rational justification, at the beginning of section 8 below.

provide sufficient justification for some actions, such as eating, without some ulterior justification having to be given (although the feeling will obviously not be sufficient justification for the action in every case, as when I am supposed to be on a diet). Category 4 involves the following cases:

> where the agent consciously sees his act or its end as desirable, good, or worth having, getting, or doing under some aspect . . . This is the sort of case where an agent consciously sees himself, upon reflection, to have a reason for doing something, and acts upon that reason. It is because the act is seen as valuable or desirable in some respect that it is done.[8]

Useful though they can be, as a way of dividing up motivating forces, Bond's categories oversimplify things. In particular, his separation of categories 2 and 4 is too strict. Bond makes two claims about category 4. It is only in category 4 'that the motivation can be, even partly, the consequence of conscious reflection'. Further, 'it is here [in category 4] only that it is appropriate to speak of rational motivation'.[9] The first claim is false because it does not acknowledge that emotions (in theory, confined to category 2, in Bond's scheme) may lead people to adopt particular reasons for action, rather than simply being led willy-nilly to react spontaneously in what Raz calls an 'expressive' way on the basis of an explanatory reason.[10] Action in anger, for example, can be the product of a degree of conscious reflection. Bond's second claim is misleading. Action taken in anger, or out of fear, can be, as Bond puts it, 'seen as valuable or desirable', and hence—following on from the point that such action may reflect an adopted reason—can be a reflection of how the balance of reasons seems to the angry or to the frightened person. In that sense, such action may be rationally justifi*able*.[11] An emotionally generated desire to do something, respecting which we are morally active, can count in favour of—as a reason for—a course of action, and thus may legitimately feature in any rational justification one seeks to give for performing that action: D says, 'I was so angry (or frightened) that intentionally shooting V was the only thing on, or uppermost in, my mind, at the time; it just *seemed* right'. None of that, of course, goes any way towards showing, in respect of such an action, that the desire in question provides adequate rational justification for the action. Indeed, when someone explains their conduct in the way D just did, they are usually all but conceding that the action taken was not in fact fully rationally *justified*. Whatever rational justification there may be for them, actions like D's can be rationally defective in a morally salient respect, in that how the balance of reasons seemed to the angry or frightened person was unduly (but,

---

[8] E. J. Bond, *Reason and Value*, 18.   [9] Ibid.

[10] The distinction between adopted and explanatory reasons was set out briefly in chapter 1.1. For Raz's use of the idea of emotions as expressive, see Joseph Raz, *Engaging Reason*, 43, discussed in section 10 below.

[11] In section 8 below, we will see how emotions can play a role in action that is fully justified, rationally.

perhaps, understandably) affected by the sheer phenomenological strength of the desire, respectively, to retaliate or to escape a threat. Whether or not the action was fully rationally justified depends on what sort of action it is, and on what else—other than the desire—there is to be said in favour of performing it.

Let me make a fresh start, then, by making the distinction between explanatory and adopted reasons (introduced in chapter 1.1 above), rather than the distinction between rational and non-rational motivation, central to an account of motivation, for the purposes of analysing excuses. In chapter 1.1 above, I said that D's conduct may come to be viewed in a relatively favourable moral light, in virtue of the way in which 'explanatory' reasons brought about D's conduct. When explanatory reasons are central to D's excuse, the excuse comes close to a plea that the conduct is involuntary, even though D's conduct may have been intentional, as when D 'instinctively' raises an arm to shield him- or herself when V suddenly advances with a raised fist, or spontaneously 'explodes with rage' and lashes out when V provokes him or her. The resemblance is due to the influence of factors with a morally passive element to them (the 'fight-or-flight' instinct; loss of self-control), even though the persistence of something about the action with respect to which D remains morally active makes it right to treat D's claim as an excuse rather than as a denial of responsibility. In that regard, in chapter 1.1 above, nothing was made of a distinction that some might think ought to be drawn between instances in which it is intentional conduct (lashing out in anger or self-defence), and instances in which it is unintentional conduct (a collision one puts down to one's clumsiness) over which one remains to a degree morally active. That might seem surprising, but the distinction between intended and unintended wrongdoing is morally much more significant if it is assumed that the intentional wrongdoing reflected an adopted reason, a consciously chosen reason, because unintended wrongdoing is clearly not chosen. When intentional wrongdoing takes the form of an explanatory reason for the wrongdoing, however, the element of evaluative control (or the lack thereof) is of much greater importance than intention itself to a moral assessment of D's conduct, because—as in the case of a clumsy accident over which D remained in evaluative control—the conduct is unchosen. In their discussion of causation in tort cases, Hart and Honoré give some illuminating examples of what I am calling intentional conduct attributable to an explanatory reason for action. They identify a category of actions stemming from 'psychological impulse' (what I am calling explanatory reason). They describe an action within this category as an 'automatic' reaction, but it is clear from the context that it is rationally related to a goal (such as escape from danger), in the circumstances. Quite rightly, because such conduct is unchosen, although rationally related to a goal, they do not regard it as breaking the chain of causation:

A purely automatic reaction is not deliberate, as when a person struck by another instinctively pushes him away. But the reaction may equally well spring from a psychological impulse, as when a wife, seeing her husband in peril, clutches him to pull him from danger . . . [T]he movement of one who, startled by a sudden noise, stumbles and clutches a rail or who, when a truck tyre comes through the front door, jumps out of bed and slips on a rug is not treated as voluntary action negativing causal connection . . . an act done under the influence of panic or extreme fear will not negative causal connection unless the reaction is wholly abnormal.[12]

Alternatively (as indicated in chapter 1.1 above), D's conduct may come to be viewed in a relatively favourable moral light, in virtue of the way in which 'adopted' reasons accounted for D's conduct. In such cases, D's conduct is not only fully voluntary but is constituted by an action intended to reflect a particular reason or reasons for so acting (the action is chosen). Where the reason in question is a reason to do the very thing prohibited, favourable—excusatory—moral light may nonetheless be shed on what was done, however serious. This can happen when a morally salient rational defect (mistake; the phenomenological strength of an emotion-based desire) explained how D came to act on that reason.[13] As we will see in chapter 5 below, favourable moral light can also be shed on an adopted reason to do the very thing prohibited, when it is a moral imperative forming part of D's system of beliefs that is thought by D to demand a particular piece of law-breaking conduct. When, by way of contrast, the adopted reasons are reasons on which D acted *in spite of which* wrongdoing occurred (as when the reasons related to a failed strategy designed to secure compliance with the law), favourable moral light may be shed on D's conduct if there was little or nothing more D could have done to avert the wrongdoing; if there was no rational or moral deficiency in the course of action adopted. As we will see, these different excusatory bases for a plea need not be 'stand alone' in the way that they operate. In some circumstances, it ought to be possible to combine an excusatory element to a plea with a morally passive factor such as mental deficiency (as in the case of diminished capacity plea, set out in chapter 4 below).

3. The Second Dimension to Excuses

The second dimension to excuse concerns differences in the way motive forces behind D's conduct connect with a judgment that D's conduct should be viewed in a relatively favourable moral light.[14] D's claim to excuse may

[12] H. L. A. Hart and A. M. Honoré, *Causation in the Law*, 2nd edn. (Oxford: Clarendon Press, 1985), 148–149 (footnotes omitted).

[13] Care must be taken in interpreting what I say when I refer to a reason as reason to do 'the very thing prohibited'. Clearly, in factual mistake cases, D believes he or she has a reason to do something that is prohibited, without knowing the facts that would reveal that it is a prohibited action; whereas, in provocation, duress and demands-of-conscience cases, D may be fully aware of the facts that make the action prohibited at the time of acting. I do not want to make more of this issue here.

[14] For reasons that will become clear shortly, though, not every theorist will accept that these differences exist. In a way, that does not matter a great deal, as less turns on the differences in this dimension than on the differences in the other dimensions.

turn in part on the fact that it is, subjectively or from the perspective of an agent, 'actively justificatory' in its motivating character. An excusatory claim may be actively justificatory in either a factual sense (mistake cases), or in a moral sense (demands-of-conscience cases; excessive defence cases). Care must be taken in understanding what is meant by 'actively justificatory' in this context. In such cases, the claim is not, of course, that D was really or truly justified in doing as he or she did. Claims of true justification are inconsistent with seeking excuse.[15] Nonetheless, D's claim has the subjective or agent-perspectival element of such a justificatory claim, in that D's contemporaneous and motivating *belief* that he or she was—factually or morally—in the right in doing as he or she did (even though D was not really in the right), plays a key role in D's defence; and that is a distinctive element in an excusatory claim.[16]

In most jurisdictions, in respect of at least some crimes, the mere fact that D acted on such a belief—however unreasonable—may suffice for an excuse (although the excuse may be a concealed one, taking the form of a denial of a morally open-textured mental element).[17] So, for example, under section 2 of the English Theft Act 1968, 'a person's appropriation of property belonging to another is not to be regarded as dishonest . . . if he appropriates the property in the belief that he has in law the right to deprive the other of it [or] . . . in the belief that he would have the other's consent'.[18] The morally open-textured character of 'dishonesty', as a mental element, makes it possible formally to present this belief as a denial of the mental element, rather than in 'confession-and-avoidance' fashion as an excuse; but the fact that one could intelligibly insist that such a belief be based on reasonable grounds before it serves to acquit, shows that it is really doing excusatory work respecting wrong—an appropriation—done. An analogous argument has sometimes prevailed where moral mistakes are concerned. Where D believed he was fulfilling his or her duty to a sick child by simply praying for the child's recovery, rather than taking the child to a doctor, Baron Pigott

---

[15] See John Gardner, 'The Gist of Excuses', 578.

[16] For the view, accepted here without further argument, that justifications must have a subjective element, in the form of a motivating belief that there is a justification for the action, see e.g. John Gardner, 'Justifications and Reasons'. As briefly explained in chapter 1.1 above, I will obviously not be concerned here with cases in which a factual mistake is best seen as a straightforward denial of the mental element, when it is not operating in a strictly excusatory way.

[17] See, further, A. P. Simester, 'Mistakes in Defence' (1992) 12 *Oxford Journal of Legal Studies* 295. Mistakes operate as true denials of the mental element only where a state of mind (such as intention) inconsistent with being mistaken is integral to the wrong itself—as in criminal attempt—and is not merely included as part of the offence out of concern for fairness to the accused.

[18] As a mental element, 'dishonesty' is sufficiently broad in scope to encompass truly excusatory claims, where the fact that one thought one was not doing wrong does not diminish the case for saying that one did in fact do the wrong prohibited. In the theft context, though, it is often hard to distinguish such excusatory claims from claims that one thought one was doing no wrong that, if accepted, mean that one simply did not commit the wrong prohibited.

said, in suggesting that D did not have *mens rea*, that:

He [D] may altogether have mistaken what his duty was; still I believe it was an honest mistake. It may be an ignorant mistake, in all probability it is the result of ignorance and superstition, but . . . he believed his duty to be in the direction in which he acted, and he carried out that duty to the utmost of his ability.[19]

Moreover (at least where factual errors are concerned) this kind of approach, treating as theoretically crucial the simple fact that D held an honest belief in facts that, if true, would have made his or conduct lawful, has received significant theoretical support.[20]

  Very commonly, though, it will not in itself be sufficient for an excuse merely to show that one acted on such a belief. Showing that one so acted is usually regarded in law as just a step, albeit an essential one, on the way to establishing one's excuse. For example, in most jurisdictions, to be excused on the grounds of factual mistake, one must show that the mistake was a reasonable one to make.[21] Similarly, for the purposes of the demands-of-conscience excuse, where moral mistakes are in issue, in chapter 5 below I shall argue that it is not enough for D honestly to believe that he or she is, morally, in the right in doing as he or she does. It must (*inter alia*[22]) also be unreasonable to expect D not to have obeyed the conscience-based demand that he or she follow a law-breaking course of action. This judg-mental element to the excuse of mistake is (in most contexts, quite rightly) *superimposed* on the basic motivational excusatory element, namely the mistaken belief itself that one was justified in doing as one did, a belief that, if sound, would have provided a true justification for one's action.[23] When this happens, excuses with an actively justificatory motivational element to them merge, at a theoretical level, with those excuses from which they would otherwise be distinguished, within this dimension. These are excuses based on an appeal for the court's judgment that no more could reasonably have been expected of D, in terms of courage, powers of self-control, or of

---

[19] *R v Hines* (1874), per Pigott B, reported (and disapproved) as part of the judgment in *R v Downes* (1875) 13 Cox CC 111, discussed in chapter 5 below, and in Alan Norrie, *Crime, Reason and History*, 2nd edn., 39 although Norrie does not point out that *Hines* was only mentioned in *Downes* for the purpose of disapproving of it.

[20] See Alan Brudner, 'Agency and Welfare in the Penal Law', in Stephen Shute, John Gardner and Jeremy Horder (eds.), *Action and Value in Criminal Law* (Oxford: Clarendon Press, 1993), 21, discussed in section 6 below.

[21] *Swann v United States* (DC App 1994) 648 A 2nd 928; *Zecevic v DPP* (Vic) (1987) 162 CLR 645.

[22] D's belief must also be representative of, or constitute an aspect of, the faith or set of beliefs in question. This issue is touched on again in chapter 5 below.

[23] It is something of an irony that English courts have recently begun systematically to root out objective requirements that beliefs be reasonable (*R v Williams (Gladstone)* [1987] 3 All ER 411; *R v K* [2001] 3 WLR 471; *R v G (and another)* [2003] 3 WLR 1060) just as Parliament has re-instated or introduced most such requirements: see the Sexual Offences Act 2003 (see also *McCann v UK* (1996) 21 EHRR 97). A classic case, then, of English judges seeking to dive into the swimming pool just as the water is being let out by Parliament.

-foresight, and so forth, whether or not there was an actively justificatory element to D's motivation for acting. For short, this can be called the 'capacity' basis for excuse (to distinguish it from the actively justificatory basis), a basis that, as we will see in chapter 3.6 below, divides into a 'subjective' version, concerned with a D's own individual capacities, and an 'objective' version, concerned with what could have been expected of someone in D's circumstances who was adequately equipped with the relevant virtues, powers, and so forth.

Provocation cases, duress cases, clumsiness cases, due diligence cases, and diminished capacity cases, are all cases in which there can be a claim to excuse without its having an actively justificatory basis (a foundation in a factually or morally mistaken claim of right). D may still claim excuse in these cases, despite having known all-too-well at the time that there was no right to do as he or she did. In such cases, D relies for excuse on a direct appeal to the court's judgment that little or no more could have been expected of (a mentally, or otherwise, adequately equipped) D, in the circumstances. As we will see in chapter 3.6 below, it is in diminished capacity cases where this appeal can be made in accordance with the 'subjective' version of the capacity theory, whereas in all the other kinds of (partial) excuse governed by the capacity theory, D's appeal is judged by reference to the 'objective' version of the capacity theory. In either case, where D relies wholly on a capacity basis for excuse, the excuse can be contrasted with an excuse that has an actively justificatory element. This is so, even though, when mistakes are in issue, in most jurisdictions D will not succeed in a claim based on a belief that conduct was justified unless it was also reasonable to act on that belief, and hence unless the capacity issue is satisfied, in that little or nothing more could have been expected of D in the circumstances. The kinds of appeals to the court's judgment that there might be, on a capacity basis alone, are familiar enough, so far as the 'objective' version of the capacity theory is concerned. Whether or not D acts for an explanatory or an adopted reason, at the heart of D's excuse may be reliance on a proposition concerning people's limited capacity to control strong emotion (provocation; duress; diminished capacity), or to see and account for all the facts that have a potential bearing on his or her actions (factual mistake cases, where the mistake was reasonably made). In these cases, the capacity in issue is rational capacity, analysed in sections 7 to 13 below.[24] Alternatively, central to D's claim may be an issue of moral capacity, the question of how reasonable it is to expect someone to abandon profound moral beliefs, in some circumstances (demands-of-conscience cases), analysed in chapter 5 below.[25]

---

[24] Diminished capacity cases, which involve partial reliance on diminished rational capacity, obviously require separate consideration, provided in chapter 4 below.

[25] Or, as we will see in chapter 3 and chapter 4 below, D's capacity-focused appeal may centre on his or her own specially limited capacities: what I will explain in chapter 3 below as the 'subjective' version of the capacity theory.

There can be some variations on and complications to this analysis. There will be some cases in which an excuse can be made to depend on the precise way in which D combines actively justificatory and capacity-focused elements. Apart from mistake cases, excessive defence cases should be like this. Where D mistakenly believes that more force is necessary to thwart a threat than is in fact reasonably necessary (the actively justificatory element), it is entirely proper to require that D be able to attribute the formation of that belief to the understandable difficulty D had in preventing sheer terror shaping his or her perception of what would be a justified response (the capacity-focused element). Exactly such a 'combined' basis for what I will, in section 4 below, be calling the 'concealed' excuse of excessive defence in English law, was set out by Lord Morris in *Palmer v R*,[26] where he said, regarding the requirement that D do no more than was necessary and proportionate to thwart an attack, that, 'if a jury thought that in a moment of unexpected anguish a person attacked had only done what he honestly and instinctively thought was necessary, that would be the most potent evidence that only reasonable defensive action had been taken'.[27] This way of expressing the requirement of necessary and proportionate force, in a way that is generous to a D caught out by a surprise attack, elegantly elides the actively justificatory element (D's honest belief in the need to do as he or she does) and the capacity-focused element (in the circumstances, almost anyone would have reacted as D did). In other cases, such as duress, in particular, it may be an open question whether or not the excuse should be made dependent on the satisfaction of an actively justificatory element, alongside a capacity-focused element. At the time of acting, should D have to believe (albeit mistakenly) that the wrongdoing done to avert the threat to him- or herself is justifiably done? Or, is it enough that D can satisfy the capacity-focused element, by showing that no more could reasonably have been expected of a courageous person, even though he or she was well aware at the time that what he or she was doing was unjustified? Most legal systems have not paid much attention to this significant theoretical issue in the way that they might.

4. The Third Dimension to Excuses

The third and final dimension to excuses is focused on a contrast between different bases on which one might judge, objectively, that D's conduct should be viewed in a favourable moral light. There is a distinction between what can be called a 'predominantly ascriptive' basis for so doing, and what

---

[26] *Palmer v R* [1971] 1 All ER 1077 (PC).

[27] Ibid., 1078. The whole question of how an explicit excuse of excessive defence might be framed has now been addressed by the Law Commission for England and Wales, *Partial Defences to Murder*, part 9.

I will call a 'predominantly normative' basis for so doing, although as the phraseology I am employing is meant to suggest, the distinction is not hard and fast. The distinction allows for excuses, like duress, that straddle the boundary between ascriptive and normative bases for viewing wrongdoing in a favourable moral light. To understand this distinction, we need to consider the distinction between normative and ascriptive rules. The classic statement of the distinction is by Raz:

Normative theory is primarily concerned with establishing what people ought to do . . . Who ought to realise which values and how is the main problem of normative theory. Its most important concepts are ought, reasons for action, rules, duties, and rights . . . The theory of ascription is concerned with the conditions in which blame or guilt can be ascribed to people . . . It is the job of normative theory to determine whose responsibility it is to realise this or that value . . . The theory of ascription deals with the ascription of blame and praise to people who have fulfilled or failed to fulfil their responsibilities. It presupposes that we have a normative theory and studies the normative consequences of failure to conform to the requirements of normative theory. The problems it studies include the relevance of mistaken moral beliefs or weaknesses of the will or mistake of fact or clumsiness, etc, on the attribution of responsibility or blame.[28]

So defined, ascriptive questions about conduct look as if they overlap substantially with what were called capacity questions about conduct, when the second dimension to excuses was discussed above. However, ascriptive questions are questions about the blame D must accept for doing wrong, *whether or not* the main focus is an actively justificatory element in D's conduct, or the understandable limitations of D's rational or moral capacities. So, it is helpful, albeit somewhat complex, to keep the idea of ascriptive questions separate from that of capacity questions *stricto sensu*.

It is tempting to map Raz's theory directly on to the criminal law, by thinking of the substantive prohibitions of the criminal law as being the normative part of the criminal law, concerned exclusively with what ought not to be done, and then by thinking of the excusatory part of the criminal law as being (an aspect of) the ascriptive part, concerned with when those in breach of legal norms are not to be blamed and convicted.[29] To do this would not, perhaps, be entirely wrong, but it would be misleading. When, say, one loses one's temper when one should not, one is in breach of a normative standard, the standard of good temper-keeping. It is just that this is not a normative standard (unlike those that make up the substantive prohibitions of the criminal law) that is in and of itself concerned with causing or threatening harm.[30]

---

[28] Joseph Raz, *Practical Reason and Norms*, 11–12.

[29] One finds such a tidy division of theoretical labour in the work, for example, of Paul Robinson: see Paul Robinson, *Structure and Function in Criminal Law*, chapter 2.

[30] However, one can obviously see a case for saying that the two kinds of normative standard are related. One could, say, call my duty not to harm others 'primary', arguing that I then have 'secondary' duties to avoid doing things that may lead me into breach of my primary

How much one is to blame, then, for losing one's temper—the ascriptive question, in Raz's terms—is a question that, at least in part, can be kept distinct from the normative question it presupposes: whether one should have lost one's temper at all in the first place. A successful plea of provocation seems to presuppose a positive answer to the normative question whether it was morally acceptable or permissible to lose one's temper at all. For, if that would not have been acceptable (surely, for example, the President of the USA should *never* lose his or her temper when one finger is hovering over the nuclear 'button', whatever the provocation), the case for a partial excuse when D has harmed another in anger does not even get off the ground. That having been said, provocation should be understood as a predominantly ascriptive (partial) excuse. Its central question, answered in the light of an assessment of the gravity of the provocation received, is how much D is to blame for losing control of the urge to kill. Not only do we take it for granted that there was no real (normative) justification whatsoever for actually killing V,[31] but any belief D had that he or she was so justified is also irrelevant. If the provocation leading D to lose his or her self-control and kill was grave enough to warrant partial excuse, it will not matter that, at the moment of killing V, D was not agent-perspectivally justified, in that he or she was well aware that the act was wholly unjustified.

For the purposes of some excuses, though, normative questions about what D did to V, and hence also questions of agent-perspectival justification about that matter, may play a more central role. Consider excessive defence. For some theorists, one should be regarded as excused respecting a mistaken act purportedly taken in self-defence, almost however disproportionate the act is to the threat believed by D to exist.[32] Except possibly as a means of permitting escape from a mandatory life sentence upon conviction for murder, such an approach seems to give D too much excusatory latitude when there has been a gross departure from acceptable standards governing the limits of a response to the threat.[33] Other than in exceptional cases, for the

---

duties, like losing my temper when I shouldn't; but this perhaps obscures the point that there are many other reasons, unrelated to the harm that I might do, not to lose my temper on inappropriate occasions.

[31] A point made with admirable clarity, escaping the ambiguity about the matter that in Jeremy Horder, *Provocation and Responsibility*, I myself unfortunately kept in circulation, by Victor Tadros, 'The Characters of Excuse' (2001) 21 *Oxford Journal of Legal Studies* 495, 507–508. The absence of justification can be explained in a number of ways. I have suggested, for example, that it stems from the fact that D acts retrospectively, retaliating in a (broadly) punitive spirit. By way of contrast, in duress and self-defence or excessive defence cases, D acts prospectively, to avert or thwart a threat to an (*ex hypothesi*) innocent person (him- or herself): see Jeremy Horder, 'Autonomy, Provocation and Duress' (1992) *Criminal Law Review* 706.

[32] See the discussion of the history of the German law governing self-defence in Markus Funk, 'Justifying Justifications' (1999) 19 *Oxford Journal of Legal Studies* 631.

[33] See, further, Andrew Ashworth, 'Self-Defence and the Right to Life' (1975) 34 *Cambridge Law Journal* 272, and the discussion by the Victorian Law Reform Commission, *Defences to*

purposes of excessive defence claims, it can be important not only that D was justified in being fearful of the threat, but also (a) that the harm D intentionally did to V did not in fact go *too far* beyond that which would have been, normatively, truly justified,[34] and (b) that D's claim is actively justificatory in character: that he or she believed that the harm done was normatively justifiable.[35] (A), in particular, is the feature of excessive defence claims that makes them predominantly normative. In order to know whether D should be excused, the most important thing we need to know is what would have been the limits of a permissible, fully or truly justified response, an inquiry with no moral significance in, say, provocation cases. For, D's claim in the typical excessive defence case is, in part, that his or her departure from what would have been genuinely permissible was not *that* great, and that such departure as there was is hence excusable, given the additional ascriptive and capacity-focused element in the plea, constituted by the effects on D of the understandable strength of his or her reasonable fear for his or her safety.

The inclusion of (a) as an element in the excuse is practically significant, in that it can seem appropriate *completely* to excuse deliberate wrongdoing, even wrongdoing involving a serious rights violation, when the excuse has the predominantly normative basis that the satisfaction of (a) gives it, even though the remaining ascriptive element to a plea of excessive defence is still vital.[36] By way of contrast, it might seem appropriate only *partly* to excuse a deliberate and serious rights violation, when the excuse has a predominantly ascriptive basis, as in provocation or diminished capacity cases. In that regard, though, we should note that although duress and

---

Homicide (Options Paper) (Melbourne, Victoria: Victorian Law Reform Commission, 2003), 159–161. See now, Law Commission for England and Wales, *Murder, Manslaughter and Infanticide*, part 5.

[34] English law secures (a) in duress cases by insisting in all cases that the threat to him- or herself that D is seeking to avoid through the wrong done is in all cases a threat of death or serious harm, and then by refusing to permit the excuse to apply in murder (or attempted murder) cases themselves: see *R v Howe* [1987] AC 417. No doubt, greater flexibility could be introduced into the law, without abandoning the normative element to the excuse, by relaxing the requirement of a threat of death or serious harm in some cases. Surely, for example, it might be right to permit the defence to operate when D is threatened that his or her daughter will be kidnapped for an unspecified period of time, unless some minor act of property damage is done by D. See, further Andrew Ashworth, *Principles of Criminal Law*, 3rd edn., 228.

[35] Subject to the point made earlier that (b) may not be as important in duress cases as it is in excessive defence cases.

[36] Notwithstanding the central importance of the normative dimension to D's claim to excuse, it is still true of excessive defence cases, as it is of provocation and mistake cases, that one admits wrongdoing, and hence makes in part an ascriptive claim to be acquitted. Moreover, the importance of this ascriptive element to the excuse of excessive defence should not be under-estimated. In such a case, it must be an ascriptive judgment that it was D's understandable terror that made him or her think appropriate what was in fact a little too much force (the predominantly normative element), and not, say, D's pseudo-justificatory view that trespassers must be dealt with ruthlessly, that completes the case for an excuse.

excessive defence provide the main examples of excuses that can operate on a predominantly normative basis, either of them could quite properly be permitted to operate in a predominantly ascriptive way. I will discuss this point in greater detail in section 5 below, but let me give one example now. Suppose D has some natural and understandable vulnerability, making him or her specially prey to the effects of fear. It could then be right to formulate D's claim to excuse in a predominantly ascriptive way, giving D greater latitude in terms of the circumstances in which the plea might be successful, by making it unnecessary for D to satisfy conditions (a) and (b) above. Consider the vexed status of duress as an excusatory plea in murder cases. Whatever the case, in general, for regarding murder as inexcusable under duress, it could still count (ascriptively) in D's favour in a murder case that the reason D did not stay faithful to the realization that he or she should never respond to a threat by killing an innocent person, to save his or her own skin, was that, say, D was so young that this realization did not have the moral significance it would have had were D an adult. Perhaps, then, D should be partially excused for murder committed under duress, in such a case, on a predominantly ascriptive basis, rather than being denied any excuse at all on predominantly normative grounds (see the end of section 5 below).

Let me return to the case for regarding excessive defence as a predominantly normative excuse. English law governing the permissible or justified limits of self-defence harbours a concealed, very limited, complete 'excuse' of excessive defence. If D has to use force to defend himself against V, in law that force must, *inter alia*, have been reasonable if it is to be truly justified.[37] English law takes a generous view, however, of how the jury should go about its task of judging the element of reasonableness in D's use of force. It is within this generous view that a complete excuse for a slightly excessive defensive reaction lies concealed. Lord Morris explained the generous view this way:

> If there has been an attack so that defence is reasonably necessary it will be recognised that a person defending himself cannot weigh to a nicety the exact measure of his defensive action. If a jury thought that in a moment of unexpected anguish a person attacked had only done what he honestly and instinctively thought was necessary that would be most potent evidence that only reasonable defensive action had been taken.[38]

In this passage, Lord Morris misleadingly implies that people acting in self-defence will tend to over-estimate the amount of force required only when their defensive act is undertaken on the basis of what I have been calling an explanatory reason (hence, the reference to what is 'instinctively' thought

---

[37] In theory, then, English law is stricter than the position endorsed by the High Court of Australia in *Zecevic v DPP* (Vic) (1987) 162 CLR 645, 661, where it was held that 'the question to be asked in the end is quite simple. It is whether the accused believed upon reasonable grounds that it was necessary to do what he or she did.'

[38] *Palmer v R* [1971] 1 All ER 1077, 1078 (PC), endorsed in *R v Shannon* (1980) 71 Cr App Rep 192.

necessary, in a moment of 'unexpected anguish').[39] Lord Morris's main point, though, is that when fear understandably takes the form of 'unexpected anguish' in the face of a sudden attack, what it is objectively reasonable to do in self-defence may begin to merge with what D 'instinctively' him- or herself mistakenly concludes that it is reasonable to do. In such cases, the question 'is D truly justified (acting just within the limits of the truly permissible), or is D to be completely excused (the normative element of what D took to be a justification being so strong)?' has something of the quality of the 'is it a duck, or is it a rabbit?' question in relation to the celebrated drawing.[40] It seems clear, though, that the limits of action that can be justified in self-defence, and the limits of action in self-defence that should be completely excused even though it was slightly excessive, will part company at the moment when D's reaction manifestly exceeds what was objectively reasonable. At that point, moreover, far from being justified or excused, in English law D is left with no defence at all.[41] Especially in murder cases, where D could be partially excused for an excessive—but not grossly excessive—reaction, there is a case for saying that the law has become too fixated by the issue of true justification. Only in extreme cases, where the force is grossly excessive, should a conviction for murder be warranted.[42] Even when excess force has been used, one ought in law to be able to say that the less excessive the force that was believed by D to be necessary to defend himself, in the moment of unexpected anguish, the better the case for at least a partial excuse. This is the predominantly normative way of conceptualizing a partial excuse of excessive defence.[43]

---

[39] It seems unlikely, though, that Lord Morris would wish to exclude someone from taking the benefit of this dictum simply because, in spite of their terror, they acted for an adopted reason, so long as that reason retains its actively justificatory character.

[40] In practice, thus, English law operates in much the same way as if it were governed by *Zecevic v DPP* (Vic) (1987) 162 CLR 645, except, of course, for its indefensible adherence to the view that D's belief in the need to use force *at all* need only be honest: *R v Williams (Gladstone)* [1987] 3 All ER 411. This decision, based on a bizarre analogy with the (equally indefensible) legal understanding of the mental element in rape cases, where a belief in consent need only be honest, runs contrary to the law governing most of the wider common law world, and has been rejected by the European Court of Human Rights. In spite of that, perhaps almost needless to say, it remains central to the Law Commission's plans for reform of the defence of excessive defence: see Law Commission for England and Wales, *Partial Defences to Murder*, part 9.   [41] See *R v Clegg* [1995] AC 482.

[42] See Ashworth's comments in Andrew Ashworth, *Principles of Criminal Law*, 3rd edn., 286–288. See also the analysis by the Law Commission for England and Wales, *Partial Defences to Murder*, where a predominantly ascriptive basis for a new partial defence of excessive defence is contemplated, in part 9.

[43] As we will see, I argue in chapter 4.10 below that if D can combine evidence of mental deficiency (falling short of evidence that would in itself warrant a diminished responsibility verdict) with evidence that the actively justificatory element was satisfied, in that he or she only did what he or she thought necessary in self-defence, there could be a case for partial excusing an excessive reaction in a much broader range of cases, but on a diminished capacity—rather than excessive defence—basis.

UNIVERSITY OF WINCHESTER

If there is an ascriptive element to predominantly normative excusatory claims, is there a normative element to predominantly ascriptive claims? There is, but it serves a different function to the function it serves in excessive defence cases. It cannot tell us how far beyond what would have been truly justified D's action went, because D's conduct (*ex hypothesi*) lacks any such justification. Instead, the normative element tells us when D's action is clearly *in*excusable. It could be, for example, that however persistent the 'provocation' one should never be excused for violently expressing one's temper by harming a crying baby.[44] It could, at least in some circumstances, likewise be inexcusable for D to commit war crimes or treason, to commit or participate in an act of mass murder, or to subject V to life-threatening or disabling torture, even when confronted by a threat of imminent death him- or herself. One of the features distinguishing excuses from pure denials of responsibility is that this underlying normative element to excuses is lacking in pure denial of responsibility claims. Insanity could be a good ground for an acquittal in any of the circumstances just mentioned: it would, indeed, clearly be unjust to deprive D of such a defence if the facts revealed evidence of it. The reason is that an excusatory claim concedes that D is still to some extent in evaluative contact with underlying guiding reasons, including reasons to refrain from some actions whatever the circumstances, in a way that is (*ex hypothesi*) not true of insanity cases.[45]

5. THE THIRD DIMENSION TO EXCUSING: HOW DURESS CASES FIT IN

How do duress cases fit into the picture, within the third dimension to excusing? They are difficult to categorize, because they can take both predominantly normative and predominantly ascriptive forms. All duress cases calling for excuse have at least one ascriptive aspect to them similar to that which characterizes excessive defence cases. The great phenomenological strength of D's fear must alter the balance of reasons in D's mind, so that he or she understandably gives priority to saving him- or herself, if need be by committing the wrong in question (see sections 10 and 11 below). Beyond that, is the basis of D's excuse simply that we do not blame D at all, or at least not all that much, for giving in to certain kinds of threats by doing certain kinds of wrongs (the predominantly ascriptive explanation)?

[44] See *R v Doughty* (1986) 83 Cr App Rep 319 for discussion of such an example, in which the Court of Appeal missed an opportunity to say that there might be some actions that were inexcusable under certain kinds of provocation, notwithstanding the changes to the law brought about by section 3 of the Homicide Act 1957. See, further, A. P. Simester and G. R. Sullivan, *Criminal Law: Theory and Doctrine*, 1st edn., 250–252.

[45] For further discussion, see Jeremy Horder, 'Criminal Law: Between Determinism, Liberalism and Criminal Justice', 166–172.

Or, is D excused because his or her reaction did not go far beyond what was truly justified, as in excessive defence cases (the predominantly normative explanation)? It is not easy to give a simple answer to these questions. Let me start with the complexity about the predominantly normative explanation.

In excessive defence cases, D can be described as acting defensively, so long as his or her reason for action has a certain, actively justificatory form. D must believe (albeit, mistakenly) that he or she is doing only what is needed to repel or ward off the attack or threat.[46] In duress *per minas* cases, by way of contrast, D's action is not defensive, because he or she is not directly repelling or warding off an attack or threat, but doing something with a different normative significance. He or she is complying with the unwelcome and unwarranted demands of the threatener, thereby (as D believes) taking reasonable steps to *negate* the threat that is backing up the demands.[47] By way of contrast, then, with self-defence (and, indeed, necessity[48]) cases, in duress cases the commission of the particular unlawful acts cannot, straightforwardly, become rationally apparent to D him- or herself by (rapid) calculation of what it will take to repel or ward off a particular threat. The commission of those acts is, instead, artificially pushed (high) on to D's agenda by the coercive nature of the threat made, a threat to which it may, or may not, then be rational to respond as D does, depending on the circumstances.[49] The very fact that D's conduct is directed at negating the threat to him- or herself, by compliance with the threatener's demands, rather than at repelling or thwarting it (as in excessive defence cases), means that D's conduct is much more readily stripped of any shred of normative justification. In a duress case, more drastic measures might more readily be justified actually to overpower or disable the threatener, thus repelling or thwarting the threat by genuinely defensive steps, than could ever be justified in committing wrongdoing—especially wrongdoing invading an innocent third party's rights—merely to satisfy the threatener's demands, thus negating the threat.[50]

[46] For general discussion, see Suzanne Uniacke, *Permissible Killing: The Self-Defence Justification of Homicide* (Cambridge: Cambridge University Press, 1994), chapter 1.

[47] See the discussion in Jeremy Horder, 'Self-Defence, Necessity and Duress: Understanding the Relationship' (1998) 11 *Canadian Journal of Law and Jurisprudence* 143, 149–150. What are, in English law, called 'duress of circumstances' cases are different again (ibid., 160–163). I shall be concentrating largely on duress *per minas* in the discussion that follows.

[48] Or by way of contrast with 'duress of circumstances' cases, cases of necessity arising in emergency situations: see the discussion in A. P. Simester and G. R. Sullivan, *Criminal Law: Theory and Doctrine*, 1st edn., 593–595, and in Jeremy Horder, 'Self-Defence, Necessity and Duress: Understanding the Relationship', 160–163.

[49] For an illuminating examination of the nature of coercion, see Grant Lamond, 'Coercion, Threats, and the Puzzle of Blackmail', in A. P. Simester and A. T. H. Smith (eds.), *Harm and Culpability*, 215.

[50] See the discussion in Jeremy Horder, 'Self-Defence, Necessity and Duress: Understanding the Relationship', 149–150.

One might wonder, then, what the argument is for saying that there can ever be a significant normative dimension to the excuse of duress at all. The argument rests on showing that what might somewhat misleadingly be called 'self-preferential' actions can sometimes be truly justified, and hence have a normative dimension. I am under a duty to give others' interests a certain moral weight (which will naturally vary, depending on who the others are, and on what the interest is), in relation to my own activities; but I am also entitled, and duty-bound, to assign some moral weight to my own interests. To wish to preserve one's own life and vital interests, because one values them highly, obviously does not involve merely a crude agent-relative preference, of the kind in issue when someone says 'I love scratching mosquito-bites'. Furthermore, the value of wishing to preserve one's own life and other vital interests cannot be equated straightforwardly with the value that an activity or pursuit takes on when people simply opt to identify with the goals associated with it, as in the case, say, of stamp-collecting or of football. One has a duty to oneself to value one's own life and vital interests (even if there are some things for which one should be prepared to sacrifice them), to assign to them the value they ought to be regarded as having. One should not be thought of as simply having 'opted' to regard them as valuable. That being accepted, the way is open to understanding some self-preferential actions as capable of having a truly justificatory character, or a predominantly normative excusatory character, when D's life or vital interests are under threat due to duress.[51] So, in cases where we are confident that the threatener will carry out the threat, if the demands are not met, there can be a true justification for preferring, say, to invade a minor property interest rather than suffer certain death or serious injury oneself.[52] Such cases can, in effect, be treated as if they were ones of necessity, in which D prefers the lesser to the greater evil, because the correct choice of evil by D is now doing the lion's share of the defence-building work, as compared with the much less significant, although not unimportant, ascriptive element of fear of the greater evil. In such a case, then (for those who attach great theoretical importance to these matters), it would be permissible for a third party who acted in order to help D save him- or herself to assist in the commission of the crime to negate the threat, whereas this would not be so if D had been required, say, to inflict grievous bodily harm on an innocent person or suffer it himself at the hands of the threatener.[53] There may,

---

[51] As Hart recognized: H. L. A. Hart, *Punishment and Responsibility*, 16, '[I]f the crime which A requires B to commit is a petty one compared with the serious harm threatened . . . by A there would be no absurdity in treating A's threat as a justification for B's conduct though few legal systems overtly do this.'

[52] See the discussion in Jeremy Horder, 'Self-Defence, Necessity and Duress: Understanding the Relationship', 155–156; Alan Brudner, 'A Theory of Necessity' (1987) 7 *Oxford Journal of Legal Studies* 339; M. Bayles, 'Reconceptualising Necessity and Duress', in M. L. Corrado (ed.), *Justification and Excuse in the Criminal Law*, 492.

[53] See Jeremy Horder, 'Self-Defence, Necessity and Duress: Understanding the Relationship', 160.

though, be little more than a question of degree separating duress cases in which the conduct in question is truly justified, and duress cases in which the conduct is unjustified, and hence falls to be excused, on a predominantly normative basis.

Suppose, for example, that a threat of death can truly justify a trespass to the person of an innocent third party in order to avoid the threat, so long as the injury is no more than transient and trifling.[54] The question of what injuries are to count as transient and trifling is, in part, one of degree. In such cases, then, the more difficult it is to say whether the commission of a given wrong was *un*justifiable, the harder it will be to say whether D is relying, as his claim to an acquittal, primarily on the fact that he made the normatively permissible choice of a lesser evil (justification), or on the fact that his great fear of a grave threat led him understandably to choose to do the wrong thing (excuse). No doubt, in borderline cases, we should give D the benefit of the doubt and treat his or her choice as one that was truly justified, but there will be limits to this. There will be cases in which we are satisfied that D has gone beyond, if not all that far beyond, what can be justified. In circumstances like this, D's excuse is still *predominantly* normative in character. A central element to it is the claim that the conduct is close to the borderline between what is truly justifiable, and what stands in need of excuse but falls just outside the scope of what is justifiable.[55] Support in English law for this way of thinking of the excuse of duress (in this case, duress of circumstances) has come from the Court of Appeal in *R v Martin*,[56] where it was said of D's actions that, 'from an objective standpoint, the accused could be said to be acting reasonably and *proportionately* in order to avoid the threat of death or serious injury'.[57] The less serious the

---

[54] Alan Brudner gives a controversial example, in the necessity context, of taking a blood sample from an unconsenting person: Alan Brudner, 'A Theory of Necessity', 365, 'taking blood from an unwilling donor would be justified if the battery were objectively necessary to the saving of life and if it imposed no real risk to the capacity for action of the victim.' This might, at best, be considered to be at the extreme end of what can count as transient and trifling.

[55] The limited nature of this departure, in point of justifiable means, given that the end or goal in view is justified, is what commentators have referred to as the element of 'partial justification'. In this phrase, the word 'partial' is a perhaps rather misleading way of saying 'predominant element of' justification. The language of 'partial justification' can be found in Andrew Ashworth's path-breaking portrayal of the defence provocation as part excuse, part justification: see Andrew Ashworth, 'The Defence of Provocation', drawing on Austin's 'A Plea for Excuses'. Ashworth's distinction is adopted and elaborated on in Jeremy Horder, *Provocation and Responsibility*, chapter 6, although as indicated earlier, my account of the normative—justificatory—element in provocation cases is now in need of substantial modification.   [56] [1989] 1 All ER 652.

[57] Ibid., 653 (per Simon Brown J) cited by K. J. M. Smith, 'Must Heroes Behave Heroically?' (1989) *Criminal Law Review* 622, 627 (with Smith's emphasis). It is possible the Court is alluding in this passage to instances where duress completely justifies conduct, although that seems unlikely. See also *A-G v Whelan* [1934] IR 518, 526, 'Threats of immediate death or serious personal violence so great as to overbear the ordinary powers of human resistance should be accepted as a *justification* for acts which would otherwise be criminal' (per Murnaghan J, my emphasis).

harm D is being required to inflict, as compared with the harm with which D is threatened, the better the (predominantly) normative case there will be for an excuse, even though D's act is still wrong. Even when D inflicts an unjustifiable harm on an innocent V, crucial to D's excuse can be the claim that there was at least a kind of normative or justificatory 'logic' to D's decision to inflict that (*ex hypothesi*, minor) harm, particularly if D did so to avoid certain *death* him- or herself.[58]

What marks duress cases out from excessive defence cases is that we will not always be able to analyse the normative element in the excuse in the simple terms applicable to excessive defence cases, namely in terms of how far beyond what would have been truly justified D has gone. This is because a simple comparison or weighing of the competing options with which D has forcibly been confronted will not always be possible. Threats can be tailored to prey on particular weaknesses or horrors that D has, perhaps in common with many others, whose effects cannot be weighed on the same set of scales as (are incommensurable with) wrongs D is required to commit to avert them. Suppose D is confronted with a choice of being forced to eat ever more putrefied amounts of rotting flesh, or agreeing to inflict bodily harm on another person. Ignoring, for present purposes, any impact on D's thinking made by the prospect that he or she may be physically harmed by eating such flesh, central to such an example is whether D can be required to (make efforts to) overcome his or her repugnance, to avoid having to inflict harm on another. It is no longer a straightforward matter of asking whether or not D has gone 'too far beyond' what would have been truly justified, because the two options are incommensurable. As we will see in section 11 below, in some instances one legitimate way of escaping the problem is to regard D's conduct in agreeing to inflict the harm as 'non-voluntary'. That would be the right approach if, say, D eats until he can (physically, and/or psychologically) go on no longer, and so complies with the coercer's demand. D is then denying full responsibility for his compliance, though, rather than seeking an excuse for it.

What if D does need an excuse for his conduct, in such circumstances? This would probably be the case if D simply refused point blank to eat the rotting flesh, agreeing in advance to do anything to avoid having to eat it, because D would ordinarily remain morally 'active' with regard to that refusal (see chapter 1.1 above). In such a case, D's claim to an excuse on the basis of duress is, as in provocation cases, predominantly ascriptive. In other words, we do not blame D much, or at all, for failing to overcome his or her repugnance and refusing to eat the rotting flesh, even though it is unjustified to inflict harm to avoid having to do so; but, as in provocation cases, what D can be excused doing to avoid eating it is bounded by at least some normative limits. So, the

---

[58] As we will see, this element of justification may even be present in some cases in which D deliberately kills V to save him- or herself. See chapter 3.8 below.

President of the USA perhaps ought not to refuse *point blank* to eat any of the flesh, if the alternative is pushing the nuclear button. Whether or not it is appropriate for the law to make mandatory such a 'counsel of perfection' is a matter considered further at the end of section 9 below, and in chapter 3.11 below. We should conclude by reminding ourselves that there is a further category of case in which duress cases could be permitted to take a predominantly ascriptive form. This is where allowance is made, or should be made, for a greater weakness in the face of a threat that arises in the course of normal human development, or that reflects natural features of human diversity, the main example being youth.[59] We cannot, for example, necessarily expect that the sacred character of human life, and the inviolability of other vital human interests, will have impressed themselves on someone who is only thirteen years of age, in the way that it should have done on someone thirty years old. So, even when a thirteen-year-old does something wholly beyond the normative pale, when threatened with death or torture, it could be right not to blame him or her for giving in, in the face of the phenomenological strength of his or her fear, and hence right to excuse him or her on a predominantly ascriptive basis. That the House of Lords did not think to make such a concession, in holding that duress could *never* be a defence to murder, is an indication that it has become too wedded to the predominantly normative view of the excuse of duress.[60]

6. Working with the Three Dimensions to Excuse

Individual excuses can be differentiated from one another in each dimension, as can different manifestations of the same excuse; and there is a surprising amount of variation. Let me give some examples. Excessive defence and most duress cases involve adopted, actively justificatory reasons for action (dimensions 1 and 2),[61] and have a predominantly normative basis (dimension 3). If an excuse claim is predominantly ascriptive in character (dimension 3), it may also be capacity-based, as in the cases of provocation, clumsiness, due diligence or diminished capacity, but that is not always so. When D pleads factual mistake, as when in a rape case D says that he believed V was consenting to intercourse when V was not, the claim to excuse is actively justificatory

---

[59] The impact of mental deficiency or disorder in duress cases is considered, as part of the analysis of diminished capacity cases, in chapter 4.10 below.

[60] *R v Howe* [1987] AC 417. The House of Lords' omission is especially culpable, given that the House acknowledged the force of analogy with provocation cases, in which allowance is made for youth, in what can be expected of the person well-equipped with powers of self-control.

[61] However, as I said earlier, in some excessive defence cases D may act for an explanatory reason (lashing out instinctively in response to a sudden threat), and in some duress cases D may have to be excused on a capacity-focused rather than actively justificatory basis, because D is aware that what he or she is doing lacks normative justification.

(dimension 2). The claim depends on being able to show that the reason for action adopted (dimension 1) was a belief[62] in the lawfulness—the consensual nature—of the intercourse, untainted by the realization that he (D) might be in error. D's claim is, nonetheless, a predominantly ascriptive claim to excuse (dimension 3). There is not a shred of justification for what D actually does, whatever the justification for D's belief. Analogously, when D's excusatory plea is focused on a mistaken belief in the need to bow to a moral imperative created by, say, D's religious beliefs (demands-of-conscience cases), D's claim to excuse is that he or she believed that the moral reason for action he or she adopted (dimension 1) actively justified his or her conduct (dimension 2). It is accepted, though, that there was in reality no true justification for what D did, and hence that D's claim to excuse is predominantly ascriptive in character (dimension 3).

It would be possible to drive a theoretical wedge between excuses, depending on whether they possess certain features in each dimension. For example, one would expect neo-Hegelian theories of excuse to lay special emphasis on those excuses that have an actively justificatory character, because (other than in demands-of-conscience cases), such excuses are inconsistent with a realization on D's part that he or she is or may be wronging another person. As Brudner puts it:

When I unintentionally wrong a person, I do not deny his capacity for rights, *but merely err as to the scope of those rights* or as to the things to which they extend . . . Accordingly, since liability to criminal punishment requires a subjective *mens rea*, a mistake concerning some fact essential to the *actus reus* excuses from liability for that crime.[63]

Brudner is obviously speaking of factual mistake here but if, as in English law,[64] one takes the absence of a 'lawful defence' justification to be an element in the *actus reus*, then a denial of *mens rea* extends to a belief in the justification for one's action in excessive defence cases. For, in those cases, just as much as in factual mistake cases, there is no 'intentional or (advertently) reckless disdain for the autonomy of another self . . . '.[65] On this view, then, there would seem to be little scope for capacity-focused excuses that are consistent with deliberate or knowing wrongdoing, such as duress and provocation.[66]

---

[62] A belief that (in self-defence cases, as in rape cases) may, in some jurisdictions, have to have been adequately grounded—see n. 40 above, and section 1 of the Sexual Offences Act 2003—creating an overlap with the capacity-focused basis for excusing within dimension 2.

[63] Alan Brudner, 'Agency and Welfare in the Penal Law', 32 and 35 (my emphasis).

[64] *R v Williams (Gladstone)* (1987) 3 All ER 411.

[65] Alan Brudner, 'Agency and Welfare in the Penal Law', 35.

[66] So, the fact that Brudner seeks to extend his neo-Hegelian theory of excuses to almost all existing excuses, even when they involve deliberate wrongdoing—such as duress and provocation—puts the theory, in my view, under considerable theoretical strain. For a theory perhaps closer to the neo-Hegelian view being expounded in the text, see R. Schopp, *Justification Defences and Just Convictions* (Cambridge: Cambridge University Press, 1998), chapter 5.

Alternatively, one might seek to develop a set of distinctions between excuses that are predominantly normative (most duress cases; excessive defence cases), *whether or not* they have an actively justificatory character, and those with a capacity-focused, predominantly ascriptive character (provocation cases; demands-of-conscience cases), confining one's understanding of the excuses for deliberate or knowing wrongdoing that should be permitted in a criminal code to the former. This would be one, narrow way of interpreting what Gardner has aptly described as the theoretical 'priority of justification over excuse'.[67] In early English law, excuses seem to have been thought of in this kind of way. There was what looks very much like a defence of excessive defence (even if it was not exactly so described).[68] The categories of provocation sufficient to reduce murder to manslaughter almost all involved an over-reaction to an incident that would have justified the use of some force, at least.[69] Finally, it was tolerably clear that duress was a defence only to crimes that could in some sense be described as lesser evils than the ones Ds sought to avoid. Murder, thus, was not counted amongst such crimes.[70] This narrow way of understanding excuses sees them as little more than the by-product of a theory of justified harming in self-defence, or under conditions of necessity. Some modern, non-liberal states have provisions setting out defences inspired by something rather like this narrow view of excuses. There is, for example, a concentration on denials of responsibility, justifications, and matters relevant only to sentencing. Excusing conditions exist only precariously, at the outer limits of the justifications.[71] In chapter 5.1 below, we will see there is nothing definitively 'illiberal' about the taking a narrow view of excusing conditions in a criminal code. A liberal state could embody the narrow view of excuses in its criminal code, if the lenient treatment of offenders with (morally speaking) good excuses for their conduct is in some other way made possible or required.

Putting this point on one side, however, Gardner himself measures what he calls the priority of justification over excuse differently. For him, one stands to be excused if one lived up to one's role as a human being, by coming up, in the circumstances, to the relevant standard (of self-restraint, of self-control, or of care in coming to certain beliefs).[72] As he puts it:

The gist of an excuse ... is precisely that the person with the excuse lived up to our expectations ... in the *normative* sense. Did she manifest as much resilience, or

---

[67] John Gardner, 'Justifications and Reasons', 118.

[68] *R v Buckner* (1641) Style 467. See the explanation of the plea in the judgment of Chief Justice Holt in *R v Mawgridge* (1707) Kel 119.

[69] See Andrew Ashworth, 'The Doctrine of Provocation'; L. H. Leigh, 'A Philosophy of Provocation?' (1993) 56 *Modern Law Review* 600, 601–602.

[70] Sir W. Blackstone, *Commentaries on the Laws of England*, 4 vols. (Oxford: Clarendon Press, 1765), iv, 30.   [71] As under the Chinese criminal code: see chapter 5.1 below.

[72] This view is analysed in depth in chapter 3.3 and 3.4 below.

loyalty, or thoroughness, or presence of mind as a person in her situation should have manifested? In the face of terrible threats, for example, did this person show as much fortitude as someone in his situation could properly be asked to show? In the face of constant taunts, did this person exhibit as much self-restraint as we have a right to demand of someone in her situation?[73]

The fact that Gardner analyses provocation in the same way as duress shows that his theory of excuses, the 'normative expectations' view, goes wider than the narrow view described just now. We can trace the historical movement in English law towards this wider view, to developments—such as the abandoning of specific categories of provocation sufficient to reduce murder to manslaughter—in the middle of the nineteenth century.[74] From that point onwards, it was no longer supposed that when D pleads provocation, he or she is doing no more than taking a genuinely justificatory warrant to use force a little too far.[75] Excuses were now permitted to vary along the three dimensions explained above, as set out below.

Some duress cases:
Adopted reason
Actively justificatory
Predominantly normative

Excessive defence cases:
Adopted/Explanatory reason
Actively justificatory
Predominantly normative

Some provocation/some duress/demands-of-conscience cases:
Adopted reason
Objective capacity-focused
Predominantly ascriptive

Some provocation/some accident cases:
Explanatory reason
Objective capacity-focused
Predominantly ascriptive

Some diminished capacity/clumsiness cases:
Explanatory reason
Subjective capacity-focused
Predominantly ascriptive

---

[73] John Gardner, 'The Gist of Excuses', 578 and 579 (his emphasis in the text).

[74] See Jeremy Horder, *Provocation and Responsibility*, chapter 5.

[75] The final nail in the narrow view's coffin, in this regard, would probably have to be the reversal of *DPP v Holmes* [1946] AC 588, and the inclusion of insulting words, alongside threatening words, as a kind of provocation fit to be considered by the jury, by section 3 of the Homicide Act 1957.

Other diminished capacity cases:
Adopted reason
Subjective capacity-focused
Predominantly ascriptive

Due diligence cases:
Adopted reason
Objective capacity-focused
Predominantly ascriptive

Mistake cases:
Explanatory/Adopted reason
Objective capacity-focused
Predominantly ascriptive

A good deal of further elaboration of the distinctions just set out should probably be provided, but I will confine myself at this point to a few observations. For example, I distinguish provocation cases into different categories, according to whether or not they involve explanatory or adopted reasons. I do this to highlight the case I will make, in section 12 below, that one should not excuse in provocation cases, if one is going to excuse at all, where D has retaliated on the basis of an adopted reason; and the same goes, as we will see at the end of chapter 4.6 below, for diminished capacity cases where the excusatory element is a provoked loss of self-control. Contrariwise, I do not distinguish between excessive defence or mistake cases in which D acts for an adopted reason, and cases of these kinds in which D acts for an explanatory reason, as the distinction has no theoretical or practical implications.[76] Finally, although there is no extended discussion of clumsiness as an excuse in this book, because—like mistake—it does not involve intentional or knowing wrongdoing, it is worth pointing out that it is an open question whether an excuse based on clumsiness should be judged by the objective or the subjective version of the capacity theory.[77] Perhaps we can only discover by investigation of an individual's circumstances how much he or she can do to avoid dropping things, bumping into people, and so forth. If so, the subjective version of the capacity theory is the appropriate excusatory yardstick. It might be, though, that we can and

---

[76] Mistake cases may involve explanatory reasons as opposed to adopted reasons, as when one changes into the wrong gear 'without thinking' when driving. Excessive defence cases involve explanatory reasons, as opposed to adopted reasons, when one just lashes out with (say) a knife one is holding when suddenly and unexpectedly attacked in some minor way. Little of theoretical or practical significance hangs on the distinction between the two kinds of case, since they may both legitimately be governed by requirements of reasonableness, on an objective, capacity-focused view of how these pleas operate as excuses.

[77] The distinction between these two versions of the capacity theory is explained in chapter 3.6 below. In chapter 1.1 above, I treated clumsiness as a case governed by the subjective version of the capacity theory.

should hold every clumsy person, who is not physically disabled in some way, to be capable of mastering their clumsiness in some situations, as when holding a baby, in which case the objective version of the capacity theory can have a role to play here.

It is now time to turn to a detailed examination of the philosophical basis of excuses that turn at least in part on a finding that there was what was called (in chapter 1.1 above) a 'rational defect' in a morally salient moving force behind an action. These are excuses, such as provocation or duress, where it is emotional pressure on the will that creates the rational defect in a key moving force behind the action, or excuses such as mistake, where it is ignorance of crucial relevant facts that creates that defect in the relevant moving force. In the latter case, the moving force behind the action is rationally defective, because D is (reasonably) unaware of vital facts that tip the balance of justificatory reasons against doing as D did.[78] In the former, the action is rationally defective because strong emotion has either (a) in the case where the emotion is the explanatory reason for the action, simply by-passed the controlling influence of reason, and hence of guiding reasons, or (b) in the case where emotion leads to an adopted reason for action, made to seem diminished the true significance of reason, and hence of guiding reasons counting against what D does. In section 7 below, I will consider two kinds of reasons that have salience in cases where rational defects of this kind are in play. Then, our concern will switch to the issue of how the claim that excuses are founded on some rational defect in a salient moving force behind the action is to be squared with the claim that, by their nature as excusatory claims, they involve the morally active side of D's nature.

7. OPERATING AND AUXILIARY REASONS, IN EXCUSING CONDITIONS

Suppose I wish to buy a particular newspaper. I believe there is one for sale in the only shop nearby. So, I now have a reason to go to the nearby shop to buy the newspaper. How should this simple example be unpacked, in terms of reasons for action? My wish to buy the newspaper provides me with what Raz calls an 'operative' reason to act, a reason concerned with my desires, values and interests.[79] Operative reasons can be contrasted with 'auxiliary' reasons. Auxiliary reasons are reasons transmitting the force of an operative reason to a particular piece of conduct, via a belief. In the example just given, my belief that the nearby shop has the newspaper connects my operative reason for action (I want this particular newspaper) with the relevant

---

[78] Ignorance of facts with a less than crucial bearing on what someone ought to do, or may do, will not undermine the rationality of a decision taken in ignorance of them.

[79] Joseph Raz, *Practical Reason and Norms*, 34.

specific piece of conduct (going to the nearby shop to buy the newspaper). Auxiliary reasons obviously presuppose operative reasons. Without the operative reason in the form of my desire to buy the particular newspaper in question, I would have 'no (auxiliary) reason' to go to the nearby shop to buy the newspaper.[80]

In true justification cases, as in the predominantly normative excuse of excessive defence, D's actively justificatory reason for action is his or her auxiliary, 'belief-reason' for action; and it is this reason, rather than D's operative 'desire-reason' for action, that has the greatest legal significance. It is the actively justificatory, auxiliary reason on which D must act, if he or she is to be found to have a defence. Suppose that D uses what he or she believes to be necessary and proportionate force to ward off V as V attacks D. If D is to be found to be justified or excused in doing as he or she does, it must be *inter alia because* D believes that V is posing a threat of imminent harm that only the immediate use of (a certain degree of) force will avert.[81] This belief must be D's auxiliary reason for using the force, the belief that gives D a reason to engage in a specific piece of (harmful) conduct, precisely because it gives D a reason to inflict harm on V it would ordinarily be unlawful to inflict. In focusing on this auxiliary reason, the law simply assumes the existence of the relevant operative reason, namely that D wishes to avoid being harmed by V. The presence of this operative reason might be said to make some normative difference, in that if D did not wish to avoid being harmed by V we could not make much sense of D's action in taking the defensive steps; but what D believes about those steps, in relation to the harm posed by V, has a much more important place in any legal analysis. The position is the same in necessity cases, where D perpetrates a lesser evil as the sole means of avoiding a much greater one. What will matter is that D acts for the relevant auxiliary reason, namely a belief that by perpetrating a lesser evil he or she can avoid a greater one. Again, D's operative reason for acting—the wish to avoid a specific (greater) evil in question—is only a background normative concern, because it is not itself a reason to perpetrate the lesser evil; only D's auxiliary reason is such a reason.[82]

Auxiliary belief-reasons also play a role in ascriptive judgments, when what falls to be explained, in a provocation, duress or self-defence case, is D's

---

[80] Famously, Antony Duff sought to provide an account of intention solely in terms of auxiliary reasons for acting (I show my intent to do X if I take certain steps in the belief that I may thereby bring X about): see R. A. Duff, *Intention, Agency and Criminal Liability* (Oxford: Basil Blackwell, 1990), 62–73. The problem with Duff's attractively minimalist account is that we cannot make much sense of acting on an auxiliary reason unless there is an operative reason lying behind it: see Jennifer Hornsby, 'On What's Intentionally Done', in Stephen Shute, John Gardner, and Jeremy Horder, *Action and Value in Criminal Law* 55, 57.

[81] This is the famous '*Dadson* principle': see *R v Dadson* (1850) 4 Cox CC 358.

[82] See, by way of example, the analysis of *R v Pommell* [1995] 2 Cr App Rep 607, in A. P. Simester and G. R. Sullivan, *Criminal Law: Theory and Doctrine*, 1st edn., 594–595.

emotional reaction: how D came to experience anger or fear of such intensity, and hence how he or she came to have the desire to do the wrong in question. If, say, I believe that you have deliberately insulted me by making some remark, then I will be understandably angrier than if I think what you said was not intended to insult me.[83] If, say, I believe that you will stop at nothing to kill me, or that you will certainly carry out your threat if I show the least signs of defiance, then I will be understandably more terrified than if I have significant doubts about your resolve. However, in predominantly ascriptive excuses, such as provocation or some duress cases, the auxiliary belief-reason for acting is not as significant as the operative desire-reason. In such cases, it is D's operative desire-reason that is the main focus. In part, this is because the motivational relationship between the auxiliary reason and the operative reason is different in such cases from their relationship in, say, the newspaper example given earlier. In the newspaper example, my belief that the nearby shop had the paper I sought gave me a reason to act that I could follow, or reject, depending on whether I remained intent on buying the paper. An auxiliary reason for acting only remains a reason for acting for so long as the operative reason underpinning it retains its exclusionary status, i.e. as something I am set to do without further sifting and weighing of the 'pros' and 'cons'.[84] This being so, it could be that either the auxiliary belief-reason, or the operative desire-reason, plays the key role for us, as agents, in particular cases. It could be that I want a newspaper, and only thereafter see the one I want (where the operative desire-reason is thought of as decisive); or, it could equally be that I see a newspaper first, and only then decide I want it (where the auxiliary belief-reason is seen as decisive). Most importantly, in the latter case, although seeing the newspaper may immediately spark off the formation of a desire to buy it, unless I suffer from some kind of pathological, 'impulse buying' condition, I will not then just satisfy the desire willy-nilly. Some kind of substantive deliberation, however swiftly engaged in,[85] will mediate between the two events (seeing the newspaper; experiencing the

---

[83] However, even if you have deliberately insulted me, if that does not induce in me a belief that this is what you have in fact done, my justification for angrily putting you in your place falls away. This is a straightforward application to an excuse case of the '*Dadson*' principle: *R v Dadson* (1850) 4 Cox CC 358.

[84] On the nature of exclusionary reasons, see Joseph Raz, *Practical Reason and Norms*, 35–48. In Bond's terms, this is 'category 4', where 'an agent consciously sees himself, upon reflection, to have a reason for doing something': E. J. Bond, *Reason and Value*, 18, discussed in section 2 above. As pointed out earlier, Bond's understanding of this kind of reason seems 'over deliberative'. In deciding to buy a newspaper, I do not need to 'deliberate' further on whether or not to go ahead having seen that the shop has the paper I want in order for my action to be an authentic reflection of value. What matters is that I am in a position to revise my priorities, having had an opportunity to give effect to them as they stand, and I simply do not revise them.

[85] Meaning, an attempt to justify (in this case, to oneself) what one is to do, on the balance of reasons, by satisfying oneself that there is enough counting in the action's favour. As a single reason could be sufficient, to this end, there need be nothing ponderous or drawn-out about 'deliberation', as I understand it. For example, a sports player may 'deliberately' direct a shot, in this sense, in fractions of a second.

desire to buy it), or will supervene in the form of a question whether the desire being experienced is worth fulfilling or not.

In provocation and duress cases, by way of contrast, the auxiliary belief-reason[86] ought to precede the formation of the operative desire-reason.[87] If I already want to kill someone before they provoke me, the provocation is likely to be regarded in law as little more than a pretext for carrying out an already formed intention. Moreover, the sparking off of the operative desire-reason by the auxiliary belief-reason *must*, not just may, occur without the mediation of substantive deliberation, if D's claim is to have any authenticity. In other words, the operative desire-reason must arise without any intervening substantive deliberation on whether it would be a 'good thing' to become angry or afraid, in the circumstances.[88] Further, and most importantly, in extreme cases when the auxiliary belief-reason has sparked off the operative desire-reason, the strength and intensity of that desire may make it difficult or impossible to remain in full deliberative control. In such cases, in other words, the power of reason to control desire on a supervening basis is weak or non-existent. For the reasons to be explained in sections 9 and 10 below, the experience of emotions such as fear and anger is part of the 'active' side of our natures, and can hence be well- or ill-grounded. In many cases where people experience great anger or fear, they still find it possible consciously to act for, or in spite of, certain reasons: the case I have been referring to as one in which people act for adopted reasons.[89] Nonetheless, when we are in the grip of these emotions, especially in extreme cases, we are not quite as free rationally to reject the goals their desire components set for us (retaliation; escape from the threat) as when we have desires of a less all-consuming character, like wanting a newspaper.[90] In the former cases,

[86] Respectively, D's belief that he or she has been insulted and should put V in his or her place (provocation), and that he or she has been threatened, and can only escape the threat by harming V (duress). .

[87] Respectively, the desire to retaliate, and the desire to escape the threat.

[88] See the discussion of L. Jonathan Cohen's thesis about beliefs, in section 9 below. An important clarification is needed respecting the claim just made. In provocation or duress cases, there may sometimes be instances in which only deliberation reveals that there has in fact been an insult, or a threat to be avoided, respectively. Perhaps only reflection reveals to me that X's cryptic comments were really an admission that he had killed a relative of mine and was proud of it; or perhaps only careful thought leads me now to believe that X's threat of death unless I comply with his demands is genuine and not a bluff. The claim in the text concerns instances in which I recognize, even if recognition is slow to dawn, that there has been a genuine insult or threat. In such cases, either I then become angry or afraid, or I do not. Cases in which I recognize that there has been an insult or threat, and then deliberate on what it would be right to feel about this, lack the necessary spontaneity to be worthy of excuse.

[89] I explore some of these possibilities in Jeremy Horder, *Provocation and Responsibility*, chapter 4. What stops such cases being straightforward examples of Bond's 'category 4' (see section 2 above), the case of rational motivation, is obviously that one did not decide to become angry or fearful in the first place.

[90] The result being, for example, that provoked angry actions, or fearful actions, may not be regarded as breaking the chain of causation from the incident that set them off, even if those actions are intentionally done: see the discussion of Hart and Honoré's analysis of what I call explanatory reasons, in section 2 above.

retaining full, deliberative, rational control is a matter of great difficulty that would require a force of will beyond most people. So, in provocation and in some duress cases, along with the fact that the operative desire-reason was simply sparked off (and was not the product of substantive deliberation), the absence of full deliberative, rational control over the desire respectively to escape the threat and to inflict retaliatory suffering, explains why the desire—D's operative reason—is the main ascriptive (excusatory) focus in such cases. Perhaps this seems most obvious in the case of provocation, where what the law requires is what it regards as a 'loss of self-control', something that appears to have no direct analogy in duress cases. Appearances are misleading. 'Loss of self-control' ought not to be associated solely with anger, and the partial defence of provocation, because its importance to that defence is in fact only one manifestation of a wider phenomenon. More widely interpreted, loss of self-control—understood as the loss of full deliberative or rational control—spans a broad spectrum of conditions from something close to involuntariness, at one end of the extreme, to relatively mild emotional disturbance, at the other. This is as true of fear as it is of anger, although some commentators have been reluctant to concede this.

In his searching examination of the rationale for the partial defence of provocation, for example, Stephen Gough objects to the law's use of the key term 'loss of self-control', because in his view this wrongly suggests that 'provocation has more in common with automatism than with excessive defence'.[91] For Gough: 'Notwithstanding its dramatic billing in the criminal law texts ... "loss of self-control" boils down to a fairly unobjectionable requirement of emotional disturbance'.[92] I will say something more general about emotional disturbance in due course. We should, however, reject the view that even the more sophisticated manifestations of emotions such as anger, fear, grief, and so forth cannot involve a genuine 'loss of self-control', albeit a loss of self-control less dramatic than when we are wholly passive with regard to the effect, as with (say) a convulsion.[93] Nonetheless, underlying Gough's concern is an important issue. I have hitherto sought to express the sense that emotions may find intentional expression in action in different ways, through a distinction between cases in which D acts for explanatory reasons (when the action is closer to the involuntary end of the spectrum), and cases in which D acts for an adopted reason (when the action is closer to a case in which D retains full rational control over his or her conduct).

[91] Stephen Gough, 'Taking the Heat out of Provocation' (1999) 19 *Oxford Journal of Legal Studies* 481, 486.   [92] Ibid., 488.
[93] In the case of fear, the experience of a loss of self-control has been analysed by LeDoux: see Joseph LeDoux, *The Emotional Brain: the Mysterious Underpinnings of Emotional Life* (New York: Simon and Schuster, 1996). He sees the experience in terms of what he calls the 'cognitive unconscious', controlled by a part of the brain known as the 'amygdala', that bypasses the influence of the higher brain functions. His examples, though, are concentrated on primitive experiences of fear/anger that make it controversial whether his analysis should be extended to the experience of anger and fear in, morally, more sophisticated cases.

Should it make an excusatory difference to provocation or duress cases, whether D acts for an explanatory or for an adopted reason? I will suggest an answer to this question in sections 11 and 12 below.

8. ANGRY OR FEARFUL ACTION AS THE RATIONAL COURSE OF ACTION

To seek to justify rationally an intentionally undertaken piece of conduct, is to claim that it adequately reflects—even if it does not fully reflect—the balance of reasons for and against engaging in that piece of conduct.[94] If, by any practically reasonable yardstick, there is not enough counting in favour of such conduct to make it worth engaging in, it is not rational to engage in it. Not all conduct, of course, calls for rational justification. Where there are no reasons against doing something, like humming or talking to myself as I work alone, I can engage in these activities without having to justify them rationally to myself or to anyone else.[95] Rational justification is, however, a kind of justification important to the criminal law. When the law insists that a mistake that led D into wrongdoing must be reasonable, if it is to excuse, the law is insisting that, to that end, D be able to give a rational justification for what he or she did, in spite of the rational defect in the moving force behind the action constituted by D's ignorance of crucial facts. D must be able to muster sufficient justification, in terms of supporting reasons for what was done, to make it possible to give what was done a rational explanation. In that regard, any appearance of paradox conjured by the notion that a rationally justifiable action could also be rationally defective can be dispelled, by bearing in mind that the reasonableness of D's belief that the crucial justifying facts exist plays a key role in the rationality of the justification given.[96] Rational justification is, then, not the same thing as true justification. One is truly justified only if the balance of reasons really does favour one's conduct (and one engages in it for that reason), and not merely if one has good grounds for believing this to be so.[97]

---

[94] If a piece of conduct fully reflects the balance of reasons, it is fully or completely justified, and not merely rationally justifiable.

[95] Of course, I might unwittingly be annoying someone I was unaware could hear me, in which case there would have been a reason against doing as I did that I failed to notice. That being so, considerations of justification ought to come into play, if I now intend to continue regardless.

[96] These points are debated, with much greater sophistication than I can muster, in Hamish Stuart, 'The Role of Reasonableness in Self-Defence' (2003) 16 *Canadian Journal of Law and Jurisprudence* 317.

[97] In that regard, Heidi Hurd distinguishes between what she calls the 'epistemic' justification for conduct (justification in terms of one's beliefs), and moral (true) justification: see Heidi Hurd, 'Justification and Excuse, Wrongdoing and Culpability', 1551, 1564; but this could be a potentially misleading way to make the distinction, if it seems plausible that the support for one's position provided by the reasonableness of one's beliefs is moral support. And where the reasonableness of the beliefs that led one into wrongdoing is concerned, it is hard to see what kind of support for what one did, other than moral support, could matter.

Exceptionally, where the balance of reasons favours doing harm, one can expect to avoid criminal liability in virtue of the justificatory strength of those reasons. Criminal lawyers have come to be familiar with the idea of truly justifying conduct, in terms of the balance of reasons, through the notion (important in jurisdictions that have the defence of necessity) of preferring a lesser evil in order to avoid a greater one; but self-defensive conduct also falls to be truly justified in this way, i.e. through the balance of reasons.[98]

Action in anger, or out of fear, can be rationally or truly justified, in that the experience of the emotions in question may be what helps us behave rationally or in a fully justified way.[99] In these cases, we see emotions playing their auxiliary role, supporting action that is in itself truly justified or rationally justifiable. It is, for example, justified to avoid torture (barring special circumstances), and fear of torture might in some circumstances give us the will to do the justified thing by escaping a torturer, when a pessimistic fatalism seems otherwise likely to keep us within his grasp.[100] Righteous indignation may help us to take steps to right an injustice we are duty-bound to right, when a wish to avoid causing trouble or making waves seems otherwise likely to deny us the courage of our convictions. Every angry outburst involves an element of self-assertion, but in cases where anger is rational or justified, alongside that self-regarding element is a spontaneous reflection of the experience of genuine injustice. It is the very fact that that experience of injustice spontaneously provoked sudden anger that

---

[98] No one doubts that I ordinarily have a reason to defend myself, if attacked, with necessary and proportionate force. However, in some instances, as when the person attacking me is sleep-walking, it can seem as if 'balance of reasons' considerations cannot generate a decisive reason for me to defend myself against an equally innocent person; but in this example, at least, this is not so. The protection given to certain interests can sometimes be lost or forfeited (albeit sometimes only temporarily) without 'guilt', or indeed any positive act attributable to the person who possesses the interest. This happens, for example, when I become liable to arrest and prosecution (losing my immunity from suit) simply by becoming ten years old. When X poses a threat of immediate harm to Y, without adequate justification, X temporarily loses his right not to be harmed, in so far as harm is a necessary and proportionate step to averting the unjustified threat to Y; and X may lose this right even though (as in the sleep-walking example) it is not his fault that he is posing the unjustified threat. That being so, Y is entitled (although not obliged) to treat the warding off of the threat as a decisive reason to take the necessary defensive steps. That is not to deny that there might be circumstances in which the balance of reasons favours staying my hand, even when I am unjustly threatened: see further, Suzanne Uniacke, *Permissible Killing: the Self-Defence Justification for Homicide*.

[99] See Michael, S. Moore, *Placing Blame*, 559, '[A]nger at unjust treatment need not make reasoned choice more difficult. It may instead make choice easier by highlighting what we otherwise might have missed. Anger at injustice is at least as effective as reciting Kant when keeping the priority of justice before one's mind as one decides how to respond.'

[100] To give another example, it is rational or truly justified to protect oneself as far as possible from injury, when under threat. It could be that, by building a high wall in front of our trench, I provide such effective protection for my soldiers from enemy fire that they gradually lose their instinctive urge to duck every time they hear the enemy gunfire. If the wall is destroyed, however, the rational or justified thing for each soldier to do would be to try to re-cultivate that instinctive urge, as a means of achieving the goal of self-protection. The spontaneous expression of the emotion serves the rational or justified end, even if not as well as some other measure (such as re-building the wall) might do.

lends anger's manifestation its intrinsic value. The fact that injustice moved someone in this way gives a sense of appropriateness to their righteous indignation, and even a certain dignity to its demonstrative expression, that cold-blooded revenge lacks.[101] For there is always the suspicion, with those who prefer calculated revenge to spontaneously acting demonstratively on angry feelings, that for them a concern for justice is much less important than (or just a pretext for) sheer self-assertion.

Even if demonstrative anger can indeed be rationally justifiable or truly justified in this way, there are few contexts in which there will be a direct implication for the criminal law. Nonetheless, the point under discussion is an important one, because it provides a context in which we can understand how provoked retaliation comes to be thought worthy of excuse. Displays of demonstrative anger may be fully justified on a variety of occasions, but as we all know, angry feelings are in general an unruly horse better reined in than let loose because they frequently give rise to what Aristotle called the desire for objectively unjustified 'retaliatory suffering'.[102] A similar point could be made about fear. Actions that are more or less spontaneous responses to one's fears may be rationally justifiable or fully justified; but great fear often leads people self-servingly to disregard the interests of others that they should be respecting. The potentially great phenomenological strength of these emotions is perhaps just as likely to lead us to act contrary to the balance of reasons, as it is to assist us to do what is rational or justified. Powers of self-control are, of course, what we have to rely on to help us match and overcome the strength of our feelings, and stay on a rational or justified course. We may find, though, that so great was the provocation and so overwhelming the urge to lash out wildly in retaliation, or so all-consuming the fear and so great the desire to save ourselves at any cost, that maintaining self-control and hence avoiding wrongdoing were beyond us. In such circumstances, where we needed to but failed to exercise sufficient control over our feelings, we have acted contrary to the balance of reasons, and have hence acted unjustifiably, whether or not it was right to feel angry or afraid. As Suzanne Uniacke has pointed out, one cannot get the balance of reasons partially, or half, right.[103] Either one's conduct was justified, on the balance of reasons, or it was not. Nonetheless, wholly unjustified conduct may be excusable, in the light of rational defects in a morally salient motivating

---

[101] On the significance of the need for anger to be demonstrative in character, to be justified, see Jeremy Horder, *Provocation and Responsibility*, 195–196, 'The righteously indignant person desires not retaliation, but to bring to the attention of the wrongdoer (and/or others), in certain characteristic ways, the wrongdoing that has been done. The righteously indignant person seeks to negate wrongdoing by an open labelling of the wrongdoer as wrongdoer, rather than through retaliation as such', cited by the Victorian Law Reform Commission, *Defences to Homicide (Options Paper)*, 100–101.

[102] Aristotle, *De Anima* 403a30, in *Complete Works of Aristotle*, Jonathan Barnes (trans.) (New Jersey: Princeton University Press, 1995).

[103] Suzanne Uniacke, 'What are Partial Excuses to Murder?', in S. M. H. Yeo (ed.), *Partial Excuses to Murder* (New South Wales: Federation Press, 1991) 1, 15–16 n. 8.

force behind it, and it is time to investigate how and why. I will start with an examination of why we should consider ourselves to be morally active with regard to beliefs and emotions, before moving on to say more about the nature of the rational defect in the salient motivating force behind an action, in mistake, provocation and duress cases.

9. ARE WE MORALLY 'PASSIVE', RESPECTING BELIEFS AND EMOTIONS?

If I asked you to try hard not to conjure up an image of a pink elephant in your mind, my request would, paradoxically, in all probability lead you to conjure up—however briefly—that very image (you are probably doing it now). If you saw me coming in through your front door, from that moment you would believe that you were not alone in the house. If a terrorist suddenly produced a gun and pointed it at your face, you would experience shock or alarm. Do such examples—instances of mental imaging, belief, and emotion—suggest that what we see, believe, and feel is confined to the realm of the 'passions', that respecting which we are passive, part of what 'just happens' to us? Is it, by way of contrast, only actions in respect of which we are active? This is, famously, the Humean line of thought ('belief is nothing but a peculiar feeling'),[104] although his simplistic equation of belief with feeling has been doubted by modern followers who nonetheless share Hume's understanding that beliefs and feelings are involuntary (they are 'passions').[105] L. Jonathan Cohen, for example, argues that:

As Hume long ago observed, belief is involuntary . . . Beliefs are said to come over you, arise in you, or grow on you, like anger or affection does. You cannot don, raise, or grow them yourself. You can plant them in others but not in yourself . . . you cannot decide to believe *that* it will rain tomorrow, or *that* it will not . . . no one can be said to decide to be disposed to feel one way or another. You cannot decide to feel joyful or suspicious.[106]

There is, of course, much of significance in what Cohen has to say about beliefs and feelings, when they are contrasted with what one *decides* to do, to achieve, to think about, to concentrate on, and so forth, a contrast emphasized (in a slightly different context) by Aristotle.[107] The contrast is best exemplified in law by the principle, in provocation cases, that D's loss

---

[104] David Hume, *A Treatise of Human Nature* (1739–1740), edited by L. A. Selby-Bigge (Oxford: Clarendon Press, 1888), 624.

[105] L. Jonathan Cohen, for example, suggests that beliefs are 'dispositions normally to feel that p' in L. Jonathan Cohen, *An Essay on Belief and Acceptance* (Oxford: Clarendon Press, 1992), part 1.

[106] L. Jonathan Cohen, *An Essay on Belief and Acceptance*, 21 (footnote omitted; Cohen's emphasis).

[107] See *Nichomachean Ethics*, iii, 1111b5-31: 'Still less is choice to be identified with temper; for acts due to temper are thought to involve choice less than any others.' For some important

of self-control must be spontaneous, rather than contrived, if it is to sat-isfy the factual or subjective condition.[108] If called on to decide the point, the courts would doubtless also say that—to be classed as 'honest'—beliefs too, like fears of threats, must arise in the holder without any ele-ment of contrivance. However, Cohen's broader contention that beliefs and feelings are involuntary, an aspect of a passive side to our nature, is unwarranted.

The Humean view that beliefs and feelings are involuntary might be thought to lend philosophical support to two well-known subjectivist crim-inal lawyer's contentions. The first is that Ds should always be judged on the facts as they believed them (however idiotically) to be.[109] The second is that, in provocation and duress cases, Ds should be judged according to how great their anger or fear in fact was, however wrong others think it may have been to have felt that (or at all) angry or fearful in the circumstances. Since we cannot help believing what we believe and feeling what we feel, so the argument goes, why blame D for believing or feeling as he or she did, and acting accordingly?[110] As Smith and Hogan put it, speaking of duress cases, 'D should surely be judged on the basis of what he actually believed and what he actually feared . . . He may have been unduly credulous or stupid but he is no more blameworthy than a person whose fear is based on reasonable grounds'.[111]

As every criminal lawyer knows, English law is consistent only in the inconsistency of its approach to the question of whether beliefs and feelings can and should be subject to evaluation (the 'evaluative element') before they can excuse. Until 2003, in English law a belief that the victim is

---

critical reflections on Humean assumptions about the pervasiveness of 'passivity' in our lives, in the thought of criminal lawyers, see John Gardner, 'On the General Part of the Criminal law', in R. A. Duff (ed.), *Philosophy and the Criminal Law* (Cambridge: Cambridge University Press, 1998), 213–214. The contrast is, of course, at the root of the distinction between cate-gory 2 and category 4 in Bond's discussion of human motivation: see section 2 above.

[108] *R v Duffy* [1949] 1 All ER 932n. This important principle has been put under considerable strain by the pressure the courts have been under to find that losses of self-control satisfy the '*Duffy*' criteria even when there has been considerable delay between the final act of provocation and the alleged loss of self-control: see *R v Ahluwalia* [1992] 4 All ER 859. This case appears to legitimate some of the dubious decisions, discussed in chapter 4.3 below, where the killer has lain in wait for V before (allegedly) losing self-control. Arguably, the doctrine has become detached from its Platonic rationale: 'the man whose anger bursts forth uncontrollably, whose action is instant, immediate, and without premeditation, resembles the involuntary killer', passage 9 (866d5–868a1), cited by T. J. Saunders, *Plato's Penal Code* (Oxford: Clarendon Press, 1991), 155. This point is picked up (although not expressed as a Platonic objection) by the Law Commission for England and Wales, *Partial Defences to Murder*, 47.

[109] *DPP v Morgan* [1976] AC 182; *R v Williams (Gladstone)* [1987] 3 All ER 411; Sir J. C. Smith and Brian Hogan, *Criminal Law* (London: Butterworths, 2002), 10th edn., 104–107.

[110] The high water mark of this kind of thinking is perhaps best represented by Brett's highly deterministic account of the effects of provocation: P. Brett, 'The Physiology of Provocation' (1970) *Criminal Law Review* 634. This is referred to as 'scientific opinion' by Smith and Hogan in their discussion of the doctrine: Sir J. C. Smith and Brian Hogan, *Criminal Law*, 10th edn., 377. [111] See ibid., 260.

consenting in rape cases needed only to be honest,[112] and a belief in the need
to use self-defensive force to ward off a threat still need only be honest.[113]
By way of contrast, although there has been some uncertainty about the
matter,[114] in duress cases the issue is whether:

as a result of what [D] *reasonably* believed [X] had said or done, he had *good cause*
to fear that if he did not so act [X] would kill him or . . . cause him serious physical
injury' [and] have the prosecution made the jury sure that a sober *person of reasonable firmness* . . . would not have responded . . . by taking part in the killing?[115]

The Law Commission for England and Wales,[116] in defiance of common law
authority from around the world (which the Commission chose to ignore),[117]
came down firmly in favour of eradicating the evaluative element at almost all
stages, in duress cases as much as in self-defence cases. Accordingly, in the
Commission's proposals for reform of the defences, matters such as whether
it was credible to think there really was a threat are judged solely from the D's
perspective.[118] The courage of the Commission's subjectivist convictions
failed it, however, when it came to rape cases. In such cases, their recommendation was that mistakes must be reasonable before they can (as I would have
it) excuse.[119] This difference of approach has been defended on the grounds
that there is a special duty of care to ensure that a potential sexual partner is
consenting, a duty that can justify a requirement of reasonableness that would
not be justified elsewhere in the criminal law.[120] As a basis for distinguishing
sex offence cases from others, this is a not a particularly strong argument. It
hardly seems more understandable and excusable that a doctor, in subjecting
a protesting patient to what turns out to be a wholly unnecessary amputation,
honestly (but entirely unreasonably and mistakenly) believed that the patient

---

[112] *DPP v Morgan* [1976] AC 182; but the Sexual Offences Act 2003 mercifully reverses this
decision, in that respect.   [113] *R v Williams (Gladstone)* [1987] 3 All ER 411.
[114] See *DPP v Rogers* [1998] Crim LR 202; *R v Safi* [2003] Crim LR 721.
[115] The words of Lane LCJ in *R v Graham* [1982] 74 Cr App Rep 235, 241 (my emphasis).
The case was damned with the faintest of praise by Lord Steyn in *R v G (and another)* [2003]
3 WLR 1060, 1086, even though *R v Graham* was approved by the House of Lords itself, in
the duress case of *R v Howe* [1987] AC 417. The approach in *Graham* has now been approved
by the House of Lords in *RvZ* [2005] UKHL 22.
[116] Law Commission for England and Wales, *Legislating the Criminal Code: Offences
Against the Person and General Principles*, Law Commission Consultation Paper No 218, Cm
2370 (HMSO, 1993).   [117] See e.g. *Zecevic v DPP* (Vic) (1987) 162 CLR 645.
[118] For critical analysis of the Law Commission proposals, see Jeremy Horder, 'Occupying
the Moral High Ground? The Law Commission on Duress' (1994) *Criminal Law Review* 334.
There has now, however, been a change of heart on the Law Commission's part. The legal
importance of the evaluative element was recognized and approved in Law Commission for
England and Wales, *Murder, Manslaughter and Infanticide*, Part 6.
[119] See Law Commission for England and Wales, *Consent in the Criminal Law*, Law
Commission Consultation Paper No 139 (HMSO, 1995), considered in Stephen Shute,
'Something Old, Something New, Something Borrowed: Three Aspects of the Project' (1996)
Criminal Law Review 684. To that extent, the Commission's views have been vindicated by
section 1 of the Sexual Offences Act 2003.
[120] See Andrew Ashworth, *Principles of Criminal Law*, 3rd edn., 370. See now the discussion of duress in Law Commission for England and Wales, *Murder, Manslaughter and
Infanticide*, Part 6.

was really consenting to a necessary operation. Much the same could be said of the supposedly well-trained firearms officer who shoots an innocent person on sight, saying afterwards 'I cannot really explain it but I just jumped to the conclusion that he must have been about to attack me'.[121] Perhaps a yet further basis for special pleading can be found to explain these last two examples, in the fact that they involve people who are meant to be professionals and hence trained to avoid the very blundering that their crass mistakes have led them into.[122] So, it could be argued, there is a special duty of care involved here too. We are all, however, under a duty of care to avoid causing unnecessary harm to others. What the examples just employed illustrate is the obvious point that more can be expected of the experienced, the trained, or the professional, than of the untrained and the inexperienced, in the discharge of that duty; and so the latitude to err 'reasonably' may vary accordingly.[123] With that important caveat, it can be argued that the right approach is to insist that in all cases beliefs, fears, and losses of self-control can and should be subject to evaluation, and hence must be found to be well grounded, before they can excuse.

The approach just outlined can profitably be associated with empirical research, and a philosophical tradition, that rejects Humean assumptions about human nature, and regards a wide range of (if not all) beliefs and feelings as having a morally 'active' dimension to them.[124] If I instinctively withdraw my hand from an unexpectedly hot surface, the movement is largely if not wholly (after all, it is not quite a 'knee-jerk' reflex action) involuntary. Beliefs and emotions—and hence the reactions they produce—could conceivably be involuntary in this way, however, only when they take a very primitive form, when their genesis does not lie in situations with complex social and moral meaning.[125] Even then, they may not be wholly beyond the realm of evaluation. Charles Darwin once gave a nice example from personal experience:

I put my face close to the thick glass plate in front of a puff adder in the Zoological Gardens, with the firm determination of not starting back if the snake struck at me; but, as soon as the blow was struck, my resolution went for nothing, and I jumped

---

[121] The European Court has indicated that the 'right to life', a right protected by the European Convention on Human Rights, requires that law-enforcement agents have good grounds for believing that they must open fire with lethal intent on supposed suspects. See *McCann v UK* (1996) 21 EHRR 97, discussed in Ben Emmerson and Andrew Ashworth, *Human Rights and Criminal Justice*, paragraph 18–25.

[122] On this point, see Jeremy Horder, 'Cognition, Emotion and Criminal Culpability' (1990) 106 *Law Quarterly Review* 469.

[123] Whether this argument has any analogy in sexual offence cases is a moot point. Assuming it is right to require beliefs in a victim's consent to be reasonable (as I believe it is), should this standard be varied according to, for example, D's age, IQ, level of previous sex education, and so forth? See now, Helen Power, 'Towards a Redefinition of the *Mens Rea* of Rape' (2003) 23 *Oxford Journal of Legal Studies* 379.

[124] This was certainly Aristotle's view, but modern defenders include Harry Frankfurt: see e.g. his 'Identification and Wholeheartedness', in Harry Frankfurt, *The Importance of What We Care About* (Cambridge: Cambridge University Press, 1988), and Joseph Raz (see Joseph Raz, *Engaging Reason*, chapter 1).

[125] See the discussion of the scientific evidence in n. 93 above, and towards the end of section 11 below.

a yard or two backwards with astonishing rapidity. My will and reason were powerless against the imagination of a danger *which had never been experienced*.[126]

Notice that even when such a primitive fearful response is in issue, Darwin
takes it for granted that one could have trained oneself to respond differently. Even the experience of quite primitive beliefs and emotions can be
made sensitive to the influence of reason.[127] Nonetheless, although I may be
able to resist the first instinct to jump back from a dangerous snake, or to
withdraw my hand from a hot stove, it seems highly unlikely that I can ever
hope to prevent myself feeling the fear or the pain that gives rise to the
instinct, in each case, in the first place.[128] By way of contrast, not only can I
hope to and be expected to resist the instinct to behave in a certain way, when
prompted by less primitive beliefs and emotions, but I can also be expected to
train myself not to come to have the beliefs or to experience the emotions at
all. The influence of reason is capable of penetrating deeper into some kinds
of cognitive and emotional reactions than into many other areas of human
experience involving bodily and mental functioning. Lest it be thought that
there is something suspiciously homespun about such philosophy, these observations are, broadly speaking, confirmed by some psychologists who have
examined the same phenomena. Dolf Zillman has suggested that:

In understanding the emotions of fear and anger, it is important to recognise their
initial function ... The initial function was twofold: to furnish energy for a bout of
action and to focus attention to the here and now of action. [Of] these two responses
... one urges aggressive action irrespective of that action's ultimate usefulness.
The other, because of cognitive preoccupation with the immediate situation, makes
individuals negligent of all non-immediate implications of their actions.[129]

According to Zillman, the evolution of emotions is associated with a relatively
primitive palaeo-mammalian brain structure known as the limbic system.
As well as having the effects mentioned in the passage just cited, the limbic
system enables us to monitor the environment for danger cues, and helps us
to respond 'appropriately': for example, through the release of adrenal hor-
mones making us ready for instant—and possibly violent—confrontation.[130]
Zillman's analysis of emotion, in terms of the continuing influence of a more

---

[126] Cited by R. Restack, 'Rapid Response', *New York Times*, 5 November 1996 (my emphasis).
[127] See the discussion in the text at the end of section 11.
[128] Perhaps one should not rule out this possibility completely. An Indian fakir is capable of
a mental discipline that fools the mind into treating the experience of pain as something else,
enabling him to lie on a bed of nails. The very exceptional character of such an example shows,
though, how differently we should treat the experience of pain, from the experience of beliefs
and emotions.
[129] Dolf Zillmann, 'Our Unique Motives for Violence Sit Beside Archaic Animal Drives for
Aggression,' *Times Higher Educational Supplement* (No 1533), 12 April 2002, 18–19.
[130] It should be noted, though, that not all scientists accept the idea of the 'limbic system',
and the idea of reasoned control over factors giving rise to anger and fear with which it is consistent: see the brief discussion of the work of LeDoux in n. 93 above. We should not discount
the possibility that such contrary theories may explain some kinds of emotional reaction. At the
heart of such theories, however, tend to be relatively simple examples—such as Darwin's

primitive dimension to our natures, goes some way to explaining why the 'phenomenological' strength of the operative reasons for action provided by extreme anger or fear is rightly cast in an excusatory light by so many legal systems (something considered in more detail in sections 10 and 11 below). Nonetheless, Zillmann does not doubt the ability of reason to control and influence the expression of emotion, in a way that makes it right to place emotions on the active side of our natures.[131]

In what guise, though, does reason operate in shaping our emotional responses? As I (with Stephen Shute and John Gardner) have sought to explain,[132] there is more than one way to be or to become morally 'active' with regard to one's conduct. In particular, one can be morally active either through one's 'causal' contribution to events, or through one's 'control' relationship to events; and it is the latter that is of central importance where the influence of reason on belief and emotion is in issue. We explained the differences between these two ways of becoming responsible thus:

The control relation is in a loose sense causal . . . There are some family resemblances. Both relations [causal and control] have counterfactual elements and both have what may be called a 'direction of operation' . . . Nevertheless, there are important differences. To be in control of something is not necessarily to be its cause, nor vice versa. Take the example of a guided missile. The missile's guidance system may be in control of the missile—the missile may be under control—even though its movements are so far entirely caused by the launch momentum . . . If we understand ourselves as complex guidance systems, which is how we must be understood if the guidance of morality and law is to apply to us and be applied by us, then it is not hard to see how the causal history of our reasoning and our conduct can be left on one side when our responsibility is being assessed.[133]

If you provoke me and I lose my self-control, I might rightly claim that my reaction was your fault. Can I, however, go further than this and claim that I was not even responsible for my action *at all* (you were)? I cannot. On another day, I might have kept my temper in the face of the self-same provocation, and

encounter with the puff adder—unmediated by social and moral meaning. So, their rejection of theories reliant on the idea of a 'limbic system', the 'learning' system that accounts for more a sophisticated—reasoned—emotional response, is not central to the thesis being developed here.

[131] In that regard, Zillmann is surely right to contrast the pacifying or moderating role of reason, in relation to the expressive emotions, with its occasional role—with or without the support of feelings—in supporting violent actions. As Zillman goes on to point out, the emergence of rational behaviour that accompanied the later development in the brain of the neo-cortex (humans have an especially large neo-cortex) has proved to be no simple 'antidote' to the more primitive influences of the limbic system. Some moral concepts, like retribution for wrongs, the intelligent development of which the neo-cortex has made possible, have dramatically increased in number and scale the occasions on which violence can supposedly be supported in individual, national and international contexts. In such contexts, though, the use of violence must be supported by the logical ('pure' justificatory) strength of the reasons in favour of the violence, or not at all, which is one of the one of the reasons we know that we ought to guard against anger's great phenomenological strength, in such instances.

[132] Stephen Shute, John Gardner, and Jeremy Horder (eds.), *Action and Value in Criminal Law*, 18–19. [133] Ibid., 19.

quite possibly a better-tempered person (of the sort I might have taken myself to be) certainly would have done. In principle, for those with adequate mental capacities, loss of temper is controll*able*—subject to direction by reason—even if its loss on a given occasion is quite spontaneous.[134] That is what I mean by saying that someone remains morally 'active' in this situation. So, in my example, we must share responsibility for the loss of temper, I on a 'control-relation' basis and you on a 'causal relation' basis, even if—when it comes to allocating blame—you must take the lion's share.

It is the same with beliefs. A judge might find she much more easily believes the evidence given by those she regards as 'well-spoken' witnesses. We would, rightly, think that this is a dispositional defect in the judge that she ought to work hard to eradicate, rather than an example of something involuntary for which she bears no responsibility whatsoever. It is something quite different from whether, say, she finds it difficult to hear in a crowded courtroom, or impossible to fix someone with an unblinking stare for an indefinite period. And, again, we might take this view even if we entirely accept that, on a given occasion, her belief in a 'well-spoken' witness's credibility is entirely spontaneously formed. So, beliefs, like emotions such as anger and fear, are sensitive to reason and are in that sense part of the 'active' side to our moral nature, subject to evaluative direction or control. As Raz puts it, in rejecting the Humean account:

The distinction between the active and the passive . . . depends, at least in part, on our responsiveness to reason (which is, like the notion of the active itself, a matter of degree) . . . We should believe only when reason warrants, be afraid only when in serious danger . . . etc. We are active when our mental life displays sensitivity to reasons, and we are passive when such mental events occur in a way which is not sensitive to reasons . . . Having thought of an incident I can become angry with John, or frightened of him, or I can come to believe that it was his fault and not mine—all of these may be rational conclusions of my thinking, yet none of them is chosen by me, nor can they be.[135]

Some might say, though, that just because beliefs and emotions *can* be subject to evaluation, because they are sensitive to reason, that does not show that they *should* be so subject, where the issue is whether or not D is to be held criminally liable.[136] There are three very different reasons why this argument should be rejected. First, at an abstract level, there is an important sense in which just to have the capacity to make one's reactions sensitive to the demands of reason is to be obliged to do so, an obligation that justifies judgement in accordance with a reasonableness standard. This is one of the instances when an 'ought' (my reactions should be sensitive to, and judged in the light of, the demands of reason) can quite properly be derived from an 'is' (I have the capacity to make my reactions sensitive to reason). The inherent

---

[134] See the discussion in Jeremy Horder, *Provocation and Responsibility*, chapter 5.

[135] Joseph Raz, *Engaging Reason*, 11.

[136] Sir J. C. Smith, 'Individual Incapacities and Criminal Liability' (1998) *Medical Law Review* 138, 156–157.

value of simply having that capacity, as a constituent element in human flourishing, bridges the gap that Hume sought to open up between the two.[137] Secondly, at a more concrete level, no criminal law theorist—whether or not a subjectivist—would deny the crucial importance of the distinction between moral activity and passivity more generally within the criminal law.[138] For example, the distinction explains in part why, when dissociative states result from psychological 'blows' (like rejection by a lover), these will not readily be regarded as external factors giving D the basis for a defence of non-insane automatism,[139] whereas physical blows or attacks having the same effect may much more readily be so regarded.[140] We are much more likely still to be mentally and morally 'active' (capable of evaluative control over our reactions) in the former case than in the latter.[141] So, it seems arbitrary simply to pick and choose which consequences of the active/passive distinction one is willing to allow to influence criminal liability, and which one is not.

Finally, it is true that requiring beliefs and emotions to be well grounded involves legal support for a moral position; and it is true that, in general, the criminal law does not seek to enforce morality for its own sake, because it respects the 'harm principle'. Nonetheless, the harm principle is not a principle that looms large when it comes to deciding what restrictions to place on the availability of excuses.[142] Legal support for judging Ds from a moral standpoint is not quite the same thing as the crude legal enforcement of morality. The harm principle restricts criminalization *ab initio*, in the interests of shielding harmless immorality from official censure and punitive sanctions. The principle has nothing—or very little—to say about the conditions in which offenders, who have admittedly breached the harm principle, should be excused what would otherwise be perfectly justified censure and sanction for their harmful wrongs. Indeed, J. S. Mill, the harm principle's inventor, might well have himself agreed with a rule that mistaken beliefs and emotions must have been well grounded before they can excuse wrongdoing, because that might do something more generally to encourage welfare-maximizing outcomes than a more subjectivist rule.[143]

---

[137] There are, of course, other examples where the is/ought divide has no application. So, for example, I can say without logical or other kind of fallacy, 'I am a teacher, therefore I should act as a teacher ought to act'.

[138] See the admirable discussion (although not employing this distinction) in Sir J. C. Smith and Brian Hogan, *Criminal Law*, 10th edn., 219–222.

[139] *Rabey v R* (1977) 37 CCC (2d) 461.

[140] *R v T* (1990) Crim LR 256; *R v Stripp* (1978) 69 Cr App Rep 318.

[141] Consistent with this approach the law requires the 'total destruction of voluntary control' if automatism is successfully to be pleaded in a driving case: see *Broome v Perkins* [1987] Crim LR 271. Reduced or imperfect awareness is insufficient: see *A-G's Reference (No 2 of 1992)* (1993) 99 Cr App Rep 429.

[142] See the discussion of Kant's view on this point, in chapter 3.8 below.

[143] See the discussion of Mill on emotion in Roger Crisp, *Mill on Utilitarianism* (London: Routledge, 1997), chapters 5 and 6.

10. Losing Deliberative Control: Reason, the 'Non-interfering Gatekeeper'

There is no single right way to characterize emotional reactions. As we have seen, on the one hand, an emotional reaction may actually help one to behave rationally. Fear for a child's safety may galvanize one into action, leading one to take the necessary steps to avert a danger; or indignation may steel one's resolve to perform a duty to rectify an injustice. On the other hand, a perfectly common emotional reaction may border on the irrational, perhaps even interfering with the voluntariness of conduct, as when I instinctively recoil in horror upon discovering an enormous spider in my bed.[144] Notice, however, that this second example is not quite like the earlier example in which I instantly withdraw my hand when it comes into contact with a boiling hot surface. Emotional reactions are 'belief-sensitive' (perhaps I would not have responded in this way had I realized the spider was a child's toy), sensitive to direction by auxiliary reasons, despite the fact that—as in the case of a phobia—the belief may be exercising relatively little normative force. Moreover, it is often within our powers to overcome phobias, even if (say) medical help is required if we are to do it. Having successfully (as I thought) undergone a course of 'aversion therapy', I might be right to chide myself for my reaction to the spider, and to resolve to be better prepared in future to exercise my new-found powers of self-control.[145] Where emotions are concerned, then, a lack of 'self-control' is a matter of fact and degree. One may have more, or less, deliberative, rational control over one's conduct, depending on the circumstances.

Let us explore some examples. Pain provides a good starting point. With a supreme effort of will, it is possible to retain more or less full deliberative control over one's conduct even when one is in great pain.[146] On the other hand, some kinds of pain may not only by-pass powers of deliberative, rational control, but may interfere with the voluntariness of conduct itself. An obvious example is the one given above, where I instinctively whip my hand away from a boiling hot surface I have accidentally touched. I certainly do not decide to remove my hand from the surface; as I have just indicated, my reaction is not a product of an auxiliary belief-reason in that respect. Moreover, the speed and direction of my hand, as I whip it away,

---

[144] Being perhaps more on the passive than the active side of people's natures, the latter kinds of reactions belong in Bond's 'case 3' (see section 2 above), i.e. that of unwilled desires and aversions that 'simply assail us'. They are scientifically analysed by Joseph LeDoux, *The Emotional Brain: the Mysterious Underpinnings of Emotional Life*, in terms of what he calls the 'cognitive unconscious', that by-passes the influence of higher brain functions: see n. 93 above.

[145] See the discussion of Darwin's example in the text at n. 126 above.

[146] Some of the novelist William 'Wilkie' Collins' best novels were written at a time when gout had so affected his whole body, including his eyes, that at regular intervals he had to replace the secretaries to whom he was dictating, because none could for long stand his constant groans of agony as he worked.

are not fully under my control either: here is the interference with the voluntariness of my conduct in reacting.[147] Slightly further along the spectrum from this example are those in which someone retains full control over the execution of conduct, but their 'will', their deliberative control over whether to engage in that conduct or not, and on what terms, is severely undermined or non-existent. Such conduct can be described as 'non-voluntary', to distinguish it from its involuntary cousin. We find non-voluntariness, for example, in your eventual compliance with my demands, only after I have been continuously twisting your arm up behind your back, or gradually increasing the strength of an electric current flowing into you, to coerce you into compliance.[148] Obviously, your spontaneous and expressive reactions as the torture continues—flinching, or shouting in pain—are involuntary, or barely voluntary, but, by way of contrast, after the torture is over, the piece of conduct that constitutes your subsequent compliance with my wishes is not *in*voluntary. It is under your executive control, and it is your decision to comply. Nonetheless, that decision is wholly dictated by me, in these circumstances, in a special sense. As in the case discussed in section 5 above, where I force you to eat ever more putrid meat until you can face eating no more, I have broken your will to resist, in that you simply cannot face the prospect of further defiance. Although such behaviour is not involuntary, the collapse of the will to resist, and with it the undermining of deliberative or evaluative control, can make it right to describe it as 'non-voluntary'.[149] Finally, further along the spectrum from this, and closest to the case in which someone retains full deliberative, rational control, are those cases in which pain does not destroy my will in some respect, but makes it understandable that I should engage in or refrain from some course of action. So, a worsening headache might make it understandable that I should give up marking examination scripts for now, even if I could do one or two more, because I rightly doubt that I could struggle much further on even if I absolutely had to. It is worth noting that cases of non-voluntary response to pain can shade into this final category. I may not, for example, as yet have caused you much

---

[147] Notice that the contrast between this example and the preceding one does not hinge on any assumption about the 'amount' of pain involved. The difference between the examples is qualitative, not quantitative. A separate point: even in the 'hot surface' example, as in the 'spider-on-the-bed' example, I could seek to train myself in techniques to control my reaction to the experience of pain in these circumstances. Presumably, though, complete mastery of one's reactions is surely impossible, something that may also be true in some cases of phobia.

[148] An example discussed by Sir J. C. Smith, 'Individual Incapacities and Criminal Liability', 159.

[149] Here, again, we may recognize a question of degree. If I hold you prisoner, torturing you continuously over a long period, my control over your will may become much more complete and pervasive than when I torture you on one occasion to wring from you a single piece of information or to get you to engage in one piece of conduct. On the other hand, if I merely threaten you with torture, as a result of which you comply with my demands, your compliance may be coerced but it is hardly non-voluntary. It would be an exaggeration, in the latter case, to say that I have broken your will to resist; I have not even had to try to do this. As indicated in section 5 above, in such cases, you need an excuse for any subsequent wrongdoing.

pain by twisting your arm behind your back, but your fear that I will do this in due course may lead you to comply with my wishes now, to avoid that possibility. In such a case I have not broken your will to resist, thus making your compliance non-voluntary, although I have certainly coerced you into voluntary compliance.

Almost all of these different points along the spectrum have some analogy where emotional responses are concerned, but there is a crucial difference between the two kinds of example. As suggested in the preceding section, emotional responses tend to be more on the 'active' than on the 'passive' side of our nature, unlike the experience of pain. At one end of the spectrum of emotional responses, we have already encountered the case in which a reaction to a phobia may interfere with the voluntariness of conduct, even if it may not be completely beyond the reach of reason to impose some self-control in such situations. Somewhat further along from this end of the spectrum are emotions with a strong 'expressive' dimension to them. Unlike behaviour manifesting a phobia, or an instantaneous recoiling from a dangerous snake unexpectedly encountered, a spontaneous display of emotion may express a good deal about character or personality, even if it has not been consciously undertaken with that end in view.[150] Consider the following example. Alan is talking to someone about the death of a close friend. Despite Alan's determination to remain calm, grief wells up and much to his embarrassment he bursts into tears. Alan's reaction spontaneously expresses his grief, and thereby says something (positive!) about his character and personality. The reaction is not controlled by him, however, even though the auxiliary belief-reason is there (he would not respond in this way if he thought he was speaking about a deadly enemy), and even though through effort and practice it is possible to gain some control over such reactions.[151] Now consider a second example. Betty maliciously harps on and on about some matter she knows very well Colin rightly feels strongly should remain closed, to the point where, despite Colin's best intentions, he flares up and snaps at Betty with some put-down he had sworn he would never mention. Is this reaction as spontaneous and lacking in control as Alan's? Yes, it is, because anger is primarily an expressive emotion, like grief. As in the case of Alan's reaction, of course, reason has its part to play. Colin's reaction obviously reflects an auxiliary belief-reason. So, if he knows Betty is talking in her sleep when she makes the offending remarks, he is less likely to, and should not, lose his cool. Further, as in Alan's case, Colin's reaction— whether or not truly justified (I leave that issue on one side)—is not extreme or outlandish. His reaction echoes, even if it does not embody, the demands

---

[150] See the discussion in Joseph Raz, *Engaging Reason*, 37–42.

[151] As Raz points out, for example, such reactions are liable to be influenced by cultural or religious factors: Joseph Raz, *Engaging Reason*, 41. In some cultures or religions, it may be 'natural' to display one's grief in a much more demonstrative way than it is in other cultures or religions.

of reason. As Raz puts it, speaking of this kind of case:

> In all, purely expressive actions are almost like actions for reasons. They differ in that while they do not involve loss of control over their initiation they involve diminution of that control ... [This] makes them differ slightly from their non-identical twins, in which the factors invoked by agents to explain their actions actually serve as reasons for those actions ... My suggestion is that we can think of people who perform normally expressive actions as people who let themselves express their emotions, feelings, or moods in action. They permit themselves to do so ... *In the case of purely expressive actions we ... allow the emotion to express itself, the will acting as a non-interfering gate-keeper.*[152]

I will return shortly to the case of someone who actually takes their emotion to be a reason to act in a certain way (an 'adopted reason' case), a way that will express their feelings more or less appropriately, this case being further along the spectrum. In the cases presently under consideration, however, this does not happen. Instead, in both Alan's and Colin's cases, spontaneity and relative lack of control stem from the fact that the emotions 'explode from within without [an] element of calculation', as Raz puts it.[153]

Here is a further example. David has promised himself he will stand up to Edgar, the terrifying bully of a Sergeant Major who is in charge of him. However, when Edgar comes into the room and summons up his most threatening manner to bark the command, 'Attention!', at David, David finds himself meekly complying by jumping to attention, as usual. In this example, the use of the term 'finds himself ... complying' is meant to indicate that the emotion has an impact much like that in the examples just discussed. There is the same spontaneity, the same diminution of control, and the same consequent sense of relative powerlessness to resist, in spite of best intentions. However, this example of the hold fear may have over someone is clearly further along the spectrum, in the direction of deliberative control, than the earlier phobia example. The auxiliary belief-reason is exercising more normative force, and David retains full control over the execution of the piece of conduct constituted by obedience to Edgar's command. So, David's compliance is not dictated by Edgar in quite the way that I dictate your compliance with my demands when I increase the strength of the electric current passing through your body until you agree to do as I say (where the consequent conduct is 'non-voluntary'). David's will is not so much broken and *thereafter* controlled, as *contemporaneously* overcome by his fear of Edgar. Reason, Raz's 'non-interfering gatekeeper', is simply overwhelmed by the short-term intensity of David's emotional reaction to Edgar's demand. Still, there would not be a great deal to separate these two examples, were it not for something David's conduct shares with Alan's and Colin's that makes us more inclined to say that his conduct is fully voluntary rather than

---

[152] Joseph Raz, *Engaging Reason*, 43 and 44 (my emphasis).
[153] Ibid., 41–42.

non-voluntary. In all these cases, the reactions reflect the morally 'active' side of human nature.

In their discussion of causation in provocation cases, Hart and Honoré give the following account:

> if one person, by suddenly appearing, startles another so that he jumps or runs away in fright, the sudden appearance would correctly be said to have made the second person behave as he did . . . in this non-purposive aspect these cases resemble causal connection between two physical events. In the law there are many examples of this borderline type of causal concept. Perhaps the most important is the case of provocation . . . It is . . . an integral part of the idea of provocation that one person arouses another's passions and makes him lose normal self-control.[154]

Now, in one sense, Hart and Honoré are right to see some similarity between the two kinds of case, in causal terms. When rage explodes from within without any element of calculation, there is a loss of self-control just as there is when X jumps when startled by the sudden appearance of Y. Beyond this basic point, though, the comparison is liable to mislead. A startled reaction is involuntary and almost wholly passive, whereas that is not true of a provoked reaction like Colin's, because in Colin's case reason is still playing its role as a 'non-interfering gatekeeper'. The fact that reason plays this role provides the link between someone's reaction, and their character and personality. David may claim not to identify with his conduct, but his compliance is an active response to or engagement with the world, an engagement that is a genuine reflection of character and personality. Your response to the pain I inflict on you, by way of contrast, is much more on the passive side of such engagements, saying little or nothing about your character and personality. So, David should be identified with his reaction, and his claim that he should not be identified with it is probably just wishful thinking.

In the case of expressive emotions, more broadly, there is an active engagement with the world, despite the fact that the emotion 'explodes' without an element of calculation. There are, for example, many instances in which we will positively identify with a spontaneously expressed emotion, in the expression of which there is some loss of self-control, whether or not it helps us (as it may do, as indicated above) to do as reason requires. Examples would be where Fred beats his fists on the floor in frustration as his team loses a crucial match in the final minute of the game, or where Graham cries at the end of a sentimental work of fiction. It could be that Fred and Graham identify with their reactions, because they see them as expressing the way they are as individuals. Fred knows he is the true follower of his team he wishes to be, just in virtue of the fact that he does not need artificially to work up a great sense of frustration at the result of the

---

[154] H. L. A. Hart and A. M. Honoré, *Causation in the Law*, 58, discussed in Jeremy Horder, *Provocation and Responsibility*, 116–118.

game. Graham finds confirmation that he is the hopeless romantic he sees himself as, precisely because he is spontaneously moved to cry over the endings in trashy sentimental novels. The fact that we can identify with our own spontaneous reactions, in such circumstances, shows that they are more to the active side of our nature than, say, a recoiling from the spider on the bed, as well as being a great distance from fits and convulsions, which are clearly on the passive side. I might accept that I tend to recoil from spiders, whereas snakes, which made you shudder, leave me unmoved. 'That is just a difference about the way we are', I might say. It is hard to see a sense, however, in which I *can identify with* this difference between us, in the way that Fred and Graham can identify with the differences between each other in terms of what moves them. What this shows is that some emotional reactions remain influenced by reason, and are hence more clearly open to evaluative scrutiny, even when there is a loss of self-control. Spontaneous reactions to fear, anger, or frustration are accountable to reason playing its role as a 'non-interfering gatekeeper'.

11. LOSING DELIBERATIVE CONTROL: PASSION AND ADOPTED REASONS FOR ACTION

At the other end of the spectrum, close to the case in which one has full deliberative control, are cases in which, even though the intensity of an emotion reduces the degree of deliberative, rational control one has over one's reaction, reason has a yet more active part to play. In such cases, reason is more than a 'non-interfering gatekeeper', in that one can act for an *adopted* reason. Nonetheless, in such cases, in spite of the more active role of reason, it may be unfair to expect D to use reason's controlling influence to hold back the dictates of an emotion, and D may be forgiven for deciding to 'go with' his feelings. We have already encountered such a case. This is the one in which a painful headache means that I doubt that I can struggle on much further with my examination marking, and so I decide to put off the remainder of my scripts until later. In this case, I may know full well I am capable of getting through just one or two more scripts, albeit with perhaps great and increasing discomfort. So, it is not a case of involuntariness, in which pain simply blurs my vision, preventing me from reading, or of non-voluntariness, in which the pain is so great that my will to go on has been eroded and I simply cannot face even a single further script. Neither is it a case in which the intensity of the pain leads me, say, suddenly to hurl aside my pen in agony (the 'expressive' case). My stopping is, instead, much more fully under my evaluative control. Accordingly, whether or not I should be excused stopping when I do, perhaps risking a failure to meet the deadline, is subject to a wider range of evaluative considerations. Excuse now depends largely, if not wholly, on what is at stake. Suppose that, by marking the very next script and immediately communicating the result (assume I am entitled to do this), I am aware that I will alleviate the great anxiety of the brilliant-but-highly-suicidal student whose script I know it is. It might then be positively wrong to stop right now, in spite of my discomfort. On the other hand, if by stopping now and resuming later, I will only miss the deadline by an hour, far less than the delay a number of my indolent colleagues will cause, my discomfort makes stopping now much more forgivable. The higher the stakes, the greater the moral strain that must be taken by the excusatory factors (whose precise nature is considered below) in play. Cases where people act in anger, or fearfully, may be found at this end of the spectrum, close to the case in which the emotion is simply urging them to do what they are still perfectly capable of deciding that it is in any event rational to do. It is well-known, for example, that the doctrine of provocation is apt to cover cases in which D has had time to map out a course of action, ultimately acting on adopted reasons, even if it can truthfully be said that his or her rage lasted from the final provocation to the moment of the killing.[155] If, and in so far as, the law's loss of self-control requirement necessitates, as Devlin J (as he then was) put it, that there have been, 'a sudden and temporary loss of self-control . . . and no time to think . . . ',[156] then the law has always been honoured more in the breach than in the observance.[157]

The more active role of reason is, of course, more explicitly acknowledged in duress cases. Few duress cases, if any, will involve the will being truly over-borne, as in the example of non-voluntariness mentioned earlier where I torture you into compliance, by subjecting you to an ever-increasing electrical current. In rare cases where one does encounter this form of duress, and its effects, the non-voluntary character of D's compliance ought to make consideration of what was at stake in D's compliance largely irrelevant. Once D's will has truly been broken, he can and should be excused *almost* anything.[158] The cases have not, however, taken up this theme, and perhaps understandably so. For, as indicated earlier, it will be difficult to say in many cases whether, say, the torture I subject you to has really so eroded your will to resist that your eventual compliance with my demands is non-voluntary; or, whether you are making a voluntary choice to comply, albeit a choice made under coercion, respecting which you need to be excused. The cases assume, as is indeed more usual, that duress involves a coerced-but-voluntary choice, a choice in which D has a residually active degree of evaluative control: D decides, upon weighing up the options, to save him- or herself from harm by doing wrong. It is a case where, as Hart and Honoré put it, 'the second actor [the one threatened] is led to believe that, if he acts as required, he will . . . escape something he dislikes . . . In this way the action in question is

---

[155] I call this kind of manifestation of anger 'outrage': see Jeremy Horder, *Provocation and Responsibility*, chapter 4.   [156] *R v Duffy* [1949] 1 All ER 932n.

[157] See Jeremy Horder, 'Provocation and Loss of Self-Control' (1992) 108 *Law Quarterly Review* 191, and the discussion in section 13 below.

[158] See the discussion in section 12 below.

rendered more eligible: he has an extra reason for doing the action'.[159] In such cases, the law acknowledges the more active role of reason in its insistence that the stakes must be very high, before D's decision to engage in wrongdoing will be excused. In English law, as in a number of jurisdictions, D must have been facing an imminent threat of death or grievous bodily harm, if he did not comply with the threatener's demand. Moreover, the demand must have been that D do something less serious than kill, attempt to kill or (arguably) inflict or attempt to inflict grievous bodily harm.[160] The excuse is, then, placed on a predominantly normative basis, something very much to do with the more active role that reason plays in what D does in such cases.

So, here, at least in theory, is an important contrast with provocation cases. In provocation cases, the role of adopted reasons is not acknowledged in law because the 'loss of self-control' requirement is wrongly assumed to prevent such reasons playing such a role in D's conduct. It is formally assumed, in other words, that when D acts in anger he or she will always be acting on an explanatory reason. Suppose, then, that we were to try to make theory fit the reality, acknowledging that anger is not inconsistent with action founded on an adopted reason. In a provocation case where D's anger has taken a form coming closer to the full 'deliberative control' end of the spectrum, we could expressly require more, by way of provocation, than when D's anger spontaneously explodes from within without any element of calculation (the case where D's anger is an explanatory reason for his or her conduct). The fact that D acts for adopted reasons, in cases where D is outraged following provocation, means that it would be quite appropriate for the law to insist that D be responding only to the gravest of provocations in such cases (the retaliatory stakes must be very high), or even to deny D an excuse altogether; whereas, the law might be understandably less insistent on this point in cases where D reacts immediately and spontaneously to an explosion of passion. For, in the latter case, when D acts for an explanatory reason, reason is reduced to (at best) its 'non-interfering gatekeeper' role. It may even be that, in practice, this is how the law does operate. As Gough has observed, speaking of several well-known cases:

The more reasons in favour of the defendant's retaliation, the less emotional disturbance he need invoke to explain his decision to act. It is no coincidence that Walters pled an 'ungoverned storm' in an effort to explain why a minor bar-room disagreement gave him reason to kill ... Equally, it is because Sara Thornton already had powerful reasons to use violence against her husband that we would expect less intense emotional disturbance to have sufficed for her.[161]

[159] H. L. A. Hart and A. M. Honoré, *Causation in the Law*, 54.

[160] See now *R v Gotts* (1992) 2 AC 412.

[161] Stephen Gough, 'Taking the Heat out of Provocation', 488, discussing *R v Walters* (1688) 12 State Trials 113, and *R v Thornton* [1992] 1 All ER 306. For further discussion of the character of Thornton's emotional reaction, see section 13 below.

More formal recognition of the distinction between the two kinds of case ought to find its way into the way in which the defence operates, as argued in section 12 below.

In ascriptive terms, what is the excusatory element, in cases where reason retains its more active role, and D acts for an adopted reason? In his searching examination of the rationale of the defence of provocation, Gough suggests that 'Anger . . . modifies perspective, directing focus towards (existing) reasons to confront and fight at the expense of reason to bite one's tongue, walk away or otherwise act sensibly'.[162] This view chimes in with Raz's observation that operative reasons can have what he calls, 'phenomenological strength, as measured by the degree of which the thought of the reason preoccupies a person and dominates his consciousness'.[163] Raz contrasts the phenomenological strength of reasons with their logical strength, the strength they derive from their ability to defeat conflicting reasons. It could be that a person knows a reason is (logically) weak in spite of the fact that it looms large on their mental horizon. It could also be, though, that the more a thought dominates someone's consciousness, the more likely they are, albeit temporarily, to think—perhaps mistakenly—that the reason has great logical strength.[164] The mental domination achieved by an operative desire-reason through its phenomenological strength, is what constitutes the rational defect in the moving force behind D's conduct, even when adopted reasons are in issue and D is acting in some sense on the balance of reasons. Although I have sought to argue that one can (seek to) educate oneself emotionally to experience such desire-reasons only in a diluted or modified form, if at all, the natural, biological tendency of emotions, to recall Zillman's words,[165] 'to focus attention to the here and now of action . . . [producing] a cognitive preoccupation with the immediate situation . . . negligent of all non-immediate implications . . . ', explains why such emotions—even when they issue in actions based on adopted reasons—so commonly excuse.

12. DURESS AND PROVOCATION AS EXCUSES: SOME CONCLUSIONS

In English law, as in many common law jurisdictions, provocation is a partial defence to murder (which carries a mandatory life sentence), reducing the crime to manslaughter, and hence setting the judge free to pass whatever sentence is thought appropriate. By way of contrast, duress is a complete excuse to any crime respecting which it is available (in England and Wales, it is not available as a defence in cases of murder and attempted murder).

---

[162] Stephen Gough, 'Taking the Heat out of Provocation', 489.

[163] Joseph Raz, *Practical Reason and Norms*, 25. See further R. DeSousa, *The Rationality of Emotion* (Cambridge, Mass.: MITR Press, 1987).

[164] Joseph Raz, *Practical Reason and Norms*, 25.   [165] See text at n. 129 above.

Although this has been the legal position for centuries, it has an illogical appearance to it. Provocation has a weaker moral claim to excusatory status than duress. In provocation cases one acts in a punitive way, retrospectively, determining for oneself the (excessive) measure of retribution for some real or imagined slight. In duress cases, by way of contrast, one is seeking prospectively to avoid a future harm to an innocent person (not necessarily oneself), by doing only what is required if that evil is to be averted.[166] In spite of this, provocation excuses the most serious of crimes, but no trivial ones, whereas with duress it is almost exactly the other way around. Naturally, things are not quite as they appear. On the one hand, duress can seem in one respect to be the weaker excuse. Given the strength of his fear, D *decides* to violate V's interests (reason having a more active role, in the form of an adopted reason), without any expressive loss of self-control propelling him or her towards that reaction. Conduct engaged in under duress can be excused when the duress does not overbear D's will, but instead leads him (in Lord Edmund-Davies's words) to make 'a conscious choice, although that choice was made unwillingly'.[167] Perhaps this is part of the explanation for the 'justificatory drift' of English duress cases, which now require that the harm done to avoid the threat must be less than the harm threatened (at least where a threat of death is concerned).[168] On the other hand, given that the stakes are so high in murder cases because a mandatory life sentence follows conviction, perhaps we are rightly reluctant to see someone convicted of this crime following a gravely provoked and purely momentary 'emotional explosion' or loss of self-control, when reason is playing only its non-interfering gatekeeper role. As Plato succinctly expressed the point, 'The man whose anger bursts forth uncontrollably, whose action is instant, immediate, and without premeditation, resembles the involuntary killer'.[169] Notice, however, that the plausibility of this rationalization of these defences depends on locating each defence close to opposite ends of the spectrum of emotional reaction that we have been considering. Unless provoked reactions do indeed, to recall Raz's phrase,[170] '*explode* from within without [an] element of calculation', *almost* (albeit not quite) as if one was reacting to putting one's hand into boiling water or to finding a large spider on one's pillow when one awakes, the case for an excuse may seem less compelling. Contrariwise, the exclusion of duress as a plea from murder cases, whatever the threat to D, makes some sense only for so long as one assumes reason plays its more active role in such cases, as an adopted reason (albeit a reason that is only seen by D as decisive because of the great

---

[166] See Jeremy Horder, 'Autonomy, Provocation and Duress'.

[167] *R v Lynch* [1975] 1 All ER 913, 951, cited by K. J. M. Smith, 'Duress and Steadfastness: In Pursuit of the Unintelligible' (1999) *Criminal Law Review* 363, 365 n. 10, where there is to be found a helpful collection of judicial analyses of the effects of duress, in a similar vein.

[168] *R v Howe* [1987] AC 417; *R v Gotts* [1992] 2 AC 412.

[169] Passage 9 (866d5-868a1), cited by T. J. Saunders, *Plato's Penal Code*, 155.

[170] Joseph Raz, *Engaging Reason*, 41–42.

phenomenological strength of his or her fear). Only in such cases is it right to judge D's conduct fully by reference to what is—morally speaking—at stake. As we now know, however, reason may retain its more active role, as an adopted reason, in some provocation cases where, despite the great phenomenological strength of D's anger, there is no loss of self-control. Likewise, at the other end of the spectrum, physical or psychological coercion—especially over a prolonged period—may break D's will to resist. This effectively silences the voice of reason, other than as a source of means–end rational guidance in complying with the coercer's demands. In such cases, D's conduct is non-voluntary. Moreover, in some cases of anger and fear it may prove difficult or impossible to say exactly whether D's emotional reaction reflected reason playing an active role, a gatekeeping role, or merely a means–end guiding role.

At the very least, what this shows is that, in so far as the law governing particular excuses is too greatly shaped by the assumption that the emotional reactions in issue fall at a particular point along the spectrum we have identified, it may need modification. As hinted above, a direction to the jury in provocation cases may need to be modified to indicate that where D did not very suddenly lose self-control and react 'instinctively', but simply made a decision to kill V, on the basis of an adopted reason that seemed decisive because of the phenomenological strength of his or her anger, only the gravest of provocations could reduce the crime to manslaughter. Indeed, it can be argued that there may be no excuse for angry retaliation in such circumstances.[171] As we will see in chapter 4 below, the distinction between the kinds of reasons on which D acts can be made to do other, related theoretical work. There may be a good case, for example, for confining instances where D may combine a provocation plea with evidence of diminished responsibility to instances in which the killing is an immediate and 'instinctive' response to a momentary loss of self-control. This is not only because (as we will see) the gravity of the provocation has no relevance to such cases, but also because such a requirement reduces the impact or relevance of strategic considerations (such as common good (iii), set out in chapter 1.2 above) that might otherwise count against permitting such a combined plea at all.

In duress cases, given the more active role of reason—D acts for an adopted reason—D's reaction can legitimately be made subject to an exacting evaluative comparison, for both normative and ascriptive purposes, between what he or she was required to do, and what he or she would otherwise suffer upon refusal to comply. In spite of the ascriptive dimension to any duress defence constituted by D's fear of the threat, D does not normally act in a moment of 'unexpected anguish' on the basis only of what he or she there and then 'instinctively' thought, to recall Lord Morris's characterization of excessive

---

[171] See Jeremy Horder, *Provocation and Responsibility*, chapter 9; and see G. R. Sullivan, 'Anger and Excuse: Reassessing Provocation' (1992) 12 *Oxford Journal of Legal Studies* 380.

defence cases.[172] If, however, the character of the coercion is such that D's will to resist is destroyed, and he or she acts non-voluntarily in complying with the coercer's wishes, the moral basis for an exacting evaluation of D's response to the threat is undermined. The more justificatory character of the rationale given for the defence in recent cases will now have no place in the analysis of D's conduct. In these circumstances, it is right to say, as judges have said in some duress cases, that D's will is 'overborne'.[173] D's claim is close to the border with a denial of responsibility *tout court*, as distinct from excuse. Such a breaking of the will seems to have been the effect duress was required to have had before it could successfully be pleaded, by the drafters of the Model Penal Code. As Professor Weschler put it: 'I emphasise those words "unable to resist" because we really mean . . . unable to resist not, would have decided not to resist, but would have been unable to resist.' [174] Where duress comes in a truly irresistible form, where it breaks the will of the person coerced in such a way that he or she wholly surrenders evaluative control over decision-making to the coercer, almost any crime might in principle be excused by such duress.[175] One perhaps finds tacit recognition of this (although the point was not directly addressed) in the decision of the Privy Council in *Abbot v R*[176] in which Lord Wilberforce and Lord Edmund-Davies agreed that, '[T]he realistic view is that, the more dreadful the circumstances of the [crime] . . . the stronger and more irresistible the duress needed before it could be regarded as affording any defence.'[177]

Strictly speaking, the rule that duress may not be a defence to murder is unaffected by this point. Involuntariness is not a 'confession and avoidance' defence but a denial of the *actus reus*, and a claim of non-voluntariness is sometimes treated in the same way.[178] So, in theory if I have truly broken your will to resist, you can deny that the *actus* was *reus* without having to rely on the defence of duress, a defence that assumes that the coerced act was

This point assumes greater significance in the light of the Law Commission's recommendation to abolish any loss of self-control requirement, *stricto sensu*, in provocation cases: see Law Commission for England and Wales, *Murder, Manslaughter and Infanticide*, Part 5. Quite rightly the Law Commission sees a corresponding need for a much higher degree of provocation if first degree murder is to reduce homicide under provocation to second degree murder.

[172] *Palmer v R* [1971] 1 All ER 1077, 1078. There can, of course, be exceptions to this, especially in duress of circumstances cases in which D responds to a sudden threat, in which case Lord Morris's dictum will have an application. But in most such cases, like *R v Conway* [1989] 3 All ER 1025, D will still be acting for an adopted reason even when he or she must act quickly if the threat is to be avoided.

[173] See the cases discussed in K. J. M. Smith, 'Duress and Steadfastness: In Pursuit of the Unintelligible', 363–364.

[174] American Law Institute, 37th Annual Meeting, ALI Proceedings 1960 127 (1961), 120, cited by Joshua Dressler 'Reflections on Excusing Wrongdoers: New Excuses and the Model Penal Code' (1988) 19 *Rutgers Law Journal* 671, 709 n. 176.

[175] The courts have wrongly failed to take up this point where those particularly vulnerable to threats, such as children and those with some kinds of mental disorder, are concerned. Arguably, the defence of duress should be much more widely available in such cases than it need be with adults who have normal mental capacities.

[176] [1976] 3 All ER 140.   [177] Ibid., 152.   [178] See *R v T* [1990] Crim LR 256.

voluntarily undertaken. Although it is perhaps unlikely that the courts would exempt such cases from the ordinary rules of the defence, this is the best course. The defence needs to be expounded in such a way that it is clear that there can be a complete acquittal, in these exceptional circumstances, even in a murder case. This is principally because the main justification for denying the defence in murder cases, that D must have the *courage* to resist coercion and refuse deliberately to take a life,[179] has no application when D's will to resist has been broken through torture, or the like. An act of courage is an act of will, voluntarily undertaken. So, when someone's will has truly been broken, they are beyond courage or cowardice, and their conduct should be treated in the same way (categorized as non-voluntary) as that of someone suffering from a serious traumatic stress disorder.[180] I return to the theoretical significance of a duress plea in murder cases, in chapter 3 below.

13. MIXED MOTIVES: WHEN FEAR TEMPERS ANGER, AS A RESPONSE TO PROVOCATION

In an age where the taking of personal retribution, even in anger, is no longer glorified, there might be thought to be little excusatory weight to a claim that one was provoked into acting on a punitive, retaliatory urge, were it not for the fact that the provocation in question may have led to a very sudden and unlooked-for loss of control of that urge, making D's reaction almost (albeit not quite) 'instinctive'. Looked at in this way, there is little to disagree with, whatever departure it may have involved from previous authorities, in Devlin J's famous direction to the jury (approved by the Court of Appeal) on the meaning on the subjective condition in provocation cases, in *R v Duffy*:[181]

> Provocation is some act, or series of acts . . . which . . . actually causes in the accused, a sudden and temporary loss of self-control, rendering the accused so subject to passion as to make him or her for the moment not the master of his mind . . . Indeed, circumstances which induce a desire for revenge are inconsistent with provocation, since the conscious formulation of a desire for revenge means that a person has had time to think, to reflect, and that would negative a sudden temporary loss of self-control which is of the essence of provocation.[182]

Yet, ironically, it is this direction (and the rationale for the mitigation provided by the doctrine of provocation that it endorses) that has come in for the most severe criticism from those who rightly perceive that, so restricted, the doctrine of provocation indirectly discriminates in favour of men. Quite simply, men are far more likely than women to lose control in the way

---

[179] See e.g. the argument of Lord Hailsham in *R v Howe* [1987] AC 417, 432.
[180] See *R v T* [1990] Crim LR 256.   [181] [1949] 1 All ER 932n.   [182] Ibid.

described by Devlin J, in the face of serious provocation, rather than—more like women, in general—being moved by great provocation to experience a more complex set of emotions for which it would be useful to use the US Model Penal Code's umbrella term 'extreme emotional disturbance'.[183] Why? Women Ds are more likely to have acted for mixed motives in provocation cases, especially when the provoker they kill—as in *Duffy* itself—is an abusive (former) partner, the motives mixed being anger *and* fear. It seems obvious that when one is being taunted by someone known to be physically more powerful and aggressive than oneself, one's anger at the provoker is liable to be tempered by a fear of the provoker's own reaction to any angry response one displays. That 'mixed' reaction is liable to ensure that one does not immediately lose control of any retaliatory impulse one experiences; but (depending, in part, on the gravity of the provocation) it may also leave one in a greatly heightened emotional state—a state of extreme emotional disturbance—in which, whilst the state endures, advantage will probably only be taken to inflict retaliation if and when the provoker is 'off his guard'.[184] By way of contrast, it seems plausible to suppose that an immediate loss of control of the urge to retaliate upon provocation will be peculiar to those for whom it is, in general, a deeply ingrained assumption that (rightly or wrongly, as things turn out) there is nothing much to fear from the provoker if they react in that way, or for whom experience has shown that an individual provoker will offer no threat in response to an immediate loss of self-control. Small wonder, then, that when one contrasts the reactions of men and women to grave provocation, particularly provocation arising out of an intimate (or formerly intimate) relationship *inter se*, more women than men will be found to have taken advantage of the provoker being 'off his guard', when they—the women—were in a greatly heightened emotional state, and more men than women will be found to have reacted with violence more or less immediately following a sudden loss of self-control.

Depending on how serious a blight on the law one considers this 'unfair advantage' conferred on men by the structure of the subjective condition in provocation cases to be, one might argue in favour of abolishing the partial excuse of provocation altogether.[185] One might look, instead, to modifications to the defence of self-defence (or of diminished responsibility) to accommodate instances in which women respond to provocation offered by someone who has also posed a continuing threat from which there was no reasonable opportunity to escape, a possibility considered in chapter 4.9 below. It might, though, be possible to reform the provocation defence to eliminate the unfair advantage. One could seek to make a virtue of the fact that Ds are more likely to act for mixed motives when they face a provoker

---

[183] See the discussion in A. P. Simester and G. R. Sullivan, *Criminal Law: Theory and Doctrine*, 1st edn., 344.

[184] See *R v Thornton* [1992] 1 All ER 306; *R v Ahluwalia* [1992] 4 All ER 889.

[185] See e.g. Jeremy Horder, *Provocation and Responsibility*, chapter 9.

UNIVERSITY OF WINCHESTER
LIBRARY

who is also believed to be a threat (although not a threat legitimately met with defensive force), by *confining* the defence to such instances. This would move the defence beyond a focus purely on sudden losses of self-control, the focus that confers the unfair advantage, however gravely provoked the loss of self-control may have been. The focus would shift to the extreme emotional disturbance produced by the combined effect of provoked anger—whether or not manifesting itself in a loss of self-control—and fear for the safety of oneself or another (say, a child of the family), a combined effect naturally associated with a violent reaction only if and when, as in *Duffy*, the provoker's guard is down. Consider the following possible replacement for section 3 of the Homicide Act 1957:

Provoked extreme emotional disturbance:

(1)   *Where, on a charge of murder, there is evidence that D was provoked to play his or her part in the killing in a temporary state of extreme emotional disturbance, the offence may be found to be manslaughter by the jury. The jury may find the offence to be manslaughter if, in its opinion, a temporary state of extreme emotional disturbance produced by a combination of provocation and D's fear for his or her own safety (or the safety of another) provided a reasonable excuse, in all the circumstances, for D's act in playing his or her part in the killing.*

(2)   *The trial judge may withdraw the issue of provoked extreme emotional disturbance from the jury when, in his or her opinion, there is no evidence that a reasonable jury could find that D was acting in a temporary state of extreme emotional disturbance produced by a combination of provocation and fear for his or her own safety (or the safety of another). However, the question whether the extreme emotional disturbance provided a reasonable excuse for the defendant's act, in playing his or her part in the killing, shall be one to be determined wholly by the jury.*

Very obviously, this revised version of section 3 of the Homicide Act 1957 does not deal with many pertinent issues (some of which, like the possible relevance of evidence of mental disorder to D's plea, are dealt with in chapter 4 below) that a full revision of the defence of provocation would need to address. In itself, though, I hope that it provides a template to work from in seeking to redress the imbalance of advantage, in the way the defence of provocation operates, between men and women. I hope that it will be thought of as doing this without reverting to such tried, and now rightly mistrusted, measures as artificially confining the kinds of provocation that can reduce murder to manslaughter to, say, 'violence' (whatever that may be construed to mean), or—even worse—to 'unlawful' actions.[186]

---

[186] I pursue the issues raised in this section in more depth in Jeremy Horder, 'Reshaping the Factual Element in the Provocation Defence' (2005) 25 *Oxford Journal of Legal Studies* (forthcoming, issue 1).

3

Which Theory of Excuses?

1. THE 'SERIAL' VIEW OF DEFENCES[1]

In this chapter, I will begin my defence of a liberal understanding of excuses. We open with a detailed examination of narrower and broader theories of excuse (I will be defending a broader theory). To that end, though, it will be important to take a view right from the start on how justification and excuses stand, in relation to one another. From a moral point of view, one should take a 'serial' view of the ethical significance of defences. Gardner explains very well why one should do this:

[I]t is best if we commit no wrongs. If we cannot but commit wrongs, it is best if we commit them with justification. Failing justification, it is best if we have an excuse. The worst case is the one in which we must cast doubt on our own responsibility. When I say 'best' and 'worst' here I mean best and worse for us: for the course of our own lives and for our integrity as people.[2]

Some theorists have rejected key aspects of the 'serial' view of defences.[3] For example, although he would obviously have acknowledged conceptual distinctions between them, Hart saw no morally significant difference in status between an excuse, a denial of voluntariness, and a denial of responsibility. All were, morally speaking, on a par as claims against the state for an

---

[1] The phrase 'serial view of defences' is gratefully adopted from Douglas Husak, 'The Serial View of Criminal Law Defences' (1992) 3 *Criminal Law Forum* 369.

[2] John Gardner, 'In Defence of Defences', in P. Asp, C. E. Herlitz, and L. Holmqvist (eds.), *Flores Juris et Legum: Festskrift till Nils Jareborg* (Uppsala: Iustus Forlag, 2002), 262. See also his remarks in John Gardner, 'The Gist of Excuses', 590: 'She [D] wants it to be the case that her actions were not truly wrongful, or if they were wrongful, that they were at any rate justified, or if they were not justified, that they were at any rate excused. A denial of responsibility rules all of this out, and that is, accordingly, the line of defence which counts as an admission of defeat for any self-respecting person.' For a different account of a 'serial' view of defences, distinguishing non-culpable right actions, culpable right actions, non-culpable wrong actions, and culpable wrong actions, from one another, see Heidi Hurd, 'Justification and Excuse, Wrongdoing and Culpability', 1551, 1560–1561.

[3] H. L. A. Hart, *Punishment and Responsibility*, chapter 2; Dennis Klimchuk, 'Necessity, Deterrence and Standing' (2002) 8 *Legal Theory* 339; Douglas Husak, 'The Serial View of Criminal Law Defences'; George P. Fletcher, *Rethinking Criminal Law*, 10.3.4, 'Decisions on justifying circumstances modify the applicable legal norm. Decisions on excuses, in contrast, leave the norm intact, but irreversibly modify the factual background of succeeding claims to excuse'.

acquittal.[4] Such a view makes it too difficult to defend the position that whilst some crimes—like genocide—are inexcusable, it ought to remain a defence to such crimes that one acted whilst insane or non-voluntarily.[5] Contrariwise, Hart's view is hard to square with the common claim that D is subjected to specially degrading treatment if classified as insane, when he or she has harmed another in the course, for example, of an epileptic fit.[6] In such a case, whilst it would, of course, certainly be very harsh to deny D a simple claim of involuntariness, there is something not so much harsh as downright insulting about classifying D's 'conduct' as that of a mad person. As (in a broad sense) a defence to crime, a denial of voluntariness should be classified and treated quite differently from a denial of responsibility.

Other theorists, like Dennis Klimchuk, believe that what fails about the serial view of defences is the claim that it is better to be justified than to be excused for wrongdoing, because one is not comparing like with like. On Klimchuk's Kantian view,[7] justifications *negate* the wrong, and are not a claim raised in respect of admitted wrongdoing, unlike excuses.[8] This is what Gardner has called the 'closure' view, according to which an action is not wrong unless it is wrong all things considered. As Gardner says, thus, on the closure view, the idea of 'justified wrongdoing' is oxymoronic.[9] One should not, though, be so prescriptive about the effect of justifications, because their intrinsic character varies a good deal. Some justifications, albeit ones unfamiliar in modern Western legal systems, have a 'transformative' character, as when it is taken to be literally true within a jurisdiction that 'the King can do no wrong'. Then, it can be the fact that it is the King himself who is engaged in some piece of conduct that makes that conduct right or justified, and dispels the impression of wrongfulness that would have otherwise characterized it, in something like the way the closure view suggests. In modern Western legal systems, the closest one is likely to get to the closure view of justifications, without actually reaching it, is in cases (a) where V can lawfully consent to what would otherwise have been an assault by D, as when D cuts V's hair whilst styling it at the salon, or (b) when, although it has the same generic character as the prohibited conduct (hence calling for a 'justificatory' argument), D's own conduct is deemed by law to fall outside the scope of the wrong, as when D is smoking in the smoking compartment of a train. In both cases, it certainly

[4] H. L. A. Hart, *Punishment and Responsibility*, chapter 2. For further discussion of Hart's theory of excuses, see chapter 1 above.

[5] See Jeremy Horder, 'Criminal Law: Between Determinism, Liberalism and Criminal Justice', 166–167.

[6] See the discussion of *R v Sullivan* [1984] AC 156, in Andrew Ashworth, *Principles of Criminal Law*, 3rd edn., 103–106.

[7] I. Kant, *Metaphysics of Morals*, (M. Gregor (trans.)), (Cambridge: Cambridge University Press, 1991), 16–17.

[8] Dennis Klimchuk, 'Necessity, Deterrence, and Standing'. See also Michael S. Moore, *Placing Blame*, 493. In spite of his well-documented 'anti-Kantian' views, Alan Norrie also endorses this view: see Alan Norrie, *Punishment, Responsibility and Justice: A Relational Critique*, 153, on which see John Gardner, 'In Defence of Defences', 256.   [9] Ibid., 252.

appears that once one is in possession of the full facts (V's consent; that D was in the smoking compartment), any impression of wrong done on D's part will be dispelled by the 'justificatory' arguments, respectively, that V consented, or that D was in the smoking compartment. One might wonder, though, whether these really are true cases of justification, where one is called to give better reasons for doing as one did, than there were reasons not to do it.[10] If the conduct fell outside the scope of the prohibited norm, as it does in these cases, what were the relevant reasons against doing as D did that must be met with a justificatory argument? The suspicion that there were no such reasons is reinforced by the fact that, given that his or her conduct simply falls outside the scope of the prohibited norm, in both cases D need not be aware of the justification when acting on it.[11] These are really cases where, given that D's conduct bears such striking similarity to that covered by the prohibitory norm, careful *explanation* (but not justification, in its true sense) may be required to show how the conduct in question is in fact permitted by law, in spite of the striking similarity it may bear, in some instances, to a kind of conduct actually prohibited.

Putting such cases aside, the arguments favour Gardner's 'serial' view of defences, over the closure view. In cases of arrest, search of premises and seizure of goods, the very fact that, except in cases of great urgency, an *ex ante* justification (in the form of a warrant) is required before such action can be taken, is a tacit acknowledgement that the invasion of the interests of private citizens is a wrong that requires a strong justification, given that, as things may turn out (perhaps as a result of the very arrest, search or seizure in question), the citizens affected may be discovered to be wholly innocent of any offence. Turning to a different example, self-defence against an aggressor can look like a case in which D's justificatory argument is to the effect that he or she does V no wrong by repelling the attack; but in fact such cases need not be so analysed.[12] It could be that D justifiably wrongs V, even in using necessary and proportionate force against him or her (imagine that V is insane, or is a child unaware that he or she is pointing a loaded gun). It is just that, in virtue of posing a threat, V's normative position has also changed, in that he or she is now morally disabled from meeting D's necessary and proportionate defensive steps with steps of his or her own to prevent D repelling the attack. *A fortiori*, then, necessity cases are cases of justified wrongdoing (*pace* the closure view), because in these instances V is posing no threat him- or herself, and yet his or her interests can permissibly be violated as the lesser of two acknowledged evils.[13] And in all these

---

[10] On this point, see John Gardner, 'Justifications and Reasons', 107–114.

[11] For a case illustrating this point in a different context, see *R v Deller* (1952) 36 Cr App Rep 184.

[12] See Jeremy Horder, 'On the Irrelevance of Motive in Criminal Law, 180 n. 17; and chapter 2.8 above. I must confess to some equivocation on this point in other writing, but I will not go into that here.

[13] See, further, Jeremy Horder, 'Self-Defence, Necessity and Duress: Understanding the Relationship', 150–155.

cases, D must act for the sake of the justification when it applies, precisely because there is a wrong done respecting which the moral—and hence legal—force of the justification for perpetrating it would be entirely lost if D did not act on the justification for its own sake.[14] In that regard, as Gardner says, the closure account of such justifications is unsatisfactory, because it embodies a misplaced optimism about the prospects for 'higher-level' rational resolution of moral problems. It makes more sense to admit, as does what Gardner dubs the 'classical' view of necessity, that one is often left 'in the unlucky position that one's life will be blemished by wrongdoing whatever one does and hence irrespective of one's competence as a rational being'.[15]

In chapter 4 below, I shall argue in favour of a greatly enhanced role for 'partial' excuses in the criminal law, by and large tied to the passing of non-custodial sentences, encompassing but going beyond the existing partial excuses of provocation and diminished responsibility (that are 'partial' in that although they acquit D of murder, he is she is convicted of manslaughter instead). Where do partial excuses fit into the serial view of defences? It is obvious that it is better to be completely excused than to be partially excused, but is it better to be partially excused than to be acquitted through a denial that one was responsible, due solely to mental disorder or infancy? If it is appropriate partially, rather than completely, to excuse in some duress, excessive defence, demands-of-conscience or provocation cases, then there is no difficulty about the place of such defences on the 'ladder' between full excuse and denial of responsibility. All these excuses are accounted for by what I will explain below as the objective version of the capacity theory, the theory that judges people by whether they came up to a relevant, morally significant standard. The line between partial excuses and denials of responsibility is liable to become blurred, however, in the case where the partial defence comes in the form of a new plea in favour of which I shall be arguing in chapter 4 below, 'diminished capacity'. This is a plea that is available even when the mitigating factor in relation to D's conduct constituted by D's mental deficiency is insufficient to warrant mitigation by itself (as it must be in the case of the existing partial defence of diminished responsibility). It would be available when D's conduct is explained by a *combination* of mental defect and the exceptional pressure of circumstances. In such cases, D's plea has an excusatory element, and is not an out-and-out denial of responsibility of the kind at issue in traditional diminished responsibility pleas. It is here, perhaps, that as Gardner remarks, when faced with the stark fact of conviction for the 1st degree offence, people are most likely to be persuaded

---

[14] See John Gardner, 'Justifications and Reasons'.

[15] John Gardner, 'In Defence of Defences', 255, where he goes on to say (255–256), 'That's the way the cookie crumbles, according to the classical view . . . They ["closure" view theorists] refused, in sum, to leave logical space for the classical idea of the tragic, which is the idea of a life unluckily blemished by wrongful actions that were performed without the slightest rational error, and may even have been rationally inescapable.'

by the cynical defence lawyer's argument that acquittal at any price, including a 2nd degree conviction partly supported on grounds of mental deficiency, is to be preferred.[16] Even so, in spite of the moral ambiguity that inevitably attends these particular cases, there is an argument that it is something we must be prepared to live with, in the interests of common humanity.[17]

A Modified Defence 'Ladder'

Rung 1: transformative justifications, negating wrongfulness
Rung 2: justifications for wrongdoing (e.g. self-defence; necessity)
Rung 3: some full excuses (e.g. duress; excessive defence)
Rung 4: some full or partial excuses (e.g. provocation)
Rung 5: the partial excuse of diminished capacity
Rung 6: denials of responsibility (insanity; diminished responsibility).

2. THE SERIAL VIEW OF DEFENCES AND THE RANGE OF EXCUSES

How do individual excuses come to be located on different rungs of the ladder, and how does their location tie in to the distinction between the objective and the subjective versions of the capacity theory? The predominantly normative character of excessive defence and most duress cases (as explained in chapter 2 above) plays a crucial role in placing them on rung 3, just below justifications for wrongdoing. By way of contrast, the predominantly ascriptive character of provocation cases, and of the demands-of-conscience cases I shall be discussing in chapter 5 below, is the key factor in placing these excuses on rung 4.[18] In spite of this important theoretical difference between the two kinds of case, in a broad moral sense, there may be little to distinguish some instances in which an excuse takes a predominantly normative form, from at least some instances in which it takes a predominantly ascriptive form. So, as we saw in chapter 2.5 above, there may be just as compelling a case for a complete excuse when D's repugnance at the prospect of being forced to eat ever more putrefied rotting flesh induces him to inflict an injury on another person, as there is when D is threatened with death unless he or

---

[16] Gardner, John, 'In Defence of Defences', 262. That the theoretical risks have turned into a reality is a claim substantiated, in relation to the plea of diminished responsibility, by R. D. Mackay, 'Diminished Responsibility and Mentally Disordered Killers', in Andrew Ashworth and Barry Mitchell (eds.), *Rethinking English Homicide Law* (Oxford: Oxford University Press, 2000), 74–77.

[17] The risk of cynical use of the diminished responsibility plea brings into play strategic considerations or common goods (i) and (ii), as explained in chapter 1.2 above. See also Martin Wasik, 'Partial Excuses in the Criminal Law' (1982) 45 *Modern Law Review* 516, 524–526.

[18] Although, in the case of the demands-of-conscience excuse, the absence of, or triviality of, a right invasion may permit an argument for a complete excuse that is not available in provocation cases.

she commits such a wrong, even though the former has a predominantly ascriptive and the latter a predominantly normative excusatory character. Similarly, where D, who is only 13 years of age, kills rather be killed him- or herself by the person making the threat, D's action is no less unjustified than it would be if performed by an adult, and if D is to be (partially) excused it must be on a predominantly ascriptive basis.[19] Even so it is wholly unrealistic to expect D to have developed the same powers of self-restraint as an adult, in the face of a threat of certain death, and so, in a broad sense, there is little or nothing to distinguish such a case from one in which an adult D is excused for an action taken under duress, on a predominantly normative basis.

To a greater or lesser degree, in spite of important differences between them, in all the excuses on rungs 3 and 4 of the defence 'ladder' we are concerned with evaluating D's conduct in the light of objective moral standards. In Gardner's terminology,[20] we are concerned with whether D has lived up to normative expectations, or to what I will distinguish below as the standards set by the objective version of the capacity theory. Contrast the examples covered by these excuses with the facts of *R v Martin*.[21] In this case, D grossly over-reacted to the presence of a young burglar by shooting him a number of times, including a shot in the back, killing him. He was initially convicted of murder, but was subsequently found to have been suffering from a paranoid disorder of which evidence had not been given at the trial. So, the Appeal Court quashed the conviction for murder, and substituted a verdict of manslaughter on the grounds of diminished responsibility. Initially, though, Martin sought to plead that the reasonableness of his reaction, in self-defence or in prevention of crime, ought to have been assessed in the light of his disorder. His plea was, thus, that his reaction was the kind of reaction, in self-defence or the prevention of crime, that one might have expected (for the purposes either of justification or of excuse) from someone with a paranoid disorder. Quite rightly, the Court cast doubt on the appropriateness of this kind of plea, for the purposes of a justificatory defence,[22] but what they said was equally applicable to an excusatory plea. Evidence of the effects of a paranoid disorder is not evidence of how D met *moral* standards—even lower than normal ones—to which he or she was expected to live up. So, as the Court impliedly found in rejecting Martin's line of argument, both the normative expectations theory, and the objective version of the capacity theory, have no application to a case such as this, and cannot be employed to explain how—if at all—D is excused. However, a finding of partial excuse on the grounds of diminished capacity (rung 5 of the ladder above), what

---

[19] For discussion of an example in which a young boy was acquitted, in such circumstances, in spite of the fact that duress is no defence to murder, see the civil case of *Halford v Brooks* [1991] 1 WLR 428, and the discussion in chapter 2.5 above.

[20] See the passage cited in chapter 2.6 above.

[21] *R v Martin (Anthony)* [2002] 2 WLR 1 (CA). This case is discussed in more detail in chapter 4.10 below.   [22] *R v Martin (Anthony)* [2002] 2 WLR 1, 16 (per Lord Woolf CJ).

were in effect the grounds for the ultimate result in *Martin* itself, can be satisfactorily explained by applying the subjective version of the capacity theory, as explained below. For, on this theory, what matters, alongside evidence of D's mental deficiencies, is whether there are still genuinely excusatory factors at work, such as the actively justificatory reason for which D acted (excusatory dimension 2, as explained in chapter 2.3 above), namely D's belief—founded in the facts, even if unreasonably held—that the force was needed to forestall an attack by V. As we will see in section 7 below, in the light of these two factors (mental deficiency; an excusatory element with a factual foundation) considered together, the issue then becomes whether greater self-restraint could reasonably have been expected of D *himself*.

As we will see in chapter 4 below, it is a matter of deep controversy whether there really is any 'excusatory' dimension to pleas on rung 5 of the ladder. On a stricter view, such pleas should be treated as denials of responsibility (rung 6) that have been illegitimately dressed up as excusatory pleas to make them appear more respectable. On such a view, if he or she really wants to be excused, D should be required to meet the objective moral standards that underpin the excuses on rungs 3 and 4. For example, in implicitly denying that there can be any distinctively excusatory element to a plea of diminished capacity, and hence denying that there is any rung 5 at all, Gardner cites an unusual, and formidable, alliance between Aristotelian and Kantian moral thinking. To cite the passage from Kant to which Gardner himself makes reference, 'We must not determine ethical duties according to our estimate of man's power to fulfil the (moral) law; on the contrary we must estimate man's power by the standard of the law, which commands categorically'.[23] Gardner's elegantly simple account of the gist of excuses is powerfully supported by his philosophical attack on the notion that one can drive a significant wedge between the question whether D did or did not act (say) courageously, and the question whether D had the capacity to act courageously.[24] Either one came up to the normatively expected standard, or one did not. Morally and (hence) legally, that is all that matters. Unless one is actually seeking to deny one's full responsibility *tout court*, through a mental disorder or infancy defence, and hence by definition not seeking a true excuse at all,[25] there can be no fallback defence that one lacked an adequate 'capacity' to come up to that standard.

---

[23] I. Kant, *The Doctrine of Virtue*, cited by John Gardner, 'The Gist of Excuses', 580 n. 9. See Aristotle, *Nichomachean Ethics*, iii, 1114a8-1115a5: 'the bad man has just as much [scope for] independence in his *actions*, even if not in his choice of end' (emphasis in the original). Kant's view was satirized by Samuel Butler, in *Erehwon*, 107, when Butler has a trial judge say to the accused, 'It is all very well for you to say that you came of unhealthy parents, and had a severe accident in your childhood which permanently undermined your constitution; excuses such as these are the ordinary refuge of the criminal; but they cannot for one moment be listened to by the ear of justice . . . there is no question of how you came to be wicked, but only this—namely, are you wicked or not?', cited in Michael S. Moore, *Placing Blame*, 503.

[24] John Gardner, 'The Gist of Excuses', 579–594.

[25] Ibid., 588: 'By making excuses people are, on the contrary, asserting their responsibility . . .'.

Gardner's strict version of the 'normative expectations' account of excuses probably describes better than any other account the direction that English law took, in developing excuses from the mid-nineteenth century up until the last two or three decades. A high point was almost certainly the passing of sections 2 and 3 of the Homicide Act 1957. That Act appeared to enshrine in statute key aspects of the strict 'normative expectations' view of provocation, and distinguished a separate plea of diminished responsibility dependent on proof of mental disorder sufficient *in itself* substantially to diminish responsibility.[26] In recent years, however, the strict reading of the 'normative expectations' view has come under attack in the courts from what Gardner describes (and himself attacks) as a 'supposedly "Kantian" view'.[27] This is the view that D's own capacity for self-control, self-restraint, and so forth, must in some cases be made relevant to the standard he or she could reasonably have been expected to reach, to deserve an excuse, a position adopted (although not because of its supposedly Kantian roots) by no lesser a modern theoretical authority than H. L. A. Hart.[28] This is the broad view of excuses that it will be the purpose of this chapter to defend. In essence, the broad view of excuses seeks to be broad by isolating for excusatory treatment some of the cases forming a significant *tertium quid*, lying between cases where D can be judged (un)worthy of excuse by the yardstick of an objective standard, and cases where D's inability to reach that standard is attributable *wholly* to mental disorder or infancy. In discussing lack of capacity to reach a standard, such as would nonetheless amount to a denial of responsibility, Gardner talks of 'people whose incapacity goes *very deep*', cases in which D suffers from a 'very specific and *deep-seated* incapacity—namely, the incapacity to reason intelligibly through to action'.[29] These are cases where, so mentally disordered is D's thinking due to an abnormality of mind, or so young is D, that the law secures a complete or partial acquittal 'by extinguishing the need . . . to rely on excuses altogether'.[30] In such cases, D relies for a complete or partial defence on a plea of insanity, diminished responsibility, or infancy. What happens, then, according to the 'normative expectations' view of excuses, if an incapacity is not deep-seated enough to amount to a denial of responsibility? The fact that it may have badly hampered D

---

[26] At about the same time, American lawyers were beginning to develop what became the Model Penal Code, in which can be found a partial defence of 'extreme mental or emotional disturbance . . . for which there is reasonable explanation or excuse'. That defence did not clearly distinguish provocation from diminished responsibility, and is objectionable to an adherent of the 'normative expectations' view, on that ground. See the discussion in Andrew Ashworth, *Principles of Criminal Law*, 3rd edn., 239; and Joshua Dressler, *Understanding Criminal Law* (New York: Matthew Bender, 1995), 2nd edn., chapter 26.

[27] John Gardner, 'The Gist of Excuses', 586. The case that calls the strict view of the normative expectations account into question is *R v (Morgan) Smith* [2000] 4 All ER 289.

[28] H. L. A. Hart, *Punishment and Responsibility*, 46–47.

[29] John Gardner, 'The Gist of Excuses', 587 and 589 respectively (my emphasis). At 589, he gives, as examples, 'profound mental illness or infancy or sleepwalking or (on some interpretations) post-hypnotic suggestion'.   [30] Ibid., 589.

in reaching the appropriate standard of conduct will not change the fact (if fact it be) that D did not reach that standard, and hence cannot hope to be excused, if his or her purported denial of responsibility is rejected. D must then be convicted of the full offence. If that seems harsh, says the adherent of the 'normative expectations' view, one must recall that, in refusing to condescend to D's incapacity the law is not directly criminalizing what is for D something impossible, in breach of rule-of-law requirements. Excuses and denials of responsibility are 'rules for courts', matters of *ex post facto* judgment of D's conduct, and are not guiding rules of conduct in themselves.[31]

The broad, liberal view of excuses that I will defend does not, unlike the version now defended by the higher courts, challenge the view that provocation and duress pleas both in some sense turn on 'normative expectations'.[32] The centrality of the need to satisfy those expectations, if one is to be excused, symbolizes a liberal society's commitment to uphold standards of conduct in the interests of the common good, whilst creating moral, cultural and legal space for the flourishing of value pluralism.[33] The importance of that symbolism outweighs the 'special pleading' argument that since the effect of provocation (unlike duress) is merely to reduce murder to manslaughter, society's commitment to uphold common standards can be set on one side in developing the excusatory conditions. The view of excuses I defend seeks to be broader than the 'normative expectations' view, by seeking to bridge the gap between those appropriately judged by normative standards, and those with 'deep-seated' incapacities not appropriately so judged. It seeks to do this by developing a new partial defence—the diminished capacity defence—with its roots in the existing diminished responsibility defence, to fill that gap. As we will see in chapter 4 below, Ds pleading diminished responsibility have always in practice been permitted to combine excusatory and denial-of-responsibility elements in that plea, thus bridging that gap, rather than being made to rely wholly on satisfying the latter element if they are to be acquitted of murder.[34] This need not be a matter of great concern, because society's commitment to regard objective standards as at the heart of the necessary conditions of excuse (see chapter 1.5 above),

---

[31] See John Gardner, 'The Gist of Excuses', 596–97; see also John Gardner, 'Justifications and Reasons', 123–126. See the discussion in chapter 2.9 above.

[32] Although, what Gardner understands by 'normative expectations' is not to be equated with what I have called the predominantly normative excuses (duress; excessive defence), as we will see shortly. He considers, as I also argued in chapter 2 above, that there is a normative dimension to, say, provocation cases, in that I can be criticized for something I did, namely losing control of the urge to kill.

[33] This theme has been most fully explored by John Gardner and Timothy Macklem, 'Provocation and Pluralism' (2001) 64 *Modern Law Review* 815.

[34] R. D. Mackay, 'Pleading Provocation and Diminished Responsibility Together' [1988] *Criminal Law Review* 411; Suzanne Dell, *Murder into Manslaughter: The Diminished Responsibility Defence in Practice* (London: Institute of Psychiatry, 1984). In chapter 4.2 below, I argue that diminished responsibility should be a verdict, not a partial defence to murder alone.

along with its commitment to promote common goods, are not so obviously at stake when the diminished responsibility defence is pleaded. For, D is not (fully) asserting his or her responsibility. It is part of the liberal vision of excuses developed in this work, though, that it would be better to give open and formal recognition to pleas that combine excusatory and denial-of-responsibility elements. This would be more likely to secure justice for 'short-comers', in terms of capacity, for whom adhering to normative expectations is unduly difficult, but whose incapacity is not so thoroughgoing or deep-seated that it amounts to a denial of responsibility in itself. As we will see, society's commitment to regard objective standards as at the heart of the necessary conditions of excuse would be no more compromised by a separate diminished capacity defence than it is by the diminished responsibility defence. For, as illustrated by the brief discussion of *R v Martin* above, the elements of an excusatory plea that may be combined with evidence of mental deficiency are the factual elements (loss of self-control; terror in the face of a threat), rather than the evaluative elements constitutive of objective standards.

3.   RIVAL THEORIES OF EXCUSES: THE 'NORMATIVE EXPECTATIONS' VIEW

Three rival theories compete for our allegiance, when it comes to explaining excuses: the 'character' theory, the 'capacity' theory, and the 'normative expectations' theory.[35] None is free from theoretical difficulty, although all may have a role to play in understanding the scope and nature of excuses. In section 6 below I shall, though, explain and defend the capacity theory, as the most important of the three (although I will say something briefly about the theory in a moment). In this section and the next, I consider the merits of the normative expectations view. This view is focused on whether, notwithstanding their failure to meet a particular obligation on a given occasion, Ds lived up to certain expectations we have of them. As Gardner puts it:

The gist of an excuse . . . is precisely that the person with the excuse lived up to our expectations . . . The question is whether that person lived up to expectations in a *normative* sense. Did she manifest as much resilience, or loyalty, or thoroughness, or presence of mind as a person in her situation should have manifested?[36]

Unexceptionable in itself, one common way to interpret this claim is to say that what is expected of someone normatively, depends on a judgment of how they exercised their *capacity* to exhibit courage, self-control, and so

---

[35] John Gardner gives some reasons for distinguishing between the idea that someone has capacities, and the idea that they should live by, or up to, certain normative expectations: see John Gardner, 'The Gist of Excuses', 576–587.

[36] Ibid., 578 and 579 (Gardner's emphasis).

forth. It is an important function of law to judge people by the yardstick of morally salient standards, especially when they claim justification or excuse.[37] On an objective version of the capacity theory, D's performance in that regard should be judged by reference to a morally salient standard (reasonable self-control, self-restraint, and so on) rather than via a wide-ranging enquiry into each D's individual capacities. Standards are morally salient, on this view, when it would be morally culpable for D's conduct to fail to come up to the level embodied in the standard. In that respect, although most adults fall to be judged by much the same standard, the central role of moral culpability to a failure to meet the standard means that the morally salient standard sometimes has to be varied (relaxed or, exceptionally, raised). There will be categories of case, in which it would not be right to expect Ds to meet the same standard as ordinary adults. Younger Ds provide the most important example. We cannot necessarily expect the same level of courage in the face of imminent death, or foresight in the face of potential risk, from someone in their early teens as from someone aged thirty-five. So, some allowance must be made for the teenager's lesser capacity, although— to retain consistency with the objective nature of this version of the capacity theory—he or she will still be judged by the standards that teenagers can be expected to reach.[38] By way of contrast, for adherents of a subjective version of the capacity theory, these kinds of exceptions are much more numerous. They include cases, such as where D has a mental disorder, in which, by way of contrast with the exception for younger Ds, there may be no lower standard (in the true sense of the word) that D could be expected to meet. To go on, normatively speaking, one may have little more than what experts with a thorough knowledge of D say is the behaviour (self-restraint, etc.) of which D could *him-* or *herself* reasonably have been expected to be capable.[39]

[37] See the discussion of this issue in chapter 1.5 and chapter 2.9 above. Explanations for the law's role in setting and judging people by moral standards have been given by many theorists. See e.g. J. M. Finnis, *Natural Law and Natural Rights*, chapter 11; John Gardner, 'The Gist of Excuses', 594–598; A. P. Simester, 'Can Negligence be Culpable?'.

[38] This point was taken by the House of Lords in *DPP v Camplin* [1978] AC 705, in which it was held that the same standard of self-control in the face of provocation could not be expected of teenagers as of mature adults. *Camplin* is the legal embodiment of the objective version of the capacity theory. Capacity theories are discussed in more detail in section 6 below. See also the defence of the objective version of the capacity theory, in Jeremy Horder, 'Between Provocation and Diminished Responsibility', 149–154.

[39] See *R v (Morgan) Smith* [2000] 4 All ER 289, which briefly moved the law governing provocation closer to the subjective version of the capacity theory, whilst seeking to retain some elements of the objective version as side-constraints. The case is extensively discussed in John Gardner and Timothy Macklem, 'Compassion without Respect? Nine Fallacies in *R v Smith*'. The case was in effect overruled in *A-G for Jersey and Holley* [2005] UKPC 23. Needless to say, it begins to become hard to see how the subjective version of the capacity theory makes much use of the idea of normative standards or expectations at all, a danger spotted by the Court of Appeal in *R v Dryden* [1995] 4 All ER 987, 998: '[I]f one adds all the characteristics of the appellant to the notional reasonable man, there is a danger that the reasonable man becomes reincarnated as the appellant' (per Lord Lane LCJ). See further, Jeremy Horder,

Gardner gives a number of grounds for rejecting the subjective version of the capacity theory.[40] In this context, the most important reason that he gives for rejecting it is because 'valid excuses . . . cannot conceivably invoke standards of character . . . which fall short of the standards for fitness for the *role* in which, by doing the wrong thing, one failed'.[41] When D is occupying a role that binds him or her to meet certain expectations (as when D is a soldier on duty[42]), then pleas that less should be expected of D because of special factors such as youth, age, inexperience or mental fragility cut no ice, when it comes to the question of whether D is to be excused for wrongdoing. It is the role-expectations alone that set the standards by which D is to be judged. In the present context, what matters is that this is not merely an argument that Gardner applies to special(ist) roles, such as that of soldier, doctor, or police officer. Gardner's argument holds respecting a more general role that we occupy 'merely as people'.[43] The normative expectations that we have of each other, in virtue of the fact that we all have a role to play as human beings, rule out special pleading for lowered expectations in the light of any individual frailties. The theory stands for the view that once one is over the age of criminal responsibility, one dons the mantle of personhood, in the eyes of the law, and must henceforth live up to the expectations of one's role as a legal person. Does that mean that Gardner also rejects the way that the objective version of the capacity theory is prepared to vary the applicable standard by which D's conduct is judged, if confronted by a category of case, like youth, in which there is a lower-but-still-general standard by which D's moral culpability can be judged? It may be that he ought to reject it, whilst arguing in favour of a significantly higher age of criminal responsibility.[44] After all, even if there are (lower) standards of courage, foresight and patience that, say, teenagers can meet and be measured against, the very employment of these lower standards, in preference to the standards applicable to adults, shows that the mantle— the role—of full legal personhood, having only just been donned, is being to some extent now modified to account for one kind of special frailty.[45] There

'Between Provocation and Diminished Responsibility', 153–154, criticized in R. D. Mackay and B. J. Mitchell 'Provoking Diminished Responsibility: Two Pleas Merging into One?' [2003] *Criminal Law Review* 745, 751–752. Even so, the subjective version of the capacity theory is correctly employed to account for the new excuse that I shall explain and defend in chapter 4 below, of diminished capacity.

[40] See, for example, the devastating critique to which (with Timothy Macklem) he subjects the endorsement of the subjective version of the capacity theory, as the governing theory for provocation cases, by the House of Lords in *R v (Morgan) Smith* [2000] 4 All ER 289, in John Gardner and Timothy Macklem, 'Compassion without Respect? Nine Fallacies in *R v Smith*'.

[41] John Gardner, 'The Gist of Excuses', 587 (my emphasis).

[42] See Gardner's discussion of this example, in ibid., 579–585.   [43] Ibid., 596.

[44] The position in England and Wales is unusual (if not that unusual, when compared with jurisdictions within the US), in that criminal responsibility begins at ten years of age, compared with about fourteen years of age in jurisdictions on mainland Europe.

[45] In that regard, it is perhaps telling that Gardner and Macklem are distinctly lukewarm in their approval for *DPP v Camplin* [1978] AC 705, the ground-breaking case in which the

seems to be little room, on Gardner's view, for the argument that so long as a child showed as much self-restraint as could have been expected of someone their age, it does not matter that the child failed to come up to the role expectations of decent (adult) human beings because that role is one children cannot fairly be expected to fulfil. The only kind of 'special' pleading with which Gardner is truly content is that which is not excusatory in character. It is the kind of special pleading that amounts to a denial of responsibility, as when one's special plea amounts to a 'very specific and deep-seated incapacity . . . the incapacity to reason intelligibly through to action',[46] a kind of special pleading that being a teenager does not even begin to amount to. What should one make of this argument, as a whole?

The occupation of a role provides a famous example of an exception to the principle that one cannot derive an 'ought' from an 'is'. If I *am* a doctor, then (barring something exceptional, like insanity intervening) I *ought* to behave as a doctor should behave; period. It follows that there is no morally troubling theoretical gap between the person D is—and Ds all vary in this—and the expectations people should have of D when D is occupying a particular role. To occupy the role in question is, morally speaking, to be bound to meet the expectations. Ironically, then, the normative expectations view of excuses might be thought to be most at home explaining why there are so *few* excuses for those who fail to meet their obligations when occupying specific roles, such as doctors, employers, police officers, and so forth. One can sometimes easily enough be justified in causing harm in the course of one's duties as a surgeon or police sniper; but, given the role one has taken on, it is harder to think of reasons for generously excusing harmful wrongdoing in such circumstances. The very nature of the expectations we have of the proper performance of the role precludes this. I will come back to this point shortly. The key issue is whether this analysis is appropriately applied to what Gardner identifies as 'the distinct role [we have] of being human beings'.[47] The idea is

House of Lords held that children should be judged by reference to lower (objective) standards, when we evaluate their responses in the face of provocation: see John Gardner and Timothy Macklem, 'Compassion without Respect? Nine Fallacies in *R v Smith*', 624, 'It may be thought by some that this was where the rot set in [i.e. the judicial application of excessively relaxed moral standards]. But we *tend* not to share this view . . . ' (my emphasis). This slight ambivalence about the correctness of *Camplin* is perhaps explained by a strong claim they make, critical of the current judicial taste for the wholesale lowering of the standards by which D is to be judged in provocation cases, that sits uneasily alongside approval for *Camplin*: 'for all defendants the all-important element of rigorous accountability to an objective (i.e. non-idiosyncratic) standard has been diluted. The defendant has no longer any option to be acquitted on the ground that he lived up to such an objective standard, for he is no longer held up to any such standard' (ibid., 627). See, further, my discussion of the 'strong' excuse theory, in Jeremy Horder, 'Between Provocation and Diminished Responsibility, 144–145.

[46] John Gardner, 'The Gist of Excuses', 589. See the detailed discussion of this view in sections 4.5 and 4.6 below.

[47] John Gardner, 'The Gist of Excuses', 594: 'whatever other roles we may have in life, we also have the distinct role of being human beings, which itself sets basic standards of character.'

that there is a role that I may fulfil or fail to live up to on a given occasion as, say, a patient, forgiving and tolerant *person*, or as a courageous and restrained *person*, whatever the nature of the particular relationship (if any) I have with people affected by whether or not I fulfil the role successfully. If what was demanded of me, in terms of the self-control or courage appropriate for the satisfactory performance of this role, went beyond what could reasonably have been expected in the circumstances, then—other things being equal— I ought to be excused wrongdoing committed in consequence. Given what was said just now, however, if I fail to meet the normative expectations constitutive of my role as a human being, then it will not be open to me to open up a second excusatory front, with the claim that there was a gap between what was expected of me, and what I personally was capable of achieving. On the normative expectations view, if such a gap exists, it is inconsistent with a truly excusatory claim (which is that I came up to expectations), and really points in the direction of a denial of responsibility plea.[48]

Gardner's theory certainly works well when applied to a society in which people are more or less constituted by their more specific roles. The theory of human nature supporting this view of how we are constituted as persons has distinctively Homeric origins, but can perhaps be said to have persisted in modern society up to the point where people ceased to be judged across the board, in terms of whether they had behaved, for example, as a 'gentleman' or a 'lady' ought to have done.[49] In such a society, it is no doubt entirely true to say that 'the question of whether and how one's actions reflect upon one just is the question of whether they point to one's fitness or unfitness for whatever role one is occupying, for whatever life one is leading'.[50] Once one distinguishes, though, between these specific roles and a more general role one has in behaving as a decent person or human being *simpliciter*, some contrast needs to be drawn between the more specific roles one has, and the human virtues and capacities—the 'you', or 'me'—being brought to bear in performing them. I am never just a husband, friend, employer, and so forth, even though I certainly can and sometimes should be judged in terms of how well I bring my virtues and capacities to bear in the performance of those roles. There is a distinctive 'me' identifying with and seeking to fulfil those roles to the best of my ability (or not, as the case may be).[51] For anyone in

<hr/>

[48] John Gardner, 'The Gist of Excuses', 587–588, and 590–592.

[49] In the 1890s, Winston Churchill still felt it to be a damning criticism of Lord Kitchener, then Commander of the Egyptian army, that (in Churchill's view), 'He may be a General—but never a gentleman'.   [50] John Gardner, 'The Gist of Excuses', 587.

[51] See, more generally, Peter Berger and Hansfried Kellner, *Sociology Reinterpreted* (Middlesex: Penguin, 1981), 61–62; Thomas Nagel, *The View From Nowhere* (Oxford: Oxford University Press, 1986), chapter 4. There are sometimes said to be some exceptions to this, such as the performance of my 'role' as a lover. How can there be a separate 'me' performing this 'role', without a detachment wholly inappropriate in context? The answer to that question is that, except when one is treating the matter with a certain ironic playfulness, there is no such thing as a 'role' one plays when in love. One does, more or less spontaneously, what one's attachment leads one to do; which is not to say that love excuses everything, as 'love-struck' stalkers so often seem to believe.

doubt about that point, imagine you are a lawyer who suddenly realizes that becoming a priest is your true vocation. *Who is it*, though, coming to that realization? Not, presumably, someone wholly identified with his or her existing roles, particularly his or her role of being a lawyer, because being so identified can hardly encompass imagining that one's true vocation lies in the priesthood. Great care must be taken, however, to understand the assumptions about modernity and the self being made, and not being made, in such a claim. The 'me' that is separate from my specific roles need not, and should not, be thought of as an ontologically prior, free-floating self, wherein virtues and capacities are analogous to the energy stored in muscles, just waiting to be deployed in any appropriate context.[52] I can only learn what it means to possess virtues and capacities through the practice of them in appropriate particular roles; and the better I fulfil the various roles, the better equipped I will be to bring the virtues and capacities to bear, whatever the occasion.[53] Indeed, there will always be something missing from a life in which someone fails to find an adequate range of valuable roles—father; husband; fanatical team supporter—with which they come to identify themselves, a point of great importance to the non-individualistic conception of liberalism relied on in chapter 5.1 below. There is, then, an apparently (but only apparently) paradoxical reciprocity or reflexivity about the way in which I understand myself as the bearer of roles, and the way in which I understand my 'self' detached from these roles.[54]

With that important caveat in mind, it is instructive to consider the way the law has moved from the one understanding of human nature to the other. Such a move is perhaps best represented by the change in the nature of the objective or evaluative criterion, in provocation cases, from a seventeenth-century test based on categories of provocation sufficient to reduce murder

[52] So, for example, there is a greatly exaggerated individualism about the contrast drawn by sociologist Peter Berger between the 'man of honour' (familiar to us from 17th-century provocation doctrines), and 'modern man': 'The . . . self, deprived or, if one prefers, freed from the mystifications of honour is hailed in Falstaff's "catechism": "Honour is a mere scutcheon." It is modern consciousness that unmasks it as such . . . Behind the "mere scutcheon" is the face of modern man—man bereft of the consolation of prototypes, *man alone*. It is important to understand that it is precisely this solitary self that modern consciousness has perceived as the bearer of human dignity and inalienable human rights. The modern discovery of dignity took place precisely amid the wreckage of debunked conceptions of honour.' (Berger's emphasis), from Peter Berger, 'On the Obsolescence of the Concept of Honour', in Michael Sandel (ed.), *Liberalism and its Critics* (Oxford: Basil Blackwell, 1984), 152–153.

[53] John Gardner, 'The Gist of Excuses', 581, 'just because we are human beings, every one of one of us has the capacity to develop new virtues by learning to recognise different rationally-significant features of situations and respond to them in our actions by acting, in a suitably positive spirit, on the reasons they give'. For the contrary view, see Michael S. Moore, *Placing Blame*, 564–565. Moreover, as we will see in chapter 5 below, there is no intrinsic value in my 'self', detached from the performance of the social roles within which I can give my life meaning.

[54] This issue has, of course, been extensively explored, as by Thomas Nagel, *The View From Nowhere*, chapter 4. In a criminal law context, it has been most extensively discussed by Norrie, in Alan Norrie, *Crime, Reason and History: A Critical Introduction to Criminal Law*, 2nd edn., chapter 2. See also Michael S. Moore, *Placing Blame*, 564–565.

to manslaughter, to a nineteenth-century test based on whether a less drastic reaction could have been expected of someone with reasonable powers of self-control.[55] The early modern categories of sufficient provocation were simplistically role-based, reliant on how people could be expected to behave as men of honour, as loyal friends, as 'manly' husbands, or as liberty-loving Englishmen.[56] The later test, based on a judgment of reasonableness, with its idea of 'self'-control (a concept unknown to early modern English law), is centred more firmly on the idea of virtues and capacities one can be expected to draw on, *whatever* one's more specific purpose in drawing on them may be (i.e. whether or not the purpose involves the fulfilment of a given role).[57] The later test embodies the view that one can, say, detach a display of virtue, or other commendable human quality, from virtuous role or commendable purpose. It makes sense, for example, for the law to say that blackmailers must show high levels of self-restraint, in the face of the abuse they receive from their potential victims, because the abuse is 'self-induced';[58] but the development of such powers of self-restraint makes sense for blackmailers in any event (it is in their selfish interests), lest they jeopardize a potentially lucrative source of income by responding aggressively to the abuse. Self-restraint, learned in the context of a virtuous role, can be shown for purely self-interested reasons, as well as for role-based or virtuous reasons. No wonder, then, that when a blackmailer loses self-control and responds violently to a provocation from one of his or her victims, he or she can hardly expect to gain credit by arguing that, up to the point when self-control was lost, as much self-restraint (and this could be considerable) was shown as could have been expected from any other blackmailer.

4. A Critique of the 'Role' Basis to Normative Expectations

I do not seek to challenge the idea that one can identify a role for people as human beings, in so far as the exercise of virtues and capacities is concerned, a role distinct in some respects from their more specific roles. What is questionable is whether, when people seek excuse for wrongdoing, they can be said to be appealing for judgment solely in the light of the role expectations of a decent human being. This is for the simple reason that role-fulfilment is primarily about *succeeding*, in the right spirit, in the achievement of the goals constitutive of the role. It is not about the plausibility of the excuses one can give for failing to succeed. For Gardner, what matters most about

---

[55] I attempt to chart the course of this change in Jeremy Horder, *Provocation and Responsibility*, chapter 5.

[56] The categories are most authoritatively, and memorably, set down by Lord Holt CJ in *R v Mawgridge* (1707) Kel 119.   [57] See e.g. *R v Kirkham* (1837) 8 C & P 115.

[58] For discussion of such an example, see *Edwards v R* [1973] AC 648.

our relationship with the life that we lead and the roles that go to make it up is that, first, 'we do not do things which people in those roles should not do', and, secondly, that we are 'fit' for those roles in that we have 'the virtues . . . as well as the physical and mental constitution which people in those roles should have'.[59] The second point seems right, but the first is more questionable, as a point about what matters most. Alongside one's fitness for a role, what matters 'fundamentally' (to use Gardner's word) to the performance of the role is surely not that we avoid wrongdoing, that we avoid failure, but that we succeed. Avoiding failure through wrongdoing, whether or not through the use of virtue, skill, and so forth, looks like little more than a pre-condition for what it really takes to fulfil one's role, which is to do what one is meant to do: to achieve the role-generated goals one has appropriately set for oneself.[60] For early modern lawyers, those who successfully pleaded provocation were those who had been a little over-zealous in the spirited performance of a role ('manly' husband, man of honour, etc.). But, as we saw in the previous section, that understanding of provocation cases could only be sustained by making mitigation depend—as early modern lawyers made it depend—on the satisfaction of a significant justificatory element to the action itself, thus making the excuse predominantly normative.[61] Once one accepts, as the modern law does, that there is no true justification for killing in anger, whatever the justification for the anger itself, that explanatory route is closed off.

As we have seen, Gardner's alternative role-based explanation is that by doing only what could reasonably have been expected, in terms of calling on my capacities and virtues to avoid wrongdoing, I fulfil my role as a person, as a human being. The problem with this view is that the very fact that I need an excuse, because I have engaged in wrongdoing, shows that I have failed in my role as a human being (albeit, perhaps, understandably so). The discussion of surgeons and police snipers above was meant to illustrate that talk of having met the normative expectations of one's role, when one is seeking excuse, is liable to confuse, because the major focus in terms of what it means to meet those expectations is not the avoidance of wrongdoing, but what it takes to be a successful surgeon or sniper. If one needs an excuse for something wrong done, the more serious the wrongdoing the more plausible it will be to say simply that one failed to meet the preconditions for successful role-fulfilment, and so the normative expectations attached to one's role are no longer of relevance. One must, then, fall back on an appeal to jury sympathy with one's all-too-human weaknesses. In that regard, there is

---

[59] John Gardner, 'The Gist of Excuses', 586.

[60] The significance of success and failure to the criminal law are analysed with great philosophical sophistication by Gardner himself, in John Gardner, 'On the General Part of the Criminal Law', 219–232.

[61] Because it is easier to justify than to excuse conduct, in terms of a role one was seeking to perform. See the discussion in chapter 2.6 above.

an asymmetry between doing, or trying to do, what is right, and avoiding, or trying to avoid, what is wrong. What we can think of as the primary or central case for the exercise of capacity and virtue, in one's role as a human being, is the effort to do what is right. When we simply try to avoid wrong-doing, however, we do no more than try to avoid violating the conditions in which we and others can securely and confidently set about right-doing in accordance with long-term as well as short-term plans, and so on. That remains true even when we find that, to avoid wrongdoing, we must draw on the virtues and capacities we have developed to date in our attempts at right-doing.[62] This is a secondary, less central case for the display of capacity and virtue in one's 'human being' role.

An equivocation on this point perhaps comes out in a subtle difference that can be highlighted between the examples Gardner uses to illustrate the things we should not do, if we wish to avoid failure in our role. He says that we must not, 'betray our friends, trip up our fellow athletes, misdiagnose our patients'.[63] Betraying a friend or tripping up a fellow athlete are things one should be found to have avoided doing, before we even come to the question whether one has proved to be a good friend or a fine example of an athlete (i.e. the question of whether one has successfully fulfilled one's role). A finding that one has not done such things, amounts to the satisfaction of a pre-condition that qualifies one for subsequent evaluation in terms of how successful one has been in the role; but one can distinguish between the two evaluative tasks, assessing wrongdoing and right-doing respectively.[64] Avoiding misdiagnosis, by way of contrast, usually only makes sense in a context in which someone is engaged in the attempt successfully to fulfil their role by making a correct diagnosis. To say of a doctor, 'she always avoided misdiagnosis' is one way of saying she mostly got things right, successfully fulfilling (part of) her role. An example that provided a true analogy with the friend and athlete examples would thus have highlighted the pre-conditions that must be satisfied, if one is to deserve unreserved and wholehearted evaluation of one's career as a doctor. Such evaluation could only have this character if, for example, a doctor were found to have avoided practising involuntary euthanasia for profit. To repeat, in cases where D needs an excuse for wrongdoing D has by definition failed, as a human being, by wronging another. It may not always be especially helpful, then, to bring reference to D's role as a human being back in, when the question arises whether D should be excused for, say, lashing out under provocation. For, this is the very role D has (*ex hypothesi*) failed in by reacting in that way. What I have to fall back on, if I seek to excuse my

---

[62] The moral asymmetry between doing right, and avoiding wrong, is pursued in relation to the virtues of the rule of law, by Joseph Raz, *The Authority of Law*, chapter 11.

[63] John Gardner, 'The Gist of Excuses', 586.

[64] So, a talented athlete, also well-known for his or her tripping of fellow athletes, can hope to receive at best only a detached assessment or muted praise for the use of his or her talents, rather than the whole-hearted recognition as an accomplished sportsperson that he or she ought to be seeking.

reaction in lashing out, is the ascriptive question of the extent to which I could have been expected to bring my virtues and capacities to bear, to avoid wrongdoing. When one claims excuse, then, one is likely to be highlighting, rather than seeking to erase, a contrast between the expectations of one's role (concerned with success), and the all-too-human weaknesses one is prey to, that led one to fail to meet one of the pre-conditions for the role's successful fulfilment. So, D says, 'I may be a judge, but even the most shrewd triers of the facts are not completely free of biases'; 'I may be a doctor, but being good at diagnosis is no guarantee one will not fall in love with a patient'; and so forth. Perhaps, in these particular instances, if D displays the weakness he or she should not be excused; but the main point lies in the nature of D's excusatory claim. In relation to this, it is worth re-emphasizing that, as we have seen in outlining the objective version of the capacity theory, there are ascriptive standards for judging whether a display of weaknesses, in a particular set of circumstances, is excusable; and, as we will see in section 6 below, it can be right to employ such standards in the criminal law. The issue need not be, as the subjective version of the capacity theory sees it, solely whether D him- or herself could have done better.[65]

The role-centred focus of the normative expectations account of excuses is not without its uses. Given what was said earlier, however, that account is, ironically, usually better at telling us when failures—such as professional failures—are inexcusable, or simply why they may be difficult to excuse. Some weaknesses may be more forgivable than others, depending on the role one occupies. So, whilst bias is always to be avoided in the exercise of public and professional functions, it is perhaps particularly unforgivable in judges. Similarly, more patience is expected of teachers dealing with students, or of priests dealing with penitents, than of police officers dealing with drunken drivers, because whilst showing great patience with their charges is part of a teacher's or priest's role, it is not part of a police officer's role to be tolerant and understanding with drunken drivers.[66] So, it might more easily be forgivable for a police officer to lose his or her temper with a drunken driver than it would be for a teacher to lose his or her temper with a student. Nonetheless, the normative expectations account of excuses also comes into its own in explaining why people may have a case for excuse, when they have committed wrongdoing only to keep faith with, say, the demands of their religion, an excuse that I call the 'demands-of-conscience' excuse. As we will see in chapter 5 below, in such cases it is indeed the fact that D is acting out his or her role as a faithful adherent of a religion that is in question, for the purposes of excuse.

Does the character theory of excuses fare better, as a theory of excuses for wrongdoing detached from role-fulfilment? Not really. The problem with

---

[65] See further, the discussion of the subjective version of the capacity theory in chapter 4 below.   [66] See John Gardner, 'The Gist of Excuses', 579–581.

the character theory, seen through the lens of the objective version of the capacity theory, is that it rests on an apparent paradox. The character theory provides grounds for excusing when D has failed to come up to the relevant standard, so long as the wrongdoing was 'out-of-character'; but it also provides grounds for denying an excuse if the wrongdoing was 'in keeping with (bad) character' even if D has come up to the relevant standards.

5. RIVAL THEORIES OF EXCUSES: THE 'CHARACTER' THEORY

One common rationale for excusing conditions is that when D acts under coercion, when intoxicated, under the influence of a loss of self-control, and so forth, it is not really 'him' or 'her'—not his or her 'true' self—acting.[67] This is the 'character' theory of excuses. The character theory has a long history, and has been developed in a number of different, more or less ambitious, ways. One version, endorsed by Hume, is that punishment is inappropriate where actions 'proceed not from some cause in the characters . . . of the person'.[68] The idea is that one must be able to identify a character trait to which the wrongdoing was attributable, if conviction and punishment are to be justified. This version can be interpreted in an expansive way, as providing grounds for inculpation as well as for exculpation. To this end, it has attracted some distinguished modern adherents. So, for Feinberg, wrongdoing can be punished 'if it reveals what sort of person he [D] is in some respect . . .',[69] and for Fletcher, 'the desert of the offender is gauged by his character—i.e. the kind of person he is . . .'.[70] Such more expansive versions of the character theory have come in for some severe criticism, and will not be considered further here.[71] It is one thing to say that the justice of imposing criminal liability for wrongdoing presupposes a wrongdoer with a sufficiently sane and mature character,

---

[67] See, for example, M. Bayles, 'Character, Purpose and Criminal Responsibility' (1982) 1 *Law and Philosophy* 1; Nicola Lacey, *State Punishment: Political Principles and Community Values* (London: Routledge, 1988); Victor Tadros, 'The Characters of Excuse'; G. R. Sullivan, 'Making Excuses', in A. P. Simester and A. T. H. Smith *Harm and Culpability* (Oxford: Oxford University Press, 1996), 131.

[68] David Hume, *A Treatise of Human Nature*, Book II, Part III, Section II. I am grateful to Ekow Yankah for this reference.

[69] Joel Feinberg, *Doing and Deserving: Essays in the Theory of Responsibility* (New Jersey: Princeton University Press, 1974), 126.

[70] G. P. Fletcher, *Rethinking the Criminal Law*, 803. See also R. Nozick, *Philosophical Explanations* (Cambridge, Mass.: Harvard University Press, 1981), 381; M. Bayles, 'Character, Purpose and Criminal Responsibility'. The inculpatory view found its way into the writings of some eighteenth- and nineteenth-century judges, but far too much has been made of this. As an authoritative view of the grounds of inculpation, the theory had been decisively struck down many years before: see the judgment of Holt CJ in *R v Mawgridge* (1707) Kel 119.

[71] See e.g. R. A. Duff, 'Choice, Character and Criminal Liability' (1993) 12 *Law and Philosophy*, 345, 361–380; Jeremy Horder, 'Criminal Culpability: The Possibility of a General Theory' (1993) 12 *Law and Philosophy* 193, 204–09; A. J. Slater, 'In Defence of a Capacity-Based Theory of Criminal Culpability', (University of Birmingham: Ph.D, 2003); Michael S. Moore, *Placing Blame*, chapter 13.

because it would be unduly harsh to visit punishment on a wrongdoer who lacked those characteristics. It is another thing to say that wrongful acts are punished simply because D is or has a bad character. The former claim is consistent with, and indeed it buttresses, the liberal underpinnings of the harm principle. The latter claim sits rather less easily alongside them. More modest and plausible versions of the character theory, those that run alongside support for the harm principle, restrict its application to excusing conditions.[72] Even so, they lack sound theoretical justification.

For opponents of the theory, that an action was out of character provides nothing more than a reason for mitigating D's sentence, if the offence was in itself not too grievous.[73] Even so, a sophisticated modern defence of the character theory, as a theory of excuses, has been provided by Victor Tadros.[74] He cites with approval G. R. Sullivan's explanation of the theory:

There are occasions when criminal liability should be precluded by invoking some version of the 'unity of the self' doctrine . . . Such a doctrine must hold that certain core values subscribed to by a particular agent are constituents of selfhood and that any sudden and fundamental change in those values for which the agent is not responsible makes for a discontinuity of the self.[75]

Tadros's particular focus in this instance (like Sullivan's) is involuntary intoxication that leads D to commit acts he would not be moved to commit when sober, although other theorists have pursued the same theme by making their focus addiction to drugs.[76] In Tadros's view, what ought to excuse D in these circumstances is that he or she was 'put into a state that did not reflect his ordinary character' (assuming, of course, that D's ordinary character did not pre-dispose him to commit the acts in question).[77] Tadros takes the same view of provocation cases, in which for him what matters is that '[D's] character whilst she is in a state of extreme anger is not like her character whilst calm. Actions done in that state do not reflect as badly upon her settled character as if they had been done whilst calm'.[78] It follows, on this view,

---

[72] See e.g. G. R. Sullivan, 'Making Excuses'; Victor Tadros, 'The Characters of Excuse'.

[73] See (on provocation) Jeremy Horder, *Provocation and Responsibility*, 131–134. See, more generally, John Gardner, 'The Gist of Excuses', 578 n. 7.

[74] Victor Tadros, 'The Characters of Excuse'.

[75] G. R. Sullivan, 'Making Excuses', 137, cited by Victor Tadros, 'The Characters of Excuse', 503. Tadros puts it this way: 'Unless one is highly erratic, which is itself an indication of a certain sort of character, one does not change character from one moment to the next but rather retains those characteristics through significant periods of one's life. I will call this one's settled character', in Victor Tadros, 'The Characters of Excuse', 503–504.

[76] Tadros's focus has been given special significance by English law's explicit refusal to countenance an excuse in these circumstances: see *R v Kingston* [1995] 2 AC 355, where the issue was whether, if D was shown to have engaged in unlawful sexual acts with a child only because he was involuntarily intoxicated, the involuntary character of the intoxication could excuse the acts even if they were committed with the relevant mental element. On drug addiction, see the discussion dedicated to the issue in (1999) 18 *Law and Philosophy*, issue 6, and (2000) 19 *Law and Philosophy*, issue 1.   [77] Victor Tadros, 'The Characters of Excuse', 503.

[78] Ibid., 507.

that if it is actually a feature of one's settled character that one is (say) aggressive or sexually exploitative, then one will not be able to rely on the fact that provocation or involuntary intoxication brought these tendencies out into the open, with the result that one did wrong.[79]

Tadros's case for the character theory is that it does the best job of explaining what he describes as the 'intuitively plausible'[80] case for regarding involuntary intoxication and provocation as excuses. This opens up his argument to an attack at more than one level. It is by no means universally the case that provocation is a complete or partial excuse to murder, still less to any other crime. Even in English law, it has been stated at the highest level that 'it is impossible to read even a selection of the extensive modern literature on provocation without coming to the conclusion that the concept has serious logical and moral flaws'.[81] A similar, perhaps even sharper, difference of opinion is likely to found amongst those asked whether involuntary intoxication should excuse those whose (say) latent paedophilic tendencies it brings out.[82] It seems questionable, thus, to rely on an appeal to 'intuitive plausibility' as part of one's case for excusing in these particular instances. Moreover, one potential problem for character theorists is that the character theory, as it stands, generates a case for excusing in some intuitively *im*plausible cases, such as unexpected and great temptation. If the normally honest D finds £10,000 in a deserted street, he or she may be sorely tempted to pocket the money. If he or she did so, this might well be aberrant behaviour for him or her, but that hardly seems to bolster the case for an excuse.[83] Or, imagine a different example in which D, a boy-monk who has not reached puberty, becomes an object of infatuation for V who, as D knows, is aged 15. V initially asks and encourages D to have sexual intercourse with him or her at the very time when D first reaches puberty; and D agrees. If intercourse takes place, and D is charged with having engaged in under-age sex, the offence may not be *very* serious; but it hard to see why the fact that the act is, for D, *ex hypothesi*, aberrant (in that D's sexual identity has not been fully formed at the time of the offence) should in itself be a ground for excuse, as opposed to mitigation of penalty.[84]

---

[79] Tadros says: Victor Tadros, 'The Characters of Excuse', 504, 'those that are violent whilst sober ought not to have an excuse for their violent behaviour whilst drunk. For in that case they cannot show that becoming intoxicated has made them responsive to reasons that they were not ordinarily responsive to'.   [80] Ibid., 499.

[81] *R v (Morgan) Smith* [2000] 4 All ER 289, 299 (per Lord Hoffmann).

[82] See *R v Kingston* [1995] 2 AC 355.

[83] Her action would almost certainly amount to theft. Section 2(1)(c) of the Theft Act 1968 says that D is not to be regarded as dishonest if he or she believes that the owner cannot be discovered by taking reasonable steps. Given the size of the sum in the example in the text, it ought to seem reasonable to take the money to the police so that further enquiries can be made.

[84] Naturally, the older D is in this kind of example, the more serious the offence becomes whether or not D's behaviour can be described as out-of-character or aberrant: see Jeremy Horder, 'How Culpability Can and Cannot be Denied in Under-Age Sex Crimes' [2001] *Criminal Law Review* 15.

Tadros seeks to fend off this kind of problem for the character theory by distinguishing what he calls an 'ordinary' claim that an action was out of character (as in the cases above), which is a matter purely for mitigation, and a claim based on proof that someone's ordinary character had been 'destabilized', which deserves excusatory treatment.[85] There is a suspicion here that Tadros is trading on an ambiguity in the metaphor of 'destabilization'. On the one hand, that term might be thought to be just another way of describing, in an especially vivid case, how such was the temptation to which one was subjected that one just—seemingly inexplicably—cast off one's normal sense of self-restraint, as in the examples just given. In that case, one's out-of-character claim is still an 'ordinary' one, and mitigation of penalty rather than excuse is appropriate. On the other hand, the term is also suggestive of some kind of mental abnormality or deficiency unexpectedly brought to the surface by (involuntary) intoxication, provocation, or the like. If the latter is the real explanation for those who engage in aberrant behaviour, of course, then the appropriate claim is diminished responsibility, and the appropriate complaint is that that defence is not available for all crimes rather than just in murder cases.[86] In this latter case, one should not be troubling oneself at all with new excuses based on claims that the act was out of character. Tadros sees this point coming, but the argument he offers in anticipation lacks real conviction.

He gives an example in which D, a devoted husband, becomes involuntarily intoxicated and consequently goes through a ceremony of marriage with another woman. Is D guilty of bigamy? Tadros believes that D needs a new kind of out-of-character excuse, and is not suffering from some kind of diminished responsibility. He analyses the example in the following way:

Suppose . . . that D had not lost his power practically to reason. Nor had he lost his ability to control himself: getting married is clearly an activity fully within his control. Ought we to say that he was not a fully responsible agent whilst performing the action? The answer it seems is no. The ability to reason and the ability to control oneself are the core concepts of agent-responsibility. And the defendant is fully capable in both respects.[87]

In this example, the fact that, for D, getting married is an activity 'fully within his control' is a theoretical distraction. In almost every case of full-blooded diminished responsibility the defendant will have performed the action in question in a controlled (means–end rational) way; perhaps even with great skill.[88] The issue in this kind of example is not whether D lost

---

[85] Victor Tadros, 'The Characters of Excuse', 502–503. He borrows the term 'destabilized' from G. R. Sullivan, 'Making Excuses'.

[86] See Jeremy Horder 'Pleading Involuntary Lack of Capacity' (1993) *Cambridge Law Journal* 298; and chapter 4.2 below.   [87] Victor Tadros, 'The Characters of Excuse', 505.

[88] See T. H. Irwin, 'Reason and Responsibility in Aristotle', in A. O. Rorty, *Essays on Aristotle's Ethics* (Berkeley, California: University of California Press, 1980), 130.

control of his conduct but whether, in respect of a perhaps perfectly executed action, D could have brought undamaged and properly developed evaluative powers of reasoning to bear on the question whether to engage in the conduct at all. In that respect, Tadros's argument against the appropriateness of a diminished responsibility plea looks like a form of 'bootstrapping'. At the beginning of the passage cited, he asks us to 'suppose' that D is in evaluative as well as physical control. By the end of the passage, however, the supposition seems to have turned into a proposition of established fact, in that D is asserted to be 'fully capable in both [evaluative and physical] respects'; and so we are asked to conclude that a diminished responsibility plea has no application. The example thus poses no special challenge to those who believe that D must either admit responsibility and hope for a light sentence, or try (were the defence available, as it should be) to plead diminished responsibility. Whether D, as claimed by Tadros, is a 'devoted' husband, or whether he is a serial adulterer (for critics of the character theory, it matters not), what will count is whether D can show that the involuntary intoxication left him substantially unable to bring evaluative powers of reasoning to bear on his choices and his conduct, and thus whether his responsibility was diminished. What Tadros, like Sullivan, may dislike about this is that, where intoxication is concerned, it involves D in an uphill legal struggle; but that is not much of an objection. In Tadros's example, D looks to be behaving irrationally, but in the absence of some underlying mental disorder that intoxication brings out, this is hardly a typical effect of intoxication. Putting aside the physiological effects, and the contested question whether, and if so to what extent, intoxicants fuel aggressiveness, intoxication alone (through alcohol, at least) is more likely to lead us simply to find some desire-based reasons for action rather more compelling than they would appear to us when sober. No wonder, then, that it is hard to construct much of a case for excusing deliberate wrongdoing attributable to intoxication, whether or not the intoxication was involuntary.[89]

Alongside this challenge to the character theory can be placed a different set of objections. To be practically useable as well as to gain theoretical purchase, the idea of aberrance as a basis for excuse must presuppose a 'settled' character, with 'core values subscribed to', and characteristics retained 'through significant periods of one's life' (to use phrases of Sullivan's and Tadros's).[90] Otherwise, one will be able to make no sense of a claim, or of a denial, that behaviour was indeed aberrant. Yet, criminal liability in England and Wales begins at ten years of age, long before someone could conceivably

---

[89] If, for example, I realize that I have become intoxicated, I should still be held accountable for deciding to go out for a drive, even if the intoxication was involuntary, and going out for a drive is something I would not decide to do just for the sake of it, when sober: see Jeremy Horder, 'Sobering Up? The Law Commission on Criminal Intoxication', 543. It would be different, of course, if the offence in question were simply 'being intoxicated', because then D's state of being is involuntary.   [90] See Victor Tadros, 'The Characters of Excuse', 504.

be regarded as having a settled character in the sense identified as crucial by Sullivan and Tadros.[91] The significance of this is obviously that 10-year-olds are just as entitled as adults to the benefit of (say) a provocation plea, in spite of the fact that it makes no sense to ask whether a killing following a provoked loss of self-control by a 10-year-old is in, or out, of character in the Sullivan/Tadros sense. The reason that the law now experiences little difficulty in handling provocation pleas by children and young people is that it adopts the objective version of the capacity theory, rather than the character theory.[92] The question is whether D lived up to the standards of self-control that could be expected of someone D's age; and to answer that question, one need know nothing at all about D's character development—such as it has been—to date.

This leads us on to the criticism of the character theory mentioned briefly at the end of section 4 above. In rejecting the view that a plea that an action was 'out-of-character' is a matter solely for mitigation of sentence, Tadros sometimes claims that what matters to a genuinely excusatory 'out-of-character' plea is that there was a *'fundamental* shift'[93] in D's character as displayed in the action (of a kind others would regard as evidence of diminished responsibility)[94]. At other times, however, he relies on a less dramatic version of the theory, saying that what matters, in provocation cases at least, is that D's actions (in losing self-control and killing) did not reflect D's settled character *'quite* as closely'[95] as his actions when calm. Tadros's equivocation on the exact effect that something—intoxication; provocation—must have had on one's character, if it is to be excusatory, is understandable. D's reaction in losing self-control, in provocation cases, must be richly merited by the provocation itself, if his or her subsequent conduct in killing is to be partially excused.[96] So, D's reaction is likely to stem from the influence of a perfectly ordinary and reasonable, more or less 'settled', aspect of D's character, namely his or her tendency to feel wounded and indignant at what was perceived to be a serious attack on his or her self-image and self-esteem, a feeling that then generated what is in such instances an all-too-common desire, the desire to 'get even' by some means or another. There is no analogy with the effects of involuntary intoxication, which exercise their influence on D in a causally passive manner, in that respect completely by-passing the kind

---

[91] Of course, in many countries the age of criminal responsibility is higher, around fourteen years of age, but that does not affect the point made in the text, as it is hardly more plausible to regard teenagers as having settled characters retained through significant periods of their lives. Significantly, something like one-quarter of all recorded crime is committed by ten-to-seventeen-year-olds, so a theory of excuses that fails to explain when and how those in this age group can be excused is one of unacceptably narrow application.

[92] See *DPP v Camplin* [1978] AC 705.

[93] Victor Tadros, 'The Characters of Excuse', 504 (my emphasis), discussing involuntary intoxication, but repeated at 507 in relation to provocation pleas.

[94] See Jeremy Horder, 'Pleading Involuntary Lack of Capacity'.

[95] Victor Tadros, 'The Characters of Excuse', 508 (my emphasis), and 507.

[96] This point is made by Tadros himself, in Victor Tadros, 'The Characters of Excuse', 508.

of actively interpretive (character-based) frame of reference through which words or actions come to be understood by a D as 'provocative'. Perhaps what is meant to matter for Tadros, in provocation cases, is that it is wholly out of character for D to retaliate violently, whether or not it was in character for D to be so angry at such a grave provocation.[97] The point is crucial, because Tadros wishes to deny the defence of provocation to Ds for whom violent reaction to a provocation was itself in character.[98] That might seem sensible enough, but problems emerge when one scratches the surface. If D is enraged, and hence loses self-control and kills, following what, by anyone's standards, is rightly regarded by D as exceptionally grave provocation, why should D automatically be denied a partial excuse because he can be proved to have a tendency to react violently to provocation? Conversely, if D is by nature non-violent, but is inexplicably so enraged by an objectively very trivial provocation that he or she loses self-control and kills, why should the fact that it is out of character for D to react violently to provocation be regarded as providing a basis for a successful plea? In this regard, Tadros appears to slide from saying that what matters is whether or not losses of self-control simply 'reflect' D's settled character (in principle, an empirical question), to saying that what matters is whether or not losses of self-control 'reflect *sufficiently badly*' on D's settled character (a straightforwardly evaluative question).[99] In the distinction between these two quite different questions, however, we find the distinction between the character and the capacity (or normative expectation) theories, rather than a refinement of the character theory. For what, other than an independent standard by which one judges the moral adequacy (as opposed to the empirical predictability) of someone's display of character in action, could provide a point of reference by which one judges whether an action reflects 'badly' on someone?

In the end, thus, Tadros finds it too difficult to resist the temptation to rely at least implicitly on an account of excuses—like a capacity or normative expectations account—that judges people by measuring their conduct against objective standards. Suppose D does something even someone well-equipped with the relevant capacities would have done, in an individual case, in that he or she only lost control and killed due to provocation so grave it would have pushed almost anyone beyond the limits of endurance.

---

[97] Tadros does say, 'Reprehensible actions in x may not reflect as closely his [D's] settled character as actions when he is settled, but *that* he is in x does appropriately reflect his settled character' (Tadros's emphasis, Victor Tadros, 'The Characters of Excuse, 508). But Tadros provides no analogous argument to deal with cases in which it might be more or less in character (and more or less reasonable) for someone to be affected by a certain degree of intoxication *per se*, whether or not—if they are reasonably affected—it is in or out of character for them to then behave (say) violently. For discussion of this point, see Jeremy Horder, *Provocation and Responsibility*, 120–127.   [98] Victor Tadros, 'The Characters of Excuse', 508.

[99] Both these ways of expounding the character theory can be found in Victor Tadros, 'The Characters of Excuse', 508, but the emphasis is mine.

In such a case, the 'character' question, the question whether he or she would have reacted in that way even if the provocation had been trivial is quite simply irrelevant: it is 'pure prejudice', as the evidence lawyers are wont to say. By parity of reasoning, if D's reaction falls short of the required standards, because he or she admittedly lost control and killed upon trivial provocation, whether D would, apart from this gross over-reaction, ordinarily be described as good-tempered is neither here nor there. There would, of course, have been nothing to stop Tadros endorsing a truly character-based excuse theory, one that excused D in the latter case but not in the former, on the grounds that, whatever the gravity of the provocation in individual cases, the doctrine should benefit the normally good-tempered and be prejudiced against the normally aggressive. Such a theory is far from being morally outlandish, even if it still faces the difficulties mentioned above in cases where D is too young not to have a settled character. That Tadros does not go down this road speaks as eloquently in favour of the capacity and normative expectations theories, as the substantive arguments addressed in earlier sections.

6. RIVAL THEORIES OF EXCUSES: THE 'CAPACITY' THEORY

The main rival to the 'normative expectation' and the 'character' accounts of excusing conditions is the capacity theory, a theory that I will divide into 'subjective' and 'objective' versions.[100] The subjective version of the capacity theory asks what could reasonably have been expected of D *him- or herself*, given his or her life history and behaviour to date.[101] The objective version judges D's actions in the light of a morally salient standard, but permits that standard to be lowered (or raised) if it can be shown that moral culpability will not otherwise be fairly assessed.[102] Suppose D's conduct is

---

[100] A comprehensive examination of the capacity theory can now be found in A. J. Slater, 'In Defence of a Capacity-Based Theory of Criminal Culpability', although my defence of it differs somewhat from his. Although we developed our ideas independently of each other, I would like to acknowledge the importance and influence of his work in convincing me that I was on the right track in defending the capacity theory. Broadly speaking, the objective version of the capacity theory is what I refer to as the 'moderate' excuse theory, and the subjective version is what I refer to as the 'weak' excuse theory, in Jeremy Horder, 'Between Provocation and Diminished Responsibility', 144–147.

[101] It is hard to say who is an out-and-out defender of the subjective version. It is perhaps most famously a view associated with George Fletcher's plea for greater subjectivity in George P. Fletcher, 'The Individualisation of Excusing Conditions'(1974) 47 *Southern California Law Review* 1269, but it may be that Fletcher is really an adherent of the kind of objective version of the capacity theory defended below. The subjective version is also favoured by some adherents of critical legal studies, or by those who, more broadly, think of themselves as developing a left-wing view of criminal law. There is a certain irony in this, because of all the theories of excuse the subjective version of the capacity is perhaps the most individualist, and 'individualism' in criminal law and theory is the strain of thought (or more properly, perhaps, 'straw target') that invites the most excoriating of the left's criticisms.

[102] The objective version is most famously defended, with some (sometimes unintentional) nods in favour of the subjective version, by H. L. A. Hart, *Punishment and Responsibility*,

partly explained by the fact that he or she is young, and cannot be expected to meet the standards that would have been observed by adults. The issue, according to the subjective version of the capacity theory, is whether D's own life to date shows that he or she could have done more to avoid engaging in the conduct in question. By way of contrast, the issue, according to the objective version of the capacity theory, is whether D's conduct came up to agent-neutral standards that can reasonably be expected of young people of D's age. Why should one prefer the objective version of the capacity theory to the subjective version? Answering that question takes us back, in part, to consideration of the strategic considerations or common goods, set out in chapter 1.2 above, that act as sufficient conditions shaping the nature and scope of legally recognized excuses.

Consider Simester's argument in favour of the element of objectivity in judging people's behaviour to have been negligent:

Whatever one takes to be the purposes of law, their achievement requires co-ordination of individuals' behaviour through the external imposition of values: by ordering ('do not') rather than asking ('unless you want to'). Individuals cannot be permitted to conduct themselves above or outside the compass of the law merely because they have different moral values ... The moral duty to avoid doing an action is derived from the fact that the action is harmful or wrong, not from the defendant's acceptance that it is.[103]

Simester is partly concerned with justifications for conduct, as a basis for denying negligence. In that regard, as far as strategic considerations or common goods are concerned, the idea is that the authoritative role in conduct-guidance that the law seeks to maintain for itself would be undermined, if made relative to the standards of conduct each individual sets for him- or herself (a matter highly relevant to 'justification' cases, as we saw in chapter 1.4 above). I will question quite how sweeping such a claim should be understood to be, when what I will call 'demands-of-conscience' excuses are in issue,[104] because value pluralism is the inevitable result of the diverse nature of the demands made on individuals by their differing faiths and sets of moral beliefs, and hence by conscience. In general terms, however, as it applies to excuses, Simester's claim is right because, by way of contrast, we will not understand the moral force behind ideas of self-control or restraint, and so forth, without presupposing that a high degree of agent-neutrality is

chapter 2, and also, by Sanford H. Kadish, 'Excusing Crime' (1987) 75 *California Law Review* 257. In the ensuing discussion, I will be concentrating on a defence of the objective version of the capacity theory, leaving discussion of the subjective version of the capacity theory to chapter 4 below.

[103] A. P. Simester, 'Can Negligence be Culpable?', 93. To similar effect, see John Gardner, 'The Gist of Excuses'.

[104] See chapter 5.2 below. A 'demands-of-conscience' excuse comes into play when D must commit wrongdoing to avoid compromising his or her beliefs, or some other value essential to his or her personal identity.

an identifying feature of those notions. Societies can remain well-ordered even though they are comprised of people with very different faiths, cultural practices and sets of moral beliefs.[105] But societies where people differ widely in the standards they set themselves (and hence by which they are judged) for the exercise of self-control and restraint, with respect to refraining from wrongdoing, are, by definition, ill-ordered. Putting aside the demands-of-conscience cases (because they raise different issues), then, it makes little moral sense to excuse wrongdoing on the grounds that although D failed miserably to come up to an adequate standard, he or she came up to the standards he or she sets for him- or herself.[106]

One might remain worried, though, that this approach will be insufficiently sensitive to differences in expected standards of self-control (many believe to be) characteristic of different ethnic or religious groups. Surely, there should be an overriding concern that any diversity of standards of self-control and restraint observed by people with different religious and ethnic backgrounds, is not erased or discounted when the conduct of one of their number falls to be judged by the criminal law?[107] Such worries may fail to account for the fact that in understanding, say, the gravity of a provocation or a threat, as opposed to judging the adequacy of the level of self-control or restraint shown in dealing with it, the law has for many years been open to evidence of, for example, ethnic or religious differences in the way certain actions are to be understood.[108] Further, as Celia Wells argues, such worries may be open to the objection that, in expecting less by way of self-control from those with different racial or ethnic backgrounds, 'we are in danger of adopting an "essentialised view of race and ethnicity, that is, the notion that there is one authentic experience of an ethnic identity for each ethnic group".'[109] Ironically, to lower the standards of control or restraint expected of D because he or she is a member of a particular ethnic or religious group may be to show D a profound disrespect, this time by patronizing D, that it was one's intention to avoid by taking that very step.[110] More broadly, as Mayo Moran argues of the pressure from radical 'outsider

---

[105] Indeed, perhaps particularly in societies with historically tolerant or welcoming immigration policies, cultural, religious and moral diversity may come to be regarded as partly constitutive of the morally well-ordered character of those societies.

[106] As we will see below, however, this claim must itself be qualified where mental deficiency forms a part of D's claim to excuse, a matter addressed more fully in chapter 4 below.

[107] See S. M. H. Yeo, 'Power and Self-Control in Provocation and Automatism' (1992) 14 *Sydney Law Review* 3.

[108] See Andrew Ashworth, 'The Doctrine of Provocation', 300, discussing *R v Uddin* (unreported), *The Times*, 14 September 1929.

[109] Celia Wells, 'Provocation: The Case for Abolition', in Andrew Ashworth and Barry Mitchell (eds.), *Rethinking English Homicide Law*, 101, citing J. Morgan, 'Provocation Law and Facts: Dead Women Tell No Tales, Tales are Told About Them' (1997) 21 *Melbourne University Law Review*, 237, 259.

[110] See further John Gardner and Timothy Macklem, 'Compassion without Respect? Nine Fallacies in *R v Smith*', 630–631; John Gardner and Timothy Macklem, 'Provocation and Pluralism'.

jurisprudence'[111] to abandon objective standards, there are significant threats to common good (i) (in chapter 1.2 above):

[I]n the context of provocation . . . subjectivization of the standard enables perpetrators to invoke discriminatory stereotypes about gender relations and sexual autonomy. Without the normative leverage that an objective standard at least theoretically provides, judges are left with simple questions of credibility. And, in this context, the prevalence of discriminatory beliefs will often lend sufficient credibility to exonerate or excuse the accused. The more widely held such beliefs, the more credible they will be.[112]

As Duff expresses it, then, 'we should take the "reasonable person" to be someone with a reasonable or proper regard for the law and the values it protects . . .'.[113]

7. How, and When, Each Capacity Theory does its Work

Hart, unfortunately, nourished a common misconception about capacity theories, when he suggested that the excuses they license 'provide for all individuals alike the satisfactions of a *choosing* system'.[114] Some theorists have gone on to defend criminal liability only when wrongdoing is chosen, and have seen excusing conditions in terms of an absence of choice; but, as Hart's own defence of criminal liability for harm done through negligence shows, the choice to do wrong is not an essential element of criminal liability and the fact that wrongdoing was not chosen does not necessarily excuse.[115] For Hart, as for many criminal lawyers and theorists, ' "I just didn't think" is not in ordinary life, in ordinary circumstances, an excuse'.[116] This is a clear indication that, for Hart as for other adherents of the capacity theory, legal responsibility in general (and criminal culpability in particular) are premised on the possession by D—to an adequate degree—of rational and moral capacity, meaning sensitivity to and the facility to be guided by considerations of moral as well as of instrumental reason.[117]

---

[111] A term coined to represent the concerns of critical race and feminist legal theory: see e.g. Mary Coombs, 'Outsider Jurisprudence: The Law Review Stories' (1992) 63 *University of Colorado Law Review* 683.

[112] Mayo Moran, *Rethinking the Reasonable Person* (Oxford: Oxford University Press, 2003), 230.

[113] R. A. Duff, 'Choice, Character and Criminal Liability', 358.

[114] H. L. A. Hart, *Punishment and Responsibility*, 49 (my emphasis); Andrew Ashworth, *Principles of Criminal Law*, 3rd edn., 28. For a pithy critique of the role Hart gives to the satisfaction of a 'choosing' system in explaining excusing conditions, see Sanford H. Kadish, 'Excusing Crime', 263–264. See also chapter 1.6 above.

[115] H. L. A. Hart, *Punishment and Responsibility*, chapter 6.   [116] Ibid., 136.

[117] For a searching examination of what the demands made on our rational capacities amount to, in the context of liability for negligence, see A. P. Simester, 'Can Negligence be Culpable?'.

Whether or not, if possessed, that rational and moral capacity issued in a free choice, is not part of the premiss on which such responsibility and culpability are founded.[118] Even when it has been freed from the illusory link with 'choice' theories of responsibility and fault, the objective version of the capacity theory is sometimes confronted by an argument against it of a different kind. This is the argument, as expressed by William Wilson, that:

Central to capacity theory it seems is an idealised notion of human beings. They are people who are morally resistant to environmental, genetic and biochemical determinations of their character and choices. Whatever their race, class, gender, upbringing, personal psychology or intellect, their range of choices are not significantly affected. Rule-breakers are punished without regard to their real capacities and opportunities to conform . . .[119]

Wilson does not cite any modern theorist who could be claimed to have expressed such a view, and that is not surprising. His portrayal of the capacity theory is just an unfortunate caricature.[120] Hence, the implicit criticism of the theory as making absurdly unrealistic assumptions about human nature, and as being excessively demanding in the standards it expects people to observe, falls a long way wide of the mark.[121] Hart, who Wilson recognizes as a central figure in the development of the capacity theory, did not see the theory in the way Wilson portrays it. For Hart, for example, a central question in the law of negligence ought to be whether D *'given his mental and physical capacities'* could have taken the precautions the reasonable person with normal capacities would have taken.[122] Perhaps, in making this observation in

---

[118] Sanford Kadish expresses the point, in a broader context, very well: 'Presumably, to say that a person is cowardly, or apprehensive, or whatever, is to say that his actions tend to be deficient in certain ways. It is certainly not to say that the person has no choice but to act in those ways. That he has once again acted in that way is the very ground for blaming him', from Sanford Kadish, 'Excusing Crime', 276. See also Jeremy Horder, 'Criminal Law', 232–235.

[119] William Wilson, *Central Issues in Criminal Theory* (Oxford: Hart Publishing, 2002), 339.

[120] It is a view frequently associated with Kant's famous claim, that '[n]ow although we believe the action to have been determined by . . . circumstances, we do not the less blame the offender. We do not blame him for his unhappy disposition, nor for the circumstances that influenced him . . . Our blame of the offender is grounded upon a law of reason, which requires us to regard this faculty as a cause, which could and ought to have otherwise determined the behaviour of the culprit, independently of all empirical conditions', from I. Kant, *The Critique of Pure Reason*, 327–328. I know of no criminal law theorist who takes such an unyielding view, if, indeed, it was truly Kant's intention to espouse such a view.

[121] Nicola Lacey suggests that determinism is a particular problem for the capacity theory, because if environmental and social factors affect our capacities this ought, at least in cases of what she calls 'extreme social deprivation', to affect our view of the scope of excuses: see Nicola Lacey, 'Partial Excuses to Homicide: Questions of Power and Principle in Imperfect and Less than Imperfect Worlds . . .', in Andrew Ashworth and Barry Mitchell, *Rethinking English Homicide Law*, 116. It was, though, the most famous modern proponent of the capacity theory, H. L. A. Hart, who suggested, albeit *arguendo*, that just such an excuse might legitimately exist (see H. L. A. Hart, *Punishment and Responsibility*, 51); and he has been followed in this by other holders of a capacity theory, such as Ashworth: see Andrew Ashworth, *Principles of Criminal Law*, 3rd edn., 255–256. See further, chapter 4.11 below.

[122] H. L. A. Hart, *Punishment and Responsibility*, 154.

the way he does, Hart wavers between adoption of the subjective and the objective versions of the capacity theory.[123] Nonetheless, what is abundantly clear is that neither he, nor any other modern theorist, adheres to the extreme version of the capacity theory taken as representative by Wilson.[124] Even so, more needs to be said about the sense in which the objective version of the capacity theory really is 'objective', something that comes out through comparing and contrasting it with its subjective counterpart.

The differences between the objective and the subjective versions of the capacity theory, important though they are, should not be over-emphasized. As Simester says, in defending his refinements of the objective version, 'the "reasonable man" is really *the defendant*, subject only to attribution of those faculties where an objective standard is warranted'.[125] The objective version seeks to judge D objectively only with respect to those failures to come up to the mark in consideration of which D is morally culpable.[126] So, that D was too young to understand, to keep control, and so forth, is a characteristic with which the reasonable person must be imbued because it is so obviously a shortcoming for which D is not morally *culpable*.[127] In that regard, though, there cannot always be an entirely constant, sharp dividing line between the two versions of the capacity theory. In some instances, empirical research may provide us with information that enables us to make generalizations about some disadvantaged people's capabilities (say, those with a low IQ), and hence to set standards and judge those people by them, in a way that would not have been possible before, because that information was lacking. So, if we wish to excuse someone (D) whose conduct is in part attributable to their low IQ, we do not now have to see this process as tied to an investigation of D's personal history, asking ourselves, 'of what standards has D shown him- or herself in the past to be capable?'. We do not, in other words, necessarily have to resort to the subjective version of the capacity theory. There may be a more general standard that research now shows that people

---

[123] A point picked up by Kadish in Sanford H. Kadish, 'Excusing Crime', 276–277, and more recently explored with great sophistication by A. P. Simester, 'Can Negligence be Culpable?'.

[124] So, for example, Kadish famously insists that 'in applying the objective standard the law does not abstract all of the circumstances in which the defendant acted. To some extent, it does individualize. A relevant physical defect of the defendant—that she was blind or deaf, for example—surely would be seen as part of the circumstances in which we imagine the ordinary person to be acting when the law assesses what her response would be.': Sanford Kadish, 'Excusing Crime', 275.

[125] A. P. Simester, 'Can Negligence be Culpable?', 91 (my emphasis).

[126] Simester gives the following examples: 'even if one is unable to rectify the causes of one's inattention, one may still be expected to compensate. Just as someone who knows of her blindness is expected to take the care that a blind person should, so too with non-physical limitations: if, for example, D should know she is likely to forget something, we may expect her to allow for that by taking additional precautions ... The naturally clumsy person ... if she has reason to perceive her clumsiness, can be expected to take extra care that her behaviour does not have unintended consequences ... By contrast, a defendant cannot be blamed for a failure of perception due to malfunctioning of the senses: one can be negligent for not looking, and for not perceiving, but not for failing to see': A. P. Simester, 'Can Negligence be Culpable?', 98 and 99.

[127] See *DPP v Camplin* [1978] AC 705.

with the D's IQ can be expected to meet; and if so, it would be right, with the assistance of expert evidence if necessary, to judge D by that standard.[128] Moreover, the emergence of such evidence, far from worsening D's position by introducing a more objective element into the evaluation of his or her behaviour, improves it (morally speaking) by treating D as a person capable of the self-respect at stake in a meaningful commitment to reach attainable standards.[129] In respect of (low) intelligence, as Simester argues, 'We do have means with which to assess intelligence . . . So there is good reason, at least in the criminal law, not to expect reasonable intelligence of the defendant but, rather, to expect *that she reasonably use the intelligence she has*'[130] (although, doubtless, in some instances, D's intelligence would be so low that one would, at best, be thrown back on the subjective version of the capacity theory once more, to assess D's culpability). That being so, it was surely an inexplicable injustice that the Divisional Court in *Elliot v C*[131] did not think that expert findings as to what could be expected of a 14-year-old girl, of low intelligence, were relevant to the question whether the risk that she might destroy property by setting light to it was 'obvious'.[132]

In fact, the courts have veered between the two capacity theories, without developing a consistent policy towards the issues on which expert evidence is admissible and relevant, in that regard.[133] Suppose that D wishes to introduce expert evidence to the effect that his or her behaviour, including (say) his or her control over temper or fear, is likely to be largely erratic and unpredictable.

---

[128] For that reason, I would reject Lacey's view that the capacity account of excuses is likely to be beset by practical difficulty in application, because it must confront 'assessments of the genuine capacities, choices, and opportunities of the defendant': see Nicola Lacey, 'Partial Defences to Homicide: Questions of Power and Principle in Imperfect and Less Than Perfect Worlds . . .', 116–117. This criticism may have some bite where the subjective version of the capacity theory is in issue, and we have no reliable independent evidence of D's capacities etc., but it misses the mark as a criticism of the objective version of the capacity theory as explained here.

[129] For this argument, see John Gardner, 'The Gist of Excuses', 590–594; John Gardner and Timothy Macklem, 'Compassion without Respect? Nine Fallacies in *R v Smith*', 627 and 630. That being so, although judgment in accordance with the subjective version of the capacity theory is the humane course, for diminished responsibility cases, there should be no doubt that it is also more demeaning for D: see the discussion in chapter 4.5 below.

[130] A. P. Simester, 'Can Negligence be Culpable?', 103. Simester rightly suggests that this view implies that more could in theory be asked of Ds whose intelligence exceeds an ordinary or average level, if that were not thought to be making too much—given that it is criminal conviction that is the issue—of a point about the way in which moral culpability varies.

[131] *Elliot v C* [1983] 1 WLR 939. The case has now been impliedly over-ruled by *R v G (and another)* [2003] 3 WLR 1060.

[132] Picking up the point made in the previous sentence, however, to be charitable one might conclude that, on the facts, given the Justice's finding in that case that D was of 'very low' intelligence for her years (*Elliot v C* [1983] 1 WLR 939, 942), there were no lower general standards by which her behaviour could intelligibly and reliably be judged, and so her plea, if anything, was really one of diminished capacity. This concession, on the facts of the case, does not detract from the injustice of the inflexible and artificially objective rule the court laid down. To use Simester's apt phraseology (A. P. Simester, 'Can Negligence be Culpable?', 104) the court confused the issue of whether Ds should be deemed to have a reasonable level of intelligence (of course not!) with the issue of whether Ds should be required to use reasonably the intelligence they have.

[133] See the decision of the Court of Appeal in *R v Emery* (1993) 14 Cr App Rep (S) 394, where it was found that, for the purposes of a plea of duress, a recognized psychiatric syndrome

That is evidence that D cannot come up to an objective standard; and so the courts have often held. Applying the objective version of the capacity theory, they have found such evidence to be inadmissible in cases (provocation; duress) where D must show that his or her reaction passes muster, when judged by the objective standard of whether no more could have been expected of someone adequately equipped with powers of self-restraint.[134] Conflicting with such an approach is what was said in the case of *(Morgan) Smith*[135] about pleas of provocation. Here, the appellant sought to rely on evidence given by a psychiatrist to the effect that his clinical depression made him, 'likely to have been rather more disinhibited . . . In a state of heightened tension and irritability, he probably would have been more prone to injure his victim and less troubled by the likely consequences'.[136] This is clearly evidence that D cannot come up to an objective standard of self-control, and so (applying an objective version of the capacity theory) the trial judge ruled that the evidence was inadmissible with respect to D's provocation plea. The trial judge indicated that such evidence could only be relevant and admissible to assist D to succeed in reducing murder to manslaughter through a plea of diminished responsibility (where, as we will see, the subjective version of the capacity theory can be given an important role to play). Yet, on appeal in *(Morgan) Smith*,[137] the expert evidence was held to have been relevant and admissible to assist the jury in answering the question whether the *objective* condition or standard was satisfied, for the purposes of the provocation defence, namely whether no more could have been expected of someone adequately equipped with powers of self-control.[138] So, (with some unclear qualifications) the subjective version of the capacity theory, which asks what could have been expected of D him- or herself, with all her weaknesses and abnormalities, was found to be applicable to provocation pleas as well as to diminished responsibility pleas.[139] We return to these issues in chapter 4 below.

---

or mental illness could be attributed to a person of reasonable firmness, the question in issue in that case being how much steadfastness could be expected of a woman suffering from 'learned helplessness'. The court is clearly attempting to apply the objective version of the capacity theory, modified to take account of a condition ('learned helplessness') still considered to be consistent with the application of (suitably) modified objective standards. In the event, though, it is unclear whether the Court really did mean to apply this theory, as distinct from the subjective version of the capacity theory.

[134] See *A-G for Jersey v Holley* [2005] UKPC 23; *DPP v Camplin* [1978] AC 705; *R v Horne* [1994] Crim LR 584; *R v Hegarty* [1994] Crim LR 353, and the discussion of this issue, as it bears on duress cases, in A. P. Simester and G. R. Sullivan, *Criminal Law: Theory and Doctrine*, 595–596. If D is to be excused in such a case, it could only be through an application of the subjective version of the capacity theory, a theory (as I shall suggest in chapter 4 below) that underpins only instances of diminished capacity.

[135] *R v (Morgan) Smith* [1998] 4 All ER 387 (CA); [2000] 4 All ER 289 (HL).

[136] *R v (Morgan) Smith* [1998] 4 All ER 387, 390 (per Potts J). See further, Jeremy Horder, 'Between Provocation and Diminished Responsibility'.

[137] *R v (Morgan) Smith* [1998] 4 All ER 387.   [138] Ibid., 399.

[139] Further discussion of the English law of provocation will be found in chapter 4.6, 4.7, and 4.8 below.

8. Liberalism, Enforcing Morals and the Capacity Theory

In judging D by objective standards, one is engaged in moral evaluation of D's conduct, but not (contrary to the opinion of some commentators) in the *enforcement* of morality. By intentionally or knowingly doing the harmful wrong, one crosses the threshold set for criminalization by the very harm principle that (for liberals) outlaws criminalization of immorality as such, hence laying oneself open to such moral evaluation at the stage when one seeks excuse.[140] Even so, the suspicion that the law is illegitimately seeking to uphold moral standards for their own sake has arisen in relation to the decision of the House of Lords to place a key normative constraint on the defence of duress,[141] making it unavailable in murder and in attempted murder cases.[142] For the House of Lords, being seen to give overriding weight to 'sanctity of life' considerations, regarding murder as inexcusable under duress, takes precedence over whatever ascriptive reasons there might be to excuse at least some intentional killings in such circumstances. Discussion of this example provides an opportunity to reflect on how the defence of the capacity theory fits with a liberal view of the relationship between law and morality.

Many theorists argue for a complete excuse for murder committed under duress, in appropriate cases.[143] Strange as it may seem at first sight, amongst their number is Kant, a philosopher associated with defence of the unyielding pursuit of the highest moral standards. His view was that in law, if not in morality, D has or should have a complete excuse. Like Bacon and Blackstone,[144] his focus was not duress-by-threats cases, but duress of circumstances cases in which D acts unjustifiably in deliberately or knowingly killing another. The classic example is where D snatches a plank (following a shipwreck) from V who is using it to prevent him- or herself drowning, purely so that D can save him- or herself, in the full knowledge that V will now drown, which V does (hereinafter, simply the 'plank' case).[145] For Kant,

---

[140] See the discussion at the end of chapter 2.9 above.

[141] On the role of normative constraints in excuses, even those taking a predominantly ascriptive form, see chapter 2.4 above.

[142] *R v Howe* [1987] AC 417; *R v Gotts* (1992) 2 AC 412.

[143] See e.g. Sir J. C. Smith and Brian Hogan, *Criminal Law*, 10th edn., 254–256. A case was briefly made for an excuse, or partial excuse, for younger defendants in murder cases, in chapter 2.4 and at the end of chapter 2.5 above.

[144] Francis Bacon, *Maxims* (London: Benjamin Fisher, 1630) Reg 25; Sir William Blackstone, *Commentaries*, iv, 186, cited by Alan Brudner, 'A Theory of Necessity', 339 n. 2.

[145] See, further, Jeremy Horder, 'Self-Defence, Necessity and Duress: Understanding the Relationship', 160–163. English law now permits a necessity plea in what would otherwise be at least one instance of intentional killing: a separation of conjoined twins designed to ensure the survival of one, in preference to tolerating the death of both, even though ensuring the survival of one entails the much more rapid death of the other: see *Re A (Children) (Conjoined twins: Surgical separation)* [2000] 4 All ER 961, helpfully discussed in Jonathan Rogers, 'Necessity, Private Defence and the Killing of Mary' [2001] *Criminal Law Review* 515.

unsurprisingly, D has no moral justification for acting in this way whatsoever. Kant drew a sharp distinction, however, between the moral and the legal point of view on this case. Kant thought that the criminal law, being by its nature coercive and reliant on the threat of sanctions, should not seek to govern D's conduct in the struggle for occupation of the plank. There exist different accounts of why Kant took this view. One account—Brudner's—is that Kant shared Bentham's view that the law would never have deterrent effect in such extreme circumstances, and it would not be right falsely to maintain a fiction that it might have such an effect, by convicting D of murder in this kind of case. In Kant's view, thus, a court, as the body charged with upholding respect for the law through the maintenance of its deterrent effect, simply has no business convicting D: it would be pointless.[146] As Brudner notes, what is odd about this account of why D should be excused is its studious avoidance of any reliance on moral reasons to acquit D. Kant seems to placing a thorough-going reliance on the 'bad man' view of the criminal law's rationale, as a simple coercive system of orders backed by deterrent threats.[147] It is wrong to do this, of course, because the law, including the criminal law, often calls upon citizens to employ their moral judgment, in either guiding their own conduct[148] or judging that of others.[149] It does not consist solely—or at all— in orders to engage in or refrain from particular actions, backed by threats.[150] So, an alternative, and perhaps more plausible, account of why Kant took this view of the limits of law denies that Kant (unlike Bentham) analysed the criminal law solely in terms of its likely deterrent effect.[151] Instead, this alternative account sees Kant as self-consciously locating himself at the extreme end of a tradition of liberal thinking which holds that the criminal law must studiously avoid enforcing the pursuit of virtue. For the criminal law to require D to die him- or herself, to spare V because V is innocent, would be to engage in just such enforcement, because only a brave act of self-sacrifice by D leaves V's rights unviolated. So, a complete excuse is warranted, even if D's conduct did wrongly violate V's rights.[152]

As it stands, though, Kant's case for an excuse in the situation where, as he puts it, '[I] take the life of another who is doing nothing to harm me, when I am in danger of losing my own life',[153] is insufficiently fine-grained.

---

[146] See the discussion of this account of Kant's position by Alan Brudner, 'A Theory of Necessity', 355–356.

[147] See Alan Brudner, 'A Theory of Necessity', 356–358. This view of law found its way into Kelsen's jurisprudence, on this point so effectively criticized by H. L. A. Hart, *The Concept of Law* (Oxford: Clarendon Press, 1961), 1st edn., 35–36.

[148] As when the criminal law requires people to take 'reasonable care' etc.

[149] As when juries are required to decide if D took an unreasonable risk, and so forth.

[150] In this regard, on the relationship between criminal law and legal positivism, see Jeremy Horder, 'Criminal Law and Legal Positivism'.

[151] See the excellent discussion in Dennis Klimchuk, 'Necessity, Deterrence and Standing', 339.

[152] Ibid., 352–353.

[153] I. Kant, *Metaphysics of Morals*, 235, cited by Dennis Klimchuk, 'Necessity, Deterrence and Standing', 341 n. 6.

To begin with, there are subtle but important differences between kinds of cases in which D kills an innocent V, when he or she (D) is in danger of losing his or her life.[154] For example, in the plank case, it may be clear that V will be saved if D does not dislodge him or her, whereas in many duress cases—*R v Dudley and Stephens*,[155] for example—V may be rightly or reasonably judged likely to die *in any event*. It is just a question of how V is to die, and whether others will survive if V is intentionally killed now.[156] This feature of such cases may permit D to give his case for excuse an actively justificatory, predominantly normative character (of the kind discussed in chapter 2.4 above) that is absent when V is as likely to survive—if uneaten—as anyone else. Arising out of this point is a broader criticism. The claim that the law lacks the authority to punish D, if only virtue would have moved D to refrain from violating V's rights, confuses two kinds of case in which the state might claim authority to act. Contrast the plank case in which D forces V off, in order to save him- or herself even though V would herself have survived, with a different example. In this example, D refuses to give the necessary permission for V (D's dependant) to have the blood transfusion that V urgently needs if V is to live, because D is a Jehovah's Witness, and thinks that blood transfusions are morally impermissible in all circumstances.[157] In the latter case, it seems plausible to say that although D misguidedly violates V's rights, so that D can remain true to his or her beliefs, there is a case for saying that the law should not seek to punish D even though he or she has done V such a wrong. This is simply because to do that would, indeed, be to use sanctions to ensure that those in D's position abandon the guidance of their deepest convictions, and are motivated instead solely by fear of the consequences.[158] In the duress cases in which V will survive if uneaten by D, on the other hand, D is not being required to act against good conscience; far from it. D simply puts a concern for his or her own safety ahead of concern and respect for V's right to take steps unhindered to secure his or her own safety. In so far as it has any justification as a necessary evil, the threat of sanctions can be said to be meant to counter the lure of just such self-serving motives. So, an alternative account of these cases in required.

An alternative, liberal account of these examples runs as follows. As indicated at the beginning of this section, in all these examples, D is in breach of the harm principle. The harm principle forbids criminalization *ab initio* on purely moral grounds. It does not, however, impose any such prohibition

---

[154] Klimchuk notices this (Dennis Klimchuk, 'Necessity, Deterrence and Standing', 341 n. 6), but perhaps does not make as much of it as he should have done.

[155] (1884) 15 QBD 273.

[156] See the discussion of this point in Jeremy Horder, 'Self-Defence, Necessity and Duress: Understanding the Relationship', 155–159.

[157] For a variation on this, see *Re T (Adult: Refusal of Medical Treatment)* [1992] 4 All ER 649 (CA), discussed in chapter 5.4 below.

[158] See further John Locke, 'A Letter Concerning Toleration', 20, cited by Dennis Klimchuk, 'Necessity, Deterrence and Standing', 352–353. For further discussion, see chapter 5.4 below.

respecting the grounds on which admitted breaches of the harm principle may or may not be *excused*. This is because the degradation involved in having one's harmless immorality officially censured by the criminal law is absent, when moral criteria are used simply to judge the degree of culpability in D's admitted breach of the harm principle. This does not mean, though, that just any criteria can be employed to judge D's culpability in such circumstances. Liberalism seeks to ensure legal processes operate in both a tolerant and a humane manner, through a sensitive appreciation of what is at stake, in relation to both of these considerations. In relation to the former consideration (tolerance), the law should seek to avoid confronting people with a 'Hobson's choice' of compromising their conscience or suffering punishment, even though not all issues of conscience justify tolerating or inflicting serious rights violations. Sometimes, as we will see in chapter 5 below, confronting people with the choice may be the lesser of two evils. In relation to the latter consideration (humanity), the law should not judge wrongdoers by reference to moral criteria that are impossibly demanding; but whether these criteria are too demanding depends on the circumstances. Where does this leave the Kantian theory of excuses?

What we need to develop out of Kant's discussion of excuses is the idea that the law, and in particular those sitting in judgment at the law's behest, may not be a good moral position to condemn by denying an excuse, because to do that would be an act of gross moral insensitivity. In that regard, Brudner modifies Kant's account of excuses by saying that we excuse, in the plank case, because D 'has not by his act empirically differentiated himself from the human community, and forbearance really would have been praiseworthy in the circumstances'.[159] Joshua Dressler's theory of excuses is structured in much the same way. He says:

> What seems to be involved in genuine cases of duress is that we believe that a person of great moral strength such as a saint . . . would refuse to give in to a threat, but that virtually every person of ordinary (but not saintly) moral firmness would commit the offense. Thus, a juror is saying more than that *he* would commit a crime in the same situation; he is asserting that . . . nearly everyone else would commit the crime . . . we are saying that normal, non-heroic, human beings lack the moral capacity to withstand the particular threat.[160]

These accounts closely resemble what I have been referring to as the objective version of the capacity theory.[161] As Dressler clearly implies, the theory

[159] Alan Brudner, 'A Theory of Necessity', 358.

[160] Joshua Dressler, 'Reflections on Excusing Wrongdoers: Moral Theory, New Excuses and the Model Penal Code', 711.

[161] In fact, Dressler links his theory to a contrast between justice and mercy, mercy being the basis for excusing: Joshua Dressler, 'Reflections on Excusing Wrongdoers: Moral Theory, New Excuses and the Model Penal Code', 699–700; but it seems likely that when we excuse we do so through a sensitive appreciation of what justice requires, and not to show mercy: see Nigel Simmonds, 'Judgment and Mercy' (1993) *Oxford Journal of Legal Studies* 52. I am grateful to Jonathan Rogers for making this point to me.

is more than a cynical appeal by defence counsel to fact-finders to admit that, like D, they might well act selfishly too, given the right circumstances. If the theory were no more than this, then in principle D could hope to succeed in a claim to excuse when he or she had found £5000 in a deserted street, and thought that the appropriation would never be discovered. The theory amounts to more than this, however, only in so far as it does involve the critical appraisal of D's conduct in the light of moral standards, and not just statistical probabilities. That does not answer the question whether it is right to place particular normative constraints on excuses: making murder, for example, inexcusable under duress. However (as I argued in chapter 2.4 above), in general, even predominantly ascriptive excuses can legitimately be subject to such constraints. This suggests that such legal constraints, if tailored to meet the special circumstances of young or mentally deficient offenders, are at least not morally impermissible.

4

Liberalism, Partial Excuses and Short-comers

1. FROM THE CLASSICAL TO THE LIBERAL VIEW OF EXCUSES

Having made the case, in this section, for moving from the 'classical' to the 'liberal' view of excuses, I want to do two things in this chapter. In sections 2 and 3 below, I will set out the theoretical structure of partial excuses, and explain what the implications of finding someone partially excused are to be. In the rest of the chapter, I will give an account of, and defend, an important theoretical distinction between different kinds of partial excuse. The distinction is between, on the one hand, partial excuses such as provocation and demands-of-conscience (explained in chapter 5 below), on rung 4 of the defence hierarchy or 'ladder' (set out in chapter 3.1 above), and on the other hand, the new partial excuse of diminished capacity that I will be proposing, on rung 5 of the ladder. The latter kind of partial excuse—discussed in detail, in due course—comes between the partial excuses on rung 4, and the more familiar partial defence of diminished responsibility, on rung 6. The distinction between partial excuses on rung 4, and the partial defence of diminished responsibility on rung 6, turns on a denial that the latter has any significant excusatory element. The success of a plea of diminished responsibility (on rung 6 of the ladder) can, and in theory should, turn solely on the cogency of evidence concerning the severity of D's mental deficiency. When it does, then the plea operates by way of denial of responsibility, and there is no truly excusatory element to it.[1] Indeed, as we will see in section 3 below, in the strictly limited account of diminished responsibility that I provide, that defence (or 'verdict': see the end of section 3 below) should replace insanity as the plea that is concerned solely with mental disorder. In general, though, I shall not be much concerned with cases firmly located on rung 6. However, also sheltering under the theoretical umbrella provided by the current diminished responsibility plea can be what amounts to a partially excusatory claim, based on a *combination* of evidence of D's mental deficiency and evidence of circumstantial pressure of some kind (such as

---

[1] This point is well explained by Gardner, in John Gardner, 'The Gist of Excuses', 587–589. It is challenged by R. D. Mackay and B. J. Mitchell, 'Provoking Diminished Responsibility: Two Pleas Merging Into One?'. Mackay and Mitchell's argument is examined more closely in due course.

UNIVERSITY OF WINCHESTER
LIBRARY

threats, or loss of self-control due to provocation)—the *factual* element in an excusatory claim—in response to which D acted. In such instances, each element, by itself, might be insufficient to warrant mitigation of the offence, so the claim to excuse can rest neither on rung 4 nor on rung 6 of the defence ladder. It is the operation of the two elements in combination that makes conviction of such a 'short-comer' as D, for the full offence, morally repugnant. To distinguish such claims (found on rung 5), from pure diminished responsibility claims (on rung 6) that are based solely on evidence of D's mental deficiency, I will call the former claims of 'excusatory diminished responsibility' or 'diminished capacity'.

Like the creation of a demands-of-conscience excuse (discussed in chapter 5 below), and the creation of a due diligence defence (discussed in chapter 6 below), the creation of a partial excuse of diminished capacity for 'short-comers'—those whose mental deficiency made them particularly susceptible to circumstantial pressure—can be explicitly tied to the opening up of an overtly liberal excusatory front in the criminal law. According to the classical view of excuses (explained in chapter 1.6 above), enshrined in the common law and defended by philosophers as otherwise very different as Aristotle and Kant, to admit that one's wrongdoing was attributable to one's shortcomings (because although one's responsibility was diminished, it was not eliminated) is already to have admitted that one has no excuse for that wrongdoing, because one is admitting a failure to come up to an acceptable standard. David Garland explains well the attitude towards short-comers that the classical view nourished in the courts:

Throughout most of the nineteenth century, individuals who appeared before the courts—however feckless, incompetent or disadvantaged—were addressed as if they were Enlightenment subjects, the only alternative category in law being the deranged, mad, non-subject.[2]

By way of contrast, according to the liberal view of excuses defended here, we should be open-minded about whether a shortcoming can have a genuinely excusatory element to it as an explanation for wrongdoing, opening the way to a diminished capacity plea.[3] It depends on the nature of the shortcoming, how it combines with other excusatory factors, and on whether or not strategic considerations or common goods (of the kind explained in chapter 1.2 above) militating against the creation of a partial excuse turn out to be decisive, in a given kind of case. Suppose D, who is 14 years old, suffers from a mental deficiency shortcoming (such as attention deficit disorder) that does not wholly undermine his or her responsibility.

---

[2] David Garland, *Punishment and Modern Society: A Study in Social Theory* (Oxford: Clarendon Press, 1990), 270.

[3] See, further, Stephen J. Morse, 'Diminished Capacity', in Stephen Shute, John Gardner, and Jeremy Horder (eds.), *Action and Value in Criminal Law* (Oxford: Clarendon Press, 1993). The gist of Morse's thesis is the liberal one defended here, although I would not endorse the precise argument that Morse employs to defend it.

In a particular case, that may open the way to permitting evidence that the factual element in a more traditional excusatory factor (say, duress falling short of the kind needed to excuse mentally well-equipped Ds) was also at work, that can be combined with evidence of the effect of the mental deficiency to form a compelling case for a partial defence plea of excusatory diminished responsibility.[4] The case for a partial excuse of this kind may be convincing, in such circumstances, in part because being put under duress, or encountering a need to defend oneself against attack, are unusual events raising few, if any, strategic considerations of the kind discussed in chapter 1.2 above. Things may look different if D, an adult, seeks to combine evidence of mental deficiency such as short-temperedness or pathological jealousy, *qua* shortcoming, with a provoked loss of self-control as the excusatory element, in a plea of diminished capacity. Should D, in principle, be able to plead a partial defence of excusatory diminished responsibility (diminished capacity)?[5] As we will see in sections 5 to 7 below, this is a far more controversial question. Situations giving rise to a risk that one may be provoked to lose self-control are considerably more commonly encountered than duress, or the need to defend oneself against attack. When, in such situations, that risk is made yet more vivid by the fact that D is also suffering from one of a certain range of mental deficiencies associated with violent temper, strategic concerns counting against granting a partial excuse for serious harm done in consequence begin to loom large; but this is to anticipate.

In broad terms, the case for promoting a liberal account of excuses is summarized by Dworkin's justly famous claim that the state must treat people with equal concern and respect, where to treat people with concern is to treat them 'as human beings who are capable of suffering and frustration', and to treat them with respect is to treat them 'as human beings who are capable of forming and acting on intelligent conceptions of how their lives should be lived'.[6] I will come to Dworkin's second injunction, the duty to treat individuals as capable of forming and acting on intelligent conceptions of how to live their lives, in chapter 5 below. For the moment, I will focus

---

[4] See section 10 below. In employing the term, 'mental deficiency', rather than mental 'disorder', I am seeking to lay stress on the fact that mental shortcomings may not come in the precise form of classifiable mental illness or disorder. They might include, for example, short-temperedness resulting from having spent one's life deaf and dumb, and hence having had to endure a lifetime of taunting and frustration at being unable to communicate with the same ease and to the same degree as others: see *R v Roberts* [1990] Crim LR 122, where the report of a psychiatrist stated that, 'irrational violence was to be expected from some immature prelingually deaf persons when emotionally disturbed'. There are some useful reflections on the meaning of psychiatric conditions in Alec Buchanan and Graham Virgo, 'Duress and Mental Abnormality' [1999] *Criminal Law Review* 517, 519–528.

[5] A straight provocation plea ought to be ruled out, in such a case, by the very fact that D has such a mental deficiency: Jeremy Horder, 'Between Provocation and Responsibility'; and *A-G for Jersey v Holley* [2005] UKPC 23; but for an alternative view, see R. D. Mackay and B. J. Mitchell, 'Provoking Diminished Responsibility: Two Pleas Merging Into One?'.

[6] Ronald Dworkin, *Taking Rights Seriously*, 272. Almost needless to say, I should not be taken necessarily to be endorsing the use to which Dworkin himself puts this claim.

on the issues raised by Dworkin's first injunction, the duty to treat individuals with concern, as beings capable of suffering and frustration. Judicial unwillingness to look beyond the classical approach to excuses led to an egregious omission at common law in England. This was the failure in the nineteenth and early twentieth centuries, alluded to in the passage cited from Garland above, to develop a partial excuse of diminished responsibility (of the kind that the Scottish courts felt perfectly free to develop),[7] for murder cases and beyond. In consequence, decades later, English criminal law became saddled with a statutory formula defining the defence notable, apart from the inadequacy of the language used to draft it,[8] chiefly for its narrowness, a narrowness that has now begun to distort (by artificial widening) the development of the parallel doctrine of provocation, and the defence of duress.[9] A defence that could have been made applicable to as many offences as the common law defence of insanity, thus became bound up with the law of murder alone.[10] Even so, limited though it is, the introduction of the partial defence of diminished responsibility rightly makes possible a significant shift away from the classical view of the nature and limits of excuses, towards a more liberal view. For, to leave Ds with a mental disorder not amounting to insanity without even the possibility of a partial excuse is to fail to treat them, in Dworkin's terms, with sufficient concern. Taking this development forward, the introduction of a generally applicable, partial defence of diminished *capacity*, a partially excusatory version of diminished responsibility, is designed to meet the challenge of showing such a liberal concern in full (not just when deciding, in the light of evidence of mental disorder, who is to receive a mandatory life sentence for murder).

In that regard, Garland has sought to characterize the liberal theory I espouse thus:

Towards the end of the nineteenth century, and at various points during the twentieth, [the] classical subject-in-law was joined by alternative figures of subjectivity and personhood. Alongside the free subject, the criminal law came to recognise (and

---

[7] See *Dingwall* (1867) 5 Irv 466; *Kirkwood v H M Advocate* (1939) JC 36.

[8] On which, see Edward Griew, 'Reducing Murder to Manslaughter: Whose Job?' (1986) 12 *Journal of Medical Ethics* 18, 19–20, who describes section 2(1) of the Homicide Act 1957, that sets out the defence of diminished responsibility as 'elliptical almost to the point of nonsense . . . The wording is altogether a disgrace'. The Law Commission for England and Wales has recommended a modernization of the wording: see Law Commisssion for England and Wales, *Murder, Manslaughter and Infanticide*, Part 5.

[9] On provocation, see the discussion of *R v (Morgan) Smith* [2000] 3 WLR 654 in section 8 below; Jeremy Horder, 'Between Provocation and Diminished Responsibility'; and John Gardner and Timothy Macklem, 'Compassion Without Respect? Nine Fallacies in *R v Smith*'; R. D. Mackay and B. J. Mitchell, 'Provoking Diminished Responsibility: Two Pleas Merging Into One?'. For the parallel development in duress, see *R v Emery* (1992) 14 Cr App Rep (S) 394; *R v Bowen* (1996) 4 All ER 837, discussed in section 10 below, and by Alec Buchanan and Graham Virgo, 'Duress and Mental Abnormality'.

[10] For discussion, see R. D. Mackay, 'Diminished Responsibility and Mentally Disordered Killers', 80–81.

help establish) other categories of persons, often with diminished responsibility . . . Thus penal institutions have witnessed the creation of categories such as 'the degenerate', 'the feeble-minded', 'the inebriate', 'the habitual offender', 'the moral imbecile', 'the psychopath', and have adopted the specific procedures of recognition and treatment deemed appropriate to them . . . [S]uch categories provide the elements for a convenient cultural framework through which normal subjects can think about abnormality and the conditions which produce it.[11]

Rich and illuminating though Garland's analysis can be, in shedding light on some dark corners in English penal history, this is far too cynical a portrayal of the endeavour to create a liberal criminal law that does not judge short-comers by the same standards it judges the mentally well-equipped, and hence deals with them more leniently or (where appropriate) just differently. For Garland, the development of doctrines such as diminished responsibility leads to, 'the modern tendency to view the self as a machinery to be maintained and repaired by specialists and to rethink what was once known as "evil" in terms of pathology rather than moral choice'.[12] By way of contrast, for Dworkin—as for all liberal theorists—such a tendency would constitute a failure: indeed, an abuse. It would be a failure, precisely insofar as it may fail to acknowledge short-comers as truly *human* ('capable [*inter alia*] of suffering and frustration'). To acknowledge the humanity of short-comers is to recognize that they may be, in some circumstances, just as deserving as the mentally well-equipped with their own partial excuse claims, of some punishment, but also of mitigation and leniency, *pure and simple*, irrespective of considerations of 'maintenance and repair'. Partially excusing, on the grounds of diminished capacity, involves a treatment with concern wholly at odds with the image Garland conjures up of the dehumanizing objectification involved in mere bureaucratic categorization for the purposes of behaviour modification.

2. PARTIAL EXCUSES AS SECOND-DEGREE OFFENCES

Having developed what was, in effect, second-degree homicide (manslaughter) in the fifteenth and early sixteenth centuries, as a way of avoiding legislative encroachment on the availability of benefit of clergy in 'first degree' homicide (murder) cases, English judges stopped there.[13] No second-degree version of other crimes was developed at common law that could have been linked with more lenient sentences. Even when legislatures worldwide began the process of codifying the criminal law in the nineteenth century (England, notoriously, excepted), a process largely completed for most jurisdictions by the early twentieth century, the opportunity was not taken to extend the use of second-degree offences outside the law of homicide.[14] Given that judges'

---

[11] David Garland, *Punishment and Modern Society*, 270.   [12] Ibid., 270–271.
[13] See Jeremy Horder, *Provocation and Responsibility*, chapter 1, for a brief discussion.

powers to pass whatever sentence they thought appropriate remained largely unrestricted for much of that period (and beyond), perhaps such a development seemed to be an unnecessary complication. If someone maimed another, or stole, in circumstances indicating strong mitigating circumstances, an appropriately light sentence could be passed (if the jury convicted at all), or would perhaps subsequently be secured through the post-sentence executive process.[15] In essence, this is the system with which we still operate today, but it is far from being entirely satisfactory. In particular, it does too little formally to permit the application to the facts by a jury or magistrate of a broad range of (moral) reasons to acquit, at the trial stage. It relies, instead, largely on reasons to be lenient, at the sentencing stage, to ensure that justice is done.[16] This fails to take the issue of conviction seriously enough.

Of what one is convicted matters, morally. It is not only the sentence that one receives that matters in that way. As Simester and Smith put it:

In addition to punishment and proscription, however, a third aspect of the criminal process, and one central to its distinctiveness from other areas of our legal system, is the conviction itself . . . a criminal conviction—at least for stigmatic offences—is regarded as a penalty in its own right . . . for it has the effect of labelling the defendant as a criminal.[17]

As things stand, in that regard, whilst conviction is in the hands of the fact-finder (jury or magistrate), moral criteria will only enter into the decision whether or not to convict when the definitional elements of the offence, by their nature, so provide, as when conviction turns in part on a question of dishonesty, or on a question of (gross) negligence, and so forth. Fact-finders should be provided with a more general, formal means of expressing an opinion about the moral appropriateness of conviction. To this end, a new general category of offence, the 'second degree' offence, ought to be created, whose function is in part to permit a wider range of moral criteria to be brought to bear at the trial stage on the question of the appropriateness of conviction for particular crimes.[18] A partial excuse is what reduces a first-degree to a second-degree offence. The prospect of such a development has been

---

[14] The main reforms concentrated on the creation of lesser, included offences. On these, see the discussion in the text following n. 25 below.

[15] For the historical picture, see e.g. P. King, 'Decision-Makers and Decision-Making in the English Criminal Law, 1750–1800' (1984) 27 *Historical Journal* 25; Thomas A. Green, *Verdict According to Conscience* (Chicago: University of Chicago Press, 1985), chapter 7.

[16] M. Wasik, 'Partial Excuses in the Criminal Law', 519–520.

[17] A. P. Simester and A. T. H. Smith (eds.), *Harm and Culpability* (Oxford: Clarendon Press, 1996), 6.

[18] As Wasik puts it, speaking of jury trial, 'it may be seen as appropriate to allow a jury the option of convicting of a lesser offence rather than being forced to choose between conviction for a greater offence seen by them to be morally inappropriate, and a perverse acquittal', in M. Wasik, 'Partial Excuses in the Criminal Law', 530. In that regard, a sophisticated theoretical examination of, and justification for, partial defences can be found in Douglas Husak, 'Partial Defenses' (1998) 11 *Canadian Journal of Law and Jurisprudence* 167. See also, Suzanne Uniacke, 'What are Partial Excuses to Murder?'.

criticized (although not on moral grounds) by the Criminal Law Revision Committee, when they considered it as an option for dealing with intoxicated offenders.[19] The Criminal Law Revision Committee criticized it on the grounds that '[t]he separate offence would add to the already considerable number of matters which a jury often has to consider when deciding whether the offences charged have been proved . . .'.[20] Whatever force it may have had at the time of the Report, this criticism lacks real bite at a time when the vast majority of offences are, and increasingly will be, dealt with in the Magistrates' Court.[21] The proposal must be considered on its substantive merits.

As I have just said, it is, of course, already the case that in many crimes the fact-finder must pass a moral judgment on D's conduct, in deciding whether D should be convicted. Any crime, for example, dependent on a finding of (gross) negligence, or on a finding of an 'unwarranted' demand made,[22] and so forth, necessarily entails such a judgment. Such crimes may reflect either the fact that some conduct is wrongful only if done for the wrong reasons (as in the case of blackmail), or the fact that there is a 'guidance' element to some criminal laws, guidance that could not be supported without reliance on moral norms in the shaping of the prohibition itself (as in the case of driving without due care and attention).[23] A further, closely related case in which the fact-finder is required to pass moral judgment on D's conduct, in deciding if D should be convicted, is the case in which conviction depends on a certain kind of negative or adverse appraisal of D's attitude to his or her conduct: such as a finding that D was, say, dishonest, wickedly reckless, or indifferent. Lastly, in instances where there is an underlying lesser (included) offence of which D can be convicted, the fact-finder's decision to convict of the lesser offence will frequently turn on a moral assessment of D's behaviour (whether or not such an assessment is an intrinsic part of the graver offence).[24] In that regard, for example, negligent homicide is in principle not so serious as reckless homicide, and in a case in which D was charged with reckless homicide but the fact-finder judges that D's conduct was not so blameworthy as to warrant conviction for that crime, a verdict of guilty of negligent homicide can be brought in.[25]

The idea of second-degree crime is not quite captured by any of these justifications for engaging the moral sensibilities of fact-finders. Consider the last example, in which conviction depends on an appraisal of D's

[19] Criminal Law Revision Committee, *Offences Against the Person*, 14th Report, Cmnd 7844 (HMSO, 1980).   [20] Ibid., para 264.

[21] See Penny Derbyshire, 'An Essay on the Importance and the Neglect of the Magistracy' [1997] *Criminal Law Review* 627.

[22] As in the crime of blackmail: see section 21 of the Theft Act 1968.

[23] For discussion, see Jeremy Horder, 'Criminal Law and Legal Positivism', 225–237.

[24] For an outstanding empirically based exploration of this issue, see Elaine Genders, 'Reform of the Offences Against the Person Act: Lessons from the Law in Action' [1994] *Criminal Law Review* 689.

[25] C. M. V. Clarkson and H. M. Keating, *Criminal Law: Text and Materials* (London: Sweet & Maxwell, 1998), 4th edn., 715–723, discussing the law of homicide in a number of US states.

conduct, in the light of the recklessness/negligence divide. In relation to the crime of reckless homicide, negligent homicide is not a second-degree version of reckless homicide. In relation to the latter the former is, quite simply, a lesser (included) offence. Negligent homicide is *ex hypothesi* a 'stand alone' offence, of which D may be convicted directly, without having also been charged with (and acquitted of) reckless homicide.[26] I shall understand partial excuses to operate in almost exactly the way that provocation and diminished responsibility currently operate as partial excuses in murder cases (reducing the crime to so-called 'voluntary' manslaughter); indeed, the idea of 'second-degree murder' ought to replace that of so-called 'voluntary' manslaughter itself. Partial excuses would come into operation only when the principal offence has been charged, and pleading them would involve no denial of the elements of *mens rea* and *actus reus*. If successfully pleaded, they are 'partial' excuses in that they avoid conviction for the main offence, but involve conviction for what can in all instances be called 'second-degree grievous bodily harm', 'second-degree arson', 'second-degree wounding', and so forth.[27] As when murder is reduced to 'voluntary' manslaughter, there is thus a formal role at the stage of *conviction itself* for the fact-finder to decide the fate of the offender on a broader range of moral criteria than is currently possible, whether or not the definitional elements of the offence in question involve some kind of moral appraisal.

3. Sentencing in Second-degree Offence (Partial Excuse) Cases

On my account, partial excuses could be brought into play whenever a serious imprisonable offence has been charged. In that regard, taking the moral significance of conviction seriously entails regarding partial excuses as no less important in the Magistrate's Court as when they are before a jury, an importance that increases as Magistrates' powers to deal with imprisonable offences become ever greater.[28] Instead of doing no more than leading to a verdict of guilty of a second-degree offence, a partial excuse should involve

[26] See further, M. Wasik, 'Partial Excuses in Criminal Law', 527–529. Although 'reckless' and 'negligent' homicide are not currently separate crimes in English law, as such, the Law Commission for England and Wales has proposed that they should be: Law Commission for England and Wales, *Legislating the Criminal Code: Involuntary Manslaughter*, Law Commission Consultation Paper No 237 (HMSO, 1996).

[27] It seems sensible to restrict the scope of 'second degree' offence in some way, perhaps to imprisonable offences against the person, or to indictable offences, or (in jurisdictions where that concept has no meaning or, as in Britain, increasingly little real meaning) imprisonable offences that have some element of '*mala in se*' at the heart of the prohibition. Given the range and variety of offences, one cannot afford to be too prescriptive about this.

[28] For a penetrating appraisal of the importance of magistrates, as compared with juries in criminal cases, see Penny Derbyshire, 'An Essay on the Importance and the Neglect of the Magistracy'. Where someone has the power both to find facts and pass sentence, it is all the more crucial that the moral issues relevant to the two stages are kept separate.

an open and explicit link to less severe sentences.[29] The unique character of a second-degree conviction will be that the judge will, other than in exceptional circumstances,[30] be obliged to impose a non-custodial penalty on D (including, for this purpose, a conditional discharge), however serious the principal—first-degree—offence.[31] As this consequence of second-degree conviction becomes more widely known, it might come to be understood to have the kind of moral standing that a voluntary manslaughter (as opposed to a murder) conviction now has.

One response to this proposal is to say that it is simply an over-refined way of making mandatory non-custodial sentences that would in any event certainly be passed, in the exercise of sentencing discretion. The answer to this goes beyond saying that such a response fails to take the moral significance of conviction itself sufficiently seriously. Even though, as we will see in chapter 5 below, the response may have some force in relation to most (if not all) demands-of-conscience cases, the proposal will in fact have an important, and sometimes radical, effect in many cases to which it is to be applied. The proposal that a finding of partial excuse should lead to a non-custodial sentence is particularly radical in its effect when provocation is pleaded as a defence. Given that, on my account, there could in theory be a conviction for a second-degree offence when any serious offence has been charged, it follows that it would be possible to broaden the categories of crime to which provocation can be pleaded as a partial excuse, to include (say), attempted murder or wounding with intent to do grievous bodily harm. For, it has ceased to matter that there may be no lesser offence to which to reduce the main offence, or only a lesser offence whose description does not accurately label what D has done.[32] D is simply convicted of the second-degree version of the principal offence charged. There might be some logic to such a development, even for 'provocation sceptics'.[33] If, morally speaking, the grounds for mitigating an offence involving delib-

---

[29] See M. Wasik, 'Partial Excuses in the Criminal Law', 529–560.

[30] Such as where D has previous convictions, particularly for similar kinds of offence. Even in such cases, it would still be open to a judge to pass a non-custodial sentence. Different considerations apply when D seeks what I will call a diminished responsibility *verdict*, where secure detention for treatment must also be an option for the sentencer: see discussion at the end of this section.

[31] I should not be taken to be implying that conviction for the principal offence, even when conviction for the second-degree offence was possible, should necessarily result in a custodial sentence. The judge should retain the power to hand down any sentence within the range of sentences (if any) appropriate for the offence in question, even if the jury rejects a second-degree conviction and hence a mandatory non-custodial sentence. It would, of course, remain open in any case for the judge to decide on an absolute discharge.

[32] As where D admits all the elements of a charge of wounding with intent to do grievous bodily harm, but is (*ex hypothesi*) convicted only of malicious wounding in the light of the gravity of the provocation. If this were the effect of a provocation plea, it would have the undesirable effect of mis-labelling what D actually *did*, in a way that a verdict of voluntary manslaughter by reason of provocation does not do.

[33] See, for example, Celia Wells, 'Provocation: The Case for Abolition', 85; Matthew Goode, 'The Abolition of Provocation', in S. M. H. Yeo (ed.), *Partial Excuses to Murder* (New South Wales: The Federation Press, 1991) 37; Jeremy Horder, *Provocation and Responsibility*, chapter 9.

erate violence, on the grounds of provocation, are weak, then they are at their weakest in relation to the most serious crimes of violence; yet, ironically, it is only in relation to the most serious offence of violence of all that the defence of provocation is currently available. Moreover, given that the result of a second-degree conviction is to be a non-custodial sentence (as the fact-finder ought to know, or to be told) there are perhaps grounds for thinking that there would be far fewer reductions from murder to second-degree murder, in undeserving provocation cases. It is worth pursuing this particular point further. As I have just implied, the effect of a successful provocation plea in murder cases should be that D is convicted of 'second-degree murder' (the term 'manslaughter' is best confined to the lesser offence of what is commonly referred to as 'involuntary' manslaughter, by recklessness or gross negligence). When D is convicted of second-degree murder, if he or she has no previous criminal record he or she will be entitled to a non-custodial sentence, a particularly dramatic and controversial result in murder cases. Even so, this revolution in sentencing in provocation cases where D admits an intentional killing, could in fact have beneficial effects, resolving some significant problems that have persistently dogged the operation of the defence in recent years.

The guidance given by the Court of Appeal, governing sentencing in cases where provocation has been successfully pleaded, is currently that the judge's starting point should be a sentence of about seven years' imprisonment.[34] This belies a sharp difference in approach between cases in which the provocation suffered by D has taken the form of violent abuse by V (typically, D's male partner), and other cases, in which the provocation has taken a non-violent form. In the latter, substantial prison sentences have indeed been the norm, whereas in the former, the measure of *first* resort has sometimes been a non-custodial sentence.[35] Although it is a matter largely for speculation, juries' awareness that a prison sentence can follow a verdict of manslaughter may have encouraged them to bring in such verdicts even though the provocation was not grave, where there was substantial delay between the final provocation and the fatal act, or where there was clear evidence of pre-planning. In relation to the first of these possibilities, the case of *R v Naylor*[36] is instructive. In this case, D received the services of a prostitute, and then refused to pay her, as agreed. She became angry, with the result that he lost his

---

[34] *R v Naylor* (1987) 9 Cr App Rep 302, discussed in Andrew Ashworth, *Sentencing and Criminal Justice*, 2nd edn., 107–108. Sentencing in provocation cases has now been reviewed by the Sentencing Advisory Panel, in their Consultation Paper, 'Manslaughter by Reason of Provocation' (2004), www.sentencing-advisory-panel.gov.uk.

[35] See Jeremy Horder, 'Sex, Violence, and Sentencing in Domestic Provocation Cases' [1989] *Criminal Law Review* 546. However, the Sentencing Advisory Panel has found that the incidence of non-custodial sentences is in fact low (see their Consultation Paper, 'Manslaughter by Reason of Provocation', paragraph 27), and almost exclusively confined to the domestic context.   [36] *R v Naylor* (1987) 9 Crim App Rep (S) 302.

temper and strangled her so hard that a bone in her neck was broken. The jury acquitted him of murder, on the grounds of provocation, even though it is hard to see what was done to him that could have provoked a reasonable person into losing self-control and killing.[37] As far as cases involving pre-planning are concerned, Ashworth's research has revealed a number of cases in which a jury has brought in a verdict of manslaughter, in spite of clear premeditation. So, in *R v Djemil*,[38] for example, where D suspected his lodger of having romantic designs on his wife, D bought a gun and hid in the bathroom on the morning of the killing. When D heard his wife tell the lodger to leave her alone, he emerged and shot the lodger a number of times. He was acquitted of murder, and convicted of manslaughter only.[39]

If the jury had been aware that in each of these cases a verdict of second-degree murder, by reason of provocation, would be followed by a *non-custodial* penalty,[40] it seems highly unlikely D would have been acquitted of murder; and a good thing too. The law rightly sets a high value on the gravity of the provocation to D, and on the spontaneity of D's reaction to it, in losing self-control and killing; but the law's currency is being debased if awareness of the possibility of lengthy prison terms being given, even when a verdict of manslaughter by reason of provocation has been brought in, is encouraging juries to bring in such verdicts despite the fact that these conditions have not been met. By making a mandatory non-custodial penalty the known norm for second-degree conviction, following a successful provocation plea, the law would be deliberately 'raising the stakes'. As the gravity of the provocation falls, or the element of pre-planning increases, so does the chance that the jury will convict of first-degree murder to avoid the non-custodial sentence that accompanies a second-degree murder conviction. In general, the change ought to mean proceedings becoming loaded in favour of bringing in second-degree convictions only when the provocation has been exceptionally grave, as when D loses control having been subjected to prolonged and serious violent treatment at V's hands. One could, then, see a situation developing in which, with some judicial encouragement, the defence begins to operate, at least in some respects, primarily in favour of battered women who kill abusive partners, and against jealous partners who lose control and take revenge when they discover their partner has been having an affair.[41] Such a development would go a long way to resolve some

---

[37] Naylor had an appalling criminal record, which meant that he received a sentence well in excess of seven years' imprisonment.

[38] 17.1.68; 4198/67, and see also the case of *Marryshaw*, 26.3.65, 2893/94, cited by Andrew Ashworth, 'Provocation in the Criminal Law', Ph.D. (University of Manchester, 1973), 463.

[39] The Court of Appeal dismissed D's appeal against a sentence of seven years' imprisonment, and said that the element of premeditation might have justified an even longer sentence.

[40] In *R v Naylor* (1987) 9 Cr App Rep (S) 302, the defendant had previous convictions for violence, and so, in my view, the judge would not in fact have been obliged to pass a non-custodial sentence.

of the seemingly intractable moral difficulties that have been identified in the operation of the provocation plea.[42]

The effect of such changes might well be, of course, that a plea of diminished capacity will begin to look especially attractive, if it allows D to combine evidence of lost self-control following something rather less than the gravest of provocations, with evidence of a mental deficiency falling short of insanity or of some other serious mental disorder.[43] For that very reason, there is a case for saying that evidence of *provocation*, as opposed to evidence of (say) a belief that a threat has to be more or less immediately negated or complied with, should not be admissible as the factual element in an excusatory plea that may be combined with evidence of mental deficiency, for the purposes of a diminished capacity plea. This issue will be considered in sections 6 and 7 below, in so far as it impacts on common goods or strategic considerations relevant to excusatory claims.[44] How, though, more broadly, is sentencing affected by the fact that there is evidence of mental disorder or deficiency, in such cases? It ought to be possible for a judge to impose a hospital order in such cases, rather than an ordinary non-custodial penalty such as a community penalty. One should avoid creating a situation in which one must rely on those responsible for detention under civil powers of commitment to be waiting outside the door of the court to take a sick D back to hospital the moment he or she leaves the courthouse, because a verdict of guilty of a second-degree offence must result in the imposition of an ordinary non-custodial penalty. In cases where hospital orders are appropriate,[45] however, they should be for a fixed period, to reflect the fact that diminished capacity is a *defence*, and hence should not lead to treatment at the hands of the legal system more severe, in effect, than D might have expected upon conviction for the full offence.[46] What if D is thought too

[41] Difficult problems remain over the nature of the loss of self-control requirement: see e.g. *R v Thornton (No 2)* (1996) 2 All ER 1023. It has been strongly argued, though, that the problem of battered women who kill abusive partners is one best addressed through imaginative use of the defence of self-defence, rather than though the provocation defence: see Aileen McColgan, 'In Defence of Battered Women Who Kill' (1993) 13 *Oxford Journal of Legal Studies* 508, and Jeremy Horder, 'Killing the Passive Abuser: A Theoretical Defence', in Stephen Shute and A. P. Simester (eds.), *Criminal Law Theory: Doctrines of the General Part* (Oxford: Oxford University Press, 2002), 283. The problems are now beginning to be addressed by law reform bodies across the common law world: see e.g. Victorian Law Reform Commission, *Defences to Homicide: Options Paper*, chapter 4; Law Commission for England and Wales, *Partial Defences to Murder*, part 10.

[42] See further: Celia Wells, 'Provocation: The Case for Abolition'. A more complex but less dramatic way of addressing the particular problems facing battered women who kill their (former) partner-abusers, by reducing the emphasis on immediate loss of self-control and introducing an emphasis on a contemporaneous fear of the threat posed by the abuser, was briefly explored in chapter 2.13 above.

[43] See the cases discussed by R. D. Mackay, 'Pleading Provocation and Diminished Responsibility Together' [1988] *Criminal Law Review* 411, 412–413, considered in section 6 below.   [44] See also the remarks about this issue made in section 1 above.

[45] As far as the present diminished responsibility defence is concerned (I shall say something about this shortly), such orders are now imposed in around 60 per cent of cases: Nicola Lacey, Celia Wells, and Oliver Quick, *Reconstructing Criminal Law: Text and Materials*, 3rd edn. (London: Butterworths, 2003), 770.

dangerous for no more than a fixed term in hospital? That, as I now go on to suggest, should be a matter for the prosecution.

It is surprising that more theorists have not argued that the so-called 'defence' of insanity, that can in theory already be alleged by the prosecution (with the accused seeking to plead guilty instead), should be acknowledged to be a verdict solely for the prosecution to seek, and should cease to be regarded as a defence at all.[47] Should diminished capacity come to be a more general partial excuse, such a development would be a perfectly natural one. An insanity verdict carries at least as much undesirable stigma as a conviction, and has remained unpopular as a plea because of the possibility—indeed, the requirement, in murder cases—that the judge orders that D be detained indefinitely in secure conditions.[48] It might make better sense, then, to return to the position in which indefinite detention in hospital is the only possible result of an insanity verdict, but make that verdict something that the prosecution alone can seek. To establish the verdict, the prosecution would have to show beyond reasonable doubt not only that D possessed full *mens rea* (where relevant),[49] but also that, in virtue of D's mental deficiency, it will remain unclear for the foreseeable future when D will cease to pose a vivid threat of serious harm.[50] Such a change would, of course, mean that a person posing no special danger who, say, under the influence of severe mental disorder had committed an offence with full *mens rea*, could not then argue that they should be acquitted completely, on the grounds of insanity, rather than being merely partially excused through diminished capacity.[51] As I have argued elsewhere,[52] such an undesirable consequence can be avoided by making a plea of diminished responsibility (as opposed to diminished capacity), on rung 6 of the defence ladder, a *verdict*—in principle available with respect to any crime—rather

---

[46] Ideally, it ought to be possible to attach to a fixed-term hospital order an ensuing community-based treatment regime to ease the offender back in to ordinary life. To that end, a sophisticated argument, along something like these sorts of lines, has been developed by Mackay: see R. D. Mackay, 'Mentally Abnormal Offenders: Disposal and Criminal Responsibility Issues', in Mike McConville and Geoffrey Wilson (eds.), *The Handbook of the Criminal Justice Process* (Oxford: Oxford University Press, 2002), 453–454.

[47] But see N. Morris, 'The Criminal Responsibility of the Mentally Ill' (1982) 33 *Syracuse Law Review* 477.

[48] Criminal Procedure (Insanity and Fitness to Plead) Act 1991; Criminal Procedure (Insanity) Act 1964, s. 5(1)(a). See R. D. Mackay, *Mental Condition Defences in the Criminal Law* (Oxford: Oxford University Press, 1995), 131–142.

[49] I agree with those who have argued that where D does not have the *mens rea* (and *a fortiori* where there was not *actus reus*), D is entitled to be acquitted outright, and dealt with, where appropriate, under civil powers of commitment: see e.g. the discussion in A. P. Simester and G. R. Sullivan, *Criminal Law: Theory and Doctrine*, 1st edn., 577.

[50] For further discussion of the degree-of-risk/degree-of-harm balance, see *R v Birch* (1989) 11 Cr App Rep (S) 202, discussed in R. D. Mackay, 'Mentally Abnormal Offenders: Disposal and Criminal Responsibility Issues', 453.

[51] It is with this possibility in mind that Simester and Sullivan recommend the retention of the insanity defence: see A. P. Simester and G. R. Sullivan, *Criminal Law: Theory and Doctrine*, 1st edn., 577.

[52] Jeremy Horder, 'Pleading Involuntary Lack of Capacity', 316–317.

than a partial excuse, a verdict that leaves open the possibility that the court can impose a range of orders (with or without the kind of restrictions currently available) appropriate to deal with D's mental disorder.[53]

We can now produce a more detailed picture of the defence 'ladder' than that set out at the end of chapter 3.1 above, concentrating on partial excuses, denials of responsibility, and verdicts, and on the consequences that flow from each of these:

The modified excuse/exemption ladder

Rung 5: diminished capacity: partial **excuse** (fixed-term hospital order; non-custodial penalty[54] or treatment order; absolute or conditional discharge), OR

Rung 6: diminished responsibility: exemption **verdict** (hospital order, with or without restrictions; non-custodial treatment order; absolute or conditional discharge).

In the interests of uncluttered criminal procedure, it would not be unreasonable to expect D to have to choose between a diminished capacity plea, and a diminished responsibility plea. D may believe that his or her mental disorder is such that he or she deserves a special verdict that reflects the inappropriateness of punishment altogether, but not the indefinite detention that (on my account) only the prosecution can seek through pursuing an insanity verdict. Alternatively, D must admit that at least some blame is deserved for his or her conduct; but, given D's mental deficiency, only such blame as would make a non-custodial penalty appropriate (should the case for a hospital or other treatment-based order not seem to the trial judge to be overwhelmingly in the public interest).

4. THE CASE FOR MIXING OIL AND WATER: EXCUSATORY DIMINISHED RESPONSIBILITY

We have seen that, for holders of the view that deserving an excuse is all about fulfilling one's role in accordance with normative expectations, an admission that one could not come up to expectations cannot be a step

---

[53] In a case of diminished responsibility D's mental disorder is, *ex hypothesi*, sufficient *in itself* to warrant the verdict, without regard to the kind of external factors that can influence a finding of diminished capacity. It is arguable that, in very trivial cases, the court should also have power to rule that prosecutions are an abuse of process, and must be discontinued, a matter that the defence should be entitled to raise (backed by appropriate medical evidence) at a *voir dire* before the trial proper begins. Being concerned with D's mental state at the time of the offence, such a procedure would, of course, be in theory separate from an inquiry into whether D is now fit to plead.

[54] As indicated in section 1 above, it is not necessarily wrong to impose punishment on short-comers, such as those suffering from diminished capacity. It is just that the punishment

on the way to establishing an excuse.[55] If one could not come up to expectations, if one is still to be acquitted one will be dependent on being able to deny one's moral responsibility for the crime, by showing that the crime was attributable to the kind of 'deep-seated incapacity' that amounts to such a denial.[56] In driving this wedge between excuses and denials of responsibility, as a part of making his case for the normative expectations view, Gardner does not make much of the legal distinction between the plea of insanity and the plea of diminished responsibility. For him, the closeness of the parallel between insanity and diminished responsibility comes from the view that, '[t]he whole point of the diminished responsibility defence is that it depends on the *unreasonableness* of the defendant's reactions, i.e. their unamenability to intelligible rational explanation'.[57] This explanation certainly rings true when applied to the defence of insanity, which is without question an out-and-out denial of responsibility. Is it equally and without exception true of all diminished responsibility cases? That seems unlikely, because of the special role volitional (in)capacities may have in a plea of diminished responsibility.[58]

Compare and contrast three examples. If D1 kills V, believing V to be the re-incarnation of Hitler, D1's cognitive deficiency is what explains his or her insanity or diminished responsibility. D1's conduct is unamenable to intelligible rational explanation, to use Gardner's words, because the belief that motivates D1's action is irrational. Contrast D1 with D2, who is unable to resist a dominant desire (whatever it may be[59]), even where this is a desire to kill, because D2 has no control over his or her desires whatsoever. There is now no cognitive defect that could form the basis of an insanity plea. It must be D2's volitional defect that explains his or her diminished responsibility (as opposed to insanity).[60] In spite of this difference, however, D2's conduct is once again unamenable to intelligible rational explanation. Someone who acts on *any* dominant desire, whatever it may be, acts irrationally.[61] Now contrast D1 and D2 with D3. D3 experiences strong desires to kill, of such

---

ought, formally, to be acknowledged as less severe in principle—even if appropriate—than that which would be imposed on a mentally better-equipped D acting in similar circumstances.

55 See the discussion in chapter 3.4 and 3.5 above.

56 See John Gardner, 'The Gist of Excuses', 589.

57 Ibid., 591 (Gardner's emphasis). For him, thus, a plea of diminished responsibility, like a plea of insanity, 'extinguish[es] the need for one to rely on excuses altogether' (ibid., 589).

58 *R v Byrne* [1960] 2 QB 396.

59 This is obviously an important rider, because if X always desires what he or she ought to desire, it will not be irrational for X to act on his or her strongest desire. The irrationality of acting on one's strongest desires comes through the fact that one gives way to them even when they have no rational justification, even when one's long-term interests clearly contradict them, and so forth. See further, John Gardner and Timothy Macklem, 'Reasons'.

60 Given the volitional nature of the defect, D cannot plead insanity in English law.

61 As Stephen put it (Sir J. F. Stephen, *A History of The Criminal Law of England*, (London: Macmillan & Co, 1883), ii, 170): 'No doubt, however, there are cases in which madness interferes with the power of self-control, and so leaves the sufferer at the mercy of any temptation to which he may be exposed; and if this can be shown to be the case, I think the sufferer ought

abnormal strength that his or her *well-developed* control mechanisms are
unable to contain them.[62] D3's conduct is irrational, because it stems from
an irrational desire; but, unlike D1 and D2, D3's explanation of how he or
she came to engage in the conduct has a perfectly intelligible, rational
dimension to it. This is that, although his or her volitional capacities—what
Michael Smith calls his or her 'back-up capacities'[63]—are intact, they
were simply not up to the task of keeping his (abnormal) desires in check.
In spite of this, D3 can, of course, still plead diminished responsibility
successfully.[64] The key will be whether or not the jury accepts that, so
strong and irresistible was the abnormal desire, D3 could not have been
expected to keep that desire in check with his or her (*ex hypothesi*) well-
developed powers of self-control. In seeking to establish this, D3 may give
an explanation designed to appeal to the jury's sense of what makes perfect
rational sense: 'given the extraordinary strength of this abnormal desire,
without super-human powers of self-control I could not have stopped
myself'.[65] So, in some cases of diminished responsibility, like D3's, D may
be able to say that there was a rational dimension to the explanation of
his or her conduct, even if in other cases, like D1's or D2's, this may not be
possible.[66]

In asking themselves the question whether D3 could have kept the abnormal
desire under control, the jury could be required to apply the objective test of
whether someone adequately equipped with powers of self-control could
have kept such an abnormal desire in check. This seems to have been
Stephen's view. Giving an apparently genuine example in which a woman
had successfully resisted a sudden and violent urge to kill a child in her care,

---

to be excused.' Stephen is obviously not using 'excused' in the sense employed here, namely as
crucial to a contrast with denials of responsibility.

[62] See, perhaps, *R v Byrne* [1960] 2 QB 396.

[63] Michael Smith, 'Responsibility and Self-Control', in Peter Cane and John Gardner (eds.),
Relating to Responsibility: Essays for Tony Honoré (Oxford: Hart Publishing, 2001), 12: 'In
agents who aren't . . . superhumanly coherent . . . we might well expect to find that they possess back-up capacities that enable them to get back on track when their desires fail to match
their beliefs about what they would want themselves to do, in their present circumstances, if
they had a maximally informed and coherent desire set'.

[64] See *R v Byrne* [1960] 2 QB 396, 403 (per Lord Parker CJ).

[65] It is in this kind of case, then, that the subjective version of the capacity theory comes closest to overlapping with the objective version, in that both make use of an objective test of what
could be expected of the person with normally developed powers of self-control; but whereas
the objective version of the capacity theory uses the test as an explicit benchmark against which
to judge D's conduct, the subjective version uses it merely as a way of trying to gain insight into
what D him- or herself could be expected to achieve. Hence, under the subjective version, the
test can be sidelined if D can produce relevant and admissible evidence showing that he or she
could not, in fact, attain the standard, whereas under the objective version, it cannot be sidelined. See chapter 3.6 and 3.7 above.

[66] See Michael Smith, 'Responsibility and Self-Control', 18: 'An agent who, though capable
of acting intentionally, remains a victim of circumstance is someone who, on the one hand,
has the capacity to act on his desires and intentions, but is also someone who, on the other
hand, has desires and intentions that are beyond the reach of the capacity he has for rational
self-control.'

he said:

I should be sorry to countenance the notion that the mere fact that an insane impulse is not resisted is to be taken as proof that it is irresistible. In fact, such impulses are continually felt and resisted, and I do not think they ought to be any greater excuse for crime than the existence of other motives, so long as the power of control or choice . . . remains.[67]

There is, though, perhaps something of an air of unreality about the notion that jurors can satisfactorily imagine what it might be like to have to resist an insane impulse with the powers of self-restraint they themselves possess (although, in practice, this kind of question may often serve as a heuristic device for testing whether D3 him- or herself could have kept the impulse in check).[68] Moreover, not enough is being done to treat D with true concern, in such cases, as someone capable of suffering and frustration, if one insists on such a judgment in accordance with the objective version of the capacity theory. So, the issue should be, as dictated by the subjective version of the capacity theory, whether D3 *him- or herself* could have been expected to keep the irrational desire in check.

The notoriously badly drafted English provisions defining diminished responsibility are apt to cover all these cases (D1's; D2's; D3's) alike.[69] By section 2 of the Homicide Act 1957:

Where a party kills or is a party to the killing of another, he shall not be convicted of murder if he was suffering from such abnormality of mind . . . as substantially impaired his mental responsibility for his acts or omissions in doing or being party to a killing.

'Substantial impairment', here, includes the case where the effect of a mental abnormality is to sweep aside the rational powers of control that D is in other respects perfectly capable of deploying (D3's case), and may have tried to employ, because his or her pathological desire to experience (say) strangling someone is impossible to resist, and so forth. Most importantly, though, the ambiguous nature of the link then made in section 2 between 'substantial impairment', 'mental responsibility', and D's 'acts or omissions in doing or being party to a killing', permits a jury to tie the degree of impairment required for a successful plea to moral consideration of the nature of what D has done. In other words, the section can be read as saying that what matters is whether D's abnormality of mind substantially reduced his *culpability* respecting his role in the killing, rather than as saying that what matters is simply whether D was suffering from a substantial impairment of mental functioning at the time of the

---

[67] Sir J. F. Stephen, *A History of The Criminal Law of England*, ii, 172.
[68] Something explicitly contemplated in *R v Byrne* [1960] 2 QB 396.
[69] On the inadequacies of the drafting, see E. Griew, 'Reducing Murder to Manslaughter: whose Job?', 19–20.

killing. The former is the 'wide' and the latter the 'narrow' view of the defence.[70] The difference between the two views can be brought out by distinguishing cases in which D him- or herself kills, and cases in which D is a mere party to a killing. Where, as in *R v Byrne*,[71] D has mutilated and killed V, the 'wide' view of the defence would require a much higher degree of mental impairment—in this case, much greater evidence of the irresistibility of the force of D's pathological desires—than if, say, under instructions from the domineering D4 the mentally sub-normal D5 (knowing of D4's intentions, but completely in awe of D4) procured a knife with which D4 then stabbed V. On the 'wide' view of the defence, the fact that D5's involvement in the killing is, *ex hypothesi*, less morally significant than D4's (or D3's) can reduce the extent to which the abnormality of mind factor must *by itself* contribute to the case for a partial excuse for that killing. On the 'narrow' view of the defence, by way of contrast, the same—'substantial'—degree of mental impairment ought in theory to be required in each case, without regard to the role in the killing that D played. In practice, the adoption of the 'wide' view by juries (and by prosecutors accepting D's plea in advance of trial) has had a very significant effect in broadening the defence, to encompass cases in which evidence of an abnormality of mind is allowed to combine with other mitigating factors to justify a manslaughter verdict. In effect, judges and juries often treat a plea of diminished responsibility as if it was a plea of diminished capacity.

Section 2 appears to be saying that D's abnormality of mind must, *by itself*, be sufficient substantially to diminish D's mental responsibility for his or her involvement in the killing (the 'narrow' view). English courts have certainly taken this approach when Ds have sought, in order to establish substantial impairment, to combine evidence of mental disorder with evidence of voluntary intoxication. The courts have ruled that the effects of the intoxication must be ignored in deciding whether there was such impairment, and that the jury must focus solely on the effects of the abnormality of mind.[72] More broadly, though, the adoption of the 'wide' view has been common since the introduction of the defence (and is not expressly ruled out by section 2). For example, Mackay's study of homicide cases in which both provocation and diminished responsibility had been pleaded together, showed that juries have been quite happy to return manslaughter verdicts

---

[70] See E. Griew, 'The Future of Diminished Responsibility' [1988] *Criminal Law Review*, 75, 77–81; Jeremy Horder, 'Between Provocation and Diminished Responsibility', 146–147, distinguishing a wide from a narrow theory of diminished responsibility. Proposals to reform section 2 have, by and large, concentrated on the narrow view, by making it tolerably clear that the nature and degree of D's mental disorder must *in itself* be sufficient to reduce murder to manslaughter: see the discussion in Law Commission for England and Wales, *Partial Defences to Murder*, 238–240.   [71] *R v Byrne* [1960] 2 QB 396.
[72] See now, *R v Dietschmann* [2003] 2 WLR 613 (HL); and G. R. Sullivan, 'Intoxicants and Diminished Responsibility' [1994] *Criminal Law Review* 156; Law Commission for England and Wales, *Partial Defences to Murder*, 149–153.

based on a combination of both factors. Indeed, in some cases, so difficult to disentangle have been the issues that judges have themselves regarded a 'mixed' verdict as entirely appropriate,[73] even though the higher courts have continued to suppose that diminished responsibility is concerned with purely 'internal' factors (i.e. the abnormality of mind) rather than 'external' ones, like provocation.[74] As Mackay and Mitchell now put it, 'it is likely that the reason why the impairment of mental responsibility was substantial will be, at least in part, because of the provocation'.[75] Cases involving provocation aside, there has for a long time been evidence that verdicts of manslaughter by reason of diminished responsibility have been brought in, in cases involving 'the depressed mercy killer'.[76] Indeed, in revising the definition of diminished responsibility, the Criminal Law Revision Committee was particularly concerned that such cases should not be excluded,[77] even though it seems obvious that most such cases will be successful only on the basis of a mixture of evidence of mental disorder *and* the exceptional pressure of external circumstances.[78] Lest this be thought to be, in general, an English aberration, the legal basis for such a 'mixed' approach to diminished responsibility, treating it as encompassing diminished capacity pleas, can be found in the way that equivalent provisions have been understood in the USA.[79]

According to the famous Model Penal Code definition, D may be convicted of manslaughter rather than of murder if:

A homicide . . . is committed under the influence of extreme mental or emotional disturbance for which there is reasonable explanation or excuse. The reasonableness of

---

[73] *R v Matheson* [1958] 2 All ER 87, discussed in R. D. Mackay, 'Pleading Provocation and Diminished Responsibility Together'.

[74] See *R v (Morgan) Smith* [2000] 4 All ER 289, 296 (per Lord Slynn), 'whereas provocation depends on a consideration of facts external to the accused, such as the acts of the deceased, the defence of diminished responsibility does not'.

[75] R. D. Mackay and B. J. Mitchell 'Provoking Diminished Responsibility: Two Pleas Merging Into One?', 756.

[76] Mackay's phrase: see R. D. Mackay, 'Diminished Responsibility and Mentally Disordered Killers', 79. As Mackay puts it, 79: 'Such cases when they come within Section 2 do so by means of a benign conspiracy between psychiatrists and trial judges which involves stretching the medical evidence in order to ensure that deserving cases do not attract a murder conviction'. Mackay found that between 1982 and 1991, of the twenty-two homicides described as mercy killings, only one ended in a conviction for murder.

[77] Criminal Law Revision Committee, *Offences Against the Person*, para 92.

[78] As Simester and Sullivan put it, in A. P. Simester and G. R. Sullivan, *Criminal Law: Theory and Doctrine*, 1st edn., 582: 'Killings induced by abusive relationships, troublesome neighbours, familial stresses, compassion for the painfully and terminally ill, and the like may . . . be recorded as manslaughter. Diagnostic labels such as reactive depression, post-traumatic stress disorder, and morbid jealousy are sufficiently accommodating, if not interrogated too closely, to encompass essentially ordinary reactions to stressful life events'.

[79] The discussion that follows relies almost wholly on the sources and commentary provided by Joshua Dressler in his admirable chapter on the 'mixed' defence, in Joshua Dressler, *Understanding Criminal Law*, 3rd edn., chapter 26.

such explanation or excuse shall be determined from the viewpoint of a person in the actor's situation under the circumstances as he believes them to be.[80]

The provision commonly forms the basis for the plea of provocation. Yet, in some US States, it has been permitted to establish a diminished capacity defence, something anticipated by the Model Penal Code in that the effects of mental disorder as a kind of 'extreme mental . . . disturbance' are referred to explicitly in the commentary on the Code.[81] Understandably enough, though, the limitation of extreme mental or emotional disturbances to those with a *'reasonable* explanation or excuse' has given rise to difficulty in explaining the diminished capacity application of the provision. It is hard to see how considerations of 'reason' come in to the question whether or not one had a mental disorder of an especially severe kind.[82] The way that the courts have met this point is what is of interest in the present context. In *State v Dumlao*,[83] D sought to introduce evidence that he suffered from a paranoid personality disorder that led him to experience 'unwarranted suspiciousness' and unusual sensitivity to criticism. Having formed an irrational suspicion that his wife was being unfaithful, he killed V when his brother-in-law and father sought to discuss his suspicions with him. The appellate court ruled that there was evidence sufficient to warrant a direction on the extreme mental or emotional disturbance defence.[84] The Court explained that the need for a reasonable explanation or excuse for the extreme mental or emotional disturbance could be met by consideration of 'the subjective, internal situation in which the defendant found himself and the external circumstances as he perceived them at the time, however inaccurate that perception may have been . . . '.[85] The final words of this passage are obviously open to criticism, in that, if D's inaccurate perception of events itself stems from his mental disorder, it should be counted as an internal and not as an external factor. Nonetheless, it is the way that situational factors are envisaged as combining with evidence of mental abnormality to amount to a 'reasonable explanation or excuse' for extreme mental or emotional disturbance that is the significant lesson to be learned from this example.[86]

---

[80] American Law Institute, Model Penal Code para 210.3(1)(b).

[81] American Law Institute, Comment to para 210.3, 71. See Joshua Dressler, *Understanding Criminal Law*, 3rd edn., 368.   [82] See ibid., 369.

[83] (1986) 715 P 2nd 822, discussed by Joshua Dressler, *Understanding Criminal Law*, 3rd edn., 369.

[84] See further Dressler's discussion of *Fisher v US* (1946) 328 US 463, in Joshua Dressler, *Understanding Criminal Law*, 3rd edn., 370–371.

[85] (1986) 715 P 2nd 822, 830. See further *State v Wolff* (1964) 61 Cal 2nd 795, in which the question was said to be whether D is unable to 'maturely and meaningfully reflect on the gravity of his contemplated act'. The use of evidence of provocation in 'jealous partner' cases of diminished capacity is critically examined in the next section.

[86] In many English cases, juries have taken precisely the same approach to diminished responsibility, usually with no objection raised by the prosecution or the trial judge: see R. D. Mackay, 'Pleading Provocation and Diminished Responsibility Together'.

It is important to stress that it is not the case that, under the Model Penal Code (any more than in the English cases), 'anything goes' where mental abnormality is concerned. As Dressler points out, the commentary on the Model Penal Code itself says that there are bound to be cases in which, even if D is mentally disordered, the disorder 'should be regarded as having no just bearing on his liability'.[87] Accordingly, proposals to reform the diminished responsibility defence in England and Wales have sought to lay similar emphasis on the need for the mental disorder or disturbance to be sufficiently severe to warrant reducing murder to manslaughter. Mackay and Mitchell's re-modelled section 2 runs on just such lines:

A defendant who would otherwise be guilty of murder is not guilty of murder if, the jury considers that at the time of the commission of the offence, he was:

under the influence of extreme emotional disturbance and/or
suffering from unsoundness of mind

either or both of which affected his criminal behaviour to such a material degree that the offence ought to be reduced to one of manslaughter.[88]

The inclusion, in this proposal, of 'extreme emotional disturbance', alongside unsoundness of mind, perhaps indicates that what Mackay and Mitchell have in mind is that D be judged in the light of the subjective version of the capacity theory. On this point, there is some ambiguity about the Model Penal Code. The Commentary on the Model Penal Code says that the defence, 'looks into the actor's mind to see whether he should be judged by a lesser standard than that applicable to ordinary men'.[89] If one assumes that all standards are largely or wholly objective, that explanation simply begs the question whether there are such things as lesser *standards* by which to judge D when an abnormality of mind is the explanation for his or her extreme mental or emotional disturbance. If, however, one extends one's understanding of judgement-in-accordance-with-a-standard to include standards that D him- or herself could reasonably be expected to meet, when extremely disturbed emotionally, there are no questions begged. The issue is

---

[87] American Law Institute, Comment on para 210.3, 72, cited by Joshua Dressler, *Understanding Criminal Law*, 3rd edn., 370.

[88] R. D. Mackay and B. J. Mitchell 'Provoking Diminished Responsibility: Two Pleas Merging Into One?', 758. A former proposal for reform of the defence, drafted by Mackay, is considered by the Law Commission for England and Wales, *Partial Defences to Murder*, 240. It is perhaps right to point out that there seems to be an ambiguity in the proposal surrounding the need for the emotional disturbance or unsoundness of mind to be affecting D's behaviour 'at the time of the commission of the offence', in so far as secondary parties before the fact are to be covered by the provision. It needs to be made clear that what matters is that a secondary party was suffering from the emotional disturbance or unsoundness of mind *at the time of his or her act of complicity*, not at the time that the offence itself was committed (which could be months, or even years, later).

[89] American Law Institute, Comment on para 210.3, 71, cited by Joshua Dressler, *Understanding Criminal Law*, 3rd edn., 368–369.

simply whether, putting evidence of provocation and extreme mental or emotional disturbance together (with the assistance of expert evidence), these factors had such an important bearing on D's conduct that it is just to regard them as having a bearing on the crime for which D is liable. In that regard, that the subjective version of the capacity theory is indeed the theory of excuse underlying the excuse of extreme emotional disturbance seems to be confirmed by the Commentary to this section of the Model Penal Code, which ends, 'to the extent . . . that the defective person is judged as if he were someone else [the reasonable person] the moral judgment underlying criminal conviction is undermined'.[90]

For Gardner and Macklem, no doubt, the objection to such a development—the creation of an excuse on rung 5 of my defence ladder, in chapter 3.1 above—would principally be that it confuses defences (provocation; diminished responsibility) with quite separate kinds of moral criteria bearing on desert of mitigation, by confusing excuses on rung 4 of the defence ladder with what ought to be regarded as denials of responsibility on rung 6.[91] One response to this objection, then, is to seek to preserve the sense in which there is something special about the criteria against which Ds are judged when pleading excuses on rung 4 of the ladder, such as provocation, because these are excuses governed by the objective version of the capacity theory, whilst leaving open the possibility that there can still be a rung 5 of the ladder, on which are located pleas with an excusatory element drawn from the provocation plea. In such instances, it is the *factual* element in a provocation plea, a loss of self-control (or some other factual element of an excusatory plea, such as fear of a threat), that is combined with evidence of mental disorder or deficiency to establish an adequate case (judged by the standards of the subjective version of the capacity theory) for what I am calling a diminished capacity excuse. There ought, thus, to be no moral confusion or ambiguity about the excuse of diminished capacity on rung 5. For, in such cases, the excusatory element constituted by the loss of self-control (or the fear of the threat, etc.) is now playing a qualitatively different—auxiliary and supporting— role from that which it plays in the provocation excuse itself on rung 4 of the ladder, justifying the court in reaching a conclusion that would not be warranted on the basis of evidence of mental abnormality or deficiency alone.[92]

[90] American Law Institute, Comment to para 210.3, 71.

[91] John Gardner and Timothy Macklem, 'Compassion Without Respect? Nine Fallacies in *R v Smith*', 627–630; John Gardner, 'The Gist of Excuses'.

[92] For further discussion of this point, see Jeremy Horder, 'Between Provocation and Diminished Responsibility', 163–166. I argue here that it is a provoked loss of self-control *simpliciter* that plays the auxiliary and supporting role referred to in the text. The gravity of the provocation must be irrelevant to an excusatory diminished responsibility plea, because to take it into account would be to muddle the separate moral criteria for excusatory diminished responsibility and for the defence of provocation. For discussion and criticism of this view, see R. D. Mackay and B. J. Mitchell 'Provoking Diminished Responsibility: Two Pleas Merging Into One?', 751–752.

5. Excuse and Mental Deficiency: the Case against Mixing Oil and Water

Even so, Gardner and Macklem give two related reasons why this kind of development of a defence of diminished capacity should be discouraged, and hence why one ought to shake oneself free of the illusion that there really is any plausibly excusatory element to a claim on rung 5 above. The first argument (one we encountered in chapter 3.3 above) is that there is no such case as a case of someone falling into a crack between the provocation and diminished responsibility pleas. For Gardner and Macklem, either someone must have a sufficient degree of mental normality to be judged by the standards of people adequately equipped with the powers of self-control relevant to a provocation plea, or that person must have a sufficient degree of mental abnormality to be classified as suffering from diminished responsibility. There is no half-way house, and hence no possibility that D can make up with factual evidence of a provoked loss of self-control what he or she lacks in terms of mental abnormality, or *vice versa*, either under section 2 of the Homicide Act 1957 (diminished responsibility) or under section 3 of that Act (provocation).[93] The argument harks back to Strawson's famous contrast between the 'reactive (moral) attitudes' appropriate for our approach to wrongdoing by fully sane and mature agents, and a more 'arm's length' moral assessment of wrongdoing by those suffering from a mental disorder, in which reactive attitudes have been suspended.[94] For Strawson, these approaches are, in theory, 'profoundly, opposed to each other',[95] as they are for Gardner and Macklem. Strawson was prepared to concede, though, that in some instances one's reaction might well be mixed.[96] So, one might, for example, say of a response to a threat by a sub-normal D, 'I can understand D being frightened (reactive attitude), but there is also something odd about the extent to which D was in thrall to the threatener (partial suspension of reactive attitude)'. In that regard, Gardner and Macklem's argument overlooks the possibility of an asymmetry between the provocation and the diminished responsibility pleas.

As I suggested at the end of section 4 above, it could be that whilst evidence of mental abnormality should have no bearing on the satisfaction of

---

[93] John Gardner and Timothy Macklem, 'Compassion without Respect? Nine Fallacies in *R v Smith*', 629–630. The argument echoes that of Lord Justice-General Normand, in *Kirkwood v Lord Advocate* [1939] JC 36, 40, 'The defence of impaired responsibility is somewhat inconsistent with the basic doctrine of our criminal law that a man, if sane, is responsible for his acts, and, if not sane, is not responsible.' See also R. F. Sparks, 'Diminished Responsibility in Theory and Practice' (1964) 27 *Modern Law Review* 9, 13. Philosophical support for the 'no half-way house' view, that has influenced Gardner's thinking on the matter, can be found in A. Kenny, 'Can Responsibility be Diminished?', in R. G. Frey and C. W. Morris (eds.), *Liability and Responsibility: Essays in Law and Morals* (Cambridge: Cambridge University Press, 1991).

[94] Sir P. F. Strawson, 'Freedom and Resentment', in Gary Watson (ed.), *Free Will* (Oxford: Oxford University Press, 1982) 59, 64–65, discussed in Jeremy Horder, 'Between Provocation and Diminished Responsibility', 163–165.   [95] Ibid., 65.

[96] Ibid., 66.

the objective condition in provocation cases, evidence of a provoked loss of self-control (*simpliciter*)—the factual element in an excusatory plea—can have a bearing on the question whether a conviction for murder is appropriate under section 2, given the mental abnormality from which D was also suffering. The provocation defence itself has, over the centuries, developed a high degree of moral integrity, being focused relatively narrowly on whether the provocation that led D to lose self-control and kill was so grave that it might have moved almost anyone with adequate powers of self-control to do likewise.[97] Maintaining that moral integrity depends on maintaining considerable exclusivity with regard to the salient moral considerations (in particular, the gravity of the provocation), in a way that is not true of a plea of diminished responsibility, even as it currently stands. To undermine the moral integrity of the provocation defence for the benefit of short-comers, then, would be to sacrifice too much for too little gain.[98] Where diminished responsibility is concerned, however, it could be that so long as evidence of mental abnormality remains an important part of D's plea[99] nothing much is necessarily lost, morally speaking, by permitting evidence of other exceptional pressures (like the experience of a provoked loss of self-control, or of being threatened[100]) to bolster D's claim that he or she is entitled to a second-degree conviction, in the circumstances. Indeed, one might go so far as to say that the influential presence of a mental abnormality makes it morally permissible to take excusatory account of other pressures on D that might not have counted in D's favour had he or she been mentally normal. Why?

The answer harks back to a point made right at the start. The intellectual labours of the common law, like those of the commentators on them, have been directed mainly at giving ever-greater moral clarity and sophistication to the legal understanding of a range of defences little changed in character

---

[97] See Andrew Ashworth, 'The Doctrine of Provocation'; Jeremy Horder, *Provocation and Responsibility*, chapters 1–4.

[98] See Jeremy Horder, 'Between Provocation and Diminished Responsibility', 161–166. It has been suggested that such moral integrity as the provocation defence retains, it retains only in virtue of a pretence that factors affecting the gravity of the provocation can be separated from factors affecting D's powers of self-control; and once that pretence has been exposed, the case for keeping provocation pleas separate from diminished responsibility pleas is undermined: see S. M. H. Yeo, *Unrestrained Killings and the Law* (Hong Kong: Oxford University Press, 1998), 60. The flaws in this attack on the case for separating pleas of provocation and diminished responsibility will be addressed in more detail in section 8 below.

[99] As I have already suggested (section 3 above), how important it must be may be permitted to depend, for example, on the degree of D's involvement in the crime, and the seriousness of the crime.

[100] Although some doubt will be cast, in section 7 below, on whether provocation in particular is evidence that should be permitted to influence the outcome of a diminished responsibility plea. If they are to be combined, in order to avoid 'moral contamination' of the provocation defence by the diminished responsibility defence, it needs to be made clear that evidence of a provoked loss of self-control is relevant to the latter defence only to show how, in combination with D's mental disorder, it explains how D *in fact* found it impossible to restrain him- or herself. The moral justification for D's loss of temper, as opposed to the mere fact that temper was lost, is irrelevant to a diminished capacity plea, whereas both are central to a provocation plea: see Jeremy Horder, 'Between Provocation and Diminished Responsibility', 165–166.

since classical times. What has always been missing from that set of intellectual concerns, a deficiency that post-Enlightenment thinking about penal
policy began to put right,[101] is a moral concern for the 'short-comer', including the person who, whilst not suffering from grossly impaired mental functioning, has a mental disorder or deficiency that makes it exceptionally
difficult to come up to standards that, for ordinary people, would be normal
or expected. For thinkers influenced by the classical tradition, short-comers
are people who, because they are not to be pitied as insane, are instead to
be blamed, if not for their short-comings then certainly for the fact that
on the occasion in question they came up short.[102] For post-Enlightenment
thinkers, by way of contrast, such an unyielding moral position fails to
show equal concern for the short-comer as someone capable, in Dworkin's
words, of 'suffering and frustration'.[103] Taking the 'narrow' view of diminished capacity effectively merges that defence with the defence of insanity
(giving one a broader insanity plea), leaving diminished capacity with no
distinctive role to play in the theory of mitigation and excuse, a role connected with concessions to short-comers.[104] By way of contrast, taking the
'wide' view of diminished responsibility, seeing it as a diminished capacity
claim, as courts in both the UK and the USA have consistently done (other,
quite rightly, than in cases where the added element is voluntary intoxication), is one way of accommodating a limited range of claims to partial
excuse by some kinds of short-comers. Mental abnormalities, and the influence they have on people's conduct, are matters of degree and almost always
influenced in some measure by so-called external factors of some kind. It is,
thus, unrealistic to expect a partial defence based on 'substantial impairment'
of mental functioning to retain a high degree of moral *integrity*, conceived as
a defence focused solely on internal disorders of the mind. Factors other than
mental disorder may be permitted to influence its operation, without a significant morally coarsening effect (just which other factors ought to be accommodated, and when, is discussed below). Nonetheless, it would be best to do
this through the development of a new, general, partial defence of diminished
capacity, to meet the claims of at least some kinds of short-comer without
moral distortion of the law's defence 'ladder', set out in chapter 3.1 above.

   That brings me to Gardner and Macklem's second argument against
diminished capacity verdicts propped up by evidence of provocation (or
other evidence of the pressure of circumstances), or *vice versa*. This is the
important argument from self-respect. Gardner and Macklem say:

[I]s it really compassionate to condescend to these rationally incapacitating conditions? A self-respecting defendant may think otherwise . . . Defendants . . . have an

---

[101] See e.g. the discussion in David Garland, *Punishment in Modern Society*, 270 and
290–292.   [102] See John Gardner, 'The Gist of Excuses', 586.
[103] See the discussion in section 1 above.
[104] See Suzanne Dell, 'Wanted: An Insanity Defence that can be Used' [1983] *Criminal Law
Review* 431, 433. R. D. Mackay and B. J. Mitchell 'Provoking Diminished Responsibility: Two
Pleas Merging Into One?', 756–759.

interest in being accorded their status as fully-fledged human beings, i.e. as creatures whose lives are rationally intelligible even when they go off the rails, and who can therefore give a rationally intelligible account of how they came to do so. Systematically to bring the criminal law's standards of judgment down to meet people's incapacities threatens this interest. It denies them the fully human measure by which to account for themselves and hold themselves out for judgment.[105]

Gardner and Macklem's argument echoes the views of the early, 'moralizing' Victorian thinkers about punishment, for whom, as Martin Weiner puts it, 'the most urgent need was to make people self-governing and . . . the best way to do so was to hold them, sternly and unblinkingly, responsible for the consequences of their actions'.[106] It is thus tempting to think of diminished responsibility as a defence embodying the contrasting, 'pathologizing' ethos of the late Victorian approach to crime, according to which greater emphasis was sympathetically to be placed on (as one contemporary commentator put it), 'an absence of power to resist criminal instincts and impulses . . . [because of] defective moral instincts . . . [that] combined with external circumstances of a more or less unfavourable character, have the effect of making juveniles what they are'.[107]

How convincing is it, though, to make a case for a sharp distinction between provocation and diminished responsibility based on an appeal to what the 'self-respecting' D (rather than the self-interested D concerned only to 'get off') may think?[108] The case seems convincing only if one makes a concern for D's self-respect an overriding concern, rather than simply one (very important) concern that must be reconciled with other important concerns, like fair labelling, in particular. Gardner and Macklem are no doubt right to imply that it would be a grotesque affront to anyone's sense of self-respect to be placed in a mental institution, or otherwise 'treated' rather than convicted, simply because they were (say) poor or from a disadvantaged social or religious group. In such cases, a concern for D's self-respect and a concern for fair labelling go hand-in-hand. There can, though, certainly be individual cases in which a concern for self-respect and a concern for fair labelling can come into conflict, and in which a concern for D's self-respect

---

[105] John Gardner and Timothy Macklem, 'Compassion without Respect? Nine Fallacies in *R v Smith*', 627; John Gardner, 'The Gist of Excuses', 588–593.

[106] M. Weiner, *Reconstructing the Criminal: Culture, Law and Policy in England 1830–1914* (Cambridge: Cambridge University Press, 1990), 55. David Garland, *Punishment in Modern Society*, 270. This was the view satirized by Butler in *Erehwon* (see chapter 3.2 n. 23, above).

[107] W. D. Morrison, *Juvenile Offenders* (New York: D Appleton & Co, 1897), 105–111, cited by M. Weiner, *Reconstructing the Criminal*, 362. See also Weiner's discussion of the difference of opinion between Baron Bramwell and Sir James Stephen over the propriety of introducing an 'irresistible impulse' defence: M. Weiner, *Reconstructing the Criminal*, 273–274. See further, K. J. M. Smith, *Lawyers, Legislators and Theorists: Developments in English Criminal Jurisprudence 1800–1957* (Oxford: Clarendon Press, 1998), chapter 10.

[108] For a further articulation of the 'self-respecting defendant' viewpoint, see John Gardner, 'In Defence of Defences', 257–262. For criticism, see R. D. Mackay and B. J. Mitchell 'Provoking Diminished Responsibility: Two Pleas Merging Into One?', 757.

must take second place to a concern for fair labelling. Suppose D is a judge famous for her scepticism about the scientific basis for diminished responsibility pleas, who has sentenced many offenders to prison having rejected as exaggerated or feigned their claims to require a medical rather than a punitive disposal. D, however, herself becomes severely mentally disordered due to illness, and kills, but then recovers fully by the time of the trial. D now seeks to insist that a plea of diminished responsibility or insanity is *not* made, because the humiliation at accusations of hypocrisy and double-standards will strip her of the last vestiges of her self-respect. In such a case, the question whether or not D's self-respect would be compromised by running the defence seems to be of marginal relevance to the question whether it should, in the interests of justice and fair labelling, in fact be run. More broadly there will be cases in which it is hard to say, given *only* the evidence of D's mental deficiency or disorder, whether we should expect D to acknowledge his or her wrongdoing in full (the self-respect issue), but, in which, when the evidence of mental disorder is combined with the pressure of circumstances in which D acted, it is also clear that it would be morally repugnant to convict of the first-degree offence (the fair labelling issue). In such cases, Gardner and Macklem do not do enough to establish a case for an overriding duty to treat D as a basically rational person who has gone off the rails, and who must thus not be permitted to employ his or her mental deficiency or disorder as a key plank in the structure of a partial excuse plea. The partial defence of excusatory diminished capacity provides a way out—and not, as we may now see, necessarily an easy one—of the dilemma posed by such cases.

6. Excusatory Diminished Responsibility: Provocation and Mental Deficiency

Cases on rung 5 of the defence 'ladder', set out in chapter 3.1 above, are pleas (in the terminology of chapter 2 above) that can involve explanatory or adopted reasons for action, and that combine ascriptive elements with elements of diminution of responsibility. They are governed by the subjective version of the capacity theory, the version that asks—as explained in chapter 3.7 above—what could reasonably have been expected of D him- or herself (rather than of a person well-equipped with the relevant rational powers), in the circumstances. For, in diminished capacity cases, as Gardner and Macklem say of diminished responsibility cases on rung 6 of the defence ladder, the Ds in question are, 'not quite among us, [they are people] who cannot quite provide an intelligible account of themselves, and whose susceptibility to the full range of human judgment is therefore in doubt'.[109] The focus is thus on D's mental condition and abilities, and in most conceivable

[109] John Gardner and Timothy Macklem, 'Compassion without Respect? Nine Fallacies in *R v Smith*', 627.

cases involves reliance on close psychiatric and/or social work assessment of the offender. What marks out diminished capacity cases on rung 5 of the ladder from diminished responsibility cases on rung 6 is that, in the former, there should be a moral element to that assessment. Someone's life history may indicate that although their mental disorder means they cannot be judged solely by rational standards,[110] they may be capable of some level of self-control or self-restraint respecting their mental disorder. If the assessment reveals that they have no such capability, the mental disorder will usually be in itself sufficient to justify conviction for a second-degree offence. In such a case, a plea of diminished responsibility is operating as a denial of responsibility, on rung 6 of the ladder. If they are capable of some degree of control, then the influence of the relevant 'external' circumstances on the commission of the offence, in determining (for the purposes of a diminished capacity plea, on rung 5 of the ladder) whether it would be morally wrong to convict D of the first-degree offence, becomes crucial.[111] This approach, characteristic of the 'wide' view of the *existing* diminished responsibility plea, explains how a successful plea can in some cases be consistent with conviction and (in my account of partial excuses, non-custodial) punishment, as well as, in other cases, a purely treatment-based disposal. What is appropriate depends on the extent to which the mental deficiency is doing the work in mitigation of the offence. On the 'narrow' view of the existing diminished responsibility plea, where the extent of D's mental deficiency must be substantial enough to do all that work, irrespective of the extent of D's involvement in the homicide (i.e. whether as perpetrator or remote secondary party), it is hard to see how conviction and punishment are justified at all.[112]

Be that as it may, in this section, I want to try to provide some guidance on the kinds of cases in which these external circumstances should exercise a telling influence, something currently lacking because of the continuing uncertainty over whether they have any relevance at all. I shall begin with

---

[110] If they can be judged by such standards, they should not be pleading an excuse on rung 5, but one on rung 3 or 4, where they are judged by the objective version of the capacity theory: see chapter 3.1 above (the excusatory 'ladder'), and chapter 3.6 and 3.7 above (the objective version of the capacity theory).

[111] The influence of those circumstances will also be crucial in determining whether, if D is successful in a plea of partial excuse on the grounds of diminished capacity, he or she should receive a straightforward non-custodial penalty, or whether some kind of treatment-based disposal is more appropriate.

[112] See Suzanne Dell, 'Wanted: An Insanity Defence that can be Used', 433. In England, in over 30 per cent of cases in which a diminished responsibility plea was successful, D received a prison sentence. This suggests that the plea is being used in many cases simply as a means of avoiding the mandatory life sentence. Ironically, in 12 per cent of cases, D was given a life sentence in any event: see Andrew Ashworth, *Principles of Criminal Law*, 3rd edn., 290. It seems that the Law Commission for England and Wales is not proposing to do anything about the issues raised by Dell, since its main concern is with the definition of diminished responsibility and the burden of proof, not with the sentencing options available to the judge: see Law Commission for England and Wales, *Partial Defences to Murder*, 237–242.

the influence of provoked losses of self-control on diminished capacity pleas. Mackay's research has yielded some telling revelations about the kinds of cases in which a plea of diminished responsibility has been successful, when combined with a provocation plea.[113] It is worth just giving a flavour of the cases Mackay examined, because of their striking similarity:

Case A: The defendant (D) who had a history of mental illness killed his wife (W) by hitting her on the head with a hammer. The offence was the culmination of prolonged marital strife, including repeated unfaithfulness and physical assaults on W's part . . . Case B: D, who was of low intellect, stabbed W during a marital row when she refused to abandon her paramour . . . Case C: D during an argument fatally stabbed the man W had run off with . . . Case D: D killed W by a blow to the head with a shovel after marital breakdown . . . Case E: D fatally stabbed W during one of many marital rows . . .[114]

The fact that in all these cases D was suffering from a mental disorder does not change the fact that he was obviously influenced by the kind of apparently 'normal' violent possessiveness and jealousy that characterizes so many defendants in provocation cases.[115] The internal experience of mental disorder can be heavily influenced by external circumstances, by culture, upbringing, and other factors that influence normal development and outlook: insane people do not nowadays claim to have been possessed by wolves.[116] If the influence of violent possessiveness is regarded as baneful in provocation cases, as it is,[117] is there any reason to change our attitude in diminished capacity cases, where D relies for partial excuse on a combination of evidence of mental disorder and a provoked loss of self-control? After a full review of the case law, Susan Edwards goes so far as to say of such cases that, 'Whichever way, reasonable man or unreasonable man, essentially what we have in this defence is moral culpability wrapped up in psychiatric nosology where instead anger, and rage and jealousy are the

---

[113] R. D. Mackay, 'Pleading Provocation and Diminished Responsibility Together'. The cases are from the period 1966–1976.

[114] R. D. Mackay, 'Pleading Provocation and Diminished Responsibility Together', 412–413.

[115] See Jeremy Horder, *Provocation and Responsibility*, chapter 9. For penetrating critique of the use of the existing diminished responsibility defence, in this regard, see Susan M. Edwards, *Sex and Gender in the Legal Process* (London: Blackstone Press, 1996), 400–406.

[116] For an incisive discussion, from a feminist viewpoint, see Deborah Cameron and Elizabeth Fraser, *The Lust to Kill* (Oxford: Basil Blackwell, 1987), chapter 4.

[117] See now, *R v (Morgan) Smith* [2000] 4 All ER 289, 309, 'Male possessiveness and jealousy should not today be an acceptable reason for loss of self-control leading to homicide, whether inflicted upon the woman herself or her new lover' (per Lord Hoffmann). Fine-sounding though it is, Mayo Moran has pointed out the difficulty of reconciling this passage from Lord Hoffmann's speech from much else that he says about the way that provocation should embrace what I am calling the subjective version of the capacity theory: see Mayo Moran, *Rethinking the Reasonable Person*, 216–220; Jeremy Horder, *Provocation and Responsibility*, 192–194. The courts have now resolved this difficulty by rejecting *Smith* and the subjective version of the capacity theory: see *A-G for Jersey V Holley* [2005] UKPC 23.

sickness'.[118] So, should a provoked loss of self-control, like evidence of voluntary intoxication, always be regarded as irrelevant to a plea of diminished capacity? I think the case for and the case against such a restrictive approach are evenly balanced.

One argument 'for' runs as follows. There are undoubtedly some mental disorders and deficiencies strongly associated with difficulty in controlling temper. It might seem unduly harsh, thus, to disadvantage people with such mental conditions by making a provoked loss of self-control irrelevant to their plea of diminished capacity, especially when the sword of Damocles constituted by the mandatory life sentence hangs overhead.[119] One could also seek to justify the relevance of provocation to diminished capacity claims, by making its relevance to a range of cases dependent on the seriousness of the offence (the partial excuse of diminished capacity could be available as a defence to more crimes than murder, according to my proposals).[120] One could then argue that the more serious the offence, the greater the moral weight that must be borne *solely* by evidence of the severity of mental disorder, if D is to deserve conviction of a second-degree offence. One could, in other words, seek to develop an approach in which, in cases where a provoked loss of self-control is the external factor, it is something close to the 'narrow' view of the existing diminished responsibility defence that must govern when a very serious offence of violence has been deliberately committed: D's claim must come close to satisfying a denial of responsibility claim on rung 6 of the defence 'ladder'. In such cases, whether D lost self-control having really been provoked in some way, as appears to have been the case in Mackay's examples, or merely—as in *State v Dumlao*[121]— irrationally believed that he or she had been provoked, has little or no moral significance. It is the extent of D's volitional or cognitive *deficiencies*, and not the adequacy of D's emotional intelligence, that would be the principal focus, where serious offences are in issue. The question would be, thus, whether D's abnormality of mind was in itself so severe, at the relevant time, that conviction for the first-degree offence is unwarranted notwithstanding the seriousness of the wrong done.[122]

Such an approach leaves open the possibility that the 'wide' view of the defence of diminished responsibility, a diminished capacity plea, could be permitted to govern when less serious offences are in issue. Suppose D's mental disorder leads him irrationally to believe that his wife, V, has bought

[118] Susan M. Edwards, *Sex and Gender in the Legal Process*, 402.

[119] See the argument in Jeremy Horder, 'Between Provocation and Diminished Responsibility', 163–166. See also, R. D. Mackay and B. J. Mitchell 'Provoking Diminished Responsibility: Two Pleas Merging Into One?', 757.

[120] See the end of section 3 above. See also Stephen J. Morse, 'Excusing and the New Excuse Defences: A Legal and Conceptual Review' (1998) 23 *Crime and Justice* 329, 397–402.

[121] (1986) 715 P. 2nd 822, discussed in section 4 above.

[122] So, in such cases, D must in effect establish a diminished responsibility plea on rung 6 of the ladder.

a vase as a present for her secret lover (all the evidence in fact points to the true conclusion, which is that the vase is for V herself). He confronts V, who confesses to the affair, upon which D loses self-control and smashes the vase. In such a case, D's mental disorder, that explains his irrational belief, is part of what may contribute to the case for a partial defence; but, given that a less serious crime (criminal damage) is in issue, in substantiating his plea of diminished capacity, it might not seem wrong to permit D to combine such evidence of mental disorder with evidence of the fact that he lost self-control upon provocation.[123] Further, as indicated in chapter 2.12 above, one can bolster the case for a partial excuse in all 'mixed' cases by drawing an excusatory distinction between provocation cases in which D acts for an explanatory reason, reacting immediately and 'instinctively' to a sudden loss of self-control, and provocation cases in which D acts for an adopted reason, allowing his or her rage to dictate his or her priorities. It was suggested that a much stronger case for mitigation might have to be made in provocation cases where D acts for an adopted reason, rather than for an explanatory reason.[124] One could make this point central to diminished capacity cases in which D seeks to combine evidence of provoked anger with that of mental deficiency, by restricting such pleas to instances in which there is evidence that D has acted for an explanatory reason. Such a restriction would go some way to dilute the strength of the strategic objections to permitting such 'mixed' pleas, objections we will consider shortly.

7. The Case for Separating Evidence of Provocation and of Mental Deficiency

What about the case against taking this more generous view? The weighty gender issues (discussed in section 6 above), raised by the typical case in which D wishes to combine evidence of a provoked loss of self-control with evidence of mental deficiency, certainly militate against taking the generous view. Although it was clear when the existing partial defence of diminished responsibility was created for England and Wales, that it was not intended to be a partial excuse for (essentially, sane) men who fly into jealous rages, the irony is that mental disorder or deficiency can become the mechanism unleashing such homicidal rages in just the kind of cases that give most

---

[123] See the end of section 3 above for discussion of the importance of distinguishing between the *fact* of a provoked loss of self-control (which may be relevant to a diminished capacity plea), and the *gravity* of the provocation (which is relevant only to a provocation plea). This is essentially the case I make for permitting 'mixed' pleas in Jeremy Horder, 'Between Provocation and Diminished Responsibility'.

[124] See chapter 2.12 above, and the discussion of this issue in Stephen Gough, 'Taking the Heat out of Provocation'. See also chapter 2.13 above for an alternative way of restricting the scope of the provocation plea, in cases where D acts for an adopted reason.

cause for gender-based concern.[125] Furthermore, even in murder cases, what is often so striking about instances in which evidence of mental disorder is combined with evidence of a provoked loss of self-control, is the mundane character of the incident that led to the loss of self-control and the deliberate killing: a marital row, or, in one recent English case, an argument about whether V had stolen some of D's tools and fishing equipment.[126] There is a strong case for saying that, whether or not D understandably had greater difficulty in controlling him- or herself than a mentally better equipped person would have done in such cases, it devalues the currency of excuse—even the currency of mere partial excuse—to permit evidence of volitional or cognitive defect to be bolstered by evidence of a provoked loss of self-control. So, the strategic considerations constituted by the maintenance of moral respect amongst citizens both for their obligations (common good (ii), chapter 1.2 above) and also for the conditions in which excuses for breaching those obligations are appropriately granted (common good (i), chapter 1.2 above), seems to be under threat when Ds are permitted to mount a case for partial excuse by combining evidence of a provoked loss of self-control with evidence of mental deficiency.

If that was not damning enough, such cases also raise in a particularly acute form the spectre of irresolvable doubt hanging over the question whether 'repeat players' have genuinely satisfied the requirement of spontaneity of response to what ought, if the excuse is to have moral plausibility, to have been a unique situation in their lives. If diminished capacity pleas remain confined to murder cases (although, on my account, they would not be), this issue is obviously not a 'floodgates' one, since only a tiny number of offenders commit homicide on more than one occasion, but it is a moral problem irrespective of the numbers of offenders involved. The moral force of an excusatory claim may be significantly undermined if D seeks to plead it again, having already done so in similar circumstances. There is a considerable risk that D will, on the subsequent occasion(s), be partly guided by what he or she thinks are the legal requirements, rather than responding more or less spontaneously as his or her emotions dictate; and to be guided by the legal requirements of an excuse is to cut away from under one the moral ground on which the excuse is founded. An example that comes close to raising this issue is *R v Hegarty*.[127] In this case, D was charged with robbery, and pleaded duress. He claimed that some men who had accommodated him while he had been 'on the run' previously attacked him, and threatened his family with violence unless he committed the crimes. The prosecution alleged

---

[125] For discussion of Parliamentary intention to exclude 'the mere outburst of rage or jealousy' from the scope of section 2 of the Homicide Act 1957, see the helpful discussion in: Law Commission for England and Wales, *Partial Defences to Murder*, 140–141. For a discussion of the gender politics of mental disorder, see Deborah Cameron and Elizabeth Fraser, *The Lust to Kill*, chapter 4.   [126] *R v (Morgan) Smith* [2000] 4 All ER 289.

[127] [1994] Crim LR 353 (CA).

that the claim was a pack of lies. In support of his plea, however, D sought to put in evidence the testimony of two medical witnesses who would testify to his mental instability. By (no doubt) an extraordinary coincidence, at a previous trial for the murder of his wife, he had secured the admission of medical evidence to the effect that he was 'emotionally unstable' and in a 'grossly elevated neurotic state', evidence that helped him on that occasion to obtain an acquittal on the murder charge and conviction for manslaughter on the grounds of diminished responsibility. If D, or his family, *really* had been threatened with serious bodily harm (or if D reasonably believed that they had), then, on a charge of robbery, D could have satisfied the elements of the defence of duress without having to rely on evidence of mental deficiency or disorder. That evidence would, at best, have been of relevance (and marginal relevance at that) only to the factual or subjective question whether D was moved to act by fear of the threats. So, one may conclude, the evidence alleged to show mental disorder or deficiency was likely to have been intended to act as little more than a convenient smokescreen or distraction, a smokescreen or distraction whose utility had been made manifest by the success of similar evidence in D's trial for the murder of his wife.[128]

Were it possible, for the purposes of a diminished capacity plea, to combine evidence of mental abnormality with evidence of a provoked loss of self-control in relation to a wide range of offences, the 'repeat player' problem raised by cases like *Hegarty* would inevitably crop up more frequently, with a consequent risk that the law might be brought into disrepute, threatening common goods (i) and (v) (chapter 1.2 above). As Jill Peay puts it, 'Offenders may be only too willing to have their behaviour treated as "uncontrollable" if there is an anticipated benefit of so doing',[129] a possibility acknowledged by Buchanan and Virgo, who observe that, 'The diagnosis of a psychiatric condition depends partly on observation but largely on listening to what the patient says. The possibility arises that people would avail themselves of [a] defence . . . simply by describing the symptoms'[130] thus also threatening common good (v). There are, though, ways of meeting this difficulty, and hence seeking to preserve the common goods at stake. As indicated in the previous section, diminished capacity pleas of the kind currently being discussed could be confined to instances in which D acted for an explanatory reason, rather than an adopted reason (the onus being on D to provide evidence that he or she acted for an explanatory reason), so as to ensure that D is not partially excused except when he or she has reacted in a purely spontaneous and instantaneous way. More realistically, perhaps, another way of meeting the difficulty is to permit the prosecution to lead

---

[128] In *Hegarty*, the Court of Appeal held that the evidence had been rightly excluded by the trial judge, and D's conviction was upheld; and the decision on this point seems vindicated by the decision of the Privy Council in *A-G for Jersey v Holley* [2005] UKPC 23.

[129] Jill Peay, 'Mentally Disordered Offenders', 775.

[130] Alec Buchanan and Graham Virgo, 'Duress and Mental Abnormality', 518.

evidence of previous attempts by D, whether or not successful, to plead diminished capacity (or provocation) when the circumstances in which the previous attempt—whether or not successful—are sufficiently similar to the current case for their probative value in undermining D's defence to outweigh their considerable prejudicial effect. Before the passing of the Criminal Justice Act 2003, whether or not, and if so in what circumstances, such a course was permitted was a difficult question to answer, because of the notoriously eccentric wording of the Criminal Evidence Act 1898.[131] In particular, it was held that the prosecution may not cross-examine using evidence that D learned from a previous trial how to deploy a defence claim to best advantage, in similar circumstances, if he or she was acquitted on the previous occasion, although (*scilicet*) this would have been permissible if D had been convicted.[132] It may be that the 'bad character' provisions of the Criminal Justice Act 2003, substituting broad inclusionary permissions to lead evidence of bad character, alongside an exclusionary discretion, will put an end to such arbitrary distinctions. Placing such an evidential weapon in the hands of the prosecution would go a long way to ensuring that a diminished capacity defence was not abused. It is, then, perhaps something of an irony that, in murder cases, the law has reached a state of development approaching the more generous view, through the development of the doctrine of provocation, on rung 4 of the defence ladder set out in chapter 3.1 above, rather than through a wide reading of the existing defence of diminished responsibility.

8. Up the Garden Path: Being Generous through the Provocation Defence

In common with many other jurisdictions, English law restricts the availability of a plea of provocation to murder cases, in which D lost self-control in circumstances where a reasonable person might also have lost self-control and killed. The propriety of this 'reasonable person test' restriction has been the subject of considerable debate.[133] Central to its justification is not, or not only, a concern about the possibility of false claims of loss of self-control not being completely disproved by the prosecution, and hence leading

---

[131] See, in general, Colin Tapper, *Cross and Tapper on Evidence*, 9th edn. (London: Butterworths, 1999), 390–392.

[132] On this, under the law as it stood before the Criminal Justice Act 2003, see *R v Cokar* [1960] 2 QB 207. But see also *R v Z* [2000] 3 WLR 117. Where this left a D who was acquitted of murder, but convicted of voluntary manslaughter was unclear.

[133] Recent contributions to the debate include S. M. H. Yeo, *Unrestrained Killings and the Law*, 60–61, J. Gardner and T. Macklem, 'Compassion Without Respect? Nine Fallacies in *R v Smith*'; R. D. Mackay and B. J. Mitchell, 'Provoking Diminished Responsibility: Two Pleas Merging Into One?'. For a seminal early discussion, see Andrew Ashworth, 'The Doctrine of Provocation'. For more general discussion, see Law Commission for England and Wales, *Murder, Manslaughter and Infanticide*, Part 5.

directly to an acquittal of murder.[134] It is the idea that provocation is, like duress, by its nature a 'two-pronged' excuse. Aside from the factual element, i.e. the loss of self-control itself (the first prong), the very thing that excuses in provocation cases is the judgment that, by losing control of the urge to kill, D did not depart from the standards adequately self-controlled people observe in their temper-keeping (the second prong). As a result of the decision of the House of Lords in *DPP v Camplin*,[135] this 'second prong' of the excuse became governed by the objective version of the capacity theory (see chapter 3.6 above). In other words, D's loss of control of the urge to kill was to be judged by the standards for temper-keeping observed by those with appropriately developed powers of self-control, a yardstick that could be used in cases where (as in *Camplin* itself), there was a lower-but-still-objectively-valid standard of temper-keeping by which it would be morally right to judge D, on account of his or her age or some other analogous factor.[136] In *(Morgan) Smith*,[137] however, the law was temporarily modified to permit the jury to apply, in effect, the subjective version of the capacity theory whenever they thought it just to do so. As Lord Hoffmann put it, in the 'Dworkinian' language of competing principles:

The general principle is that the same standards of behaviour are expected of everyone, regardless of their psychological make-up ... But the jury should in an appropriate case be told ... that this is a principle and not a rigid rule. It may sometimes have to yield to a more important principle, which is to do justice in the particular case. So the jury may think that there was some characteristic of the accused ... which affected the degree of control which society could reasonably have expected of *him* and which it would be unjust not to take into account.[138]

In this passage, we see Lord Hoffmann watering down the commitment to the objective version of the capacity theory, endorsed in *Camplin*. He purports to do this in the interests of allowing a jury freedom to do justice (as they see it) in an individual case in which, say, a mental abnormality or

---

[134] For this defence of the condition, see H. L. A. Hart, *Punishment and Responsibility*, 33. One should not, though, dismiss this objection out of hand. Provocation cases often involve no witness to the events leading up to the killing other than D and V, and it is well-known that problems have arisen in virtue of the fact that the jury is necessarily reliant on D's own account of events in court. The fact that D now loses his shield against cross-examination on his character if he blackens the name of the victim only in part meets the difficulties. Moreover, one cannot so easily infer from the fact that a reasonable person would not have lost control that D did not. So, it is no answer to the objection to say that the 'reasonable person' test can play the kind of evidentiary role that it does when a fact-finder is deciding whether, say, D intended or foresaw something.   [135] *DPP v Camplin* [1978] AC 705.

[136] See the decision of the Court of Appeal in *DPP v Camplin* [1978] 1 QB 254, 261, 'youth, and the immaturity which naturally accompanies youth, are not deviations from the norm; they are norms through which we must all of us have passed before attaining adulthood and maturity' (per Bridge LJ). In the House of Lords, gender was mentioned as a factor that might affect the general standard of self-control that could be expected, although it is not clear why, and this view has been rightly rejected by the High Court of Australia: see *Stingel v R* (1990) 171 CLR 312, 331.

[137] *R v (Morgan) Smith* [2000] 4 All ER 289. The decision was effectively overruled in *A-G for Jersey v Holley* [2005] UKPC 23.   [138] Ibid., 313 (Lord Hoffmann's emphasis).

deficiency meant that D him- or herself could not have been expected to reach the kind of standard of self-control that would have led a mentally well-equipped person to hold their temper in check, in the circumstances. In such a case, what matters is whether, as the subjective version of the capacity theory dictates, more could have been expected of D *him- or herself*, with his or her particular capacities.

Accordingly, Lord Hoffmann sees no reason to criticize the decision of the Court of Appeal in *R v Dryden*,[139] in which D, an eccentric and obsessive individual, had become fixated with the idea that the planning authorities were prejudiced against him, even though (as he was aware) he was in flagrant breach of the planning regulations. Dryden deliberately shot dead a planning officer visiting the property in question in order to demolish it in accordance with an enforcement notice. The Court of Appeal quashed the murder conviction, on the grounds that the jury should have been directed to take account of psychiatric evidence of D's eccentricity and obsessiveness, in considering D's provocation plea. Crucially, the Court of Appeal drew no distinction between the relevance of D's eccentricity and obsessiveness to the gravity of the 'provocation' constituted by the planning officer's actions, and the relevance of these characteristics to the level of self-control that D could have been expected to maintain: a failure turned into a positive virtue by Lord Hoffmann, in *(Morgan) Smith*.[140] On Lord Hoffmann's view, the jury was entitled to be told (putting it in the language of the theories employed hitherto: see chapter 3.6 above), that whilst the objective version of the capacity theory is ordinarily the right theory to apply, with the result that D is to be judged by the standards of those with adequately developed powers of self-control, it is for the jury to decide if justice demands that the subjective version be applied instead. If the jury decides on the latter course, the result is that D is judged (assisted, if need be, by expert evidence concerning D's condition) by the standards he or she was him- or herself to be regarded as capable of reaching, bearing his or her (*ex hypothesi*, abnormal) characteristics in mind.[141]

The gloss on *Camplin* introduced by *(Morgan) Smith* was meant to avoid confronting the jury with the supposedly difficult distinction between the characteristics of D that are relevant to the gravity of the provocation,[142] and those characteristics (if any) affecting D's level of self-control.[143] This approach found its way into clause 58 of the Draft Criminal code for England and Wales 1989, which requires no more than that, 'the provocation is, in all the circumstances (including any of his personal characteristics

---

[139] [1995] 4 All ER 987.   [140] *R v (Morgan) Smith* [2000] 4 All ER 289, 310.

[141] This kind of approach is defended as an approach to duress cases by Alec Buchanan and Graham Virgo, 'Duress and Mental Abnormality', 529–531.

[142] Which are in all cases relevant: see *R v Morhall* [1995] 3 All ER 659.

[143] Which were, after *Camplin*, not (other than in the case of age and gender) relevant in a provocation case, but which could be relevant to a plea of diminished responsibility.

that affect its gravity), sufficient ground for the loss of self-control'.[144] Under this formulation, the characteristics the jury may take into account are not limited to those bearing on the gravity of the provocation, and may—through the requirement to have regard to 'all the circumstances'— include characteristics affecting D's level of self-control. Even so, the problem with *(Morgan) Smith* is that it replaces the usually perfectly intelligible distinction between characteristics affecting the gravity of the provocation, and characteristics affecting levels of self-control, with an almost unintelligible distinction. By way of contrast with the generous view taken of a provocation plea as it arose on the facts in *R v Dryden*, in *(Morgan) Smith*, Lord Hoffmann held that in a case in which D's obsession is rooted in 'male possessiveness and jealousy',[145] the jury is to be directed to ignore those characteristics. In the Australian case of *Stingel v R*,[146] D became obsessed by a woman who had ended their relationship. He stalked her, and she obtained a court order restraining him from coming near her. In breach of the order, seeing her in a car with another man, he went to his car, fetched a knife, and stabbed the man to death. The High Court of Australia held that the trial judge had been right to withdraw the issue of provocation from the jury. Lord Hoffmann, agreeing with this result, suggests that in a similar case in England, although the question of provocation must be put to the jury, 'a direction that characteristics such as jealousy and obsession should be ignored in relation to the objective element is the best way to ensure that people like Stingel cannot rely upon the defence'.[147] Why is it, though, that D's obsessive behaviour is to be taken into account in cases such as *Dryden*, whereas it is to be ignored in cases like *Stingel*? Surely, the *source* of D's obsession (planning controls, as opposed to relationship failure) cannot intelligibly be regarded as the distinguishing mark?[148] If not, the difference between the two cases can only be the extent to which D's obsession is explained by mental disorder (although that explanation is not to be found in Lord Hoffmann's speech).[149] It is, though, hard to see why that distinction is not regarded as one whose moral significance relates primarily to the strength of the case for a finding of diminished responsibility (on rung 6 of the defence ladder, set out in chapter 3.1 above) or of diminished capacity (on rung 5 of the ladder, where the fact of loss of self-control is relevant), rather than to a finding that D had been so *gravely*

---

[144] Law Commission for England and Wales, *A Criminal Code for England and Wales*, Law Com no. 177, (1989) clause 58.

[145] Lord Hoffmann's terms: see *R v (Morgan) Smith* [2000] 4 All ER 289, 309.

[146] *Stingel v R* (1990) 171 CLR 312.

[147] *R v (Morgan) Smith* [2000] 4 All ER 289, 309. The Court of Appeal has already seen fit to ignore this part of Lord Hoffmann's speech: see *R v Weller* [2003] Crim LR 724, saying (per Mantell LJ), that 'characteristics such as jealousy remain with the jury as matters which fall for consideration in connection with the second objective element of provocation'.

[148] See the incisive discussion in Mayo Moran, *Rethinking the Reasonable Person*, 216–220.

[149] This explanation of the distinction appealed to the Privy Council in *Paria v The State* [2003] UKPC 36.

UNIVERSITY OF WINCHESTER LIBRARY

provoked that he could not reasonably have been expected to restrain an urge to kill.[150]

For sure, in retrospect, too little was said in *Camplin* to indicate that factors other than age may lower the level of self-control that can be expected of someone with perfectly ordinarily developed powers of self-control, such as the cumulative effect of (say) violent or abusive behaviour over a long period. Sometimes, the effect of such factors may be to produce in D what Simester and Sullivan helpfully call a 'life experience' syndrome,[151] a condition falling short of mental disorder, but which expert evidence may indicate is likely to lead D—as it would any normal person—to have a 'short fuse' until some time after D escapes from the abusive situation.[152] Such cases can fairly be judged through an application of the objective version of the capacity theory, because there is no need (to recall Strawson's language[153]) to suspend one's reactive attitudes in coming to a judgment. With expert assistance, if need be, a jury is perfectly capable of putting itself firmly in the shoes of a D whose powers of self-control have been eroded by long-term subjection to violence and/or abuse from which it has been impossible to escape, and then asking itself what kind of provocation might well spark off in D a loss of control of an urge to kill.[154] What is much more difficult for the jury, even with the benefit of expert evidence, is to imagine what it would be like to be a mentally disordered, eccentric person with an obsession about planning controls.[155] In some cases of this kind expert evidence can only show the extent to which the jury does indeed need to suspend its reactive attitudes if it is to understand D's behaviour; and that is an indication that it is diminished responsibility, on rung 6 of the defence ladder, that is, morally as well as legally speaking, the most appropriate plea. In other such cases, where D's mental deficiency is not quite so severe, the jury's attitude will be a mixed one—partly reactive (as far as D's provoked loss of self-control is concerned), and partly a suspension of reactive attitudes (with regard to D's mental deficiency). It is in such cases that the diminished capacity defence, on rung 5 of the defence ladder, is meant to come into its own, because the provocation defence was never intended to account for, and cannot (morally) be asked to account for, the range of mitigating circumstances at issue.

---

[150] See further, Jeremy Horder, 'Between Provocation and Diminished Responsibility', 161–166, and *A-G for Jersey v Holley* [2005] UKPC 23.

[151] A. P. Simester and G. R. Sullivan, *Criminal Law: Theory and Doctrine*, 1st edn., 351.

[152] In *R v (Morgan) Smith* [2000] 4 All ER 289, 307, Lord Hoffmann discusses a good example, the New Zealand case of *R v Rongonui* [2000] NZLR 385, in which D, who had developed post-traumatic stress disorder following a history of violence against her, stabbed a neighbour to death when the neighbour produced a knife in a non-threatening context. An English case coming close to this (although there was some provocation directed at the characteristic in question) is *R v Humphreys* [1995] 4 All ER 1008. See also *R v Emery* (1992) 14 Cr App Rep (S) 394; *R v Thornton* [1992] 1 All ER 306. For further discussion, see Jeremy Horder, 'Between Provocation and Diminished Responsibility', 158–161.

[153] Sir P. F. Strawson, 'Freedom and Resentment', in Gary Watson (ed.), *Free Will*, 64–65.

[154] See the discussion in Jeremy Horder, 'Between Provocation and Responsibility', 158–161 and in *A-G for Jersey v Holley* [2005] 2 AC 580, 594.

[155] The facts of *R v Dryden* [1995] 4 All ER 987.

An increasingly influential line of argument against this way of theorizing the provocation defence has been developed by Stanley Yeo, according to whom the distinction between characteristics affecting the gravity of provocation, and characteristics affecting levels of self-control, cannot be sustained because, 'it is inconsistent with the opinion of behavioural scientists that the accused's personality must be taken as a whole and cannot be dissected into the way he or she would view some provocative conduct on the one hand and the way he or she would respond emotionally to that conduct on the other'.[156] Invoking the opinion of (some) 'behavioural scientists' cannot be regarded, however, as shielding this line of argument from evaluative scrutiny, so that the argument becomes one to be won or lost solely on the balance of behavioural scientific evidence. Even if what Yeo's behavioural scientists say is true of those with mental disorders or deficiencies of certain kinds (who, on my account, should be pleading diminished capacity, in any event), the scientists' arguments will have to overcome a formidable methodological objection before we also accept them as an account of how mentally well-developed and well-equipped persons respond to provocation. Simply, the objection consists in the fact that behavioural science has mistakenly sought to challenge a distinction that, on the contrary, it ought to be seeking to explain. We saw in chapter 2 above that anger requires, in part, a biological account, because otherwise we would be unable to explain what Aristotle refers to as its 'material conditions'.[157] We also saw that the circumstances in which anger comes to be expressed, what Aristotle refers to as its 'form or account',[158] are influenced by environmental and cultural factors, and are hence amenable to social scientific (or behavioural) analysis. For mentally well-developed people, however, there is a value-laden, cognitive dimension to anger (an aspect of the way one 'views' provocative conduct, to use Yeo's language) that cannot be collapsed into the experience of feeling anger (an aspect of the way one 'responds emotionally' to anger, to use Yeo's language). Failure to attend to this distinction will inevitably lead into methodological error any purported scientific analysis of anger.

Consider this example. Suppose a Jewish person is angered by a tasteless joke about the Holocaust, intended as a 'put down', that he or she hears at a meeting. Now if, as Yeo says that the behavioural scientists are claiming, personality is indeed indivisible, so that it makes no sense to distinguish between the gravity of the provocation to someone, and that person's emotional reaction to it, this has the following consequence. Someone who says to the Jewish person, 'I am not surprised you became angry; that was an offensive remark', is to be regarded ('scientifically') as saying something that

---

[156] S. M. H. Yeo, *Unrestrained Killings and the Law*, 60. The passage just cited is relied on by R. D. Mackay and B. J. Mitchell, 'Provoking Diminished Responsibility: Two Pleas Merging Into One?', 746.
[157] Aristotle, *Rhetoric* 2.1012.11, in Jonathan Barnes, (trans.) *The Complete Works of Aristotle* (New Jersey: Princeton University Press, 1995).   [158] Ibid.

is, in effect, much the same as if they had said, 'I am not surprised you became angry; you were being emotional'. Both responses are true, but whereas the latter response is, itself, a degrading insult, the former takes the Jewish person's reaction seriously in a moral sense. The *moral* importance of respecting the contrast invoked here is what constitutes the core of good sense in Gardner and Macklem's claim that the provocation defence respects D's 'interest in being accorded their status as fully-fledged human beings'.[159] One might add that to collapse the distinction between the gravity of the provocation and someone's emotional reaction to it, leaves one unable to account for the exceptional self-control that people may (be required to) exercise in the face of grave provocation, in some circumstances, in order to remain calm. So, to employ a variation on an example used in chapter 2 above, if a black President of the USA is racially abused as she has her finger on the nuclear button, we trivialize her ability to remain calm, in these circumstances, by suggesting that the provocation was nothing to become worked up about; but we give her the praise due to her if we acknowledge that, in the face of very grave provocation, she managed to keep her self-control.[160] In that regard, then, good behavioural science ought to be seeking to shed light on sound moral thinking, rather than seeking to undermine it, a point reinforced by the argument that ever more subjective standards, whether or not backed by scientific opinion, will always favour violent men more than they favour abused women. As Moran puts it:

The cases suggest that the equality of the defence will not be enhanced either by substituting ordinariness for reasonableness nor by subjectivising the self-control component of the standard so that the hypothetical more closely resembles the actual person. In fact, such responses seem to make it more difficult to ensure that the standard is egalitarian, so much so that many equality seekers now suggest completely abolishing the defence, rather than opening it up.[161]

Quite so.

9. DIMINISHED CAPACITY: MERCY KILLING CASES, AND KILLING VIOLENT ABUSERS

What external factors other than provocation can, on the 'wide' view of a diminished capacity plea (a diminished capacity plea on rung 5 of the defence ladder), be less controversially combined with evidence of mental disorder to warrant a partial excuse? We have already seen that the Criminal Law Revision Committee was concerned to ensure that a diminished capacity plea should be flexible enough to encompass at least some instances of the

---

[159] John Gardner and Timothy Macklem, 'Compassion Without Respect?: Nine Fallacies in *R v Smith*', 627.

[160] See the discussion of normative constraints on predominantly ascriptive excuses, in chapter 2.4 above.   [161] Mayo Moran, *Rethinking the Reasonable Person*, 220.

'depressed mercy killer'.[162] There is certainly some evidence that the effects of long-term care on someone in a close relationship with a terminally ill (or otherwise sick) person may lead to mental health problems.[163] In Dell's study of diminished capacity, the typical cases in which the plea is successful are ones in which, 'men in their 60s or 70s . . . had reached breaking point under the continued strain of looking after wives with severe mental or physical illnesses', and killed impulsively.[164] One should not overlook the gender politics at issue in such cases, in that, as in instances of half-completed suicide pacts, when a killing has taken place the D is usually a man exercising what is, in effect, a decision-making prerogative over a woman's destiny. Even so, for the purposes of a diminished capacity defence, or on the 'wide' view of the existing diminished responsibility defence, where there is some credible evidence of mental disorder, mercy-killing cases are ones in which there are strong grounds for permitting the external pressures on D to influence the decision whether or not to partially excuse. This is, perhaps, especially so where V has over a long period continually pressured D into taking just this course of action.[165] One must be careful, though, not to assume that a diminished capacity defence is operating, *faute de mieux*, solely as a kind of poor substitute for a euthanasia defence. The external pressure on D need not take so specific a form as the moral force of the case for ending V's life. As we will see in chapter 5 below, insofar as such cases can be suitable for partial excuse, it is best if they are dealt with as demands-of-conscience claims to partial excuse, and not as claims based on diminished capacity. The latter can perfectly well encompass cases in which V is not 'better off dead', and where there is no demands-of-conscience case for a partial excuse. The central excusatory issue will be whether the problems of caring for V (as in the case of a disturbed and violent child) have led D him- or herself into inescapable

---

[162] See section 4 above. The phrase is Mackay's: see R. D. Mackay, 'Diminished Responsibility and Mentally Disordered Killers', 79. For reasons to be given at the end of this paragraph, the phrase is potentially misleading, in that it may confuse diminished capacity cases with ones in which a demands-of-conscience partial excuse is more appropriate.

[163] See, by way of analogy, the discussion of 'folie à deux' in *R v Windle* [1952] 2 QB 826, although the idea mooted in that case of a 'communicable' form of insanity is obviously absurd. For discussion of the cases, see also Glanville Williams, *Textbook of the Criminal Law*, 2nd edn., 692–693. One potential difficulty that has recently arisen is that the mental health problems associated with the debilitating effects of long-term care tend to take the form of so-called 'reactive depression', a psychological condition difficult to square with what may have recently become a requirement in English law that the abnormality of mind have an organic cause: see *R v Sanderson* (1994) 98 Cr App Rep 325, 336, 'We incline to the view that the phrase [in section 2] "induced by disease or injury" must refer to organic or physical injury or disease of the body including the brain' (per Roch LJ), critically examined by R. D. Mackay, 'The Abnormality of Mind Factor in Diminished Responsibility' [1999] *Criminal Law Review* 117. Mackay may be right to think, however, that the court did not intend expressly to exclude 'reactive depression' from the scope of section 2.

[164] Suzanne Dell, *Murder Into Manslaughter*, 35–36, cited by Andrew Ashworth, *Principles of Criminal Law*, 3rd edn., 295. See the extensive discussion of such cases in Law Commission for England and Wales, *A New Homicide Act for England and Wales?*, Part 8.

[165] See the discussion in Jeremy Horder, 'Mercy Killings: Some Reflections on Beecham's Case' (1988) 52 *Journal of Criminal Law* 309.

mental illness or disorder;[166] although, in these kinds of cases we should note the higher-than-normal risk, threatening common good (v) (set out in chapter 1.2 above) of collusion between lawyers and other experts involved who are sympathetic when a euthanasia defence seems to have been warranted, as they see it, to ensure that D does not encounter difficulties with the cogency of the evidence of mental disorder or deficiency.

Another important kind of case in which the pressure of external circumstances could combine with evidence of mental disorder to warrant a partial excuse, on the grounds of diminished capacity, is the case of prolonged (and violent) abuse. There has understandably been a great deal of discussion of the appropriateness of particular defences for those who have had little choice but to endure violent abuse at the hands of a partner, or parent, and who have eventually killed the abuser to escape the continued—often escalating— abuse.[167] In many cases, the most appropriate defence ought to be self-defence. In English law, self-defence probably gives D considerable latitude to react in a pre-emptive way that anticipates future attacks, even if at the moment of the pre-emptive strike V is posing no threat, if the only alternative is to wait for a murderous attack by V on D that will in all probability be impossible to neutralize when it comes (as, *ex hypothesi*, it almost certainly will).[168] A plea of self-defence obviously requires neither that D has lost self-control at the time of the killing (for the purposes of a provocation plea), nor that at that time D has been suffering from a mental deficiency (for the purposes of a diminished capacity plea).[169] It may also be pleaded successfully so long as D honestly (and in most countries other than England, reasonably) believed that a future attack could not by other means be avoided than by the lethal pre-emptive strike, even if this was not in fact the case.[170] There is a further advantage to a plea of

[166] See, by way of example, the case of *R v Price*, *The Times*, 22 December 1965, discussed in Glanville Williams, *Textbook of the Criminal Law*, 2nd edn., 692–693. I say, 'inescapable' desperation, and mental illness, in that D may rightly or understandably have felt that there was a personal obligation to care for V on an ongoing basis, irrespective of whether the resources of the social services would have been sufficient to lift the burden.

[167] For an authoritative discussion, see A. McColgan, 'In Defence of Battered Women Who Kill'; Robert F. Schopp, Barbara J. Sturgis, and Megan Sullivan, 'Battered Women Syndrome, Expert Testimony and the Distinction Between Justification and Excuse' (1994) *University of Illinois Law Review* 45.

[168] See the discussion of the possible differences between English and American law in Jeremy Horder, 'Killing the Passive Abuser: A Theoretical Defence', in Stephen Shute and A. P. Simester (eds.), *Criminal Law Theory: Doctrines of the General Part*, discussed in Law Commission for England and Wales, *Partial Defences to Murder*, 204–207. See also, E. Schneider, 'Equal Rights to Trial for Women: Sex Bias in the Law of Self-Defense' (1980) 15 *Harvard Civil Rights-Civil Liberties Law Review* 623; Aileen McColgan, 'In Defence of Battered Woman Who Kill'; Victoria Law Reform Commission, *Defences to Homicide*, chapter 3. Law Commission for England and Wales, *Partial Defences to Murder*, part 10.

[169] Both requirements have given rise to difficulties in English law, and to a number of appeals. See e.g. *R v Thornton* [1982] 1 All ER 306; *R v Thornton (No 2)* [1996] 2 All ER 1023; *R v Ahluwalia* [1992] 4 All ER 889.

[170] *R v Williams (Gladstone)* [1987] 3 All ER 411; *Beckford v R* [1987] 3 All ER 425 (PC); *Zecevic v DPP* (Vic) (1987) 162 CLR 645.

self-defence, on the basis of pre-emptive strike. This is that it gives D's plea a rational, justificatory structure, emphasizing the moral soundness of her reasons for action, rather than seeking to portray them as essentially as aberrant or pathological.[171] It is important to make these comments in the present context, since it would be wrong to give the impression that a diminished capacity plea is, in some sense, the appropriate plea for battered women who kill, whether or not it is the most common one. Nonetheless, in some cases a plea of self-defence may be inappropriate, for a variety of reasons.

In *R v Ahluwalia*,[172] following years of violent abuse D killed her husband (V) by setting fire to him as he slept. Self-defence was not pleaded. This may have been because there was considerable evidence of advance preparation for an attack of a specific kind (burning), and because D admitted in a letter to her mother that the reason she had set fire to V was to give him 'a fire bath to wash away his sins', evidence that her primary motivation was not self-defensive.[173] The defence of provocation was rejected by the jury. There was, however, evidence of diminished responsibility that, because it had not been given at the trial, led to the quashing of D's conviction for murder and the substitution of a verdict of manslaughter. A doctor who had examined D found that she was suffering from 'endogenous depression at the material time, a condition which, in the opinion of some experts would be termed "a major depressive disorder"'.[174] In such cases it is, though, likely to be hard to disentangle the evidence of mental disorder, and the effect of the 'external' element constituted by the pressure of having lived under constant threat from an increasingly violent, unpredictable and domineering individual. If the evidence of mental disorder is not decisive, in such a case, it seems right to consider whether the combination of evidence of mental disorder and evidence of extraordinary external pressure is sufficient to justify a judgment that a first-degree conviction would be wrong, and a partial excuse by way of diminished capacity would be more appropriate. By way of contrast, perhaps, with cases in which it is evidence of a provoked loss of self-control that D seeks to combine with evidence of mental deficiency, there is relatively little risk of a D who has been abused over a number of years becoming a 'repeat player' in so dramatic a context. Hence, the risk that, on a subsequent occasion, D will anticipate the granting of the defence in the way she shapes her conduct and the explanations she gives for it is, to say the least, remote in the extreme. In such cases, as in the 'depressed mercy killer' cases, the origins of the mental disorder from which

---

[171] On the importance of this, in the context of a choice between provocation and diminished responsibility, as pleas, see John Gardner, 'The Gist of Excuses', 590–592. I gave insufficient consideration to the discussion of this point in Jeremy Horder, *Provocation and Responsibility*, chapter 9.   [172] [1992] 4 All ER 889.

[173] Ibid., 893. I do not put much stress on this point, since self-defence was never raised in the case itself and so her motives were not tested in evidence.

[174] Ibid., 900. The court also took account of her strange behaviour after her attack on V, in finding that the conviction for murder should be quashed.

D suffers are closely tied to the evidence of the abuse D had to endure at V's hands, over a lengthy period. Such cases can, then, be contrasted with ones in which D uses objectively excessive force in self-defence or under duress, in a relatively isolated incident, and then seeks to combine evidence of having been attacked or threatened with substantially independent evidence of mental disorder explaining the nature and/or degree of force used.[175] In spite of these differences, there is a case for regarding the partial excuse of diminished responsibility as sometimes appropriate in the latter cases as well.

10. Diminished Capacity: Excessive Defence and Duress Cases

As far as the defence of self-defence is concerned, the courts have rejected the view that evidence of mental disorder can (save in unspecified exceptional circumstances) be relevant to the question whether the force used in a given set of circumstances was excessive.[176] However, employing what appears to be the 'wide' view of the plea, in murder cases the courts have permitted D to combine evidence of a relatively minor mental disorder with evidence of the pressure exerted by the effect of an unlawful attack, to make a case of diminished responsibility where excessive force has been used. They have, in other words, allowed D to succeed in what is, in effect, a diminished capacity plea on rung 5 of the defence ladder masquerading as a diminished responsibility plea on rung 6. An example is *R v Martin (Anthony)*.[177] In this case, D had used excessive force in making what he believed to be a pre-emptive strike in self-defence, but there was some evidence that he did so whilst suffering from clinical depression that aggravated a paranoid personality disorder. Further, the defence adduced expert opinion to the effect that these mental characteristics would have led D to perceive the threat to his safety to be much greater than an ordinary person would have thought that it was.[178] However, there was conflicting expert testimony on a key issue. Although D might have had psychological problems in the past, there was little evidence of mental illness at the time of the offence, when D was (it was argued) suffering no more than the natural anxiety that is 'a normal reaction to grossly abnormal circumstances'.[179] Significantly, faced with this conflict, in finding that the issue of diminished responsibility should have been left to the jury, the court observed that 'the distinction between the doctors is only one of degree, since Professor Maden

---

[175] On self-defence, see *R v Martin (Anthony)* [2002] 2 WLR 1.

[176] Ibid., 16, discussed on this point in chapter 3.2 above.

[177] [2002] 2 WLR 1. See the discussion of this case in Law Commission for England and Wales, *Partial Defences to Murder*, 171–173.

[178] *R v Martin (Anthony)* [2002] 2 WLR 1, 14.   [179] Ibid., 13.

accepts that [D's] feelings were consistent with severe anxiety although he would not describe this as a paranoid personality disorder'.[180] This suggests (albeit without proving) that the court is prepared to see the jury adopt the 'wide' view of diminished responsibility, according to which evidence of a less severe mental disorder may form part of a successful diminished responsibility plea, when combined with evidence of exceptional or abnormal external pressure. As the court said, albeit solely in relation to the matter of sentence, 'we take into account not only the evidence of [D's] medical witnesses, but also the conduct to which he had been subjected'.[181] In effect, this makes D's plea one of diminished capacity on rung 5 of the defence ladder, in all but name.

It seems highly likely that a similar approach would be taken to duress cases, in which D was suffering from a mental disorder, perhaps particularly in murder cases where the defence of duress is not available.[182] In theory, in relation to the objective question in duress cases whether D acted as a person of reasonable firmness might have done, if the (character-based) evidence does no more than show that D was 'more pliable, vulnerable, timid or susceptible to threats than a normal person . . .',[183] that evidence will not be admissible. The Court of Appeal in *R v Bowen*[184] held that to admit such evidence would be simply inconsistent with adherence to the objective standard of reasonable firmness. In that respect, the courts' approach to duress does not differ much from the approach taken to factors relevant to the degree of force regarded as reasonable in self-defence.[185] However, following the decision in *R v Bowen*, the two defences now part company to a substantial degree, if there is evidence that D's response to the threat was affected by a 'mental illness, mental impairment or a recognised psychiatric condition . . . provided persons generally suffering from such a condition may be more susceptible to pressure and threats'.[186] If so, then that evidence will be admissible in relation to the objective question, in a way (at present) it would not be in self-defence cases.[187] It is meant to be 'just' to take the characteristic into account in the latter case (where mental disorder is involved), in a way it would not be in the former (where D is mentally normal, but 'cowardly').

---

[180] Ibid., 17.   [181] Ibid., 19.   [182] See *R v Howe* [1987] AC 417.

[183] *R v Bowen* [1996] 4 All ER 837, 844 (per Stuart-Smith LJ). See also *R v Emery* (1992) 14 Cr App Rep (S) 394; *R v Horne* [1994] Crim LR 584; *R v Hirst* [1995] 1 Cr App Rep 82; *R v Hegarty* [1994] Crim LR 353.   [184] *R v Bowen* [1996] 4 All ER 837.

[185] *R v Martin (Anthony)* [2002] 2 WLR 1, 14.

[186] *R v Bowen* [1996] 4 All ER 837, 844. The court's reliance on the notion of a 'mental illness, mental impairment or a recognised psychiatric condition' as the key to characteristics with which the person of reasonable firmness can be endowed has been subjected to searching criticism by Alec Buchanan and Graham Virgo, 'Duress and Mental Abnormality'.

[187] Although, in that regard, the Court of Appeal in *R v Martin (Anthony)* left the door open a fraction, when it was suggested that 'in exceptional circumstances which would make the evidence [of psychiatric illness] especially probative, in deciding whether excessive force has been used', such evidence would be admissible: *R v Martin (Anthony)* [2002] 2 WLR 1, 16. See the discussion in Law Commission for England and Wales, *Partial Defences to Murder*, 173.

In *R v Bowen* itself, D was convicted of obtaining property by deception. At a comparatively late stage in proceedings, he had claimed that he had acted under duress at the time. He said that two unknown men had accosted him in a public house and told him that if he did not commit the offences, he and his family would be petrol-bombed, and that he had not initially mentioned this to the police because of fear of reprisals. A witness (himself with a conviction for dishonesty) testified that D was a 'simple' man who required a great deal of assistance to cope with his job as a taxi-driver (D was said to have had an IQ of 68). On appeal against his conviction, defence counsel accepted that evidence that D was abnormally suggestible and vulnerable was irrelevant, but argued that his low IQ (something not mentioned at the trial) was something admissible to show that D might have been inhibited in his willingness to seek help from the police. The Court of Appeal disagreed, saying:

We do not see how low IQ, short of mental impairment or mental defectiveness, can be said to be a characteristic that makes those who have it less courageous and less able to withstand threats and pressure . . . It would not have assisted [the jury] . . . if [the judge] had added, without qualification, that the person of reasonable firmness was one who shared the characteristics of the appellant.[188]

In justifying the exception for cases of mental illness, with the proviso (mentioned earlier), 'provided *persons generally* suffering from such condition may be more susceptible to pressure and threats',[189] the court in *R v Bowen* was guilty of confusing the objective version of the capacity theory with the subjective version (see chapter 3.7 above). In deciding whether more could reasonably have been expected of D *him- or herself* (the issue under the subjective version), what others suffering from the same condition are capable of may be relevant in a supporting D's case in an evidential way, but cannot be legally decisive. The court did not make this clear, preferring instead misleadingly to hint, in the reference to the capabilities of 'persons generally' that what are in issue are objective, moral standards by which D can be judged (the issue under the objective version of the capacity theory). The hint is misleading, of course, because there are no firm moral standards by which people suffering from serious mental disorders can, in relation specifically to the effect of those disorders, be judged (as opposed to standards by which their behaviour can be predicted, empirically, and so on); that is the difference discussed in chapter 3.6 and 3.7 above between such individuals, and those capable—because, say, of their young age—of reaching only lower (but still objectively determinable) moral standards.

The court's equivocation over whether to adopt a subjective or an objective version of the capacity theory is not surprising, of course, given that whilst duress is a defence meant to be governed by the objective version of

---

[188] *R v Bowen* [1986] 4 All ER 837, 845.
[189] Ibid., my emphasis.

the capacity theory, on rung 3 of the defence ladder above, it can seem harsh to judge some short-comers by objective standards.[190] D, in *R v Bowen*, was potentially exposed to such harshness, because he had not intentionally killed and thus could not plead diminished responsibility. Yet, as indicated in the passage just cited, in relation to D's duress plea, the court set its face against saying that D's low IQ had any bearing on the case, even though (as the court conceded) it can be relevant when it edges into mental defectiveness, and IQ *is* a matter of degree. The difficulty of knowing when to be 'tough' and when to be 'tender', when trying to relate mental impairment or deficiency to the satisfaction of the objective conditions in excuses on rungs 3 or 4 of the defence ladder is, then, nowhere better illustrated than in this case. If diminished capacity were a partial excuse to any crime, then the courts would have fewer difficulties in such cases. Defendants suffering from mental deficiencies making them peculiarly vulnerable to threats could—always assuming their behaviour was truly voluntary[191]—be invited to plead diminished capacity, in order appropriately to be judged by the subjective version of the capacity theory. Consistent with what has been said hitherto, in relation to such a plea, they could then legitimately seek to combine evidence of their mental deficiency with evidence of the external influence of the unlooked-for threat, in bolstering the case that the plea of diminished capacity should be successful.[192]

11. DIMINISHED CAPACITY AND DEPRIVATION

To be poor is not, *ipso facto*, to have failed to respond to the demands of reason, and still less is it to be a short-comer. So, deprivation hardly features in this, or in any other, mainstream liberal discussion of excusatory doctrines. As modern liberalism became a more established and widely held political philosophy during the twentieth century, the supposedly 'positive' effects that tinkering with the criminal law, or of introducing forms of nominally non-punitive incarceration, were meant to have on disadvantaged people became increasingly questioned, even as (for a variety of reasons)

---

[190] The decision is extensively criticized, on this ground, by Alec Buchanan and Graham Virgo, 'Duress and Mental Abnormality'.

[191] See the discussion of this issue in chapter 2.12 above.

[192] It follows that evidence of threats of adverse consequences less severe than death or serious injury could be relevant to pleas of diminished capacity, in a way they would not be to a plea of duress *simpliciter*. For the role the threats play, in relation to each defence is different. In diminished capacity cases, evidence of threats made which exert pressure on D's will simply bolsters the case, to a greater or lesser degree, for saying that little blame is to be attached to him or her for involvement in the crime, given that D's claim to partial excuse has been anchored in the influence of a mental deficiency on his or her conduct. By way of contrast, in duress cases proper on rung 3 of the defence ladder, the threat must play a predominantly normative role, and in the eye of the law, nothing short of a threat of death or really serious harm adequately does this.

these kinds of experiments continued.[193] Modern liberals' idea of the positive collective action needed to address the problems associated with deprivation has increasingly come to be shaped almost exclusively by public policies
on education, employment, housing, social security, and the involvement of
the voluntary sector, along with other bureaucratic measures far removed
from penal and quasi-penal detention, however well-intentioned.[194] It is,
then, something of an irony that one sees modern critical legal theorists
seeking to find some kind of intellectual blindness or moral deficit in the
comparative lack of attention paid by modern liberal criminal law thinkers
to the possibility that deprivation itself might be an excuse.[195] For, by raising the very question whether deprivation could or should in and of itself be
a justification or an excuse for crime, one shows oneself, in some sense, to
be a thinker firmly within the liberal tradition (and at the late nineteenth
century rather than late twentieth century end of it, at that), rather than—like,
say, Pashukanis[196]—a genuinely critical thinker from outside that tradition. In
that regard, the critical legal (and sociological) preoccupation with poverty
and crime has been scathingly mocked by some left-wing thinkers themselves.
So, for example, Vincenzo Ruggiero, speaking contemptuously of what he
calls the 'sociology of misery', says of this preoccupation:

I am alluding to a sociology which is always prepared to focus on other people's
predicaments, while regularly ignoring its own; a sociology which believes itself to be
needed by its objects of study more than it needs them. In criminology this is exemplified by the propensity of some researchers to study marginalized communities with
a missionary zeal and a honeyed paternalism which derive from traditional philan-
thropy. This propensity, which in Britain is prevalent even among critical and radical
criminologists, is akin to that guiding eighteenth-century reformers, religious milit-
ants, sewer-cleaners, and the Salvation Army.[197]

  A philanthropic bent to criminal law scholarship, so out of place—as
Ruggiero rightly suggests—in the critical scholarly thought of soi-disant
radical left thinkers, is sometimes to be found in the law reform proposals
of more than one thinker within the liberal tradition, although not—most
importantly—in the simplistic form of a proposal to make 'poverty', as
such, an excuse. One way to make sense of the idea that the experience of

---

  [193] See Sir L. Radzinowicz and Roger Hood, The Emergence of Penal Policy in Victorian and
Edwardian England (Oxford: Clarendon Press, 1990), chapter 19.
  [194] Although these well-intentioned efforts to make detention work continue to have
their supporters, and have retained an importance place in public policy, not least because they
can be all things to all people: see M. A. Crowther, The Workhouse System 1834–1929:
The History of an English Social Institution (London: Batsford Academic and Educational,
1981), 90.
  [195] See e.g. Alan Norrie, Crime, Reason and History, 2nd edn., 171–173. The liberal cast of
Norrie's supposedly non-liberal thought will be further considered in chapter 5.1 below.
  [196] E. B. Pashukanis, The General Theory of Law and Marxism, trans. Hugh W. Babb
(Cambridge, Mass.: Harvard University Press, 1951).
  [197] Vincenzo Ruggiero, Crime and Markets: Essays in Anti-Criminology (Oxford: Oxford
University Press, 2000), 7.

deprivation can feature within a (broadly) excusatory framework is with an argument that deprivation can be channelled into a diminished responsibility plea:

Consider the proposal for a defence of 'social deprivation', based on the assertion that many offenders fail to acquire the capacity to resist offending because society fails to provide the conditions . . . for their proper moral and social development . . . it seems that the argument is not that they should be excused because they achieve the standard of a person of reasonable firmness in that situation, but rather that there was an absence of a fair opportunity, stemming from diminished capacity to conform their behaviour to the law.[198]

The fact that many people from deprived backgrounds do not commit indictable offences in spite of the disadvantages under which they labour, may not undermine the case for saying, as Ashworth puts it, that 'the pressures on *some* defendants are so great as to diminish capacity significantly'.[199] Both biological and environmental factors may combine to create such pressures, in different ways, perhaps particularly in young people when the influence of attention deficit disorder, hyperactivity, and low IQ are met with long-term parental indifference or hostility;[200] and the influence of the environmental factors in the mix has been shown to be aggravated by the effects of social and economic deprivation.[201] In theory, then, for the purposes of a diminished capacity plea, these factors could legitimately be combined together, or added to evidence of the influence of some kinds of external factors such as threats or provocation, to add up to a case for at least a partial excuse, in cases where their effects are thought to have been very severe.[202]

The objection to developing the defence of diminished responsibility in this way is that, as Ashworth puts it, 'It seems to be because the effect of social deprivation is less urgent and more diffuse (insufficiently "explosive") that it is widely assumed that this matter is better taken into account in mitigation

---

[198] Andrew Ashworth, *Principles of Criminal Law*, 3rd edn., 255–256. See also H. L. A. Hart, *Punishment and Responsibility*, 51, 'The admission that the excusing condition may be of no value to those who are below a minimum level of economic prosperity may mean, of course, that we should incorporate as a further excusing condition the pressure of gross forms of economic necessity'. On the face if it, it looks as if Hart is going even further than Ashworth, by proposing a special 'deprivation' excuse, rather than adopting the 'shoe-horn' approach that favours looking at deprivation in terms of diminished responsibility; but without further elucidation, which Hart did not provide, it is hard to say.

[199] Andrew Ashworth, *Principles of Criminal Law*, 3rd edn., 256 (my emphasis).

[200] See the discussion in David J. Smith, 'Crime and the Life Course', in M. Maguire, R. Morgan, and R. Reiner (eds.), *The Oxford Handbook of Criminology*, 3rd edn. (Oxford: Oxford University Press, 2002), 724–726. As Smith puts it (ibid., 728): 'It is possible to argue that this anti-social trait then becomes self-sustaining, because it sets in train further interaction sequences that again reinforce coercive behaviour in situations outside the family as well as within it.'

[201] David J. Smith, 'Crime and the Life Course', in M. Maguire, R. Morgan, and R. Reiner (eds.), *The Oxford Handbook of Criminology*, 3rd edn., 733–734.

[202] See e.g. Stephen J. Morse, 'Diminished Capacity', 265–266.

of sentence'.[203] This is, perhaps, not an entirely persuasive objection, in relation to a diminished capacity plea, because there is no special need for any 'explosiveness' in D's reaction, or in the circumstances that led to it, if such a plea is to be successful. Broadly speaking, all that matters is that D's capacity was substantially diminished at the time of the offence. In any event, people would seem to be entitled to expect fair labelling considerations to take some account of longer-term effects that diminish capacity, as well as to account for short-term factors having this effect, much as the new-car buyer is entitled to expect safety protection from the longer-term effects of rust-proofing failure as well as from the short-term effects of a crash. Even so, as in the case where the effects of provocation are mixed with those of mental disorder, a more substantial objection comes from the special need to guard against 'repeat players' whose claims raise too starkly strategic considerations, such as common goods (i) and (ii) (set out in chapter 1.2 above), militating against the extension of an excuse or partial excuse. No one should be excused whose claim is disingenuous, in so far as D is more or less self-consciously shaping his or her self-perception, and the narrative constituted by his or her account of events leading up to the incident in question, in accordance with an understanding of what the law governing excuses requires.[204] Moreover, for the modern (rather than late nineteenth-century) liberal thinker, whatever the justification might be on fair labelling grounds for such a development of the defence, it is always going to be over-shadowed by the knowledge that, as Peay puts it, 'piecemeal tinkering may provide solutions for the problems posed by specific offenders; it is insufficient as a basis for addressing problems across the ordered-disordered offending continuum'.[205]

No doubt, for the critical legal scholar, the very fact that one finds here a discussion of deprivation in the context of diminished responsibility, shows that I have missed the point. In many liberal societies, deprivation stems largely from the failure of the free market to deliver relative economic equality and stability across the board. So, to regard the victims of market failure with 'recognized' psychiatric problems, such as attention deficit disorder and so forth, as to be excused on that ground, wrongly gives explanatory priority to individual pathology over socio-economic critique. No one seriously doubts the importance of socio-economic critique, but the weakness in this argument is that it regards the ideals of liberalism as something more than merely contingently connected to institutional support for the free market. As we will see in chapter 5.1 below, liberalism is conceptually connected to a vision of society in which what matters most is the long-term realization of (often) incommensurable forms of intrinsic value in people's

---

[203] Andrew Ashworth, *Principles of Criminal Law*, 3rd edn., 256, citing Stephen J. Morse, 'Culpability and Control' (1994) 142 *University of Pennsylvania Law Review* 1587, 1652–1654.; Stephen J. Morse, 'Diminished Capacity', 266.

[204] See the passage cited from Peay, in chapter 1.7 above. This is the so-called 'reverse *Dadson* principle'.   [205] Jill Peay, 'Mentally Disordered Offenders', 785.

lives; and its approach to deprivation, howsoever caused, is shaped by that vision. The vision entails the recognition of individuals' inter-dependence, and their partial dependence on thriving traditions, structures, social forms, and so on, without which the pursuit of value is unlikely to be able to take adequate root, and hence bear the weight of people's individual and collective commitments. However, neither the generation and accumulation of wealth, nor the participation in paid employment (as opposed to simply remaining 'active' in wholehearted pursuits: see chapter 6 below), necessarily have intrinsic value, *as such*. Their value can be purely instrumental value, important though they can be to us, in that regard, in the pursuit (individually and collectively) of that which has intrinsic value.[206] So, there is no special theoretical connection between the world of the free market place and the ideals of liberalism. As a political philosophy, liberalism might become the dominant ideology even in a society without a developed market. That is, in part, why so much of liberal social and economic policy is directed at compensating for the effects of market failure. Such connection as exists between liberal ideals and marketplace activity is, at best, indirect. It comes about because the world of (capitalist) work is capable of generating new social forms—'entrepreneur', 'personnel manager', 'stress counsellor', 'shop steward'—that individuals can endow with intrinsic value through their wholehearted participation in the activities associated with the form. What matter for liberals, though, are the consequent long-term possibilities for giving one's life intrinsic value through such participation, not the market/work context in which that value is to be realized.

This point is perhaps overlooked by Jock Young, when, as he rightly says:

To suggest that any work is better than no work, and that work has this essential redeeming quality, is bizarre in the extreme. Work ... is largely repetitive and demeaning; the use of 'work' by the 'contented classes' to describe their highly-paid, creative, and self-fulfilling activities in the same breath as the low-paid, oppressive chores of the working poor is a fraud of the first order.[207]

From a liberal perspective, the point missed here is that whilst it is obviously unrealistic to expect all work to be capable of being endowed with intrinsic value, it is not necessary that it should be, if an individual's life is to have sufficient long-term intrinsic value. The investment fund manager, just as much as the parking attendant, may find little or no intrinsic value in their work-related activities, but no one is obliged to seek or find such value in their work. Quite enough of that value may, for any individual, lie elsewhere (as it is made pointedly to do for the barristers' clerk, Mr. Wemmick, in

---

206 Although, as we will see in chapter 6.6 below, it is possible to endow one's work with intrinsic value, in the way in which one approaches it, through the spirit in which one carries it out. See also Jeremy Horder, 'Strict Liability, Statutory Construction and the Spirit of Liberty'.

207 Jock Young, 'Crime and Social Exclusion', in Mike Maguire, Rod Morgan, and Robert Reiner (eds.), *The Oxford Handbook of Criminology*, 3rd edn., 457, 473.

Charles Dickens' *Great Expectations*): in their family lives, friendships, hobbies, sports, religious faith, and so forth.[208] This point is an important one, in this context, in that it can do something to block one kind of argument that the state does not have the moral authority to punish—and really ought to excuse—those who reject a conventional, largely law-abiding lifestyle because, as Ruggiero puts it, they 'have found an alternative lifestyle and income through participation in illegal economies . . . [rejecting] the alternative offered by the sociologists of misery (poorly paid, dull, and humiliating jobs)'.[209] No one is obliged to find intrinsic value in their work, in order to generate sufficient long-term intrinsic value in their lives, and no one may seek to give their own (working) lives 'alternative' intrinsic value by invading the autonomy of others. So, there is no excuse for such a choice, even if the market failure that makes that choice seem so attractive for some people means that it is always wrong to regard those who do make it as necessarily 'evil', or as necessarily 'them'-as-opposed-to-'us'.[210]

---

[208] Obviously, this claim depends on a number of contingencies that cannot be explored further here, such as limitations on the hours someone is required to be at work, safeguards against 'hard' work adversely affecting employees' prospects for realizing intrinsic value in their lives through wholehearted participation in activities outside work, and so forth.

[209] Vincenzo Ruggiero, *Crime and Markets: Essays in Anti-Criminology*, 5.

[210] See, in that regard, the passage cited from J. M. Finnis, *Natural Law and Natural Rights*, 262, in chapter 5.1 n. 19, below. In his otherwise excellent discussion, Ruggiero's brief critique of the 'harm principle' objection to such alternative lifestyles is regrettably marred by a woefully cavalier dismissal of Mill's interpretation of the limits of that principle: Vincenzo Ruggiero, *Crime and Markets: Essays in Anti-Criminology*, 80–83. That Mill's thesis is recognizably a product of its time (isn't every theory?) hardly goes to show that we have nothing to learn from the harm principle itself. Further, that prohibitions on drugs or alcohol can, at best, only controversially draw support from the harm principle discloses no weaknesses in the principle itself. The harm principle was always intended as a guide—whose principal purpose was to secure toleration—and not as an exclusionary 'bright line' rule: see further Stephen Shute and John Gardner, 'The Wrongness of Rape'.

5

Liberalism and the
Demands-of-conscience Excuse

1. LIBERALISM, AND THE SCOPE OF EXCUSES

It is a commonplace amongst critical criminal lawyers that the excusing conditions to be found in Anglo-American criminal law reflect a narrow, peculiarly individualistic (and hence, supposedly, 'liberal') view of what should count as a defence. Alan Norrie has made the point in a particularly vivid way:

> The criminal law's currency of judgment is that of a set of lowest common denominators. All human beings perform conscious acts and do so intentionally. That much is true, and there is logic in the law's denial of responsibility to those who, because of mental illness or other similar factor lack voluntariness (narrowly conceived) or intentionality. But such an approach misses the social context that makes individual life possible . . . Necessity and duress are significant precisely because they push at the line between context and agency . . . the law permits these defences as a kind of safety valve . . . to take the pressure off the narrow paradigm of physical involuntariness with which it standardly operates.[1]

In the terms in which defences have been explained here, Norrie sees the central case of a 'defence', within individualistic thinking, as one that involves a denial of responsibility, of voluntariness, or of the mental element, rather than a claim to excuse. In Norrie's view excuses (and justifications) are pushed to the margins by such thinking, because they may involve contextualization. The potential for contextualization involved in such defences is by law kept purposefully to a minimum, in order to keep at bay 'the opposing political and ideological reasons that individuals would give for their actions if they could'.[2] As we will see in section 6 below, it is certainly true that the law cannot grant excusatory space to political or ideological reasons for law-breaking, as these are reasons that oppose the law at a strategic level. Yet, that does not entail that a legal system that refuses to excuse acts so motivated must also limit the scope of excuses more generally, in such a way that an individual is treated as 'an isolated homunculus, an individual without past or future, a solitary atom capable of acts and intentions and responsible for them'.[3] The scope, explored in the sections below,

---

[1] Alan Norrie, *Crime, Reason and History*, 2nd edn., 171, 173.
[2] Ibid., 173.   [3] Ibid., 172.

for the law to grant space for considerations of personal conscience to excuse gives the lie to that suggestion. As important, for present purposes, is the conflation in Norrie's work of, on the one hand, the kind of extreme libertarian or existentialist outlook that might well regard an individual as nothing more than 'an isolated homunculus . . . without past or future', and, on the other hand, liberal political philosophy.[4] In fact, these two strains of thought have always been fundamentally opposed ideologically and politically. This is because of the importance attached by liberalism to personal autonomy ('freedom to'), rather than to mere negative liberty ('freedom from').[5] The anti-individualist element integral to this latter vision of liberalism comes through its insistence that personal autonomy cannot be achieved, except through wholehearted engagement in some combination of the personal, social, religious, educational, occupational, cultural, and political relationships, institutions and activities that give meaning, stability, depth, and a sense of belonging to people, and to their plans, aspirations and attachments.[6] So, how could the conflation between individualism and liberalism possibly have come about? The conflation comes about through the drawing of a mistaken inference from what Norrie rightly, if somewhat misleadingly, refers to in the passage just cited as the criminal law's 'lowest common denominator' currency.[7]

On the one hand, in almost all liberal societies, the law's excusing conditions are said to be very narrow, mainly taken up with defects of the will (broadly construed) or of reason. On the other hand, in such societies, sentencers' powers to make allowances for matters of mitigation going well beyond such defects are typically very much wider, encompassing almost any aspect of D's past, or future prospects, as well as broader matters of the public interest. Norrie sees this as the way in which the modern liberal state can claim formally to be committed, in the interests of all, to a (narrow) individualistic vision of formal equality, legal certainty, and extensive freedom of the

---

[4] Norrie refers, for example, to the law's 'liberal individualism' (Alan Norrie, *Crime, Reason and History*, 2nd edn., 29), which he sees as having at its core something he calls a 'logic of individual right' (ibid.). [5] Joseph Raz, *The Morality of Freedom*, 425

[6] For a liberal critique of individualism, see e.g. Joseph Raz, 'Rights-Based Moralities', 182. In this regard, the phoney nature of Norrie's war on liberalism comes through in his support for the supposedly alternative view that '[t]here is no getting away from our existence in families, neighbourhoods, environments, social classes and politics. It is these contexts that deal us the cards which we play more or less effectively. Human beings, it is true, are not reducible to the contexts within which they operate, but nor are they or their actions intelligible without them' (Alan Norrie, *Crime, Reason and History*, 2nd edn., 172). A comparison with Raz's strikingly similar analysis of positive freedom shows up Norrie for the thorough-going liberal that he really is: Joseph Raz, *The Morality of Freedom*, 319, 320,

> All I argue for is that individuals inevitably derive the goals by which they constitute their lives from the stock of social forms available to them, and the feasible variations on them . . . Who then is a moral person? . . . At a superficial level one is inclined to say that he is a person among whose pursuits there are many non self-interested ones . . . A better answer is that the morally good person is he whose prosperity is so intertwined with the pursuit of goals which advance intrinsic values and the well-being of others that it is impossible to separate his personal well-being from his moral well-being.

[7] He does not make it clear whether he really means 'lowest common denominator', or whether he means 'highest common factor' instead.

will, whilst ensuring substantively—through individual sentences and the sentencing system more generally—that the flagrant injustices produced by such a commitment are kept to a minimum in particular cases.[8] In fact, there is no special connection between 'doctrinal minimalism' (as I will refer to the lowest common denominator approach) and the emergence and mainten-ance of the liberal state; far from it. Modern *non*-liberal states exemplify the tendencies Norrie identifies far better than most liberal states do.[9] If any-thing, the latter have by and large somewhat more generous formal excusing conditions, no doubt (ironically) because of the liberal state's somewhat greater sensitivity to the adverse consequences for the individual of convic-tion itself. Let me briefly give some examples.

In the criminal code adopted for the People's Republic of China in 1979 (as amended), in section 1, dealing with 'Crimes and Criminal Responsibility', one finds provisions dealing with denials of (full) responsibility on the grounds of infancy and insanity, of a reasonably familiar kind (articles 17–19). In articles 20 and 21, dealing with confession-and-avoidance defences, however, the defences included are almost wholly justificatory in nature. The only mention of a recognizable excuse is of excessive defence, said to warrant lesser punishment:

Article 20. Criminal Responsibility is not to be borne for an act of legitimate defence that is undertaken to stop present unlawful infringement of the State's and public interest or the rights of the person, property or other

---

[8] See Alan Norrie, *Crime, Reason and History*, 2nd edn., 46:

> The possibility of mitigation of sentence is a marvellous mechanism for allowing the criminal process to 'have its cake and eat it'. Having convicted the accused by a strict, unbending set of rules, the rule books are cleared away and judicial or governmental discretion comes in to do 'real' justice to the individual . . . The sentencing style represents the 'scandal' of the liberal criminal justice system, yet is a scandal that is necessitated by the very certainty of the rest of the law.

In one sense, here, Norrie does no more than show a rule-of-law-driven concern about juris-dictions in which excessive sentencing discretion is given to judges, a discretion that may then be used inconsistently by them without a proper system of accountability; something that lib-eral reformers, such as Ashworth, have been criticizing for many years. There is, moreover, a very obviously exaggerated contrast between Norrie's vision of the criminal law as a 'strict, unbending set of rules', and the idea that when it comes to sentencing the rule books are 'cleared away'. Like any rule, a rule of criminal law may be subject to as-yet-untested-or-acknowledged exceptions, and propositions of logical entailment, and may in itself be highly open-ended, such as a rule preventing driving 'without due care and attention'. Contrariwise, sentencing discretion may, although it need not, be highly structured (even involving mandat-ory sentences) in a way that gives the sentencer little discretion. Here, then, is another example of Norrie's phoney war on liberalism: see n. 6 above.

[9] In this respect, there is a lopsidedness to Norrie's examination of the issues. His aspiration is to confine himself to 'presenting [English] law as a social and historical practice emerging in the first half of the nineteenth century': Alan Norrie, *Crime, Reason and History*, 2nd edn., ix, but he nonetheless claims that English law reflects 'liberal *Western* modernity and legality' (ibid., 29, my emphasis). The latter claim is not backed up by detailed comparison with non-Western criminal law codes. In that regard it should be noted that countries, like Nigeria or Pakistan, that inherited a rel-atively modern Western criminal code, but then abandoned liberal democracy for a lengthy period or never became liberal democracies, retained much of the 'General Part' of their Western liberal criminal codes. That simply reinforces the point that there is no tight connection between the main-tenance of a Western liberal government, and the liberal theory of excuses and justifications.

rights ... Criminal responsibility shall be borne where legitimate defence noticeably exceeds the necessary limits ... However, consideration shall be given to imposing a mitigated punishment ...

Article 21. *Criminal responsibility is not to be borne for damage resulting from an act of urgent danger prevention.*

The character of the Chinese Code to some extent reflects its Germanic origins;[10] but the emphasis in non-liberal jurisdictions on justifications, excuses being left as matters solely for mitigation, is also to be found, for example, in the Criminal Code of the Republic of Belarus (a code that came into force in 1961). As in China's criminal code, the so-called General Part of the Belarus code exempts the insane and young children from criminal responsibility, and places its primary emphasis, where confession-and-avoidance defences are concerned, on setting out the circumstances in which justifications entitle someone to avoid criminal liability ('Necessary defence', Article 13; 'Extreme necessity', Article 14). Excusatory matters, spelled out in detail (by way of contrast with the criminal code of the People's Republic of China), are made a matter purely for 'attenuating responsibility', in the sense of justifying a less severe sentence.[11] In that regard, it is interesting to note that the same bias towards justifications is to be found in many pre-liberal societies (even though some categorized what would now be called justifications as excuses).[12]

One should not become carried away with the idea that non-liberal states focus on justifications, playing down formal excuses, whereas liberal states embrace justifications and excuses with equal enthusiasm. For example, some non-liberal states with criminal codes influenced by English law reformers of the nineteenth century, have inherited a rich legacy of excusatory claims, as is the case with Pakistan;[13] but these continue to be

---

[10] See D. C. Clarke and J. V. Feinerman, 'Criminal Law and Human Rights in China', in S. C. Lubman (ed.), *China's Legal Reforms* (Oxford: Clarendon Press, 1996), 137: 'the major statutes in the fields of criminal law are the Criminal Law (CL) and the Criminal Procedure Law (CPL), both passed in 1979 and effective from 1980. The CL [is] a Western-style penal code on the German model . . .'.

[11] Article 37. Circumstances which attenuate responsibility. When prescribing punishment the following circumstances shall be regarded as attenuating responsibility: (1) prevention by the culprit of harmful consequences ... or voluntary reimbursement of the damage caused ... (2) committing of a crime due to a coincidence of grave personal or family circumstances; (3) committing a crime under a threat of coercion or owing to material or other dependence; (4) committing of a crime under the influence of strong emotional feeling caused by illegal actions of the sufferer; (5) committing of a crime in defence against a socially dangerous encroachment though with excess of the necessary defence limits ... (8) sincere repentance or giving oneself up ...

[12] So, in early English law, self-defence was regarded as an excuse: see Thomas A. Green, *Verdict According to Conscience*, 89–90. In other respects, the heavy emphasis laid in early English law on justifications for killing escaped felons, burglars, and so forth, follows ancient Greek law very closely: see T. J. Saunders, *Plato's Penal Code*, 243–244 and 255. Plato's eloquent case for regarding homicide in anger as a lesser former of killing (partially excused) would have been regarded as a major innovation.

[13] The Pakistan Criminal Code of 1860 makes formal provision not only for mistake and accident (sections 79 and 80), but also for involuntary intoxication (section 85) and compulsion

claims that—most significantly, for the purposes of this discussion—the states in question have *not* thought it essential to eradicate as inconsistent with their non-liberal political constitution. Nonetheless, what could a critical legal scholar conclude from a finding that codes in non-liberal jurisdictions at least tend to place greater emphasis on justifications, and regard excuses as matters merely for sentencing discount? He or she might seek to change the emphasis of his or her thesis. He or she might suggest, first, that the absence of a significant role for excuses in non-liberal codes reflects an authoritarian instinct normally to some extent resisted in liberal societies; but, secondly, he or she might claim that that does not change the special political and moral dilemmas besetting liberal society that drive the urge to grant excuses, but then to severely restrict their scope. I will say something directly about this view in a moment. First a preliminary point. Societies that, in modern times, have moved from liberal to non-liberal forms of government, have *not* commonly found it in consequence necessary or desirable to change the liberal cast of the provisions in their codes dealing with excuses.[14] Why? Narrowly drawn defences of duress, provocation, mistake, and so forth, still exemplify a kind of doctrinal minimalism. It is simply a minimalism better suited than that to be found in more authoritarian non-liberal codes to the creation of at least a modicum of space for D to exculpate him- or herself, without compromising whatever overall strategic aims the criminal code itself may have (on which I say a little more shortly). One should thus certainly not strain to find, in the extra generosity, the influence of distinctively 'liberal' thinking.[15] A pre-modern society preoccupied, unlike a liberal one, with whether wrongdoing reflected honourable or dishonourable motives, might wish to grant D much the same kind of excusatory space, in order to bring the issues central to that preoccupation more sharply into focus.[16] So, given its 'one-size-fits-all' character, one is likely to find doctrinal minimalism widely employed, to set limits to the excuses, by states of very different political complexions and traditions throughout history; and one is as likely to find it employed by liberal states as by any other kind.

More broadly, one should not infer a commitment to the supposedly liberal values of formal equality, legal certainty and extensive freedom of the will from the excusatory narrowness of a criminal code. Instead, one may hypothesize that such narrowness stems from the (mistaken) assumption

by threats (section 94), alongside private defence (section 96), consent (section 87) and necessity (section 81) and the denials of responsibility (infancy, section 82/83; insanity, section 84). See also M. Akida, 'Criminal Law', in N. Bernard-Maugiron and B. Dupret (eds.), *Egypt and its Laws* (The Hague: Kluwer, 2002). Akida points out that under Egyptian law, duress is a valid plea, and intoxication may be pleaded as a denial of specific intent. See also, B. O. Nwabueze, *Constitutional Law of the Nigerian Republic* (London: Butterworths, 1964).

[14] See n. 9 above.

[15] Although, as I have already said, such thinking may be at work if the justification for the excusatory or justificatory space is sensitivity to the adverse consequences for individuals of conviction itself. [16] I owe this point to John Gardner.

that a generous set of excusing conditions will seriously impede what has proved to be a dominating strategic concern in all developed societies, past and present, liberal and non-liberal alike. This is the concern to maintain the legal system's authority over the use or threat of force, by effecting a transfer of people's desires for revenge against (or, perhaps less luridly, for the compulsory incapacitation of) wrongdoers into a desire for the state *itself* to punish wrongdoing (or to incapacitate). Such a concern militates against the generous development of excuses for wrongdoing, in that such a development might weaken the 'transfer effect', leading people to fall back on self-help remedies, threatening common good (vi) (see chapter 1.2 above). As Gardner puts it:

That people are inclined to retaliate against those who wrong them, often with good excuse but rarely with adequate justification, creates a rational pressure for social practices which tend to take the heat out of the situation and remove some of the temptation to retaliate, eliminating in the process some of the basis for excusing those who do so . . . [T]his displacement function of the criminal law always was and remains today one of the central pillars of its justification.[17]

In that regard, in authoritarian societies, whether of a right- or left-wing outlook, whatever serves to maintain that authority—even the harshest of punitive measures—may come to be regarded as a good thing in itself. In liberal societies, by way of contrast, the picture will inevitably be more complicated. In liberal societies being true to themselves, the strategic concern outlined above is simultaneously bound up with, and mediated by, the requirement that the public be educated not to expect wrongdoing to be controlled solely or largely through the exercise of state authority to punish, incapacitate or (for that matter) to rehabilitate,[18] and the requirement that the dignity and needs of wrongdoers, as continuing members of society, be acknowledged. As Finnis puts it:

The legal system, then, is to be a human response to human needs, not modelled on a campaign of 'social defence' against a plague of locusts, or sparrows . . . [S]anctions are part of the enterprise of legally ordering society, an enterprise rationally required only by that complex good of individuals which we name the common good. The criminal is an individual whose good is as good as any man's, notwithstanding

---

[17] John Gardner, 'Punishment: In Proportion and In Perspective', in Andrew Ashworth and Martin Wasik (eds.), *Fundamentals of Sentencing Theory* (Oxford: Clarendon Press, 1998), 31–32.

[18] Liberalism, unlike socialist-authoritarian theories of governance, does not necessarily regard the state as the sole, or even the best, means of securing the conditions in which personal autonomy will flourish. A liberal state may thus be more likely to accept that the best 'deterrent' to crime is appropriate parental education, peer pressure, decent employment prospects, and so forth: see Andrew Ashworth, *Principles of Criminal Law*, 3rd edn., 16–17, '[T]he criminal law should not be regarded as a primary means of protecting individual and social interests. In terms of prevention, more can probably be achieved through various techniques of situational crime prevention, social crime prevention, and general social and educational policies'.

that he ought in fairness to be deprived of some opportunities of realising that good.[19]

Accordingly, there will, for example, always be a tension between the strategic concern, and a concern about the negative effects of conviction on the largely blameless. This simply reflects the widespread liberal perception that 'crime control', through the use of the blunt instrument that is the criminal law, is a necessary evil, and not a political or moral good in itself.[20]

In spite of this perception, there are other reasons why liberal would-be reformers, having inherited a doctrinally minimalist set of criminal law excuses from a non-liberal past, may have left them substantially unreformed. That is, quite simply, that they have been rightly focused primarily on much more important defects of that non-liberal past: a moralistic and discriminatory substantive law of offences, and a harsh or arbitrary set of criminal procedures and punishments.[21] Reform of the excuses has come, and may rightly even now remain, well down the list of liberal reformers' priorities. Naturally, that does not mean that a liberal state is stuck with doctrinal minimalism. I hope to underscore the claim that doctrinal minimalism has no special connection with the criminal law systems of liberal societies, by suggesting three ways in which the law should be developed to become *distinctively* liberal in its excusatory outlook. One way we have already considered, in chapter 4 above: partially excusing the 'short-comer'. Another, we will look at in chapter 6 below: excusing in cases where 'due diligence' has been shown in seeking to avoid committing a regulatory offence.[22] In this chapter, I will consider the case for (partially) excusing in what I call 'demands of conscience' cases. In any event, whether or not they

---

[19] J. M. Finnis, *Natural Law and Natural Rights*, 262; and see John Gardner, 'Crime: In Proportion and in Perspective' for a similar analysis.

[20] Norrie himself has rightly drawn attention to the tension: see e.g. Alan Norrie, *Crime, Reason and History*, 2nd edn., 28–31, 32.

Obviously, in liberal societies there will be other tensions that do not afflict authoritarian societies in quite the same way. The desire to constrain the scope of criminal liability to genuinely harmful or harm-threatening activity, whilst recognizing the importance of the set-backs to people's lives that other kinds of wrongdoing can cause, is another familiar tension in liberal societies. Norrie perhaps never quite explains why the recognition of never-ending tensions or conflicts between important goals is such a problem for liberal (or any other) society. Is the ruthless, monomaniacal pursuit of one set of goals (say crime control) at the expense of another (say, the promotion of negative liberty) always in principle more 'rational' than a willingness to keep each in a perpetual battle for supremacy? I hope, for all our sakes, that it seems highly unlikely.

[21] See e.g. Sir L. Radzinowicz, *A History of the English Criminal Law: The Movement for Reform* (London: Stevens & Sons, 1948). In common with many others (myself included), Norrie's almost exclusive historical and critical concern is with the substantive law, and with some aspects of punishment. The arguably much more significant nineteenth-century reforms of the trial, and of pre-trial procedure, the legal profession and advocacy, barely get a look in.

[22] In chapter 6 below, I will tie an exposition of the 'due diligence' defence to crimes of ostensibly strict liability, to the 'active' account of well-being integral to a liberal theory of well-being; although it is perfectly possible to give a non-liberal account of the 'due diligence' defence.

concur in the merits of the case for developing any given one of these excuses, liberal criminal law theorists should have confidence that, far from undermining the authority of the criminal justice system, the development of any or all of them has the potential to enhance that authority, by better fulfilling the state's duty of humanity to punish people only in proportion to the crimes.[23]

2. THE CASE FOR A 'DEMANDS-OF-CONSCIENCE' EXCUSE

To develop a partial excuse of diminished capacity is to have constructed only one side of a liberal theory of excuses. Dworkin's second injunction, outlined in chapter 4.1 above, that people should be treated with respect, as capable of forming and acting on intelligent conceptions of how their lives should be lived, also has implications for a liberal theory of excuses. These implications are followed through here. In chapter 1 above, we saw that a commitment to the common good of the rule of law, forsaking unrestrained individualism, entails a willingness to be guided by good faith efforts to provide communal legal solutions to political and social problems (such as poverty or poor housing provision), rather than seeking to define and resolve such problems through 'self-help', i.e. taking it upon oneself to act single-handedly in the name of supposedly higher values.[24] Support for this vital strategic consideration sets limits on the scope of excuses, as well as on the scope of justifications; but those limits need not be as extensive as some theorists have suggested. As we have seen, Simester argues that:

Individuals cannot be permitted to conduct themselves above or outside the compass of the law merely because they have different moral values . . . The moral duty to avoid doing an action is derived from the fact that the action is harmful or wrong, not from the defendant's acceptance that it is.[25]

Depending on the work that 'merely' is doing here, this claim could be taken to be ruling out any provision for conscientious objectors to avoid conscription in the army; to entail an insistence that Sikhs take off their turbans and don motorcycle helmets when riding on motorcycles; to be outlawing the ritual slaughter of animals for religious purposes, if it involves cruelty to those animals; and so forth. No doubt, I am being unfair, and Simester had nothing so sweepingly illiberal in mind; but, as we saw in chapter 1.2 above,

---

[23] On the duty of humanity, in this regard, see John Gardner, 'Crime: In Proportion and in Perspective', 47–48.

[24] See common good (vi), in chapter 1.2 above. The claim to be supporting a 'higher' code of morals was the justification given by duellists for engaging in the practice: see Jeremy Horder, 'The Duel and the English Law of Homicide' (1992) 12 *Oxford Journal of Legal Studies* 419.

[25] A. P. Simester, 'Can Negligence be Culpable?', 93. The fuller citation can be found in chapter 3.6 above.

there is a difference between saying that people cannot be justified or excused in acting wrongly if they put their *personal convenience* ahead of the law's demands, and saying that people cannot be justified or excused if their *genuinely moral values* dictate that they must act in a way the law regards as wrong. It is not, of course, in every such case that someone should be found to have a justification or (partial) excuse; but there are strong arguments for a justification or for a (partial) excuse in at least some cases, and it is those arguments that are examined here.

Dworkin's second injunction finds familiar expression, then, in demands for recognition of the right to conscientious objection, in cases where people find themselves bound to insist on remaining true to important moral or religious beliefs, and hence refuse to comply with a law that requires them to compromise those beliefs.[26] Liberal political theorists seek to acknowledge the significance of value pluralism, in such instances, by making it possible for people to be exempted from criminal or civil liability in circumstances where they adhere to a system of belief that will necessarily bring them into conflict with particular (in other respects perfectly fair) legal demands.[27] The justification for liberal tolerance of conscientious objection is linked to the liberal concern to enhance people's prospects of achieving and maintaining a life characterized by personal autonomy.[28] To insist, in all instances, that someone sacrifice their beliefs in order to comply with what might be a relatively trivial legal demand, is to place disproportionate emphasis on the importance of law-abidingness, thereby unduly affecting people's prospects for achieving personal autonomy; requiring individuals to be sacrificed on the altar of the greater good simply because their conception of the good goes against the grain. Tolerance of moral pluralism, and a commitment to regard the flourishing of each and every citizen as a matter of moral significance, requires that this approach be softened.

[26] The domain of conscientious objection is comprised of familiar examples, such as those mentioned above, involving religious or moral objections to particular kinds of conduct, such as active service in war, the wearing of crash helmets, the requirement that one work on particular days, and so forth. Almost certainly essential to a valid claim to be a conscientious objector is proof that one adheres to a *system* of belief (Islamic beliefs; Roman Catholic beliefs; Quaker beliefs) that naturally generates the objection in question. I say, 'almost certainly', because in the case of war service it may be that anyone with a profound enough aversion to fighting ought in practice to be exempted because they may compromise the effectiveness of fighting units. This, though, is a special case.

[27] For full discussion, see Joseph Raz, *The Authority of Law*, chapter 15; Ronald Dworkin, 'Civil Disobedience and Nuclear Protest', in Ronald Dworkin, *A Matter of Principle* (Cambridge, Mass.: Harvard University Press, 1985), chapter 4.

[28] Raz has suggested that the domain of personal autonomy is, 'The areas of a person's life and plans which . . . are central to his own image of the kind of person he is, and which form the foundation of his self-respect': Joseph Raz, *The Authority of Law*, 280. Raz has had to broaden this account, in order (partly) to acknowledge the importance of the space for small decisions and trivial activities, alongside very significant ones, in an autonomous life; but the first instinct, to emphasize the importance of values central to someone's self-respect to personal autonomy, is not misplaced: see the passage cited from Joseph Raz, *The Morality of Freedom*, n. 6 above.

Liberal thinking requires that individuals be shielded from liability in at least some instances in which, were compliance demanded, those individuals would be required to sacrifice profound (albeit, perhaps, misguided) beliefs, action in accordance with which is for them essential to the maintenance of their personal autonomy. There are two ways in which this might be done, each having different theoretical and practical consequences.

The first, and normal, way to acknowledge the moral and political importance of conscientious objection is through legislative anticipation of the problem, and the creation of a specific exemption or justification, when a law is passed that touches on practices dictated by moral and religious belief;[29] but legislatures are not omniscient. Laws may unexpectedly clash with minority moral or religious practices,[30] or the law may be, or may even have to be, left ambiguous on the question whether a criminal offence is committed, in a particular set of circumstances (as in the case of neglect of a child), if religious convictions are followed.[31] In the event, then, people may find themselves prosecuted when their conscience compelled them to do as they did. So, secondly, a demands-of-conscience excuse ought to be available to ensure D is acquitted in at least some such cases. In that regard, the courts have made clear their commitment—in theory, at least—to the protection of conscience against coercion through the criminal law. In *R v Graham John*,[32] for example, Roskill LJ (as he then was) said:

For a man to be punished for an offence which is committed by reason only of his adherence to his own religion or belief can only be justified if the court is satisfied that the clear intention of the Statute creating the offence was in the interests of the community as a whole to override the privileges otherwise attaching to freedom of conscience and belief, *which it must always be the duty of the courts to protect and defend*.[33]

It will, though, be in relatively unusual cases that a demands-of-conscience excuse is appropriately granted.[34] In a case where D is given a specific justification for ignoring a legal demand, in order to preserve the lawfulness of a minority religious practice, his or her engagement in the practice could be a more or less calculated act of defiance in the face, for example, of objections by those who disagree with the justification.[35] By way of contrast, if D is to

[29] As is commonly done, for example, when legislation is brought in introducing conscription. See Joseph Raz, *The Authority of Law*, 288.

[30] As was the case in England, at first, when the wearing of motorcycle helmets was made compulsory, necessitating the passing of the Motor Cycle Crash Helmets (Religious Exemption) Act 1976.

[31] See Jonathan Montgomery, *Health Care Law* (Oxford: Oxford University Press, 2003), 2nd edn., 431–432, discussing parents' obligations to their children.

[32] *R v Graham John* [1974] 2 All ER 561 (CA).

[33] Ibid., 564 (my emphasis). The facts of that case did not warrant protection of the accused from coercion of his conscience, for reasons discussed shortly.

[34] Some possibilities are discussed in section 4 below.

[35] Such as going out for a ride around town just for the sake of it, with one's turban on in place of a helmet.

be excused on a demands-of-conscience basis, his or her engagement in the law-breaking religious practice must have more or less spontaneously reflected, in terms of reasons for action, solely and simply a sense of moral obligation. The reasons for D's conduct must, as Article 9(2) of the European Convention for the Protection of Human Rights and Fundamental Freedoms (1950) puts it, '*manifest* religious beliefs' (my emphasis).[36] D may well have known at the time that his or her actions were prohibited by law, but that knowledge is distinct from D's motivation. Unlike the justification, the excuse is inconsistent with deliberately ostentatious defiance of the norm governing those who do not share the beliefs in question, whether or not the defiance is cloaked in excusatory language.[37] Confined in that way, the excuse can be granted without threatening at least some important common goods.[38] Being an excuse (in which wrongdoing is admitted) sought *ex post facto*, rather than a justification of the kind sought *ex ante*,[39] it will not involve a claim that those with minority beliefs can conduct themselves, in Simester's words, as 'above or outside the compass of the law'.[40]

Even so, there may be further common good or strategic consideration-based objections that an argument for the excuse has to surmount, before it is appropriate to grant it, such as the risk that the law will be brought into disrepute by the success (or simply by the making) of too many specious claims.[41] D's claim in *R v Graham John*[42] failed because of the strength of such an objection. In *R v Graham John*, D had been charged with and convicted of failing without reasonable cause to provide a specimen of blood, in circumstances where it was suspected that he had been drinking alcohol whilst driving. He claimed to be a follower of eighteenth-century German physician Mesmer (most commonly associated with the practice of hypnotism), as a consequence of which D believed that he had healing powers related to the presence in his blood of divinely given gifts, a belief inconsistent with voluntarily giving blood. The court accepted his *ex post facto* plea as having been made in good faith, but affirmed the conviction on the grounds that 'in the interests of the community as a whole' (see the passage cited above) he should not be regarded as having had reasonable cause to fail to provide a specimen of blood. No doubt, the court could have been

---

[36] The full version of Article 9 states, '2. Freedom to manifest one's religion or beliefs shall be subject only to such limitations as are prescribed by law and are necessary in a democratic society in the interests of public safety, for the protection of public order, health or morals, or for protection of the rights and freedoms of others'. See now the Human Rights Act 1998, schedule 1.

[37] See further, the discussion in sections 6 and 7 below, and see Peter Alldridge, 'Rules for Courts and Rules for Citizens', 501, 'The weakness of the case of the "knowing" defendant is that the more his/her behaviour is attributable to reliance upon the supposed norm, the less causal influence will the real defence upon which s/he relies have had'.

[38] Such as common goods (i) and (ii), in chapter 1.2.

[39] See chapter 3.1 above, and George P. Fletcher, *Rethinking Criminal Law*, 10.3.4.

[40] See the passage cited at n. 25 above.

[41] Common good or strategic consideration (v) in chapter 1.2 above.

[42] [1974] 2 All ER 561 (CA).

more forthcoming about the interests of the community that were at stake in this case, but the decision seems right. In relation to an offence that is part of a group of road traffic offences notorious for the effort and ingenuity that people put into evading their requirements and conviction for breach of them, there is too great a risk that people would be tempted to claim that they, too, held the kind of beliefs D held, bringing into needless disrepute both the law and the *bona fide* followers of Mesmer's doctrines. This is a weighty strategic objection to permitting a demands-of-conscience excuse in this case, whether or not, more generally, the efficacy of the law itself would be seriously impaired (which does not seem all that likely).

In the cases to which the demands-of-conscience defence can be permitted to apply, however, D ought to have a complete excuse, so long as the offence in question involves no violation of individual rights,[43] and at least a partial excuse in some (rare) instances involving a rights violation. To create an excuse to deal with such cases may seem to some to be 'overkill'. Surely, in the rare instances in which such cases crop up, they are best dealt with by way of prosecutorial discretion, pending legislative amendment? Not necessarily. There may be an argument for an excuse, in demands-of-conscience cases, even if it was no mere legislative oversight that led to the conflict between the law and the demands of conscience. It is always possible, for example, that a legislature will be found to have preferred to avoid making, in a very public way, the difficult moral choices involved in exempting certain groups of people from legal demands, hence leaving it to the courts to deal with such cases as they arise,[44] in pursuance of the duty to respect conscience affirmed in *R v Graham John*.[45] Further, defended in terms of the importance of personal autonomy, we will also see that the demands-of-conscience excuse can extend beyond circumstances in which a belief in the overriding moral significance of, say, a minority religious practice, leads D into wrongdoing. Also sheltering under its broad umbrella, are circumstances in which it is a belief that the integrity of one's *personal moral identity* is at stake that leads one to commit wrongdoing; and in such cases, as I have just indicated, there is a case for partial excuse even when a serious violation of rights was involved, of a kind not appropriately dealt with simply through the exercise of prosecutorial discretion.

---

[43] Although, as we will see, in a restricted range of cases in which there is a relatively minor violation of the rights of a family member or member of the same religious community, for whose moral or spiritual welfare D is responsible, there can still be a case for a complete excuse on a demands-of-conscience excuse basis: see section 4 below. For a recent case rejecting the view that there can be a *justification*, in such circumstances, see *R (on the application of Williamson and others) v Secretary of State for Education and Employment* [2003] 1 All ER 385 (CA), a case dealing with corporal punishment in religious schools.

[44] See, generally Simon Gardner, 'Necessity's Newest Inventions'. Law Commission for England and Wales, *Criminal Law: Codification of the Criminal Law*, Law Com No. 143 (1985), para 13.25-13.29.

[45] [1974] 2 All ER 561 (CA). See the examples discussed in section 4 below.

In considering this second aspect of the demands-of-conscience excuse, we may start with Raz's observation that:

moral convictions . . . [do not] have a claim to respect superior to all personal goals. On the contrary, most adults' vision of themselves is built around some aspects of their life or personality and around some goals such that the preservation of these is crucial to their sense of identity and self-respect.[46]

Sensitivity to value pluralism, then, in relation to religious convictions, would make little sense within liberal theory if, underlying that sensitivity, there was no concern, as such, for the importance people attach to the crucial role a broader range of values may play in the constitution of their personal identity.[47] That being so, a liberal theory of excuses ought to be open to the possibility that an excuse can be appropriate in at least some instances in which D can only avoid a sacrifice of his or her personal identity by committing wrongdoing. What kinds of examples do I have in mind? Half-completed suicide pacts, which are manslaughter rather than murder in virtue of section 4 of the Homicide Act 1957, provide an instance in which one finds the law willing partially to excuse in circumstances of the sort under discussion. The paradigm case for partial excuse under section 4 of the Homicide Act 1957, would seem to be where both D and V have agreed that neither of their lives would be worth living without the continued presence of the other—where the personal identity of each has become, in their eyes, inextricably bound up with the identity of the other—and the life of one or both is under threat, say, from terminal illness, or there is for some other reason to be a permanent and irreversible separation. So, with V's consent, D kills V, then intending (but failing, obviously) also to kill himself, so that neither party has to endure separation. The partial excuse formally acknowledges what was, for D, the personally compelling force of the reason for the sake of which, with V's consent, he acted.[48] The excuse (on rung 4 of the defence ladder set out in chapter 3.1 above) is only partial, however, because D's action involves a serious violation of V's individual rights. So, on the account of partial excuses provided in chapter 4.2 above, D would be guilty of second-degree murder. Here is the contrast with the effect of a demands-of-conscience excuse in the conscientious objection cases where D's wrongdoing (*ex hypothesi*) involves no such violation. It follows, though, on the account of sentencing in partial excuse cases provided in chapter 4.3 above, that, other things being equal, nothing worse than a non-custodial penalty

[46] Joseph Raz, *The Authority of Law*, 281. Raz goes on to say (ibid.), 'such personal goals have an equal claim to respect by the state.'

[47] In that respect, Raz has suggested that the domain of personal autonomy is, 'The areas of a person's life and plans which . . . are central to his own image of the kind of person he is, and which form the foundation of his self-respect': Joseph Raz, *The Authority of Law*, 280.

[48] See chapter 4.2 above and the discussion of such cases in Law Commission for England and Wales, *A New Homicide Act for England and Wales?*, Part 8.

must be imposed when D is partially excused. I will be discussing a further case in which a partial excuse could be countenanced, in not wholly dissimilar circumstances.

3. THEORIZING THE DEMANDS-OF-CONSCIENCE EXCUSE (1)

In the terminology of chapter 2 above, when the complete excuse of demands-of-conscience operates in conscientious objection cases, it is an adopted reason, actively justificatory and predominantly ascriptive claim to be excused: D's excuse is based in part on the claim that he or she intentionally put into practice a moral belief mistakenly thought to provide adequate justification for his or her action. D's excuse is also based in part on the claim that although there was, in law, no justification for the action, D ought not to be blamed for acting as he or she did, in the circumstances: i.e. the ascriptive dimension to the claim. As we will see in the next section, it is the role-focused, 'normative expectations' account of excuses (as explained in chapter 3 above) that explains the demands-of-conscience excuse when it covers law-breaking motivated by convictions founded on religious beliefs, and the like. In breaking the law, D is (*ex hypothesi*) living up to the role of a member of his or her faith. By way of contrast, when the demands-of-conscience claim operates as a partial excuse, in cases where D has committed harmful wrongdoing rather than compromise a value central to his or her personal identity, D's claim to excuse is an adopted reason, and a *capacity-focused*, predominantly ascriptive claim. D admits—or should be admitting—that he or she knew there was no element of justification for what was done. Instead, D claims that such was the understandable phenomenological strength of D's and V's mutual desire not to carry on living without the presence of the other, that it was not reasonable to expect D to withstand the emotional pressure to act for the reason he or she adopted, at the time and in the circumstances.[49] In such cases, as we saw in chapter 3.7 above, it can be either the subjective or the objective version of the capacity theory that explains the excuse, depending on whether or not D is seeking to combine evidence of mental disorder with evidence of emotional pressure under which he or she acted, in claiming excuse. In the more theoretically significant cases where D does *not* seek to rely on evidence of mental disorder, the case for partial excuse rests on the claim that, even though D may be betraying his role as, say, V's father, husband, brother, or the like, someone well-equipped with powers of self-restraint might nonetheless have done likewise, in the circumstances.

---

[49] The reliance on the role emotional pressure played in D's action, in the 'personal identity compromise' case, is what distinguishes that case from the 'conscientious objection' case, where D relies on the moral force of what was taken to be an adequate reason for action.

Above all others, the demands-of-conscience (partial) excuse can be particularly hard to reconcile with traditional accounts of excusing conditions, such as the 'choice' theory, criticized in chapter 1 above. For Hart:

[B]y attaching excusing conditions to criminal responsibility, we . . . introduce the individual's choice as one of the operative factors determining whether or not those sanctions shall be applied to him . . . we provide that, if the sanctions of the criminal law are applied, the pains of punishment will for each individual represent the price of some satisfaction obtained from breach of the law.[50]

On this view, in demands-of-conscience cases in which D refuses to compromise his or her beliefs simply in order to remain law-abiding, criminal conviction, and punishment are the price D must pay for the 'satisfaction' of staying true to his or her convictions, because in such cases there can usually be no question but that D's decision is an authentically chosen one. That one is not, morally, free to abandon one's deepest convictions in order to avoid adverse consequences, casts no doubt on the authenticity of one's choice. So, Hart's 'doctrinal minimalism', in relation to excuses, provides an insufficiently rich set of theoretical resources on which to draw, in explaining the justification for, but also the limits of, the demands-of-conscience (partial) excuse, for the purposes of a truly liberal theory of excuses. One must start, instead, with the necessary conditions for excuse, set out in chapter 1.1 above. These are satisfied if D's reason for acting sheds favourable moral light on what he or she did. If D's claim to excuse satisfies these conditions, as I take it that a demands-of-conscience claim will certainly do, one then goes on to ask whether the sufficient conditions have been satisfied, whether there are any over-riding strategic considerations that count decisively against formally granting an excuse, or in favour of granting an excuse on only a limited basis.

By proceeding in this way, one will avoid the appearance of artificiality in explaining why some claims to excuse that can speciously be presented as demands of 'conscience' ought to be denied. In relation to, say, the poor thief, who 'high-mindedly' makes a way of life from stealing from the rich to give to the poor, Dressler argues:

Although he does not have a fair opportunity to live an economically satisfactory, much less safe and serene, life, he does have the opportunity to consider whether he wishes to continue to embrace the values of his immediate antisocial subcommunity or, instead, to move closer to the larger community. He has a greater opportunity to behave lawfully on any particular occasion than does the person suddenly thrust into a coercive situation.[51]

Whether or not one agrees with this, to put oneself in the position of having to argue that the thief has a fairer opportunity to avoid law-breaking than

[50] H. L. A. Hart, *Punishment and Responsibility*, 47.
[51] See Joshua Dressler, 'Reflections on Excusing Wrongdoers: Moral Theory, New Excuses and the Model Penal Code', 714.

the person acting under duress, involves undertaking an uphill struggle to show that the difference between them is not just a matter of degree, and that the two situations are not simply incommensurable.[52] The theoretical task Dressler sets himself is easier to perform if one argues that, even if acting as 'Robin Hood' could in theory show up one's actions in a favourable moral light, thus satisfying the necessary conditions for an excuse, so acting is excluded from the domain of excuse by the sufficient conditions. 'Robin Hood' has no moral grounds whatsoever for deciding *himself* whose rights can be violated, and to what degree and how often, in the interests of distributive justice (as *he* defines it).[53]

As I suggested in chapter 1.2 above, such strategic considerations—threats to common goods—loom large in both sorts of cases in which I am suggesting that the demands-of-conscience excuse may arise. Where the moral beliefs of minorities are concerned, it is the force of strategic considerations that explains the restriction of the complete excuse (barring exceptional cases) to instances in which there is no rights violation. As is well-known, some practices involving what would otherwise be regarded as violations of individual rights, such as male circumcision, are regarded in law as justified, and not merely as excused.[54] The reason for this is, in part, that such essentially family or community-based religious practices do not diminish V's prospects for a fully autonomous life (and may, in some respects, enhance those prospects), whether or not V remains a member of the faith in question. Accordingly, no such justification is held out to more serious violations of individual rights in the name of cultural or religious belief or practice, violations that set back too far V's prospects for a fully autonomous life outside V's faith or culture: hence, the ban on female circumcision.[55] An illustrative

---

[52] Moore has a different argument against excusing in this kind of case: see Michael S. Moore, *Placing Blame*, 545–546. On his view, double standards may be at work when left-wing theorists argue that a deprived background should be the basis for an excuse. For, in so saying, they studiously ignore the excusatory possibilities in claming, say, that it was the very fact that one came from a privileged background where everything was done for one, that made it almost inevitable that one would turn into a criminal when one was left to make one's own way in life. The argument foreshadows Ruggiero's 'causality of contraries': see Vincenzo Ruggiero, *Crime and Markets: Essays in Anti-Criminology*, 6–8.

[53] By way of contrast, it is axiomatic in duress cases that the person acting under duress has no reasonable opportunity or grounds for seeking official help, and must him- or herself act, or suffer the consequences: see the discussion in Jeremy Horder, 'On the Irrelevance of Motive in Criminal Law'.

[54] For a general discussion, see S. M. Poulter, *English Law and Ethnic Minority Customs* (London: Butterworths, 1986).

[55] See ibid., 148–152. These are not the only justifications for restricting harmful practices inspired by religious faith. For example, mild forms of corporal punishment do relatively little to harm V's autonomy in the medium or long term, and are regarded by some as having a basis in scriptural authority: see *R (on the application of Williamson and others) v Secretary of State for Education and Employment* [2003] 1 All ER 385 (CA). Even so, when it is someone in authority at a school who is to administer the punishment, this could be seen to lend unwarranted support to the view that an organ of the state (or a body performing a state function, in lieu of the state) is entitled to use retributive violence in pursuit of its objectives: see *Christian*

case to consider, in this regard, is *R v Downes*.[56] In this case, D was charged with the manslaughter of a two-year-old child, by neglect. V had been wasting away for some 8–9 months, before dying, as a result of a lung inflammation that might have been cured by prompt medical attention. V's parents had not called for medical assistance, due, as the court put it, to 'a conscientious religious belief' in the power of prayer to heal such ailments (it was admitted in cross-examination that a doctor would have been called in, had V broken his leg). The conviction was affirmed.[57] In the light of the foregoing argument, the conclusion seems right. No evidence was given that, had V received medical assistance, it would then not have been possible later to receive V into the parents' faith. This weakens any supporting conscience-based claim that it was as important for V as for D that medical assistance was not sought on this occasion. Further, a grave threat to V's health had obviously developed. Hence, the failure to secure V's right to proper care, leaving the illness to progress without medical attention for so long, was a grievous one.[58] We will re-consider the facts of this case, along with the strategic considerations relevant to it, below.

When D claims partial excuse on the grounds that demands of personal moral identity led him or her into wrongdoing, strategic considerations loom, if anything, even larger, because such demands are likely to be more frequently encountered. An example is usefully discussed by Antony Duff.[59] Suppose a court must decide if D is guilty of theft when he has stolen from his employer to pay for a life-saving operation that is urgently needed for V, a close relative, an operation that would not be performed without payment and could not otherwise be afforded.[60] D may feel compelled to steal to avoid what he sees as a serious compromise of his moral obligations to V, and hence of his own personal moral identity in a case where (let us suppose) his life is bound up with V's. Sympathetic though we might in one way be to D's plight, we need not regard it as even partially excusable that D violated V's rights in order to save the relative. If the facts of such a case were regarded as providing the basis for a 'Robin Hood' defence, as Sir Matthew Hale put it centuries ago 'men's properties would be under a strange insecurity,

---

Education South Africa v Minister of Education [2000] 9 BHRC 52. This could provide a justification for prohibition of such punishment under article 9(2) of the European Convention (1950): see n. 36 above, and the discussion in J. M. Eekelaar, 'Corporal Punishment, Parents' Religion and Children's Rights' (2003) 119 *Law Quarterly Review* 370.

[56] (1875) 13 Cox CC 111.

[57] Disapproving of *R v Hines*, reported in the judgment in *R v Downes* (1875) 13 Cox CC 111, 114–115, where an acquittal in similar circumstances was justified on the grounds that D honestly believed that prayer would be effective.

[58] On the potential importance of this point to the issue of *mens rea*, see *R v Sheppard* [1981] AC 394.   [59] R. A. Duff, 'Choice, Character and Criminal Liability', 377.

[60] Even under the existing law, it is possible that a sympathetic court might find that D was not dishonest, because 'dishonesty' is apt to cover a broad range of excusatory questions; but I leave aside this doctrinal point here. If D is to be excused, it is better that the excuse is openly acknowledged as such, and not hidden behind what purports to be a *mens rea* issue.

being laid open to other men's necessities, whereof no man can possibly judge, but the party himself'.[61] There is, in other words, a risk that knowledge of the excuse may corrupt the normally high regard people have for the very legal obligations in respect of which D successfully gained excuse, threatening common good (ii) (set out in chapter 1.2 above). So, there is a weighty set of common good-based objections to excusing in this case. A case illustrating the same point, but with different strategic considerations at stake, is *Re B*.[62]

In *Re B*,[63] B was almost completely paralysed, and her life sustained only by a ventilation device. Eventually, she asked for the device to be removed, although she knew that this would mean almost certain death. Despite accepting that the request had been made by a mentally competent adult, those treating her did not comply with her request, because they had become emotionally very attached to her and '*could not . . . bring themselves to contemplate* that they should be part of bringing Ms B's life to an end . . .'.[64] The court held that the ventilation device had been unlawfully kept in place, and awarded a small sum of damages against the relevant Health Service Trust for the assault constituted by the unlawful failure to remove the device.[65] The decision is correct. To have found an excuse, or, *a fortiori*, a justification, for the carers' actions would undermine the law's commitment to the right of a competent adult to refuse treatment (about which I will say more in section 4 below). Further, however personally identified carers have become with the task of keeping alive a mentally competent, adult patient, to excuse them for committing an assault, on demands-of-conscience grounds, would put at risk common goods (ii) and (iii) (explained in chapter 1.2 above), by appearing to undermine respect for the inviolability of personal interests and for the culture of law-abidingness that protects them. In a case such as this, moreover, where the carers are not unqualified relatives, but professionals, the risks to common goods are all the greater. Professional carers are bound together by shared ethical values and commitments, as well as common standards, shared working practices, and so forth. To excuse professional carer A on certain grounds, then, is likely to have ethical and working-practice implications for carers B, C, D, and so on, in the same and in similar situations, respecting which they

---

[61] Sir Matthew Hale, *Pleas of the Crown*, i, 54. Arguments to the same effect were made by the Criminal Law Commissioners in the nineteenth century, who argued in their Second Report in 1836 against allowing a defence of necessity to murder on the grounds that people might then 'overrate the danger to which they are exposed, and . . . place too low an estimate on the life of another when placed in the balance against the prospect of additional safety to themselves': Criminal Law Commissioners, Second Report, *Parliamentary Papers* XXXVI, (343), (1836), 36. See, further, in this regard, the discussion of the necessity defence in chapter 1.2 above, and Jeremy Horder, 'On The Irrelevance of Motive in Criminal Law'.

[62] [2002] 2 All ER 449.   [63] Ibid.

[64] Ibid., 463, per Dame Elizabeth Butler-Sloss P (my emphasis). B's carers wished to transfer her to a spinal rehabilitation unit.

[65] The court went out of its way, though, to lay stress on the excellence of the treatment by, and the devotion of, the individual carers.

may (rightly or wrongly) consider that they have a permission or even duty to adjust their own thinking and approach. I will return to this point in section 7 below. Nonetheless, although common good-based objections to the applicability of the demands-of-conscience excuse ought often to be a decisive factor against excusing, there are some cases that are not subject to them in quite the same way. When D is partially excused under section 4 of the Homicide Act 1957, despite having intentionally killed V, D is excused not only in virtue of the extreme emotional pressure in response to which the action was performed, but because this is a unique situation in which V's *consent* to the violation of the right plays a crucial role, in setting the boundaries to the partial excuse. Naturally, V's consent is legally ineffective to justify D's conduct; but that does not mean V's consent also ceases to have any moral relevance to the case for an excuse, especially insofar as strategic concerns relevant to excuse are in issue. The fact that, for D, V's consent is crucial, means that there is *not* an almost limitless list of possible unwitting victims whose rights can be excusably violated (by way of contrast with Duff's example).

The less weighty or compelling nature of strategic considerations is also characteristic of the kinds of 'mercy' killing, or assisted suicide,[66] cases to which I believe the partial excuse of demands-of-conscience should be extended:

> Example 1: D has been married to V for 50 years. They have devoted their joint lives to the relief of the suffering experienced by the terminally ill. Each is thus well aware of what awaits them should they find themselves dying of certain kinds of incurable disease. Further, each would regard it as a monstrous betrayal of the relationship if their partner were to fail to perform euthanasia on the other, if he or she had reached a certain point of decline attributable to one of these diseases, and they have exchanged promises to perform euthanasia at that point. V reaches that point of decline, having such a disease, and asks D to honour his or her promise by giving her a fatal dose of painkiller, or assisting him or her to take one. D does so. Is this murder, or assisting in suicide?[67]

It is understandably rare to find any legal system in which D's decision to kill V in such circumstances, being one of great and wide-ranging moral import, is regarded as having been taken *justifiably*, when taken without reference to a legal framework within which the decision can be openly approved of *ex ante*, on medical and ethical grounds.[68] When it comes to

---

[66] Contrary to section 2 of the Suicide Act 1961.

[67] See *R v Smith* [1979] Crim LR 251; *R (on the application of Pretty) v DPP* [2002] 1 All ER 1 (HL). The example is intended to revive the Criminal Law Revision Committee's proposal for a partial excuse in such instances: see Criminal Law Revision Committee, Fourteenth Report, Cmnd 7844 (HMSO, 1980), 53.

[68] See the discussion in Jeremy Horder, 'On the Irrelevance of Motive in Criminal Law', and in *R (on the application of Pretty) v DPP* [2002] 1 All ER 1 (HL). See also the discussion in section 7 below.

UNIVERSITY OF WINCHESTER
LIBRARY

ex post facto partial excuse, however, as in instances of half-completed suicide pacts under section 4 of the Homicide Act 1957, if V consents to be killed—or to be assisted to die—by D, then the range of strategic considerations against which a partial excuse offends is significantly narrowed, albeit certainly not eliminated entirely. One can, accordingly, find an impressive cast of thinkers who believe that an excuse is appropriate on facts such as those in example 1.[69] For some, of course, any indication that the law does not treat the sanctity of life as a basic good, and does not regard as wholly inexcusable any intentional attack on it, offends against strategic consideration (ii) (see chapter 1.2) in an unacceptable way.[70] Apart from anything else, against a background in which the passing of a life sentence for murder is mandatory, such an approach is too unyielding: juries already routinely convict of manslaughter rather than of murder in these (and similar) cases.[71] Its unyielding character once persuaded the Criminal Law Revision Committee, albeit tentatively, to propose in a working paper that D should be convicted only of 'mercy killing' (an offence to be punishable with up to two years' imprisonment), when, from compassion, he or she unlawfully killed another who was, or was reasonably believed to be (a) subject to great bodily pain or suffering, (b) permanently helpless from bodily or mental incapacity or (c) subject to rapid and incurable bodily or mental degradation.[72] Even so, problems of proof may pose great difficulties in such cases, raising the objection to creating an excuse at the heart of common good (vii), in chapter 1.2 above, since (perhaps especially in half-completed suicide pact cases) we are likely to have only D's word that V consented to be killed to separate the case from one of outright murder. There are, though, ways of addressing such difficulties, as by placing an evidentiary burden of proof on D to show consent, and making it possible to cross-examine D as to credit if he or she pleads that V consented, just as if D had thrown away the shield protecting him or her from such cross-examination.[73]

---

[69] See e.g. Joseph Raz, *The Authority of Law*, 285, 'a person who claims, however erroneously, that it was his moral duty to aid a friend to commit suicide or to commit voluntary euthanasia has an overwhelming claim that his offence shall not make him liable to the normal legal consequences. His claim must be recognised as exceptionally strong even by those who support the existence of such laws'. See also the short but powerful case made for a partial excuse, in Sir J. C. Smith, *Justification and Excuse in the Criminal Law* (London: Stevens & Sons, 1989), 79–82.

[70] J. M. Finnis, Joseph Boyle, and Germain Grisez, *Nuclear Deterrence, Morality and Realism* (Oxford: Clarendon Press, 1987), chapters 4 and 11.

[71] From 1982 to 1991, of the twenty-four homicides categorized by the police as 'mercy killings', there were sixteen convictions for manslaughter only (when murder had been charged), one conviction for infanticide, two acquittals, and three cases in which no proceedings were taken at all: Jonathan Montgomery, *Health Care Law*, 2nd edn., 466–467.

[72] Criminal Law Revision Committee, *Offences Against the Person*, 53. This helpful summary has taken direction from Sir J. C. Smith, *Justification and Excuse in the Criminal Law*, 80.

[73] See now the evidentiary provisions concerning 'bad character' in the Criminal Justice Act 2003. The strategic problem is addressed at some length in Glanville Williams, *The Sanctity of Life and the Criminal Law* (London: Faber & Faber, 1958), 271–276.

4. THEORIZING THE DEMANDS-OF-CONSCIENCE EXCUSE (2)

Every liberal accepts that people who possess the capacity for personal autonomy, people who can be part authors of their own success in goals, relationships, and so forth, with which they identify, may simply fail to achieve personal autonomy, as things turn out. We all have to accept that ill-luck, tragedy and disaster may set back our prospects for achieving personal autonomy, without any infringement of our rights having taken place.[74] It might be suggested, accordingly, that minorities may have to forego the achievement of personal autonomy through adherence to their beliefs, in the interests of maintaining respect for law through uniformity in its application irrespective of personal moral circumstances. That is just the way the 'cookie crumbles', in a rule-of-law state.[75] Is this kind of simplistic theorizing enough to dispose of any case for excuse (or partial excuse) when D's conscience or beliefs place demands on him or her inconsistent with remaining law-abiding? No. As Raz puts it:

It is necessary to contrast one's inability to satisfy many personal goals and desires which is regarded as bad luck and unfortunate . . . with one's inability to conduct normal life (i.e. out of gaol) while avoiding moral wrongdoing which is perceived as humiliating and degrading.[76]

First, the standards of conduct by which we stand to be judged under law are rarely created on a *tabula rasa* and set down for uniform application by the law itself. More commonly, the law draws on *existing* moral standards (or, where relevant, professional standards, and so forth) to set binding benchmarks,[77] and such standards are plural in character. In the setting of benchmarks, then, there has never been a theoretical or practical requirement that, for self-control, courage, foresight, and so on, a *single* benchmark—one standard understood to be observed in common—be identified as the sole criterion for moral assessment.[78] So, if the question is whether a doctor lived up to the standards expected of doctors in treating patients, there is always moral elbow-room for a doctor to concede that she did not follow what the majority would regard as good practice, but to go on to argue that she should nonetheless be acquitted because her conduct was

---

[74] As I have already suggested, what makes the ideal of personal autonomy a non-individualistic one, in spite of appearances, is the essential (and welcome) dependence of the achievement of the ideal on the existence of inter-personal or communal practices, institutions, and other facilitating structures that shape people's goals, give them value, and make possible their realization: see section 1 above. See also Joseph Raz, *The Morality of Freedom*, 198–207 and 307–313.

[75] Ironically, perhaps, it tends to be opponents of liberalism, rather than liberals themselves, who make this claim about the nature of law in the rule-of-law state.

[76] Joseph Raz, *The Morality of Freedom*, 281.

[77] This is a frequently encountered example of the dependence of the criminal law, as well as the civil law, on morality. For further discussion, see Jeremy Horder, 'Criminal Law and Legal Positivism'.   [78] See, in this regard, John Gardner, 'The Mark of Responsibility', 164–166.

bona fide regarded as acceptable by a substantial minority of doctors.[79] In so far as it still draws on the idea of the professional acceptability of a practice, such an argument is a quite different sort of argument from the argument that she should be acquitted solely and simply because she personally believed she was in the right.[80] Tadros has put the point nicely, this way, 'in assessing liability, we are not interested in the agent's reasons for or against treating morally significant reasons as reasons. We are only interested in whether or not he actually acted for or against morally significant reasons'.[81] In that regard, what goes for the justifiability of medical or other practices may also go for the excusability of actions. In the present context, what matters is whether the reasons for the sake of which D acted have sufficient moral significance to make it unacceptable to blame D for committing wrongdoing, even if those reasons cannot justify D's conduct, and whether or not those reasons reflect a 'common' or 'majority' moral viewpoint.

Secondly, as Raz indicates in the passage cited above,[82] it seems obvious that one should (at least to some extent) distinguish between the effects of brute ill-luck, tragedy, and disaster on our prospects for personal autonomy, and the effects that *the law* itself has on those prospects. The law is meant to reflect and be relatively sensitive to reasons—including moral reasons—that apply to us.[83] As we saw in chapter 3.8 above, that entails accounting for the fact that reasons that have moral significance may bind us to act in certain ways, such that we are not free to disregard them, even at a cost to ourselves or to others. A classic case in which the law effectively recognized this is *R v Blaue*.[84] In this case, V had received stab wounds so serious that only a blood transfusion could save her. As V was a Jehovah's Witness, however, she refused to have a blood transfusion even though she knew that meant she would die, which she did. D appealed against his conviction for homicide, on the grounds that her refusal to have a blood transfusion broke the chain of causation. His appeal was dismissed. As explained by Hart and Honoré, the decision is correct because:

The question is not whether it is reasonable, as in this case, to believe that blood transfusion is wrong, but whether a person whose life is in danger can reasonably

---

[79] *Bolam v Friern HMC* [1957] 2 All ER 118, 121, 'A doctor is not guilty of negligence if he has acted in accordance with a practice accepted as proper by a responsible body of medical men skilled in that particular art'. See further *Maynard v West Midlands RHA* [1985] 1 All ER 635, and the discussion in Jonathan Montgomery, *Health Care Law*, 2nd edn., 169–177.

[80] See John Gardner, 'The Mark of Responsibility', 164–166. Of course, I am not saying that every practice a substantial body of professionals regards as acceptable is therefore an acceptable practice, but that issue takes us too far from the present discussion. See the discussion in Jonathan Montgomery, *Health Care Law*, 2nd edn., 169–177, and (more broadly) in David Miller, *Principles of Social Justice* (Cambridge, Mass.: Harvard University Press, 1999), chapter 6.

[81] Victor Tadros, 'Practical Reasoning and Intentional Action' (2000) 20 *Legal Studies* 104, 105.   [82] See text at n. 76 above.

[83] See Joseph Raz, *The Morality of Freedom*, chapter 4.   [84] [1975] 3 All ER 446.

be expected to abandon a firmly held religious belief. The answer must surely be no . . . In view of the high value attached in our society to matters of conscience, the victim, though free to accept any belief she wished, is not thereafter free to abandon her chosen belief merely because she finds herself in a situation in which her life may otherwise be in danger. So, it was not her free act to refuse a transfusion.[85]

If D is not free to abandon her belief when she herself stands to suffer by adhering to it,[86] she may equally not be at liberty to abandon it even when someone else in her family or religious community may suffer thereby. An illustrative example arises out of the facts of *Re T*.[87] In that case, T was a pregnant Jehovah's Witness, who had been involved in a car accident. Her injuries would put both her and her child at risk, without a blood transfusion. Following consultation with her mother, she signed a form indicating that she did not wish to receive a blood transfusion. Her child was stillborn, and her condition deteriorated. A Court Order was obtained authorizing a non-consensual transfusion of blood to save her life. The Court Order was granted on the somewhat flimsy grounds that the court remained unpersuaded that her mental condition had not deteriorated, along with her physical condition: hence, given that there was doubt over whether she was taking an informed and intelligent decision in continuing to refuse the transfusion, the court resolved the case in favour of life-preservation.[88] The decision does little to support—indeed, it undermines—the principles set down in *R v Graham John* that are meant to bind the courts to defend the right of individuals to act as their conscience dictates.[89] Most importantly, for our purposes, it puts someone in the mother's position in the case described at risk of criminal conviction (especially in a case where V is a dependent

---

[85] H. L. A. Hart, and A. M. Honoré, *Causation in the Law*, 361.

[86] Where 'freedom' is, of course, being understood in its richer sense of absence of autonomous choice, not absence of mere obstacles to choice. In as much as an autonomous life is a life lived, in part, through adherence to the values one holds most dear, then to be prevented from showing one's continuing commitment to those values is to be deprived of a valuable freedom. Joseph Raz, *The Authority of Law*, 280.

[87] *Re T (Adult: Refusal of Medical Treatment)* [1992] 4 All ER 649 (CA).

[88] The court also professed itself to be concerned about what it thought might often be the over-bearing influence of parents and religious advisers in such cases. The decision to resolve the issue in favour of life-preservation because of doubts about T's capacity hardly does justice to what is meant to be a presumption of mental capacity in such cases: see *Re MB (an adult: medical treatment)* [1997] 2 FCR 541, 553, 'Every person is presumed to have the capacity to consent to or to refuse medical treatment unless and until that presumption is rebutted' (per Butler-Sloss LJ). See also *Re C (adult: refusal of medical treatment)* [1994] 1 All ER 819 (68-year-old paranoid schizophrenic permitted to refuse what would have been a life-saving amputation of his leg. Apparently, he wished to die a biped).

[89] *R v Graham John* [1974] 2 All ER 561, 564, cited in section 2 above. The court should perhaps have been reminded of Lord Reid's homage to the importance of liberty to English law, in *S v S, W v Official Solicitor* [1970] 3 All ER 107, 111: 'English law goes to great lengths to protect a person of full age and capacity from interference with his personal liberty. We have too often seen freedom disappear in other countries not only by coups d'état but by gradual erosion; and often it is the first step that counts. So it would be unwise to make even minor concessions.'

minor[90]) if, before V is placed under professional care,[91] she advises or insists that V avoid medical treatment in circumstances where such treatment will involve a blood transfusion, or other potentially life-saving treatment. In such a case, of course, once V is under medical care, doctors can avoid a serious rights violation by simply overriding the absence of parental consent, in the patient's best interests, as in *Re T*.[92] However, the mother's conduct in seeking to influence V's behaviour prior to that point may still fall foul of legal prohibitions, such as 'child neglect',[93] especially if she was aware that a reasonable parent would have advised or insisted on V receiving medical care.[94]

Ideally, perhaps, as indicated earlier in section 2 above, cases of conscientious objection to medical treatment for oneself or for relatives would be dealt with in advance specifically by medico-legal rules that provide those in charge of minors with a justification for the objection, in specified circumstances. However, such rules could probably only apply to minors already under medical care. Furthermore, as indicated earlier, it seems likely that the legislature will continue to prefer to leave such difficult issues to case-by-case resolution in the courts, especially when the conduct alleged to be criminal took place prior to V's admission into medical care. That being so, the demands-of-conscience excuse can come into its own. In theory, the excuse could have an application on facts not unlike those in *R v Downes*,[95] with the important difference that the rights violation involved would have to be much less serious than it was in that case, for an excuse to be warranted. The excuse would have an application, because one is dealing with parents for whom fervent belief in the power of prayer to cure children's illnesses 'manifests' their faith (to use the language of Article 9(2) of the European Convention), and, in some cases, with parents whose claim to excuse lies in part in the fact that they were, like the mother in *Re T*,[96] not free to cast off responsibility to avoid jeopardizing the chance that their offspring can become members of their faith. In that regard, I hope that it goes almost without saying that there is no quick-and-easy route to dealing with conscientious objection to medical care for minors, by re-casting the claims as simple denials of neglect or of cruelty, as denials of the crime itself rather than

---

[90] The courts do not regard the conscientious objection of a minor him- or herself to blood transfusions as having any moral significance: see *Re E* [1990] 9 BMLR 1, 8, where the judge said of a 15-year-old who wished to refuse a blood transfusion, 'I cannot discount at least the possibility that he may in later years suffer some diminution in his convictions'.

[91] It has been claimed that once V is under medical care and supervision, a parental refusal to consent to treatment cannot give rise to criminal liability, although it is not clear why there should be an absolute bar: see Andrew Bainham, *Children, Parents and the State* (London: Sweet and Maxwell, 1988), 135.

[92] *Re T (Adult: Refusal of Medical Treatment)* [1992] 4 All ER 649 (CA). For a closely related discussion, see Simon Gardner, 'Necessity's Newest Inventions', 127–130.

[93] Child neglect is an offence contrary to section 1(2) of the Children and Young Persons Act 1933.   [94] *R v Senior* [1899] 1 QB 823.

[95] (1875) 13 Cox CC 111: see text at n. 56 above.

[96] *Re T (Adult: Refusal of Medical Treatment)* [1992] 4 All ER 649 (CA).

as claims to excuse for wrong done. For, that would be to confuse the role the law has in setting *over-arching* standards ('reasonable care', and so forth) with the sometimes incompatible and incommensurable standards one is expected to live up to as a member of a faith.[97] In such cases, the question when—i.e. in relation to what kind and degree of illness—putting such a belief into practice will *not* be permitted to take excusatory precedence over a judgment, in law, of criminal neglect of or cruelty towards a child or other dependant, may be to some extent one of fact and degree; but it may really be a question of competing principles between which judges or juries must choose (or it may be a mixture of both). One way or another, as long as D's conduct involved no more than a minor violation of a child's rights (where D has not let V's condition deteriorate as far as it did in *R v Downes*),[98] placing at the court's disposal a demands-of-conscience excuse goes some way to ensuring that the law is sensitive to the binding character of the moral reasons to which D felt bound to respond. Such a step (along with the courts' new obligations under Article 9(2) of the European Convention, via the Human Rights Act 1998) would, perhaps, also go some way towards persuading the courts to take the demands of conscience and religion, in the field of sickness and treatment, rather more seriously than they have to date.[99]

In these kinds of demands-of-conscience cases, the excuse is based, in part, on the role-based 'normative expectations' account of excuses. D's religious obligations mean that he or she is not free to do otherwise, but they also constitute a kind of role that D can live up to, in refusing to comply with the law's demands: his or her role as a Jehovah's Witness, a devout Muslim or Catholic, and so forth. When D seeks excuse respecting law-breaking conduct, then, a crucial question—albeit, not the only one—will be, 'is D living up to the expectations of a true believer in his or her religion, by refusing to comply with the law's demands?'. If so, there is at least a plausible case for excuse.[100] In assessing the plausibility of the case, there

---

[97] This point is particularly well explained by John Gardner, 'The Gist of Excuses', 593–594.

[98] (1875) 13 Cox CC 111.

[99] For critical discussion, see Jonathan Montgomery, 'Healthcare Law for a Multi-Faith Society', in J. Murphy, (ed.), *Ethnic Minorities, Their Families and the Law* (Oxford: Hart Publishing, 2000), 161.

[100] Does that mean that however 'far out' the demands of D's religion, the law must excuse (assuming there is no, or only a relatively trivial, rights violation) if D lived up to the demands of the role carved out for him or her by that religion? No. To embrace cultural pluralism, by showing sensitivity to the binding character of the demands made of adherents by a variety of faiths, is not to buy into cultural relativism wholesale. There is no duty to shield Ds from liability, especially in a case of rights violation, if the character of their beliefs is radically morally mistaken. The value of criminalizing wrongdoing without excuse may rightly take precedence, in such a case, even if it is acknowledged that D's belief in the obligatory nature of his or her conduct was sincere. For a helpful discussion of this point, see Joseph Raz, *The Authority of Law*, 281–282. Here, then, we see the law having to weigh competing principles (the value in tolerating conduct based on [misplaced] faith in a set of beliefs, as against the value in upholding law-abidingness, in general) in a way that, for reasons yet to become clear, adherents of critical legal studies find so objectionable. As we have seen, for them, it seems, either one should

will be a need to have regard to a number of competing factors. Let us go back to the variation on *Re T*,[101] in which, on religious grounds, D insists or urges that a dependent minor avoid medical treatment, if that will involve a blood transfusion. D violates V's rights by seeking to insist that V refuse the chance to receive the treatment, and (at least, in theory) may thus fall foul of laws prohibiting cruelty to children.[102] However, D's beliefs are not wholly outlandish, and, perhaps most important of all, D may be, in common with those who practise male circumcision, seeking to ensure that, should she recover, V can be received on the appropriate terms into the faith that she (D) sincerely regards it as her solemn responsibility to bring V up to share.[103] Moreover, although she violates V's rights, D does not directly harm V in simply advising or insisting as she (D) does. Crucial to the case for an excuse, then, as in the variation on *R v Downes* given above, may be D's awareness that, whatever she advises or insists on, V is likely to receive sufficiently prompt medical intervention in any event (suppose that V's father—who is not a Jehovah's Witness—is certain to alert the medical services). So, in spite of the rights violation that may be involved even when D advises or insists that V avoid treatment, there can be a case for excuse. In some cases, however, even if there is no rights violation, D's beliefs will be too badly mistaken or ill-supported (meaning there is no established role for D to live up to) to be worthy of legal accommodation;[104] or, in other cases, such as those involving female circumcision, even though D's beliefs have genuinely moral content, the non-consensual rights violation they dictate may be too serious to warrant even partial excuse.

By way of contrast, in demands-of-conscience cases in which it is for the sake of values central to his or her personal identity that D acts, a partial excuse must be explained by the objective version of the capacity theory (see chapter 3.6 above). We have already seen how if the burden of long-term care for the terminally ill V brings about a mental disorder in D which, in combination (*inter alia*) with the pressures associated with, say, V's incessant demands that he put an end to her life, leads D intentionally to kill V, D may have a case for a partial excuse of diminished capacity, in virtue of the subjective version of the capacity theory (see chapter 4.9 above). It may be, however, that D kills V in circumstances such as those in example 1 above, and hence does not seek partially to deflect responsibility for the action by putting forward evidence of mental disorder. On the contrary, D accepts full

be in the business of governing through a single set of exception-less and/or overriding principles, or one should scarcely be in the business of governing at all, because one's principles of government must be, by definition, in crisis: see section 1 above.

[101] *Re T (Adult: Refusal of Medical Treatment)* [1992] 4 All ER 649 (CA).

[102] See text at n. 93 above.

[103] This last point is, perhaps, one overlooked by Raz in his discussion of conscientious objection, in Joseph Raz, *The Authority of Law*, chapter 15. See further, section 9 below.

[104] One might make this claim in support of the decision in *R v Graham John* [1974] 2 All ER 561.

moral responsibility for the action, and rests the claim for excuse squarely on the demands-of-conscience basis that he was bound to honour his promise to V, and could not have lived with the betrayal of what he and V stood for that would have been involved in refusing to perform euthanasia. On the particular facts of example 1, we could seek to explain the partial excuse, in terms of the normative expectations theory (see chapter 3.4 above), by reference to D's role as V's life-long partner; but the weakness in this argument is that it is the very demands of that role that are in question, when what is sought is an excuse for deliberately killing the partner, V. In one sense, D's act is the ultimate *betrayal* of that role, undermining the very foundations on which such relationships are based. It makes better theoretical sense, thus, to explain the basis of D's partial excuse in terms of the objective version of the capacity theory, in terms of a judgment that almost any person, despite being well-equipped with powers of self-restraint, might have felt compelled to comply with V's wishes, in the circumstances.

As I have already made clear, the case for a demands-of-conscience excuse, and *a fortiori* for its application in cases of rights violations, faces a formidable array of common good-based or strategic objections. On the one hand, when D puts conformity with his or her religious beliefs ahead of compliance with legal obligations, if D could be excused this would be the only instance in which D can be excused despite choosing to place his or her moral priorities above those of the law, other than when those priorities have been dictated by another's threats, distorted by a provoked loss of self-control, undermined by mistake, and so forth. As Hart did,[105] one might wonder how a claim to excuse taking that form, could ever be consistent with support for the authority of the law's commands. On the other hand, even when emotional pressures distorting D's determination of moral priorities do form a part of the claim to (partial) excuse, as in example 1 above, making the claim capacity-based rather than actively justificatory (see chapter 2.3, and section 3 above), other strategic considerations of a familiar kind come into play. Problems of proof with regard to V's consent cannot easily be overcome, leaving an inevitable shadow of doubt in many cases over the claims of both prosecution and defence, threatening common good (vii) (in chapter 1.2 above). Moreover, the difference between example 1 and half-completed suicide pacts already covered by section 4 of the Homicide Act 1957, is that the cases like example 1 are much more clearly and unambiguously a kind of euthanasia. At least some of the strategic or common good-based objections to euthanasia must thus be met, if they are not to count decisively against even partially excusing, in example 1. In the next section, I will begin with some general theoretical considerations, before showing in section 6 below how strategic considerations bear on the right legal response to civil disobedience, as opposed to conscientious

---

[105] H. L. A. Hart, *Punishment and Responsibility*, 47.

objection or the demands-of-conscience excuse. I will then go on to look at more specific problems raised by each variant of the demands-of-conscience excuse in later sections.

5. THE AUTHORITY OF LAW TO COERCE CONSCIENCE: A BRIEF OVERVIEW

I will follow Raz in supposing that law is a system of exclusionary reasons for action.[106] A law both provides a reason to act or refrain from acting in a certain way, and also provides a reason—an exclusionary reason—not to act for conflicting moral or prudential reasons. The authoritativeness of law stems from its status as a set of exclusionary reasons. In general, for X to be treated as an authority on a subject by Y is for X to have his or her opinion on the subject regarded as decisive by Y, simply because it is X's opinion, whether or not an evaluation of the merits by Y (or anyone else) leads to the same opinion. For its part, the law claims authority over conduct, in that its claim is to be regarded as a decisive reason for (not) acting in a certain way, even if someone subject to the law believes that conflicting moral or prudential considerations ought to be followed, in an individual instance.[107] Why should any citizen treat the law as an authority, so defined? In Raz's view, crucial is what might be called the 'expert' or 'resources' reason for so doing.[108] The law is commonly in a much better position than any individual citizen to account for all the relevant reasons, for and against, requiring or prohibiting an action. The law's resources in terms of its ability to draw on the widest possible range of expertise, to conduct consultative exercises, to plan for the long term, to inject democratic input into a decision, and so forth, are so much greater than those of any individual citizen or group of citizens. Suppose that one is a citizen of a state that, as part of its rule-of-law commitment to reciprocity, makes use of the kind of resources just mentioned in giving shape to legislation. One will then be much more likely to do the right thing, by obeying the law in a given situation, than by seeking to resolve issues *de novo* for oneself, on a case-by-case basis, paying no special heed to the law's demands;[109] and that will remain true even if, as must

---

[106] See Joseph Raz, *Practical Reason and Norms*, 140–146.

[107] This is not to equate law with authoritarianism. The law may itself rightly limit the scope of the exclusionary character of its reasons, so that moral considerations are in some circumstances capable of straightforwardly outweighing legal demands, as through the provision of a defence of necessity.

[108] There is, I believe, also a moral reason for deferring to the law's judgment on an exclusionary basis that can easily be confused with the 'expert' or 'resources' reason. This is that the very idea of a state is of a body that has the supreme moral right to take decisions, for better or worse, on behalf of a community as a whole, supplanting the claims of any individual or group to do this. I will not pursue this point here.

[109] This point represents the truth in Bentham's famous claim that one should obey promptly, but criticize freely. Needless to say, nothing said here compels the conclusion that the

inevitably happen, the law sometimes ends up making the wrong demand. As Raz puts it:

[T]he normal way to establish that a person has authority over another person involves showing that the alleged subject is likely better to comply with reasons which apply to him (other than the alleged authoritative directives) if he accepts the directives of the alleged authority as authoritatively binding and tries to follow them, rather than by trying to follow the reasons which apply to him directly.[110]

It goes almost without saying that when D should—as he or she ought to know—comply with the law rather than contravene it by seeking to follow his or her own assessment of the applicable reasons directly, the law's authority will be undermined unless it is (re)asserted through action taken against people such as D, on a sufficient number of appropriate occasions.[111]

For our purposes, two crucial questions arise out of this thesis. First, when are people more likely to follow the reasons that apply to them by submitting to the authority of law, rather than by seeking to weigh up the reasons for themselves directly? Secondly, in a criminal case, must the law always seek to (re-)assert its authority by convicting in full and punishing when the law has been broken intentionally, as a result of someone following conflicting reasons directly? Turning to the first question, in discussing the role of rules in practical reasoning, Raz says:

The advantage of normally proceeding through the mediation of rules is enormous. It enables a person to consider and form an opinion on the general aspects of *recurrent* situations in advance of their occurrence. It enables a person to achieve results which can be achieved only through an advance commitment to a whole series of actions, rather than by case to case examination.[112]

This is one of the important 'strategic' dimensions to the authority of law. No one is a moral island or morally omniscient, and a willingness to submit to legal rules—as communal solutions to complex and/or recurrent problems with wide-ranging ramifications—is to demonstrate one's practical reasonableness as a citizen, ruling out (*inter alia*) morally simplistic 'Robin Hood' solutions to injustice and other social or political problems, except in the event of a dramatic breakdown of the moral or practical authority of the state.[113]

---

obligation to obey the law generated by its authority is conclusive or overriding: see Joseph Raz, *The Authority of Law*, 236–237. I am concentrating here on the authority of legislation. Common law crimes have authority as laws, but a slightly different account of their authority is required given the way that the common law develops.

[110] Joseph Raz, *The Morality of Freedom*, 53.

[111] In some instances, those where private, civil liability is appropriate, it may be enough to rely on the incentives citizens have to seek compensation from one another, in cases of breach, to uphold the authority of the law's reasons. In other cases, only regulatory or criminal offences may suffice.   [112] Joseph Raz, *The Morality of Freedom*, 58 (my emphasis).

[113] See J. M. Finnis, *Natural Law and Natural Rights*, 319, whose discussion relies more on the moral than on the 'expert' or 'resources' reason to defer to the law as a system of exclusionary

There are, though, those who believe that when faced with betraying a friend or betraying one's country, one should have the courage to betray one's country.[114] For them, although we may indeed sometimes do better to follow the law than try to follow the relevant reasons directly (in so far as such reasons bear, for example, on the best *definition* of treason), the law cannot authoritatively determine whether loyalty to one's country is to be preferred to loyalty to one's conscience or to one's most significant relationships. Even if the law is unique as an institution claiming authority, in recognizing few practical limits to that claim,[115] the argument is that in this context the law has no authority to place the reasons for refraining from treason outside the balance of reasons, treating them as protected. For many perfectly sincere and honourable people, because one's loyalties are a 'purely personal' matter, reasons for refraining from treason must remain in the balance, as against other important values such as remaining true to one's conscience or to a friend. Arguing along these lines, a case could perhaps be made that D has no reason to accept the law's authority in *any* demands-of-conscience cases, precisely because the law is seeking to set D's conscience-based moral priorities. The case is that the relative moral importance of such priorities (keeping a clear conscience, as against other moral values, such as remaining law-abiding), is something on which D does best to follow his or her assessment of the balance of reasons directly, rather than following the law's authoritative guidance. Surely, then, at the very least, D should not be blamed if he or she refuses to submit to having his or her conscience coerced, or if he or she (as in example 1) attaches overriding moral significance to an aspect of a relationship with V—how it should end—that has come to define the shared part of their personal identity that D has autonomously created with V?

In general terms, the moral authority of the criminal law to coerce conscience *can* be established, principally by showing that harm will be averted if D submits to having his or her conscience coerced.[116] As we have seen, in this regard, Finnis explains the law's moral authority in this way:

Such an ambitious attempt as the law's can only succeed in creating and maintaining order, and a fair order, inasmuch as individuals drastically reduce the occasions on which they trade off their legal obligations against their individual convenience or conceptions of social good.[117]

---

reasons (see n. 108 above). The moral reason seems to be at least as central to the rejection of the 'Robin Hood' defence as the 'expert' or 'resources' reason. See also chapter 1.2 above. For general discussion, see Jeremy Horder, 'On the Irrelevance of Motive in Criminal Law'.

[114] See, most famously, E. M. Forster, *Two Cheers for Democracy* (London: Edward Arnold & Co, 1951), 76, 'I hate the idea of causes, and if I had to choose between betraying my country and betraying my friend, I hope I should have the guts to betray my country'.

[115] See Joseph Raz, *Practical Reason and Norms*, 150–151.

[116] See further, the discussion in section 8 below, and, for discussion of a particular example, see J. M. Eekelaar, 'Corporal Punishment, Parents' Religion and Children's Rights'.

[117] Joseph Finnis, *Natural Law and Natural Rights*, 319, cited in chapter 1.2 above.

In response, then, to the argument made above, one might reply that the very viability of long-term relationships such as D's with V in example 1, the fruitfulness of long-term planning, the reliability of indefinite commitments, the freedom of minorities to follow their conscience free from persecution, and so on, depends on the willingness of all to submit to the law's ambitious attempt to sustain a reasonably fair order (outlawing discrimination, persecution, causing harm, and acts of dishonesty, providing a legal framework for making binding agreements, and so on). That being so, respect for the attempt to sustain this order, and acknowledgement that one cannot simply pick and choose when to regard oneself as a part of it and when to feel free to disregard it, entails that one should not engage in harmful conduct running contrary to the demands of that order. It might be argued, then, that one should not engage in such conduct even for the sake of one's conscience, or for the sake of an intrinsically valuable element in a long-term relationship. In the passage just cited, though, Finnis does not completely rule out the possibility that legal obligations can, exceptionally, be traded off against a conception of the good, perhaps particularly where such a conception of the good touches on a matter of conscience. Instances where this could be excusable (let alone, justifiable) would certainly be rare. Standing in the way of any excuse, or, *a fortiori*, justification, in these circumstances, is a strategic concern that the law will come to be regarded as placing a higher value on people being able to keep a clear conscience or to resolve personal tragedies, even by ignoring the law in order to do so, than on protecting innocent people more generally from rights violations, thus violating common good (ii) (chapter 1.2 above). In that regard, on the one hand, I have sought to restrict the 'conscientious objection' instances of the demands-of-conscience excuse to cases in which rights violations are not involved, or are relatively trivial and confined to a restricted range of morally significant family or community religious practices. On the other hand, even when a serious rights violation is in issue, as in example 1, two factors play a role in diminishing the moral significance of strategic objections to excusing: V's consent, and the fact that D is a private citizen responding to intolerable emotional pressure in a situation that is, for him or her, unique or 'one-off'. These are all points worthy of further consideration, and I will turn to them in ensuing sections. Before doing so, however, we can shed light on the relevance of strategic considerations to excuses and justifications by exploring a contrast between the demands-of-conscience excuse, and partly conscience-based civil disobedience.

6. The Authority of Law to Coerce Conscience: Civil Disobedience

An act of civil disobedience is 'a *politically motivated* breach of the law designed either to contribute directly to a change of the law or of a public policy or to express one's protest against . . . a law or a public policy'.[118] In such instances, individuals commonly seek to challenge or to protest against the way in which the state has used—or proposes to use—its authority to determine one kind of strategic issue (the nature and extent of the steps that should be taken to pursue social or political goals on the community's behalf), by challenging its authority over another strategic issue (the maintenance of law-abidingness). As we will see, there are significant differences between civil disobedience and conscientious objection,[119] but there can be no doubt that acts of civil disobedience can be motivated at least in part by conscience. So, should such acts not be worthy candidates for excuse or justification? The natural way in which to express a legal claim to a confession-and-avoidance defence, respecting an act of civil disobedience, is in terms of necessary defence, of necessity, or of duress of circumstances. In that regard, Norrie has claimed that to permit the defences of necessity or duress in law is to bring a 'Pandora's box' into the legal system.[120] In the box are a whole variety of subversive political and moral claims against the state, all of which (given a dash of relativism) have the potential to cause embarrassment for the law in making a claim to govern through its prohibitory norm, in the situation in which necessity or duress is being pleaded. Naturally, Norrie argues, the law seeks to keep these claims shut inside the box, by keeping the defences within tight bounds; but how convincingly can it do so? As he puts it:

Beyond the excuse of dire social need, it [the defence] has the potential to open up a whole area of political controversy for the law because it allows broader accounts and contextualisations of agency to be raised in the courtroom. In the United States, the necessity defence has been used to challenge political choices made by the state concerning the support of Apartheid, intervention in Central America, and nuclear power and weaponry . . . The existence of a necessity defence . . . allowed the defendants the legal space to make their case before a jury, with the chance of appealing to their broader sense of justice.[121]

An ambiguity at the end here means that it would be right first to acknowledge the possibility of so-called 'jury nullification' in the examples of civil disobedience to which Norrie alludes. A jury may always acquit, in any given case, to 'cock a snook' at the establishment. What Norrie principally

---

[118] Joseph Raz, *The Authority of Law*, 263 (my emphasis).

[119] Two modern accounts drawing a theoretical distinction between them are to be found in Joseph Raz, *The Authority of Law*, chapters 14 and 15, and Ronald Dworkin, 'Civil Disobedience and Nuclear Protest'.

[120] Alan Norrie, *Crime, Reason and History*, 2nd edn., 159–162. In spite of his well-known opposition to Kant's moral and legal philosophy, Norrie takes the very Kantian view that 'viewed as a justification, necessity is understood as involving a choice between two evils in which the accused's act is *held not to be wrong* where the lesser evil is selected': ibid., 154 (my emphasis). Like Kant, Norrie does not allow for the possibility that one can justify (as well as excuse) wrongdoing: see John Gardner, 'In Defence of Defences', 256 n. 10.

[121] Alan Norrie, *Crime, Reason and History*, 2nd edn., 160–161.

wishes to bring into focus, however, is the question whether the defence of necessity ought, in fairness, to have been available in principle (even if then rejected in substance by the jury), when pressed into service to justify wrongdoing perpetrated in the name of one of an array of—at one time or another—fashionable left-wing causes that have led to civil disobedience.[122]

In one way, Norrie might simply be mistaken to think that there is anything in the supposedly liberal structure of English law that entails keeping such claims inside Pandora's box, as opposed to out in front of the jury. There is a long-standing argument that it is just an old-fashioned, conservative distrust of juries that leads judges to treat defences as if they were Pandora's boxes, and hence to hedge their applicability with all manner of legal restrictions in the form of determinative rules.[123] That very distrust, as a reason for maintaining such restrictions, has been recently criticized by the House of Lords itself.[124] Such an explanation is unlikely to appeal to critical legal critics of the criminal law, however, who are prone to be as distrustful of juries or other lay fact-finders—albeit for very different reasons—as the most reactionary of judges.[125] The analysis offered here, however, provides a different way of explaining how the contours of duress (and necessity) ought to be shaped, when acts of civil disobedience are in issue. One is not simply faced with an impossible choice between three options: arbitrarily restricting such cases to life-or-death emergencies, more or less recklessly putting one's whole trust in juries to reject unmeritorious claims, or unfairly abolishing the defences altogether in favour of prosecutorial discretion. Whilst putting one's whole trust in juries does risk inconsistent verdicts in similar cases, undermining the moral standing of an excuse,[126] the restriction of defences such as duress to emergencies is not arbitrary. It reflects a rational choice to confine such defences to situations in which there is no reasonable opportunity to seek the intervention of the authorities: one must take action oneself (perhaps violating another's rights) if even greater harm done is to be avoided.[127] Further, and most importantly, for reasons explained in the preceding section, in a democratic state only the legislature

---

[122] I put the matter in this way, because although Norrie studiously avoids mentioning it, it seems obvious that a wholly open-ended defence of necessity might give a foothold in law to rather less fashionable right-wing claims to take the law into one's own hands, doing only what is necessary to prevent abortions taking place, or to prevent attacks by 'terrorists' that the government has supposedly culpably failed to prevent, and so forth. As Dworkin has rightly observed, a theory of civil disobedience cannot turn on whether those engaged in the disobedience are in the right, and the same goes for politically motivated uses of the defence of necessity: see Ronald Dworkin, 'Civil Disobedience and Nuclear Protest', 105–106.

[123] For the contrast between determinative and facilitative rules, see chapter 1.4 above.

[124] See *R v (Morgan) Smith* [2000] 4 All ER 289, 310–311 (per Lord Hoffmann).

[125] The most common source of dissatisfaction—shared to some extent with liberals—is, predictably enough, with the tendency of juries to rely on unappealingly conservative, 'common sense' intuitions about the credibility of certain kinds of witnesses.

[126] See the discussion of facilitative and determinative rules, in chapter 1.4 above.

[127] See Jeremy Horder, 'Criminal Law: Between Determinism, Liberalism and Criminal Justice', 174–175.

has the supreme moral right to take strategic ('political') decisions on behalf of the whole community, and to decide how these should affect individual rights (the moral basis of the state's authority). A state's legislature is also better placed than any individual or (protest) group adequately to account for all the reasons that bear on what is to count as the right guidance to follow in that regard (the 'expert' or 'resources' basis of the state's authority). In a democratic state, thus, activists who break the law for such political reasons cannot expect to be able to avail themselves of an excuse (or *ex post facto* justification), because political explanations for conduct *themselves* have by their nature at least some strategic motivation, directly challenging the law's legitimate claim authoritatively to guide conduct for strategic reasons.[128] Moreover, were there such an excuse, the likelihood of being excused would hence in itself provide a (strategic) reason for other would-be protestors, whether or not like-minded, to engage in the law-breaking conduct to further their political aims, undermining the authenticity of the claim to excuse; and there might be further unwelcome follow-on threats to common goods, such as a greater willingness amongst protest movements at large to forego a preference for law-abiding protest in favour of rights violations.[129]

Civil disobedience cases should be contrasted with demands-of-conscience cases. In these cases, as in many cases of civil disobedience, D is motivated by moral (or religious) demands of great personal importance. By way of contrast with cases where civil disobedience is involved, though, this motivation does not amount to a 'political' motivation, in the sense explained here. The person claiming a demands-of-conscience excuse will *not* have been breaking the law in the interests of the community at large because—as the political protester does—he or she (no doubt, passionately and sincerely) regards the democratically elected government's policy as dangerous or misguided. Putting aside cases in which the government is seeking actively to suppress action based on conscience, those acting purely for reasons of conscience do not seek to challenge the state's supreme right, through law, to take decisions on behalf of a whole community, either generally or on some particular issue. So, they do not choose (for purely strategic reasons) the laws that are to be disobeyed. Instead of actively *seeking confrontation* with the political establishment through law-breaking, they

---

[128] Other things being equal, they are entitled to expect a degree of leniency from prosecutors and sentencers, in recognition of the sincerity and personal significance of their views. On this point, see Ronald Dworkin, 'Civil Disobedience and Nuclear Protest'. Nothing I have said should be taken to cast doubt on the view that, although there is no case for a 'legal right to' civil disobedience, civil disobedience may simply 'be right' in certain instances where grave injustice may thereby be avoided: see Joseph Raz, *The Authority of Law*, 266–267.

[129] See common good (ii), set out in chapter 1.2 above. It may be that Norrie himself would welcome such developments as a destabilizing influence undermining the legitimacy of the liberal state, and opening up the possibility of socialist revolution, even though there would be a risk of a right-wing authoritarian backlash. His writing does not reveal such a preference, however, but then neither does it disclose an alternative theory of the authority of the criminal law in large, democratic, plural societies.

are themselves *confronted by* a clash between the demands of particular laws and the demands of their conscience, in an individual instance. Their claim is not that it is right or excusable pro-actively to coerce the authorities into abandoning a law or policy said to be wrong in principle, if need be by breaking selected laws—such as the laws of trespass—quite unconnected with it. Their claim is that whether or not a particular law is right in principle, it can be excusable to disobey it in circumstances when to obey it would be unconscionable. Although it is thus easy to see how demands-of-conscience claims are not effectively ruled out by the need to satisfy the sufficient conditions for excuse, unlike claims that acts of civil disobedience should be excused, important strategic arguments against both kinds of demands-of-conscience (partial) excuse must be met if those excuses are to satisfy the sufficient conditions for a formal excuse to be merited. In the next two sections, I will consider the most important of those arguments.

7. LEGAL AUTHORITY AND STRATEGIC CONCERNS IN EXAMPLE 1

In example 1, the fact that V consents to be killed, and the requirement that D's act in killing V must be partly a reflection of conscience-driven emotional difficulties D experienced in preventing him- or herself from giving in to V's request (arising from the special character of D's relationship with V), both serve to restrict the range of cases in which such a demands-of-conscience partial excuse would be available. Together, in the way that they restrict its availability, these factors also serve sharply to reduce the strategic concerns that might otherwise count against granting any kind of excuse in such a case. A claim to excuse can have reason-focused strategic objections or considerations, or outcome-focused strategic considerations or objections, counting against granting it. An excusatory claim has a reason-focused strategic objection to it, if D or others could in future come to regard the likelihood of an excuse being granted as itself a reason to engage in law-breaking conduct, in similar or analogous circumstances, thus undermining the moral integrity of any claim to excuse.[130] An excusatory claim has an outcome-focused strategic objection to it, if granting it will lead to morally troubling consequences in the same or in other areas of life. Let me give examples of each kind of strategic consideration, starting with the reason-focused kind.

Consider 'example 2':

Example 2: D is a doctor who deliberately gives a fatal dose of painkiller to a terminally ill patient, in order (at the patient's request) that the

---

[130] See common good (vi), set out in chapter 1.2 above. As we saw in the preceding section, this reason-focused strategic objection is one that counts against excusing those engaged in civil disobedience.

patient should die, even though the doctor knows all too well that this amounts to euthanasia. Should D be excused on the grounds that he or she was doing only what he or she took to be in V's best interests, given (*inter alia*) V's express consent?[131]

This is a different kind of case from example 1. D's decision is likely to be guided by a principle, the 'best interests of the patient', with an application going well beyond the particular facts, in ways that are difficult to predict. To begin with, if D adheres to the principle, he or she (and others who learn of the case) may regard the fact that a defence has been granted in the present case as a reason to continue performing euthanasia, whenever they regard the circumstances as governed by the principle in the same way. Further, the principle is capable of generating both professional and ethical reasons for D (and others) to perform euthanasia that are unconnected with any compromise of personal conscience, even if in this particular case D's conscience guided him or her. Such developments undermine the moral integrity of any *excusatory* defence, because the *ex ante* reliance by D on the likelihood of such a defence being granted as itself a reason for action is an abuse of what is meant to be—as it would be in example 1—a purely *ex post facto* humanitarian response by the court to the uniqueness of D's moral situation.[132] In that regard, whilst it may be appropriate for citizens to rely directly on (some) *justificatory* legal reasons, it is inappropriate for them to rely on reasons to excuse, because the latter are reasons for courts to respond to wrongdoing in a certain way, and not reasons to be relied on by citizens.[133] To use the equity lawyers' phrase, when D claims an excuse when such reliance has taken place, he or she does not do so with 'clean hands'. As Eric Colvin puts it:

A defence of justification modifies the rules of conduct . . . A person is entitled to do whatever is covered by the defence. A defence of excuse . . . permits an *actus reus* to be excused because the special circumstances under which it was committed happen to make conviction inappropriate. Nevertheless, persons are still expected to observe the rule. [So,] they are not supposed to make reference to the defence in determining what they are entitled to do.[134]

---

[131] A recent discussion of the issues is to be found in R. H. S. Tur, 'The Doctor's Defence and Professional Ethics' (2002) 13 *King's College Law Journal* 75. A 'best interests of the patient' explanation obviously looks justificatory in nature, and it is, but we need to keep this point in suspense for the present. I will return to it shortly.

[132] We will consider an exception to this rule, where one's excuse is that one showed 'due diligence' in seeking to avoid wrongdoing, in chapter 6 below.

[133] See John Gardner, Justifications and Reasons', 123–124; George P. Fletcher, *Rethinking Criminal Law*, 768 and 776–777; M. Dan-Cohen, 'Decision Rules and Conduct Rules: On Acoustic Separation in Criminal Law'; Peter Alldridge, 'Rules for Courts and Rules for Citizens', 499–501.

[134] Eric Colvin, 'Exculpatory Defences in Criminal Law' (1990) 10 *Oxford Journal of Legal Studies* 381, 385. In suggesting here, that those who are excused are still required to observe the rule, whereas (by implication) those who are justified are not, Colvin flirts with the suggestion—criticized in chapter 3.1 above—that there is no such thing as a justification for wrong-*doing*; but I do not want to pursue that point again here.

As Colvin rightly points out (just before the passage cited), one of the key reasons for distinguishing justification and excuse is severely to restrict the scope for compassionate acquittals to blur the line between rightful and wrongful conduct. An instructive example, in that regard, is provided by the well-known case of *R v Bourne*.[135] In that case, a 14-year-old girl had been raped, and fell pregnant in consequence. She was taken to see a member of the medico-legal council of the Abortion Law Reform Association, who secured a fellow member's—Bourne's—agreement to perform an abortion, contrary to section 58 of the Offences Against the Person Act 1861. Bourne said, 'I have done that before and shall not have the slightest hesitation in doing it again. I have said that the next time I have the opportunity I will write to the Attorney-General and invite him to take action'.[136] Bourne performed the operation, and then reported the matter to a senior police officer who had come to stop the operation going ahead. Bourne said to him, 'I want you to arrest me'. Famously, Bourne was acquitted, following the judge's direction to the jury that they should acquit if, '[a] doctor is of the opinion, on reasonable grounds and with adequate knowledge, that the probable consequence of the continuation of the pregnancy will be to make the woman a physical or mental wreck . . . '.[137] For our purposes, what is important is that Bourne's behaviour is wholly inconsistent with excuse, in this context at least, because his was not simply an all-too-human emotional response to the exigencies of a particular dilemma. Instead, Bourne characterizes the act as one done in the best interests of the patient, and hence as an act that it is a part of his professional responsibility to perform, as in example 2.[138]

So, if D is to be acquitted in example 2, it ought to be—as in *R v Bourne*—on grounds that explicitly permit D later to rely *ex ante* on the likelihood that an acquittal will be forthcoming in similar cases, precisely because the principle that motivates D is a professional and ethical reason for repeatedly administering the 'treatment' in such cases. An acquittal on such grounds would inevitably have a justificatory cast, as it did—in the form of 'therapeutic abortion', in *R v Bourne*—rather than an excusatory cast. That is, naturally, why it ought to be regarded as, in a way, so much more controversial than granting an excuse in cases such as example 1, even if the V—like the mother in *R v Bourne*—likewise consents, because the justificatory cast of the grounds for the acquittal carries an implication that the conduct was not (*prima facie*, or all-things-considered) wrongful. As James Griffin puts it, rhetorically, speaking of what I am calling the reason-focused strategic objections:

Instead of reacting, when forced, the surgeons' policy [will be] to go out into the world and find opportunities . . . And a policy like that makes enormous demands on

---

[135] [1939] 1 KB 687. The detail given here is gratefully borrowed from J. Keown, *Abortion, Doctors and the Law* (Cambridge: Cambridge University Press, 1988), 49–52.

[136] 'Charge of Procuring Abortion' [1938] 2 *British Medical Journal* 97.

[137] *R v Bourne* [1939] KB 687, 694 (per Macnaughten J).

[138] Bourne was really engaged in an act of civil disobedience, for which there can be no excuse: see section 6 above.

knowledge. It also spreads naturally through life. If the surgeons do it today, why not tomorrow? If this group of surgeons does it, why not others? If surgeons do it, why not, say, politicians when their moral sums come out the same?[139]

Diane Pretty's application to the court to ensure her husband would not be prosecuted for assisting in her suicide, during her last few months when dying of motor neurone disease, failed, in part, for much these kinds of strategic reasons.[140] As Lord Bingham put it, 'It is not hard to imagine that an elderly person . . . might opt for a premature end to life if that were available, not from a desire to die or a willingness to stop living, but from a desire to stop being a burden to others'.[141] Ironically, then, Pretty died unaided, in the undignified manner she had sought to avoid, precisely because she and her husband misguidedly thought that the thing to do was to seek legal immunity from prosecution under the Suicide Act 1961, on the basis of a justificatory argument for the ending of her life. Suppose, instead, that her husband simply continued to care for her until—if such a point ever came—the emotional pressure on him became intolerable, and for that reason he, with his wife's full consent, assisted in her suicide. On my view, he would then have been entitled to a partial excuse, leading to a conviction for assisting in suicide in the second-degree (see chapter 4.2 above), and hence to a non-custodial sentence (see chapter 4.3 above). Similarly, in example 1, an excusatory as opposed to a justificatory approach is entirely appropriate. As the granting of the excuse is in part linked to the experience of conscience-driven emotional pressures arising from D's special relationship with V, the uniqueness or 'one-off' character of the situation means that reason-focused strategic objections cannot really arise in quite the same way. The reason D is excused does not provide a morally secure basis that can be relied on by others, in analogous cases. To return to Raz's argument for the authority of legal rules, namely that they are apt to deal with *recurrent* situations, part of the case for saying that in example 1 D ought to be partially excused is that the special combination of excusatory factors (D's emotional difficulties as well as V's consent) makes D's situation *non*-recurrent, and hence no real threat to the authority of the law's prohibition on murder.[142]

At the end of the passage just cited, Griffin points to one outcome-focused strategic consideration at stake in euthanasia cases. Granting an excuse to those who perform euthanasia, or (say) transplants-for-profit, when they share the patient's sincere belief that it is in his or her best interests, may lead to a coarsening of moral attitudes across the board, in the form of an

---

[139] James Griffin, *Value Judgement: Improving Our Ethical Beliefs* (Oxford: Oxford University Press, 1996), 99. Griffin's points are directed as much at the possibility that a doctor might be regarded as justified in committing euthanasia, as at the possibility of an excuse. See further, Jeremy Horder, 'On the Irrelevance of Motive in Criminal Law', 180–183.

[140] *R (on the application of Pretty) v DPP* [2002] 1 All ER 1.   [141] Ibid., 18.

[142] D may even rely on this assumption in acting, a kind of reliance that (unusually) would strengthen the case for an excuse.

increased willingness to regard all values as commensurable (the disvalue of pain versus the value of life; the value of a complete set of organs versus the staving off of poverty; the sacrifice of a few to save many). Even if one is sceptical about the ability of the law to influence people's behaviour and attitudes in this way, there is still the important matter of symbolism. In terms of maintaining common goods (such as (ii), in chapter 1.2 above), the law should not be *seen to be* insensitive to issues such as the coarsening of moral attitudes. So, to give a different kind of example, one good outcome-focused reason for refusing to excuse killings sparked by trivial provocation is that, however remote the chance that over-generosity in one such case may lead people to make less effort to keep their tempers more generally, the law should be seen to care about the standards of temper-keeping to which people adhere, thereby upholding common good (i) (chapter 1.2 above).[143] Is the case for an excuse in example 1 defeated by this kind of outcome-focused strategic consideration? It seems unlikely. As a moral philosopher, Griffin may well be concerned with the ethical objections to a policy on euthanasia (or on organ transplants, and the like) that amounts to reliance on little more than the conscience of the surgeon, as a guide to acceptable practice. A raft of strategic objections stand in the way of such a policy, not least because the law must account for the possibility or likelihood that those dealing with considerable numbers of cases, on a professional basis, will too easily be *wrongly* convinced in at least some (kinds) of them that the situation they confront is a morally compelling one for euthanasia, when it is not (see chapter 1.2 above). Notice, though, how Griffin contrasts his objections to such a policy, with an instance in which the hand of the surgeon is 'forced' when he or she performs the euthanasia or transplant, as when the surgeon is acting under duress. In the latter case (as in example 1), the purely reactive, as opposed to proactive, nature of D's conduct means that any 'slippery slope' objection is unlikely to be of great moral significance. As we saw in the discussion of the contrast between civil disobedience and conscientious objection, reactive as opposed to pro-active conduct has fewer—if any—guidance implications for D or for others (the reason-focused strategic consideration), and is liable to have insignificant follow-on consequences of a morally troubling kind (the outcome-focused strategic consideration).

This brings me to the second issue, referred to in section 5 above, arising out of the passage from Raz explaining the authority of law. The law need not always seek to (re)assert its authority in every kind of case in which D has followed conflicting moral reasons directly, by convicting and punishing D as if D had has no conscience-based reasons of that kind for acting as he or she did. The fact that, as in some of the examples discussed so far,

[143] Although, as pointed out in chapter 1 above, the insistence that D must meet standards of temper-keeping, in order to be excused, is one of the necessary, rather than one of the sufficient, conditions of excuse.

the outcome-focused strategic considerations counting against claims to excuse in such cases are non-existent or remote possibilities, means that there is less reason for the law to assert its authority in full against D. On the contrary, when, for such reasons, the challenge to the authority of a specific prohibition is weak, providing a partial or even a complete excuse may actually enhance the moral authority of the criminal law as a whole, by showing the extent to which it takes the demands of moral agency seriously.[144] That being so, in demands-of-conscience cases such as example 1, granting D a *partial* excuse, partly in the light of D's emotional difficulties arising from his or her special relationship with V, preserves the residual sense that the law has authority to govern in such instances, whilst recognizing that the challenge to the authority of the law was weak, whereas the demands of conscience were strong. The law can stigmatize what D has done as wrong (D wrongly acted as if he or she was a moral island), but in the special circumstances, it can also acknowledge the compromise of autonomy that would have been involved in obedience to law, through the granting of the partial excuse.

8. Raz's Argument against Conscience-based Defences

An act motivated by conscientious objection is 'a breach of the law for the reason that the agent is morally prohibited to obey it'.[145] What is the reason for the distinctively liberal concern about conscientious objection? As Raz argues,[146] the humanistic liberal concern for personal autonomy, the ideal of (in substantial part) self-authorship of one's commitment to, shaping of, and participation in valuable relationships, goals, and so forth, leads to a concern for the flourishing of value pluralism. A commitment to value pluralism involves a commitment, *inter alia*, to creating the conditions in which people can, consistent with the demands of social co-operation and equal rights, seek to remain true to the values, projects, relationships that are central to their self-image and form the foundation of their self-respect.[147] In that regard, however, Raz argues that there is an insufficiently strong case

---

[144] See the discussion of this point, in the discussion of common goods, in chapter 1.2 above.

[145] Joseph Raz, *The Authority of Law*, 263. Raz adds that the moral prohibition may relate to the general character of the law, as when absolute pacifists object to conscription, or to particular applications of the law, as when pacifists oppose conscription into an offensive rather than self-defensive war.　　　　　　　　[146] Joseph Raz, *The Authority of Law*, 280.

[147] Joseph Raz, *The Authority of Law*, 280–282. See also section 1 above, on the non-individualistic understanding of this claim. As Raz points out, however, this concern could not be overriding, since it may involve shielding from liability individuals who hold morally mistaken views, and must therefore take second place on some occasions to securing what is right. In their pursuit, respectively, of ideological purity and of social and cultural stability, genuinely socialist or conservative political theories usually find it necessary or desirable to place an emphasis on promoting and enforcing a homogeneity of thought and action that is inconsistent with such liberal commitments.

for a general right to conscientious objection, detached from particular objections that might arise in relation to specific laws. Raz suggests that it is better, when creating or amending such laws, to anticipate and meet an obligation to address the issue in advance.[148] Some of his arguments to this end are the very kind of outcome-focused and reason-focused strategic concerns that are capable of undermining the case for an excuse, at the stage when the sufficiency conditions must be met. The legalism that would develop, in relation to the question of what conscientious objection amounts to, would make the right 'open to abuse', and might lead to greater 'self-doubt, self-deception, and in general undesirable forms of introspection' (both reason-focused strategic concerns).[149] Further, where political activism must be the necessary concomitant of the conscientious objection, 'given the potentially grave consequences of such actions', and the fact that 'too much is usually at stake in such cases' (outcome-focused strategic concerns), such instances should not be given formal legal recognition in a liberal state.[150] One might add that, as the product of a coherent and established system of moral beliefs, conscientious objection may commit one to the repetition of particular (in)actions, in a way that in itself raises reason-focused strategic concerns militating against granting of an excuse (the 'clean hands' problem).

At the end of the preceding section, I suggested that, given the right factual background, the argument for an *excuse* in demands-of-conscience cases is not undermined by objections of this sort. So, does that mean that in such cases Raz would support the provision of an excuse, or partial excuse, along the lines that I have suggested? There is a degree of equivocation in his attitude. On the one hand, he is a strong supporter of an excuse on facts such as those in example 1, describing D's claim as 'overwhelming'.[151] On the other hand, apparently flying in the face of such support, he makes it clear that the duty on the state not to coerce the conscience of any citizen applies only when the moral obligation to break the law stems from the perception that the law itself is wrong. There is no such duty, 'if the obligation to violate the law is thought to be due to *a rare combination of circumstances* or to any other conditions which cannot be expected to be met by amending the law'.[152] Why? Raz claims that what I am calling demands-of-conscience cases are not worthy of special legal recognition because they are most often and most easily avoidable by the citizen. One can usually control the circumstances that have led to the conflict between the law and one's deeply held convictions or values, and 'if one desires to remain faithful

---

[148] See section 2 above.   [149] Joseph Raz, *The Authority of Law*, 287.
[150] Joseph Raz, *The Authority of Law*, 282–283. This argument thus mirrors the one made above against formally excusing civil disobedience. Like Dworkin (see Ronald Dworkin, 'Civil Disobedience and Nuclear Protest'), Raz does not believe that law-breaking political activists need especially deterrent sentences, although (unlike Dworkin) he does not seem to believe they deserve special leniency either.   [151] Joseph Raz, *The Authority of Law*, 285.
[152] Ibid., 282 (my emphasis).

to one's moral principles one could, even if at a cost to oneself, prevent [the circumstances] from arising'.[153] Naturally, one should not stand ready to excuse those who seek out opportunities to put their convictions in conflict with the law. They are excluded by the 'clean hands' doctrine applicable to excuses. It seems unduly harsh, however, to rule out a demands-of-conscience excuse in every case where, albeit at a cost to oneself, one could prevent the conflict arising, because the 'cost' concerned may not be one that can be counted in simple terms of time and effort. The cost to D of avoiding the conflict may necessarily be moral. It may necessarily involve a sacrifice of self-respect, as it would if the D in example 1 was simply to walk away from the situation, and let the chance slip by respectively to end V's life as V wishes and as D has promised. For that reason, it is better to take the view that, as Raz candidly admits, his stance, 'may [involve] no more than an arbitrary distinction or one which at best is justified in terms of . . . administrative difficulty'.[154] In demands-of-conscience cases, one can underline this point through the analysis of excuses provided in chapter 2 above, by understanding the (partial) excuse as predominantly ascriptive (dimension 3), whether it is actively justificatory or capacity-focused (dimension 2). The jury or other fact-finder is predominantly concerned with whether it would be morally repugnant to convict for the (full) offence, because D is not to be blamed for acting wrongly.

9. The Demands-of-conscience Excuse and Individual Rights

From two very different theoretical perspectives, one can find what might be considered strong arguments for restricting the scope of a demands-of-conscience excuse to law-breaking that involves no (serious) rights violations. Let us begin with Raz's analysis. For Raz, the criminal law is for the protection of 'vital interests', and where vital interests are at stake, autonomy-based justifications for invading such interests can, and should, be overridden, unless (in a limited range of cases) V consents to the interference with his or her interests.[155] For Raz, vital interests are those directly concerned with individual rights. For him, the rightness or wrongness of criminalizing autonomy-based justifications for the invasion of vital interests centres on the question whether 'the matter affects *sufficiently* vital interests of the victim to justify the further intrusion into the liberty of the offenders which such measures involve'.[156] Things may be different where offences against the public interest are concerned. Such laws protect all of our

---

[153] Joseph Raz, *The Authority of Law*, 282.   [154] Ibid.   [155] Ibid., 284–285.
[156] Ibid., 284 (my emphasis). See the end of this section, for a discussion of the significance of the concession that 'sufficiency' may matter.

interests collectively, so one individual's contribution or efforts (by way, say, of tax contribution or abstaining from unauthorized disposal of garbage) are insignificant. There is, then, potentially more room for manoeuvre for the legislator to draft the laws in question in such a way that they tolerate conscience-based justifications for wrongdoing by minorities. Raz has in mind laws such as those permitting compulsory taxation, or those preventing speeding, and so forth. So, if my argument for a demands-of-conscience excuse were to track very closely Raz's argument for tolerating conscientious objection, I would seek to confine its application to laws of this kind, those protecting the public interest. Raz's argument is merely that there is a stronger case for tolerating conscientious objection when the public interest is at stake than when vital individual interests stand to be compromised. Such an argument cannot easily be shown to be wrong (indeed, it seems broadly to be right), but I think it involves some over-simplification.

It is clear, for example, that the present law sometimes permits conscientious objection in cases where each and every individual's contribution to upholding the public interest at stake is significant. This is so, for example, when the law exempts Jews and Muslims from strict animal cruelty laws, permitting them to practise ritual slaughter.[157] Animal cruelty laws are not 'public interest' laws in quite the sense in which Raz describes them, namely as laws providing for a public good 'whose availability to an individual does not depend on his personal contribution'.[158] In principle, every instance of law-breaking, however isolated, in some way undermines the integrity of the public good that is refraining from cruelty to animals. No doubt, Raz would reply that such a law does not touch and concern people's 'vital' interests, but the category of vital interests in Raz's theory is in itself not uncontroversial. It includes 'violation of property or contractual rights',[159] but excludes inchoate offences such as 'unlawful possession of firearms',[160] along with spying, counterfeiting, and polluting rivers[161] ('public interest' offences) that may be considered to be very serious offences in themselves. Given, thus, that the category of crimes that protect vital interests, as Raz defines them, does not coincide with the—necessarily vaguer—category of crimes that should be described as very serious, it is unclear that only the former can or should bear the moral weight that Raz wishes to place on it, namely the full burden of overriding claims to exemption based on conscientious objection. In short, the case for shielding crimes that protect so-called vital interests from conscientious objection claims, or from a demands-of-conscience excuse, however trivial the invasion of the interest and however compelling the demand of conscience, remains unproven.

---

[157] See the discussion in S. M. Poulter, *English Law and Ethnic Minority Customs*; Slaughterhouses Act 1974; Welfare of Animals (Slaughter and Killing) Regulations 1995.
[158] Joseph Raz, *The Authority of Law*, 285.   [159] Ibid., 284.   [160] Ibid., 286.
[161] Ibid., 283.

I put in question the strength of the case for relying on a hard-and-fast distinction between offences concerned with 'vital' interests and those concerned with 'public' interests, because it has been my case that in some rare instances there can be a case for wholly excusing some minor rights violations, particularly but not necessarily solely when it is ethical or religious objections to some kinds of medical care that are in issue. This is in the limited context where D is bound in conscience to refuse to give V up for, or to advise V to take, the medically appropriate course of treatment, as when, according to D's faith, it is his or her responsibility to ensure that, should V recover, V will not be excluded from the possibility of becoming a member of the faith by having received the treatment. In such instances, the excuse could (although it perhaps need not) be restricted to instances in which, as D is well aware, the authorities will in fact step in to ensure that V will receive what is officially regarded as the right treatment, thus preventing D's conscience-based stance from having too serious an impact on V. Perhaps noteworthy, in this regard, is the emphasis Raz places, in discussing offences against the public interest, on the insignificance of D's own contribution, as a factor militating in favour of granting an exception for conscientious objectors.[162] In these special cases, in the medical treatment context, where D knows (or, *a fortiori*, does something to ensure) that the authorities will step in to override his or her decision to refuse treatment for V, it can be precisely the moral insignificance of D's invasion of V's interests that, combined with the exceptional pull of conscience in the circumstances, provides grounds for an excuse.[163] As I set out by indicating, it was only ever when 'sufficiently' vital interests of V's were at stake that, for Raz, the state had a duty to override or ignore conscience-based reasons for invading such interests.[164]

Alan Brudner also argues from a neo-Hegelian perspective that actively justificatory reasons of a moral kind for law-breaking, as opposed to actively justificatory explanatory reasons of a factual kind (mistake cases), cannot excuse rights violations. For Brudner, 'the basis of criminal liability has nothing to do with one's moral worth or dangerousness and everything to do with one's denial of equal liberty as the basis of rights (thus a saint who performs a mercy killing is a murderer)'.[165] On this view, the explanation for an excuse or denial of responsibility must be that it in some way blocks the conclusion that, in doing the wrong, D was intentionally denying the victim's equal right to liberty. So, for Brudner, 'Insanity excuses if . . . there is lacking the devaluation of personality that alone implies the

---

[162] Joseph Raz, *The Authority of Law*, 285–286.

[163] The distinction between D's duty to follow the dictates of his or her faith in relation to V, and the duty of care D is under towards V under the general law, was explained in section 4 above.   [164] See text at n. 160 above.

[165] Alan Brudner, 'Agency and Welfare in the Penal Law', 38–39. See also chapter 2.6 above for a brief discussion of Brudner's views on the actively justificatory element to excuses.

nugatoriness of one's own rights',[166] and more broadly, 'the conceptual basis of excuses ... [is] ... that the accused, through lack of intention, meant no challenge to the intersubjective basis of right'.[167] I will come back to the excuses that this conceptual foundation supposedly supports in a moment. What of regulatory or public welfare offences? Here, in virtue of the fact that such offences do not involve a challenge to equal liberty rights, Brudner anticipates a potentially much wider range of excuses, based on 'capacity to conform to the law'.[168] In principle, picking up the point about the moral worth of the saint that he makes in the passage cited above, perhaps Brudner might regard this capacity as including moral capacity and the effects of the demands of conscience. So, although in a rather more sharply defined sense than Raz, he would institute a regime for conscientious objection and excuse claims with a very different character, depending on the nature of the offence (individual right-based, or public welfare).

As I have already indicated in discussing Raz's views, it is hard to doubt the case for making some distinction between offences against individual interests, and offences against public welfare, when considering how wide in scope excuses (and permissible claims to exemption on the grounds of conscientious objection) should be. Nonetheless, there are weaknesses in the way that Brudner makes his case for an unbridgeable gulf between the two (as we have seen, Raz does not go quite that far). First, it is unclear that all the excuses Brudner is prepared to see continue to apply to invasions of individual rights really do entail that there is, to use his words cited above, 'through lack of intention, no challenge to the intersubjective basis of right'. Provocation, for example, is merely thought to '*simulate* the conceptual basis of excuses', in that regard.[169] Further, in duress cases, it appears that there *is* a challenge to the intersubjective basis of right, but one based on D's reasonable judgment that he or she 'is entitled to treat his life or health as inalienable when they conflict with another's property in some particular things; he will not be entitled to do so if they conflicted with another's life'.[170] In my terms, then, Brudner confines duress to instances in which the excuse has an actively justificatory, predominantly normative basis. Fair enough; but as we saw in chapter 2.5, Brudner is in fact prepared to extend the excuse to at least some kinds of invasion of personal (bodily integrity) rights, and does not confine it to instances where property is sacrificed for the sake of personal rights. So, it is not as clear as it might be that the excusatory character of duress has quite the strength of justificatory backbone to it that Brudner would have us believe it must have. What these points indicate in general terms, is that Brudner underplays the significance

---

[166] Alan Brudner, *The Unity of the Common Law* (Berkeley, California: University of California Press, 1995), 238.   [167] Ibid., 244.

[168] Alan Brudner, 'Agency and Welfare in the Penal Law', 47.

[169] Alan Brudner, *The Unity of the Common Law*, 244 (my emphasis).

[170] Ibid., 243.

of ascriptive factors in excusing conditions, even where normative factors play a crucial role. In principle, excuses can excuse rights-violations just as surely as they can excuse anything else.

As the 'saint' example shows, Brudner shares with a number of other theorists the view that wrongdoing, rather than the moral worth of or threat posed by the offender, is one of the criminal law's defining concerns. In developing this view, however, in Brudner's theory the contrast between the so-called domain of agency, and that of welfare, becomes way too sharp. It seems to rest on a distinction between what is of ultimate value (agency), and what is of merely instrumental value (welfare). Properly construed, the liberals' harm principle involves drawing more subtle distinctions. Some actions, such as polluting rivers, desecrating graves, or killing endangered species, may be *mala in se* and in a relevant sense harmful, even if they involve no attack on human agency as such.[171] This is because they may involve an unjustified attack on or damage to things of *intrinsic* (not merely instrumental) value, and other things being equal,[172] that can set back human interests in a way as serious as an attack on agency itself.[173] That being so, a theory of excuses should not be made to hinge on a rigid distinction between agency and welfare interests.

---

[171] See Stephen Shute, John Gardner, and Jeremy Horder (eds.), *Action and Value in Criminal Law*, 4–5; 19–20.

[172] They may not always be equal. For example, one justification for damaging interests of intrinsic value, a justification of great importance to liberal theorists, is that the damage is partly constitutive of an activity or way of life that itself has intrinsic value. So, for example, one might permit people to kill whales, to make use of their flesh and bones for various purposes, if those peoples' intrinsically valuable way of life depends on that activity. Unlike commercial whaling, the justification for the activity is genuinely social and cultural, not merely economic.

[173] This issue has explored with great sophistication by John Gardner and Stephen Shute, 'The Wrongness of Rape', in Jeremy Horder (ed.), *Oxford Essays in Jurisprudence*, 4th Series, chapter 10.

6

Excusing Strict Liability Crime: A Liberal Account beyond the Common Law Agenda

1. THE NARROWNESS OF THE COMMON LAW'S PERSPECTIVE

Perhaps a shade unfairly, the history of excuses could be summarized as the history of judicial and academic preoccupation with seeking to shed ever-increasing concentrations of light on what ought to be regarded as just one part of the excusatory domain. It has been the legal limits and theoretical basis of defences designated and discussed as such by classical thinkers—insanity, mistake, intoxication, provocation, necessity, and duress—that have attracted the lion's share of the attention. As well as regarding short-comings as inexcusable (see chapter 4.1 above), and hence outside the excusatory domain, classical thinkers paid little attention to excuses that might be regarded as having special moral importance in relation to the kinds of wrongdoing they knew could be created through the operation of the 'pro-active', bureaucratic-administrative state.[1] Mentally imprisoned, for the most part, by the confines of classical thinking, English judges have shown little concern for such excuses either. Consequently, 'definitional minimalism' (see chapter 5.1 above) continues unacceptably to restrict the range of lawyers' and theorists' concerns, in the shaping of excuses. The excusatory agenda remains much the same as it was when Plato and Aristotle turned their attention to the matter. An instructive example is the well-known case of *Sweet v Parsley*.[2] In this case, D was charged with and initially convicted of 'being concerned in the management of premises used for the purpose of smoking cannabis'.[3] She had allowed a group of students

---

[1] So, for example, Aristotle was accustomed to draw a distinction of a kind that would now be regarded as a distinction between *mala in se* and *mala prohibita*: (*Nichomachean Ethics*, v, chapter 7), 'Of political justice part is natural, part legal—natural, that which everywhere has the same force and does not exist by people's thinking this or that; legal, that which is originally indifferent, but when it has been laid down is not indifferent, e.g., that a prisoner's ransom shall be a mina, or that a goat and not two sheep shall be sacrificed', cited by Stuart Green, 'Why it's a Crime to Tear the Tag off a Mattress: Overcriminalisation and the Moral Content of Regulatory Offences', (1997) 46 *Emory Law Journal* 97 1533, 1570.

[2] [1970] AC 132 (HL).

[3] Contrary to section 5(b) of what was then the Dangerous Drugs Act 1965.

to sub-let a farmhouse she did not herself use, and they were the ones who—wholly unknown to her—had been smoking the cannabis. The House of Lords quashed her conviction, on the grounds that the offence implied knowledge or awareness on the part of the person concerned in the management of the premises that cannabis was being smoked there. It was held to be open to the defendant to deny such knowledge by arguing that, say, she believed (on reasonable grounds) that cannabis was not being smoked on the premises, and hence put the prosecution to its proof on the *mens rea* point.[4] So, a *mens rea* requirement having been read into the statute, the case was decided in accordance with the narrow common law understanding of *mens rea* as subjective fault (knowledge), the requirement being regarded as brought into play only by evidence of an equally narrow common law understanding of denial of subjective *mens rea* (mistake). The real issue in *Sweet v Parsley* could have been regarded as being not (a) whether a *mens rea* requirement of a subjective kind could or should be implied into the wording of the statute, but (b) whether D had taken all the steps it would be reasonable for her to have taken to ensure that the offence (on its ordinary wording) was not committed. In other words, the issue should have been whether justice required that the courts make available to D a 'due diligence' defence.

Half a step towards such a position was taken by the Australian High Court in *Proudman v Dayman*,[5] where the Court abandoned (a) above, i.e. the rigid (and frequently artificial) approach of asking simply whether the legislature has expressly or impliedly excluded traditional *mens rea* requirements. Instead, the court indicated that the issue was whether D could be exculpated by way of excuse. Dixon J said:

There may no longer be any presumption that *mens rea* . . . is an ingredient in an offence created by a modern statute; but to concede that . . . does not mean that the rule that honest and reasonable mistake is prima facie admissible as an exculpation has lost its application also.[6]

The final words of this passage indicate that the High Court remained sufficiently in thrall to the narrow common law perspective on excuses, to regard mistake as the paradigm example of the kind of plea that ought to exculpate in cases where the legislature has ostensibly imposed strict liability. It was not

---

[4] See the speech of Lord Diplock, *Sweet v Parsley* [1970] AC 132, 164.

[5] (1941) 67 CLR 536.

[6] Ibid., 540–541. Morris and Howard have claimed that, far from being exceptional, this kind of approach is one that the Australian High Court had adhered to consistently over the sixty years since its inception, however trivial the offence: Norval Morris and Colin Howard, *Studies in Criminal Law* (Oxford: Clarendon Press, 1964), 201. The important advance in *Proudman v Dayman* can be contrasted with the intellectually idle approach of Donovan J in *St Margaret's Trust Ltd* [1958] 2 All ER 289, in which the judge apparently found compelling the following non sequitur: '[t]here would be little point in enacting that no one should breach the defences against a flood, and at the same time excusing anyone who did it innocently.'

until the decision in *R v City of Sault Ste Marie*[7] that the Canadian Supreme Court fully broke free from common law shackles. The Court held that even when *mens rea* is not an ingredient of an offence, exculpation was still possible, if D could show on the balance of probabilities that he took all reasonable care: 'The defence will be available if the accused reasonably believed in a mistaken set of facts which, if true, would render the act or omission innocent, *or if he took all reasonable steps to avoid the particular event*'.[8] Let us put on one side the question that loomed disproportionately large in the Law Lords' speeches in *Sweet v Parsley* when they considered alternative approaches, namely whether at common law a legal burden of persuasion can be placed on an accused person with respect to exculpation.[9] The key advance, then, in *R v Sault Ste Marie*, is the recognition that, in theory, even if D is only too well aware that he or she may be committing an offence (i.e. D has subjective *mens rea*), if all reasonable steps were taken to avoid committing it then that in itself is a sufficient ground for excuse. One of the tasks of this chapter will be to give this approach a sound theoretical foundation, one that goes beyond Hart's alternative to common law subjectivism, the 'fair opportunity' doctrine (see chapter 1.6 above). Although it could be defended in other ways, in section 6 below I will connect that foundation to the liberal defence of an 'active' account of well-being, wherein the (excusatory) emphasis is on people's wholehearted efforts; and I will suggest that it ought to be regarded as opening the way to other excuses whose primary relevance is to regulatory offences, such as reasonable ignorance of the law.

2. Approaches to Regulatory Crime: Legislative Interest in 'Fault'

According to one influential, but superficial, reading of the history of English criminal law in the nineteenth century, whilst (from the mid-century onwards) Parliament was creating ever more 'pro-prosecution' crimes of strict liability, with scant regard for the mental element,[10] the courts and law

---

[7] (1978) 85 DLR (3rd) 161.   [8] Ibid., 182–83 (my emphasis).

[9] See e.g. *Sweet v Parsley* [1970] AC 132, 158 (Lord Pearce), and 164 (Lord Diplock).

[10] See e.g. the observations of Lord Pearce in ibid., 156, 'Since the Industrial Revolution the increasing complexity of life called into being new duties and crimes which took no account of intent'. See also H. L. A. Hart, *Punishment and Responsibility*, 176: 'this is a development of the last hundred years, the general principle that for criminal liability there must be *mens rea* has been qualified by the admission into the body of the law of a number of offences where liability is said to be "strict" . . . They concern the maintenance of standards in the manufacture of goods . . .'. Hart's use of the image of strict liability offences being admitted into the 'body' of the law conjures up a vision of an unpleasant virus liable to infect the otherwise healthy whole if left unchecked, a vision that accords with his generally hostile approach to strict liability. Neither Lord Pearce nor Hart is, of course, saying that Parliament never paid attention to the mental element in crime when it created regulatory offences, but that is not unfairly regarded as the impression they (wish to) give.

reformers were developing a more 'pro-defendant', subjective approach to liability for crimes *mala in se*.[11] In fact, what are now thought of as the core elements of the objective dimension to liability and excuses where crimes *mala in se* are in issue, were more or less confirmed at this very time.[12] More importantly, although many ostensibly strict liability crimes were indeed introduced in the late nineteenth century, Parliament also introduced to the criminal law new ways of thinking about the mental element in crime and about excuses, as these bore on regulatory offences, developments over-looked in the hail of protest that was to meet the increasingly frequent use of strict liability. However, these new ways of thinking about culpability in the regulatory context made no impact whatsoever on common law theory and practice. Broadly speaking, judges (supported by a number of commen-tators) continued to trumpet their belief that the common law could be relied upon by the individual as a bastion of liberty, without any develop-ment of its understanding of culpability. At the same time, though, judges failed entirely to draw lessons from changing legislative practice, to develop the kind of robust and sophisticated approach at common law to the inter-pretation of criminal statutes, and hence to excusing regulatory offences, that could have given their belief real substance.

In developing this thesis, I shall begin with some brief and somewhat frag-mentary historical reflections on the significance of the late nineteenth cen-tury period to the development of the regulatory state in Britain. On an older view, according to A. J. P. Taylor:

> Until August 1914 a sensible, law-abiding Englishman could pass through life and hardly notice the existence of the state, beyond the post office and the policeman. He could live where he liked and as he liked . . . The state intervened to prevent the cit-izen from eating adulterated food or contracting certain infectious diseases. It imposed safety rules in factories, and prevented women, and adult males in some industries, from working excessive hours. The state saw to it that children received education up to the age of 13 . . . This tendency towards state action was increasing . . . Still, broadly speaking, the state acted only to help those who could not help themselves. It left the adult citizen alone.[13]

In this famous passage, we can see a tension between Taylor's wish to pre-sent the First World War as an epoch-making event, in terms of the effect it had on the role of the state in the regulation of 'ordinary life', and his

---

[11] The classic statement of this view would be that of Turner, in J. W. C. Turner (ed.), *Kenny's Outlines of Criminal Law*, 16th edn., (Cambridge: Cambridge University Press, 1952), 118, in which he claims there was 'the stage, stretching into the nineteenth century, when the law came to adopt a subjective test; that is to say, it now looked primarily at the attitude of the defendant's mind which inspired his conduct.' For a more detailed examination, presenting a more balanced picture, see K. J. M. Smith, *Lawyers, Legislators and Theorists*, 159–172 and chapter 5.

[12] See Jeremy Horder, 'Two Histories and Four Hidden Principles of *Mens Rea*' (1997) 113 *Law Quarterly Review* 95, 108.

[13] A. J. P. Taylor, *England 1914–1945* (Oxford: Clarendon Press, 1965), 1.

acknowledgement that the state was already heavily engaged in such regulation by the end of the nineteenth century.[14] By then, large numbers of people were being prosecuted for failing to ensure that their children attended school.[15] There had been riots over the legal requirement (backed by a threat of criminal sanction) to vaccinate children.[16] The storm of protest that met the introduction of regulation of publicans and the liquor trade, under the Licensing Act 1872, led Gladstone to attribute his defeat at the polls to the view that 'we have been borne down in a torrent of gin and beer'.[17] If, then, what Taylor refers to as 'pass[ing] through life' includes being a parent, and trying to run a business (such as one concerned with food, or drink or drugs), by the mid-1870s the regulatory role of the state had already become both visible and controversial. As José Harris argues, whilst influential politicians still thought of this as a libertarian age, 'economic *laissez-faire* did not necessarily entail moral *laissez-faire*, and many mid-Victorian social policies were explicitly designed to reward or punish certain kinds of rational moral behaviour on the part of individuals'.[18] In that regard, as Harris says, a concern for physical and moral health permitted 'a very elastic interpretation of legitimate public action' (including slum clearance and re-housing).[19]

These developments represent, like the late nineteenth-century concern for those suffering from what we now call 'diminished responsibility' (see chapter 4.1 above), the movement from a largely libertarian to a liberal state. This is a state committed to the view that personal autonomy will never in practice be widely realized in a large market economy without state-sponsored promotion of 'public goods', such as education, health and housing (see chapter 4.11 above). It is, though, one thing to support state-sponsored promotion of public goods, as liberals do. It is another thing to assume, as the Victorians did, that the *criminal law* should spearhead the attempt to secure citizens' participation in reaching that goal;[20] and it

[14] For a contrary view, see José Harris, *Private Lives, Public Spirit: A Social History of Britain 1870–1914* (Oxford: Oxford University Press, 1993), 252, 'In so far as there have ever been great chasms rather than mere subterranean murmurings in the deep structures of British social history, it seems to me that they occurred in the 1870s and 1880s, and then again in the 1960s and 1970s, rather than in the apparently more dramatic and cataclysmic happenings of either of the two world wars.'

[15] The legal basis for this was section 74 of the Education Act 1870.

[16] Vaccination (Amendment) Act 1867, section 16; Roysten Lambert, 'A Victorian National Health Service: State Vaccination, 1855–71' (1962) 5 *Historical Journal* 1.

[17] Cited by John Morley, *Life of Gladstone* (London: Greenwood Press, 1971), vi, chapter 14. The bishop of Peterborough spoke for many, in memorably declaring, in the debate over the Licensing Bill, that he would rather see 'England free, rather than England sober,' cited by Sir R. Ensor, *England 1870–1914* (Oxford: Clarendon Press, 1936), 21.

[18] José Harris, *Private Lives, Public Spirit: A Social History of Britain 1870–1914*, 197 and 198. For discussion of this theme, in the context of the development of diminished responsibility, see chapter 4 above.   [19] Ibid., 199.

[20] The modern 'locus classicus' on the proper sphere of the criminal law, as far as liberal thinking about this issue is concerned, is Joseph Raz, 'Autonomy, Toleration and the Harm Principle', in Ruth Gavison (ed.), *Issues in Contemporary Legal Philosophy* (Oxford: Clarendon Press,

would, of course, be a yet further thing to believe that the criminal law should play this role, without there being any proper opportunities for citizens under the threat of conviction and sanction to excuse their non-participation. The Victorians frequently eschewed this last view,[21] and rightly so. For it would have set one liberal aim, the securing of valuable and flourishing public goods, against another liberal aim, maintaining a 'plural' view of criminal law.[22] This is a view (examined below) according to which there is always room for the more or less unforeseen exigencies, or other extenuating features, of the situations in which individual Ds come to commit the *actus reus* of crimes against the public good to shape perceptions of adequate fault requirements and applicable excuses. In that regard, as K. J. M. Smith's diligent research has revealed, when creating regulatory offences, Parliament sometimes gave careful consideration to whether or not to include a fault element in the offence in question.[23] For example, in the process leading up to enactment of the (in)famous provision making it an offence to sell intoxicants to a drunken person, contrary to section 13 of the Licensing Act 1872, a requirement of knowledge that the purchaser was drunk was originally argued for and included at the Committee stage, but then later withdrawn in response to a proposed amendment.[24] By way of contrast, the Government of the day resisted attempts by some to remove the requirement of knowledge from the offence under the same Act of 'keeping a disorderly house'.[25]

Even more significantly, in pursuing its regulatory agenda, Parliament introduced new varieties of excuse hitherto unknown to the common law (except in so far as, where relevant in an evidentiary way, they amounted to a denial of negligence). Under the Food and Drugs Act 1872, mixing or selling food injurious to health was not an offence unless done 'wilfully' or 'to the knowledge' of the D: standard, (broadly) subjective *mens rea* terms, at the heart of the definitional element. When the offence was repealed and replaced by the Sale of Food and Drugs Act 1875, however, the analogous offences created were ones of seemingly strict liability, but then by section 5

1987), chapter 8.1. His views on 'public goods' can be found in Joseph Raz, 'Rights-Based Moralities'.

[21] Most regulatory criminal laws of the nineteenth century provided, if not *mens rea* elements like knowledge, then excuses, such as 'reasonable diligence' shown, or 'reasonable excuse' provided; but they did so very inconsistently: see *Sherras v De Rutzen* [1895] 1 QB 918.

[22] In this regard, a persistent, almost wilful, failure to appreciate that one can wholeheartedly support the promotion of public goods, but (perfectly consistently) also regard as disproportionate the indiscriminate or unbending use of the criminal law to coerce individuals in seeking to promote those goods, continues to blunt the force of much 'critical' discussion of liberal criminal law theory.

[23] K. J. M. Smith, *Lawyers, Legislators and Theorists*, 211–213.

[24] Hansard, Parl Debs (1872) 212, 1701–1703 & 660–662. As Smith rightly observes, it is hard not to conclude that, at the root of Stephen J's celebrated judgment in *Cundy v Le Cocq* (1884) 13 QBD 207, which held this offence to be one of strict liability, must have been an awareness of this legislative background.

[25] K. J. M. Smith, *Lawyers, Legislators and Theorists*, 213.

of the Act, a D was not to be held liable, 'if he shows to the satisfaction of the justice of the court . . . that he did not know . . . and that he could not with reasonable diligence have obtained that knowledge'. Here, then, is both a switch in the burden of proof, and a new 'due diligence' defence to which the burden relates, that, as we have seen, did not become firmly established at common law for another 100 years (and then, almost needless to say, only outside England).[26] There was nothing unique about this Act. Under section 16 of the Vaccination (Amendment) Act 1867, a parent was placed under a positive duty to have a child vaccinated within three months of birth. Section 29 of the Act, that made a failure to comply with section 16 a criminal offence, read, 'Every parent . . . who shall neglect to take such child . . . to be vaccinated . . . *and shall not render a reasonable excuse* for his neglect shall be guilty of an offence' (my emphasis).[27] In one sense, the structure of offence and defence established by such statutes represented a radical break with common law thinking, because such defences were unknown to the common law. Yet, in another way, in virtue of their very general and largely facilitative (see chapter 1.4 above), 'case-by-case' rather than specialized and highly determinate character, the defences fitted the mould of already existing common law defences, such as, say, duress. In other words, with these defences, not only was the list of instances in which they might be available always open to addition, but there was also a not inconsiderable element of evaluative work to be done by the fact-finder in deciding, in each case, whether the element of 'reasonableness' was satisfied. It would, I believe, have been a relatively uncontroversial matter (at a time when Parliament scarcely had that much more democratic legitimacy than the courts) for the courts to have taken a lead from Parliament, and by a relatively minor act of judicial law creation held that a 'due diligence' defence—or the like—was also available at common law, in cases where justice and good conscience so required but Parliament had omitted to provide for it. No such development, of course, was forthcoming. Why not?

3. APPROACHES TO REGULATORY CRIME: THE COURTS' CAPITULATION

Following the French Revolution, English lawyers took it upon themselves to puff up the common law as the epitome of a code devoted to the protection of the individual's traditional liberties, as against state authoritarianism.[28]

---

[26] See *R v Strawbridge* [1970] NZLR 909; *Civil Aviation Department v MacKenzie* [1983] NZLR 78; *R v City of Sault Ste Marie* (1978) 85 DLR (3rd) 161.

[27] A similar, 'reasonable excuse' defence is also to be found, for example, as a defence to a number of offences under the Public Health Act 1875.

[28] I pursue this theme in Jeremy Horder, 'Strict Liability, Statutory Construction and the Spirit of Liberty', 461–463.

So, for Sir James Stephen, 'the spirit of French Legislation ... is very favourable to persons in authority', and 'a dictator like Napoleon [is] placed in such circumstances that he can practically impose his own will on a great nation'.[29] By way of contrast, he thought, with such a top-down, command-based system characterized by purely means–end rationality, the common law was (naturally) 'formed by very slow degrees and with absolutely no conscious adaptation of means to ends', having 'an organic unity which seems to me to be wanting in the French system'.[30] Furthermore, he opined, in England 'it is unnecessary to distinguish between the morality of the Legislator and that of the persons legislated for, for the two may be considered practically identical'.[31] Yet, ironically, at the very time Stephen was writing, the British state was engaged in creating what José Harris has called a 'great chasm ... in the deep structures of British social history',[32] imposing its will through its often controversial experiments in regulatory government and bureaucratic managerialism.

Take, by way of example, the introduction of a professional police force, from the time of the creation of the Metropolitan Police in 1829 onwards, one of the developments that marked what has been called, in relation to late nineteenth-century Britain, the rise of the 'Policeman State'.[33] Initially, this generated understandable public hostility. It was not just a matter of distrust of the kind of state intervention derided in Parliament itself as 'the teasing vigilance of the perpetual superintendence of the law',[34] or dislike of plain-clothes detectives (often seen at this early time as more or less unregulated official spies).[35] Over time, there was clear evidence of corruption amongst the existing police, who sometimes stooped to the old thief-takers' device of organizing both the crime *and* the apprehension of the offender, creating a series of scandals in the early part of the nineteenth century.[36]

---

[29] Sir J. F. Stephen, *History of the Criminal Law of England*, ii, 77.   [30] Ibid., i, 565.
[31] Ibid., ii, 77.
[32] José Harris, *Private Lives, Public Spirit: A Social History of Britain 1870–1914*, 252.
[33] Gatrell's phrase: see V. A. C. Gatrell, 'Crime, Authority and the Policeman-State', in F. M. L. Thompson (ed.), *The Cambridge Social History of Britain, 1750–1950* (Cambridge: Cambridge University Press, 1990), cited by M. Weiner, *Reconstructing the Criminal*, 262. See Stephen's discussion of summary offences found in Sir J. F. Stephen, *History of the Criminal Law of England*, iii, chapter 32, where he identifies a category of what he calls 'police' offences, offences principally concerned with public order, created by Acts setting up, modifying or regulating the police.   [34] Hansard, xix, col 647 (29 March 1811).
[35] See Clive Emsley, 'The History of Crime and Crime Control Institutions', in Mike Maguire, Rod Morgan, and Robert Reiner (eds.), *The Oxford Handbook of Criminology*, 217–218.
[36] Clive Emsley, 'The History of Crime and Crime Control Institutions', 211–212; Ben Bowling and Janet Foster, 'Policing and the Police', in Mike Maguire, Rod Morgan, and Robert Reiner (eds.), *The Oxford Handbook of Criminology*, 982. It was not until much later that their legitimacy gradually became more widely accepted. For example, in 1912, it was claimed that, 'Forty years ago, it was an every-day occurrence for defendant's counsel, when there was no defence, to attack the credit of the policemen witnesses. To-day this practice has become almost obsolete': Sir C. S. Kenny, *Outlines of Criminal Law* (Cambridge: Cambridge University Press, 1929), 14th edn., 446 n. 3. Even then, this greater degree of legitimacy came about in part through police acceptance that their principal role was to concentrate on the

In spite of this, there was no judicial move to create anything remotely resembling a defence of entrapment, as one kind of defence for the citizen against the outcome of police malpractice.[37] Yet, for Stephen, it was French rather than English law whose criminal proceedings are 'instituted secretly and carried on oppressively'.[38] So, it was Stephen who was, in this respect as in others, (as the modern phrase goes) simply 'in denial'. In consequence, perhaps, in so far as he acknowledged the existence of the regulatory state at all, he saw no need whatsoever for the common law values that were meant to be in part constitutive and in part supportive of the value of individual liberty, to play a role in defining and limiting the reach of regulatory crime. Notoriously, for Stephen, the 'true' realm of the criminal law was that of 'gross outrages against the public and against individuals which we commonly associate with the word crime'.[39] So, following a brief discussion of regulatory offences, Stephen concludes (with the weak pun on 'summary' highlighting the dismissive nature of his approach):

Probably all the acts which regulate particular trades or branches of business . . . create offences punishable on summary conviction. I pass over these large subjects in a cursory and summary way because the offences in question do not form part of the criminal law properly so called, but are merely the sanctions by which other branches of the law are, in case of need, enforced.[40]

So, as far as Stephen was concerned, 'the definition of offences of this class is a special matter little related to broad principles of any kind, especially moral principles'.[41]

Not all judges, of course, took such a blinkered and complacent view. Famously, in *Fowler v Padget*[42] Lord Kenyon strongly defended the application of the common-law-as-natural-law, and in particular the maxim

---

'criminal classes' living in certain areas, so that 'they guarded the elegant areas of St James by watching the slums of St Giles': Clive Emsley, 'The History of Crime and Crime Control Institutions', 217.

[37] Such an excuse was familiar enough in other jurisdictions: see *Jacobson v US* (1992) 112 S Ct 1535, and the discussion in Andrew Ashworth, *Principles of Criminal Law*, 3rd edn., 248–250. It should, though, be noted that entrapment is not really an excuse for crime, in the way in which that notion is understood here, because although 'entrapment' can be a reason for which D acts that falls be to be evaluated in a sympathetic light, it is only when we discover that it was (unknown to D) police instigation that led D to commit the crime that this becomes of great moral significance. In and of itself, without some element of threat or undue influence, showing that someone else egged one on to commit a crime is not saying much in mitigation. This suggests that the real basis of an entrapment defence is not an explanation-based excuse, but an 'abuse of legal process' by the police themselves that makes the subsequent criminal proceedings unfair: see further Andrew Ashworth, 'Testing Fidelity to Legal Values: Official Involvement and Criminal Justice', in Stephen Shute and A. P. Simester (eds.), *Criminal Law Theory: Doctrines of the General Part*, chapter 13. Under moral pressure following the passing of the Human Rights Act 1998, the House of Lords belatedly recognized an 'abuse of process' basis on which D could plead entrapment as a defence: *R v Looseley* [2001] UKHL 53.

[38] Sir J. F. Stephen, *History of the Criminal Law of England*, i, 565.   [39] Ibid., i, 4.

[40] Ibid., iii, 266.

[41] Sir J. F. Stephen, *A General View of the Criminal Law of England*, iii, 100, cited by K. J. M. Smith, *Lawyers, Legislators and Theorists*, 217.   [42] (1798) 7 TR 509.

that *actus non facit reum nisi mens sit rea*, to regulatory offences, in the following terms:

It is a principle of natural justice, and of our law, that *actus non facit reum nisi mens sit rea* . . . I would adopt any construction of the statute that the words will bear, in order to avoid such monstrous consequences as would manifestly ensue from the construction [favouring strict liability].[43]

Drawing on the legacy of Coke,[44] Lord Kenyon's approach is to apply to the criminal law a tradition of supposedly 'anti-positivist,' common law thinking that is tied to a distinctive method of statutory interpretation, i.e. straining to give statutory words a meaning that acknowledges the common law value in question: here, the incorporation of an implicit mental element into the definition of the offence.[45] This is what can be called the 'static' version of 'anti-positivist' common law thinking, according to which it is traditional conceptions of fault and excuse, those already known to the common law, in the light of which statutes are to be interpreted. The static version of common law thinking found some supporters amongst the judiciary during the period under discussion. So, in *R v Morris*,[46] for example, Byles J held that statutes were to be construed 'in conformity with the common law rather than against it, except where and so far as the statute is plainly intended to alter the course of the common law'.[47] However, the attempt to weave the Blackstonian vision of a rights-based, 'natural' common law into the interpretation of criminal statutes was only ever half-hearted. The consequences of a finding of strict liability often turned out to be viewed as 'monstrous' (to use Lord Kenyon's word) only when Ds themselves

---

[43] In *Fowler v Padget*, D stood to be found bankrupt—a criminal matter then—if the offence in question was found to be one of strict liability. So, there is a whiff of *mala in se*, or of stigma attached to conviction, about this case. See further, *Bowman v Blyth* (1856) 7 E & B 26.

[44] See the passage from Coke cited in *Margate Pier v Hannam* (1819) 3 B & Ald 266, 270, 'Acts of Parliament are to be so construed, as no man that is innocent, or free from injury or wrong, be by a literal construction punished or endamaged.'

[45] For the historical and theoretical background to this approach, see Gerald Postema, 'Classical Common Law Jurisprudence (Part II)' (2003) 3 *Oxford Journal of Commonwealth Law* 1, 18, 'Typically, common lawyers in this era [the seventeenth century] contrasted the reasoned and considered judgments of the courts with the arbitrary and heedless legislation of Parliament. The latter they regarded as the product of a temporary aggregate of wills rather than the product of publicly deliberated common judgment.' I use the term anti-positivist only with reluctance (hence, the inverted commas), since it has become common to contrast positivist and common ('natural law') approaches to statutory interpretation: see David Dyzenhaus, 'The Politics of Deference: Judicial Review and Democracy', in Michael Taggert (ed.), *The Province of Administrative Law* (Oxford: Hart Publishing, 1997), 280. However, as we will see, there is nothing really anti-positivist in Lord Kenyon's approach at all.

[46] (1867) LR 1 CCR 90.

[47] Ibid., 95. See also *A-G v Bradlaugh* (1885) 14 QBD 667, 689 (per Brett MR), 'it is contrary to the whole established law of England (unless the Legislation on the subject has clearly enacted it), to say that a person can be guilty of a crime in England without a wrongful intent—without an attempt to do that which the law has forbidden', cited in A. P. Simester and G. R. Sullivan, *Criminal Law: Theory and Doctrine*, 1st edn., 158. Other cases to a similar effect are cited by them at 159 n. 14.

generated great sympathy, in highly unusual cases such as *R v Tolson*.[48] When D's activities attracted less sympathy, he or she was likely to be treated much less sympathetically, like the 'cad', Prince.[49]

Moreover, there is an inherent weakness in this way of seeking to apply the static version of common law thinking to regulatory offences, the root cause of which is that it is not really an 'anti-positivist' approach at all. Those who were prepared to continue to assert the legal importance of what they took to be common law values, did not challenge the view that the legal *validity* of the statutes they were construing was one thing, and the moral merit of those statutes a rather different thing. In other words, they implicitly affirmed rather than denied a positivist analysis of these statutes. What they were in fact doing was, perfectly permissibly (legally speaking), using their 'ultimate' discretion[50] to decide that the background against which those admittedly valid statutes would be interpreted was a background in which common law values would be taken to have a great and continuing importance. This interpretive background they preferred to the background, favoured by judges with more Benthamite sympathies, in which (broadly speaking) the seemingly more value-neutral history of the efforts to make legislative intent clear took interpretive priority.[51] The implicit positivism in the *Fowler v Padget*[52] approach proves to be a weakness, because the willingness to acknowledge that the wording of statutes binds whether or not it has merit means that it is always likely that many judges will find that they lack the courage of their supposedly 'anti-positivist', common law convictions about the importance of *mens rea*, when faced with the argument that there is nothing particular in the language of the statute to indicate that *mens rea* is required. As Avory J was later to put it, in *R v Forde*:[53]

The words of a statute cannot be construed, contrary to their meaning, as embracing cases merely because no good reason appears why those cases should be excluded. It is not the duty of the court to make the law reasonable, but to expound it as it stands, according to the real sense of the words.[54]

The temptation to acquiesce in a prosecutorial 'ordinary language' argument will be all the greater, of course, if it is coupled with an argument of a kind supported by the passage cited from Stephen,[55] that where regulatory

---

[48] (1889) 23 QBD 168.

[49] *R v Prince* (1875) LR 2, 154, discussed in illuminating detail by K. J. M. Smith, *Lawyers, Legislators and Theorists*, 207–211.

[50] Judges' ultimate discretion is the discretion to decide what rules and principles shall govern the interpretation of binding law, including, say, a law that purports to lay down interpretive principles binding on judges. The discretion is 'ultimate' in the sense that it is not derived from any higher legal norm: see further, Joseph Raz, *The Authority of Law*, 96–97.

[51] It has, of course, frequently proved tempting to seek to merge these two backgrounds to some extent, by speaking of what the legislature *would have* intended, had it given the matter thought: see further, Ronald Dworkin, *Law's Empire* (London: Fontana, 1986), 325–327.

[52] (1798) 7 TR 509.

[53] [1923] 2 KB 400. See further, the discussion of sexual offences at the end of this section.

[54] Ibid., 404.   [55] See n. 40 above.

UNIVERSITY OF WINCHESTER LIBRARY

offences are in issue the consequences of conviction for D are relatively trivial, when compared with the (supposedly) great inconvenience that will be caused to regulatory authorities by the implication of fault requirements.[56] It can, thus, prove all too easy for a judge to mask a failure, in point of courage of common law conviction, with a claim that he or she is doing no more than faithfully construing a statute in accordance with Parliament's intention. In turn, such an approach (what one might call 'weak-kneed' positivism) can easily be turned by more means–end rationalist judges into a basis for embracing a more full-blooded 'Benthamite' version of positivism. On this view, the enactment of a statute should be regarded, at least presumptively, not as having preserved common law values, but as having destroyed in its wake every last vestige of such so-called 'natural law' or custom to the contrary.[57] In that regard, the fact that it is criminal liability that is being imposed is to make not a scrap of difference to the deference that must be shown to the ordinary meaning of statutory wording. So, for example, in *Bond v Evans*,[58] in discussing whether an absentee landlord could be liable if gaming took place on his licensed premises to the knowledge of the person in charge, Stephen J said, 'I think the meaning [of the Statute] is that the landlord of licensed premises must prevent that which the act prohibits from being done on his premises, and if he does not prevent it so much the worse for him';[59] and in *The Gauntlet*[60] it was held that:

[A] penal enactment is to be construed, like any other instrument, according to the fair common-sense meaning of the language used; and the court is not to find or make any doubt or ambiguity in the language of a penal statute where such doubt or ambiguity would clearly not be found or made in the same language in any other instrument.[61]

The combination of judges who preferred to take refuge in the weak-kneed 'ordinary language' approach to criminal statutes, and judges who embraced a more hawkish Benthamite positivism in that regard, led to what can only be described as a lengthy period of moral abdication by judges (and commentators) with respect to their responsibilities to argue in favour of and defend the value of liberty and the importance of fault requirements, when

---

[56] See e.g. the well-known case of *R v Woodrow* (1846) 153 ER 907, 913, 'public inconvenience would be much greater if in every case the officers were obliged to prove knowledge'. Of course, in some instances such an argument has real force, as in relation to the question whether it should be necessary to show that someone knew that the person to whom he or she was selling an intoxicant was 'drunk': see n. 24 above.

[57] Notoriously, as far as the common law was concerned, for Bentham [cited by P. Schofield and J. Harris, ' "Legislator of the World": Writings on Codification, Law and Education', in P. Schofield and J. Harris (eds.), *The Collected Works of Jeremy Bentham* (Oxford: Oxford University Press, 1998), 20–21], 'so long as there remains any, the smallest scrap, of unwritten law unextirpated, it suffices to taint with its own corruption—its own inbred and incurable corruption—whatsoever portion of *statute* law has ever been, or ever can be, applied to it [Bentham's emphasis].'   [58] (1888) 21 QBD 249.

[59] Ibid. In almost exactly analogous circumstances, of course, a very different view was taken years later in *Sweet v Parsley* [1970] AC 132, as we have seen.

[60] (1871) 4 PC 184.   [61] Ibid., 191.

interpreting penal statutes. So, by 1910, Kennedy LJ could confidently say, 'in construing a modern statute this presumption as to *mens rea* does not exist'.[62] Ironically, such prolonged judicial passivity had some beneficial side-effects in that, in the longer term, it forced Parliament itself to pay attention to fault requirements. Consider, for example, the case of some of the successive Acts passed by Parliament concerned with food quality.[63] The Fertilisers and Feeding Stuffs Act 1893 made it an offence under section 3(1), *inter alia*, for a seller to cause or permit an invoice relating to, or a description of, fertilizer or foodstuffs to be false, to the prejudice of the purchaser, or to sell for use as cattle food any article containing an ingredient deleterious to cattle. In spite of the fact that the former offence hinged on a positive duty to provide information in a specified form, a bureaucratic formality epitomizing the 'mesh-thinning' effect of ever-increasing state superintendence,[64] the offence was duly held by the courts to be one of strict liability.[65] It was left to the legislature, by section 7(1) of the Fertilisers and Feeding Stuffs Act 1926, to create a defence to the latter offence by putting the burden on D to show that he or she 'did not know and could not with reasonable care have known that the article contained a deleterious ingredient'.[66] Similarly, under the Sale of Food and Drugs Act 1892, the courts had held that D was criminally liable for selling adulterated milk even when the adulteration has taken place as a result of an employee acting against his orders.[67] A conviction was also upheld when the milk was pure when D had in good faith left it on a train to be delivered, but adulterated (by persons unknown) by the time it reached its destination.[68] It was left to later legislation, the Food and Drugs Act 1955,

---

[62] *Hobbs v Winchester Corporation* [1910] 2 KB 471, 483.

[63] Discussed in R. M. Jackson, 'Absolute Prohibition in Statutory Offences', in Sir L. Radzinowicz and J. W. C. Turner (eds.), *The Modern Approach to Criminal Law* (London: McMillan & Co, 1945), 262, 267–268.

[64] It would, in other words, have been perfectly possible for the legislature to insist that the provider give warranties, deemed to have certain effects under the contract, without a fussy insistence on a detailed and precise form in which the warranty should be made, backed up by a criminal penalty.

[65] *Laird v Dobell* [1906] 1 KB 131; *Korten v West Sussex County Council* (1903) 72 LJKB 514. These cases were concerned with the 'causing or permitting' offence under section 3(1)(b), but the offence of selling cattle food with an ingredient deleterious to cattle contrary to section 3(1)(c) was, if anything, seemingly even more strict in the liability it imposed than the offence under section 3(1)(b). See Sidney Wright, *The Law of Landed Estates* (London: Frank P. Wilson, 1897), 273. No doubt, the courts were influenced by the fact that under section 3(1)(a), the offence of failing to provide an invoice before, at, or just after the time of delivery of the article in question was not an offence unless the failure occurred 'without reasonable excuse'. No such inhibitions held the court back from implying fault requirements, in analogous circumstances, in *Sherras v De Rutzen* [1895] 1 QB 918.

[66] This might not have changed the outcome on the facts of *Laird v Dobell* [1906] 1 KB 131, but the point of principle remains the same. For a further contemporary statutory foray into the provision of defences, in such a context, see also section 12 of the Sale of Food (Weights and Measures) Act 1926. [67] *Brown v Foot* (1892) 66 LT (n s) 649.

[68] *Parker v Alder* [1899] 1 QB 20. Lord Russel CJ said, no doubt inspired by Sir J. F. Stephen's dismissive approach to statutory offences, 'This is one of the class of cases in which the Legislature has, in effect, determined that *mens rea* is not necessary to constitute the offence.'

and the Food Safety Act 1990, respectively to reverse the effects of these decisions: by providing a defence of 'due diligence' (in the supervision of employees) under the 1955 Act, and a more general defence that D took all reasonable precautions and exercised all due diligence under the 1990 Act.

It is, of course, always possible to rationalize judicial indifference to a concern for liberty, or for other intrinsic values at risk in the regulatory state. In the cases under discussion, this can be done through a quintessentially neo-Weberian argument that, in the bureaucratic-administrative state, the courts are not sufficiently expert in the areas in question to create defences that will protect liberty whilst not undermining a carefully crafted regulatory scheme. Such an argument fails to draw a distinction, noted in chapter 1.7 above, between specialized defences based on highly context-specific concerns requiring expert knowledge for their resolution,[69] which it is indeed beyond the competence of the courts to create, and more general defences (impossibility; due diligence; reasonable ignorance of the law) respecting which the courts may be perfectly competent to ensure that the conditions in which those defences can successfully be pleaded are limited, in a way that permits the regulatory scheme to continue to flourish. Having created, say, an impossibility or due diligence defence to offences that are part of a scheme to improve food safety, it would have been perfectly possible for a court to insist that Ds produce expert evidence to support their case,[70] evidence that deals with policy issues relating to the potential for certain kinds of excuse or justification to frustrate the common good underpinning the scheme of regulation.[71] Such an approach we could call the 'dynamic' version of common law thinking about statutory interpretation, an approach endorsed in chapter 1.7 above. There was, though, to be no such creative development of the courts' role as the self-professed defenders of liberty.[72] Indeed, as every English criminal lawyer knows, in a blatant betrayal of their professed concern (in rhetoric, at any rate) for individual liberty and for the stigma of conviction, the courts found

[69] Such as the defence, in sub-section 4, to the offence under section 444(1) of the Education Act 1996 of failure to ensure that a child attends regularly at school: 'The child shall not be taken to have failed to attend regularly at school if the parent proves—(a) that the school at which the child is a registered pupil is not within walking distance of the child's home' ['walking distance' is then defined in sub-section 5]. See, further, section 4 below.

[70] As the courts do in cases where automatism is being claimed: see *Hill v Baxter* [1958] 1 QB 277.

[71] Such evidence would, for example, have been of consideration assistance in *Laird v Dobell* [1906] 1 KB 131, where D's claim was that he had relied on an analyst's assessment that the food contained the prescribed statutory minimum amount of certain ingredients.

[72] For example, in 1929, Kenny noted the dramatic increase in the number of indictable as well as summary offences tried before justices, who convicted in eight out of nine cases, but saw no reason to comment on this other than—perhaps predictably—to cite a French authority for the view that there was much to commend in the paternalistic way in which magistrates dealt with poor defendants, 'A French eyewitness . . . found "quelque chose de frappant à voir la confiance qu'ont les malheureux dans la bonté des magistats. C'est pourquoi la justice reste toujours populaire" (Franqueville, *Sys Jud G-B II* 326)', in Sir C. S. Kenny, *Outlines of Criminal Law*, 13th edn., 442 n. 1.

that even when D stood to be convicted of a sexual offence under statute, that in itself became no bar to a finding that the offence in question was one of strict liability.[73] Invoking a kind of crude Benthamite positivism, the courts now sometimes expressly disassociated themselves from the view that questions of justice should ever enter into matters of statutory construction in such cases, as we have seen.[74] Far from being exceptional or anomalous, thus, the decision in the well-known case of *R v Larsonneur*[75] should be regarded as all-too characteristic of the period. In this case, D was convicted of being an alien in the UK without permission, even though she was only in the UK because she had been brought there compulsorily from Eire in the custody of the police. Here, then, was an ideal opportunity for the development of an excuse of 'impossibility', or the like, an excuse that would go somewhat beyond the narrow 'denial of responsibility' claim—understandably supported by most critics of the decision—that D's presence in the UK was not voluntary.[76] For Lord Hewart CJ, however, in spite of the clear stigma attaching to conviction, the element of compulsion was 'perfectly immaterial' to the question whether D ought to be found guilty.[77]

Even at a time when pro-defendant subjectivism was beginning to dominate academic understanding of how the criminal law governing *mala in se* should be developed, the weak-kneed positivist approach that was agnostic about strict liability had some academic apologists. For R. M. Jackson, whilst the new approach would have surprised a previous generation of judges, even in sex cases where conviction involved considerable stigma he thought that, 'So long as proper use is made of nominal punishment in cases of inadvertent offences there seems no reason to object to such stringent provisions'.[78] He rather lamely concluded, on the matter of how courts should approach the question whether liability in a criminal statute was strict, that, 'in statutory offences nothing more, and nothing less, is required than that the statute should be carefully read and the rules of statutory construction properly applied in each case'.[79] Such timidity, a failure of nerve

---

[73] *R v Prince* (1875) LR 2 CCR 154; *R v Wheat and Stocks* (1921) 15 Cr App Rep 134; *R v Forde* [1923] 2 KB 400; *R v Maugham* (1934) 24 Cr App Rep 130. All of these cases were called into question by the decisions of the House of Lords in *B (A Minor) v DPP* [2000] 2 AC 428, and in *R v K* [2001] 3 WLR 471, although fortunately those paedophiles' charters have been swept away by the Sexual Offences Act 2003.   [74] *R v Forde* [1923] 2 KB 400, 404.

[75] (1933) 24 Cr App Rep 74.

[76] See e.g. the discussion in A. P. Simester and G. R. Sullivan, *Criminal Law: Theory and Doctrine*, 1st edn., 17, and 71–73.   [77] *R v Larsonneur* (1933) 24 Cr App Rep 74.

[78] R. M. Jackson, 'Absolute Prohibitions in Statutory Offences', 270. Jackson points out that Larsonneur received a sentence of three days' imprisonment, Wheat and Stocks one day's imprisonment each, and Maugham two days' imprisonment (see n. 73 above).

[79] R. M. Jackson, 'Absolute Prohibitions in Statutory Offences', 272. Jackson seems to have overlooked or ignored Sayre's appropriate riposte to these kinds of arguments, that, 'When it becomes respectable to be convicted, the vitality of the criminal law has been sapped': F. B. Sayre, 'The Present Significance of *Mens Rea* in the Criminal Law', in R. Pound (ed.), *Harvard Legal Essays* (Harvard, Mass.: Harvard University Press, 1934), 409, cited by A. P. Simester and G. R. Sullivan, *Criminal Law: Theory and Doctrine*, 1st edn., 174.

all too typical of lawyers, when considering the evaluative backdrop to be employed when construing criminal statutes, makes simply laughable Stallybrass's later claim, when comparing the proposed new Italian Criminal Code with English criminal law, that:

England too has played her part in the progress of the world towards a rational system of criminal law . . . Her glory is that thanks to the integrity and ability of her judges, the high standard of honour and public spirit of her bar . . . and the efficiency of her police, there is no country in the world where an innocent man is less likely to be convicted or a guilty man is less likely to escape punishment for his crime.[80]

4. A 'PLURAL' APPROACH TO REGULATORY CRIMES

The preceding section was taken up largely with the question of when courts have been willing to imply fault requirements into statutes, rather than with—my main concern—excusatory defences to regulatory crimes. It should now be clear why. The perceived need to squeeze statutory language, to find fault requirements implicit in it, was always likely to give so-called 'anti-positivist' judges who nonetheless accepted Parliamentary sovereignty, a mountain to climb, in search of a means to give common law values a continuing role in the regulatory state. Inevitably, judges would in the end take the easier route: meek acceptance of weak-kneed positivism and the ordinary language approach, coupled with (as often as not) the merely pious hope of further statutory intervention. By way of contrast, as we saw in section 1 above, courts in other common law jurisdictions have been able to re-affirm the significance of a common law agenda (be it 'static' or 'dynamic' in character) through the application of excuses to statutory crimes, crimes whose language need thus not be strained to find evidence of hidden fault requirements, narrowly construed. So, by way of contrast with the reasoning and hence the result in *R v Larsonneur*,[81] in the New Zealand case of *Finau v Department of Labour*,[82] when D was prosecuted for remaining in the country after the expiry of her visitor's permit, it was held to be a good defence to show that it was *impossible* for her to leave, because she was pregnant and no airline would carry her. The advantage of this

---

[80] W. T. S. Stallybrass, 'A Comparison of the General Principles of Criminal Law with the "Progetto Definitivo di un Nuovo Codice Penale" of Alfredo Rocco', in Sir L. Radzinowicz and J. W. C. Turner (eds.), *The Modern Approach to Criminal Law*, 390. This kind of bombast was reinforced by eager citation of any 'foreign' praise for English criminal procedure: see e.g. Sir C. S. Kenny, *Outlines of Criminal Law*, 13th edn., 442.   [81] (1933) 149 LT 542.
[82] [1984] 2 NZLR 396, discussed by A. P. Simester and G. R. Sullivan, *Criminal Law: Theory and Doctrine*, 1st edn., 72–73.

approach is that it opens up regulatory offences to a range of possible defences—impossibility, due diligence, reasonable ignorance of the law—that can be applied in a context-sensitive way by fact-finders, having had their determinative rules shaped by judges in such a way that they account for any strategic concerns bearing on the continued success of the regulatory scheme.[83] Such a 'dynamic' approach to statutes is surely to be preferred to the 'static' approach, since the latter usually amounts to little more than the very occasional wielding of the sledge-hammer constituted by a finding through statutory interpretation that the prosecution must prove actual knowledge or intention.[84]

What theoretical commitments are involved in taking the excuse-based approach to regulatory crimes? I argued in chapter 1.7 above that (especially in a jurisdiction with an active common law tradition tolerated by the legislature) judges are under a continuing interpretive obligation to use their discretion to develop the law in a morally sound way. In so far as such developments touch and concern the creation and application of excuses in criminal law, the use of that discretion is no more or less than what I have meant in referring to as the 'dynamic' understanding of common law values, or the common law agenda. The obligation to use interpretive discretion to develop the law in a morally sound way, ought to be regarded as ruling out the agnostic approach towards fault and excuses inherent in the weak-kneed positivism of Jackson,[85] *R v Forde*,[86] and *The Gauntlet*.[87] In a theoretically more detailed sense, the obligation can be expressed in terms of what can be called a commitment to a 'plural' view of the criminal law. Implicit in both in weak-kneed positivism and its more hawkish Benthamite counterpart, is an understanding of the criminal law as primarily concerned with the legislative imposition of prohibitions and sanctions (the 'one-way projection of authority'[88]), and concerned only at the margins with the range of justifications, excuses or other explanations defendants may seek to give for their alleged wrongdoing.[89] Expounding the view that common law defences

---

[83] See chapter 1.4 above for an explanation of 'determinative' rules, and chapter 1.2 above for an explanation of strategic concerns.

[84] For two examples of the English courts determination to press ahead with this thoroughly discredited approach, see *B (A Minor) v DPP* [2000] 2 AC 428; *R v K* [2002] 1 AC 462, both of which have lost their authority as a result of the Sexual Offences Act 2003.

[85] R. M. Jackson, 'Absolute Prohibitions in Statutory Offences'.   [86] [1923] 2 KB 400.

[87] (1871) 4 PC 184.

[88] Lon Fuller's phrase: see Lon Fuller, *The Morality of Law* (New Haven: Yale University Press, 1969), revised edn., 209.

[89] This is, of course, very much the picture of the criminal law portrayed by legal theorists, such as Kelsen and Austin, for whom all laws have an ultimate single source, such as a supreme sovereign. It did, however, perhaps unintentionally creep into Hart's conception of law (even though, famously, he broke from the 'single source' tradition) as a result of an exaggeration of the contrast he made so central to his theory, the contrast between criminal law, on the one hand, and the civil law governing agreements and property transfer, on the other: see Jeremy Horder, 'Criminal Law and Legal Positivism'.

can be of little relevance to crimes of strict liability, Jackson gives the following example of just how marginal that relevance will be:

If, for instance, a butcher in a fit of somnambulism exposes tainted meat for sale in his shop, presumably he will not be liable for that offence . . . that is only another way of saying that the act must be one which can in law be imputed to the accused.[90]

No doubt, the possibility of such a concession would have come as a great relief to the vast majority of blameless butchers faced with prosecution. By way of contrast, I side with a tradition—the plural view—of looking at the criminal law in a way that sees a concern for both offences *and* an adequate range of defences as primary, and that hence portrays as a virtue the sometimes conflicting elements of intrinsic value—the 'plurality' of value—within the criminal law.[91]

On the plural view of criminal law values, there will often be a tension between the value (to law-enforcement officials) of a broad-ranging offence, and the value (to Ds and to their advisers) of having a range of defences at their disposal. As Gardner says, of the criminal law:

It is primarily a vehicle for the public identification of wrongdoing . . . *and* for responsible agents, whose wrongs have been thus identified, to *answer for* their wrongs by offering justifications and excuses for having committed them.[92]

The tension between offence and defence is a natural and healthy product, in a system of criminal law founded on recognition of the intrinsic value of reciprocity, alongside the value of (in an evidentiary sense) procedural due process.[93] A system of criminal law is morally deficient, not only if—disproportionately—it employs criminal modes of definition, procedure and punishment to attack trivial wrongs (where fault in committing them is indeed a side issue), but also when it excludes utterly the possibility of raising fault-based excuses when it criminalizes more serious wrongs. To do the latter is to threaten the pivotal place and value of the common good of reciprocity within a plural system of criminal law.[94]

In this context, reciprocity entails openness in the construction and interpretation of criminal offences to excusatory (as well as, obviously, to justificatory) arguments. It involves ensuring that D has appropriate opportunities

---

[90] R. M. Jackson, 'Absolute Prohibition in Statutory Offences', 270–271. In his choice of example, he is obviously alluding to the case of *Hobbs v Winchester Corporation* [1910] 2 KB 46.

[91] The classic statement of this liberal theory is H. L. A. Hart's 'Legal Responsibility and the Excuses', in *Punishment and Responsibility*, chapter 2.

[92] John Gardner, 'In Defence of Defences', 254 (my emphasis on 'and'; his emphasis on 'answer for').

[93] A well-ordered legal system involves, as Finnis puts it, '*reciprocity* and procedural fairness . . . valuable for its own sake', in J. M. Finnis, *Natural Law and Natural Rights*, 274 (my emphasis). We came across this value as strategic consideration, or common good (iv), in chapter 1.2 above.

[94] For a broader discussion, see R. A. Duff, *Trials and Punishments* (Cambridge: Cambridge University Press, 1986), chapter 4.

to 'answer for' (as Gardner puts it) his or her wrong in a substantive sense, and not just in a procedural sense. If, whatever efforts one may have made or precautions one may have taken, there is simply no answer one can make to a criminal charge, the substantive fairness of one's trial is threatened, in that one has no self-sufficient moral reason, *qua* individual D, to engage constructively and co-operatively in the trial process.[95] So, for example, it has been said in the Divisional Court, in relation to the offence of failing to ensure one's child attends regularly at school,[96] that if the offence were held to be one of strict liability, 'it may be thought positively to discourage parents who need encouragement from taking responsibility for their children for them to know that they may be taken to court even if they do all they can to secure the child's school attendance'.[97] A point of considerable profundity is being made here, even allowing for the obvious point that too few parents will be aware, in advance, of the precise nature of their legal obligations for such discouragement to have an *ex ante* conduct-guiding effect. Wholly strict liability may discourage co-operative and constructive engagement with the legal system itself, on the part of a blameless D charged with an offence, doing nothing to encourage compliance *ex post facto* except through the brute (and last resort) mechanism of deterrence. As Finnis observes, a willingness to rely solely on the deterrent effects of conviction and punishment, in the regulatory context, as elsewhere, is wrong, because:

The idea of the Rule of Law is based on the notion that a certain quality of interaction between ruler and ruled, involving reciprocity and procedural fairness, is very valuable for its own sake; it is not merely a means to other social ends, and may not lightly be sacrificed for such other ends. It is not just a 'management technique' in a programme of 'social control' or 'social engineering'.[98]

Very obviously, this does not mean that there must a defence that *every* D has some prospect of using in answer to the criminal charge, whatever the reason that he or she came to commit the offence. To carry on with the same example, the Education Act 1996 makes provision for a number of specific justificatory and excusatory answers to the charge of failing to ensure one's child attends regularly at school.[99] It could well be that, taken together,

---

[95] See R. A. Duff, 'Law, Language and Community: Some Preconditions of Criminal Liability' (1998) 18 *Oxford Journal of Legal Studies* 189, 194.

[96] Contrary to section 444 of the Education Act 1996.

[97] Per Elias J in *Barnfather v London Borough of Islington Education Authority* [2003] EWHC 418, paragraph 53. In fact the offence in question in this case was not one of wholly strict liability, because the Education Act 1996 provides for a limited range of justifications and excuses, but the point made in the text is unaffected.

[98] J. M. Finnis, *Natural Law and Natural Rights*, 274. It follows that the Court of Appeal was wrong in *Barnfather v London Borough of Islington Education Authority* [2003] EWHC 418, to find that the guarantee of the right to a fair trial under Article 6 of the ECHR does not permit the courts to review the status of crimes as ones of strict liability, on the narrow grounds (as the court saw it) that under Article 6(2) the idea of a fair trial relates to matters of procedural or evidential fairness alone. The need for 'reciprocity' is equally important. See further, section 5 below.

[99] See the discussion of section 444(5) of the Education Act 1996, later in this section.

these provide adequate opportunities to 'answer for' the wrong and hence to engage constructively with the legal process in a way that satisfies the requirements of reciprocity. So, it may be that a parent who could not have done more to ensure their child attended regularly at school, but cannot make use of any of the specific defences, is simply unlucky. The courts should, however, not be too quick to reach such a conclusion.

The duty to respect the value of reciprocity, and the plural character of criminal law, is a duty to protect and promote a common good in the fair operation of regulatory crime (see strategic concern or common good (iv), in chapter 1.2 above). This is the maintenance of respect for the intrinsic moral soundness and fairness of structuring law in terms of offence and defence (whatever the substantive content of the offence) amongst all those connected with its enforcement, not just amongst those to whom it applies. In that regard, in terms of human rights considerations, the absence of *any* defence to a crime does not, as commonly argued, really threaten the fairness of trials in virtue of Article 6(2) of the European Convention on Human Rights (guaranteeing the presumption of innocence), but does so in virtue of an analogy with the justification for a right to be present in any proceedings—including criminal ones—in which 'personal character and manner of life' issues are at stake.[100] Where such issues are at stake, as one or other of them must be in almost all criminal proceedings against individuals (on which see section 6 below), that right stems from the understanding that, as Duff puts it:

The criminal trial should be understood not merely as an inquiry *on* the defendant—and inquiry in which she has no active role to play—but as a process in which she is to be an active *participant*. She is called to *answer* a criminal charge: either to admit the charge by pleading guilty, or to defend herself against it by denying the facts alleged, or by offering some legally recognised defence . . . A criminal trial purports to be, and ought to be, a rational process of communication in which the defendant is actively involved.[101]

Reciprocity being itself a common good ((iv), in chapter 1.2 above), the importance attached to defences under the plural view of criminal law is very far from being, *ipso facto*, a simple assertion by courts of the rights of the individual as against the 'truly' common good-based regulatory claims of state prosecutors.

In that regard, I cannot stress too strongly that it is not an essential aspect of the plural view of the criminal law that the plurality in question emerge through a constant clash or tension between legislators' values, on the one hand, and 'dynamic' common law values (as I am defining them), upheld by

---

[100] *X v Sweden*, Appl No 434/58 (1958–1959) 2 Yearbook 354; *Muyldermans v Belgium*, A/214-B (1993) 15 EHRR 204, 215, both discussed in Jason Coppel, *The Human Rights Act 1998* (Chichester: John Wiley, 1999), 255.

[101] See R. A. Duff, 'Law, Language and Community: Some Preconditions of Criminal Liability', 194.

the courts, on the other. There is always scope for legislative 'schizophrenia', in which whilst enacting (say) strict liability offences, or even what are by many people's standards repressive crimes, the legislature still *itself* provides for or tolerates the application to those offences or crimes of a range of defences whose existence owes something to the desire to protect intrinsic values threatened by too literal a reading of the offence itself.[102] Indeed, there is a special duty on the legislature to make space for appropriate defences when creating offences, because it is in by far the best position to decide whether and how specialized defences should be created to meet the demands of the particular regulatory context.[103] Only the legislature, for example, was in a position to make it a defence under s.444(5) to show, in response to a charge under s.444(1) of the Education Act 1996 of failing to ensure that one's child attends regularly at school, that the school at which one's child was a registered pupil was not within walking distance, namely, '(a) in relation to a child who is under the age of eight . . . 3.1218688 kilometres (two miles), and (b) in relation to a child who has attained the age of eight . . . 4.828032 kilometres (three miles), in each case measured by the nearest available route'. It ought to be acknowledged, however, that tensions arising between offence and (possible) defence must often be resolved by the courts, applying the values they think appropriate to settle the case, drawing on the 'dynamic' version of common law values. This is simply because the tension cannot always be artificially smoothed away at the time of enactment, by seeking in Benthamite fashion to anticipate once and for all every likely defence in the definition of the offence itself. That being so, when it comes to the creation of defences to crimes, in any pluralistic legal culture it would be wrong for the courts to come to see themselves—or for the legislature or for citizens to come to see the courts—as no more than 'the mere handmaidens of public officials'.[104] In jurisdictions such as England and Wales that have an active common law tradition, and a duty to interpret the law in the light of human rights considerations (on which, see section 6 below), it is especially likely to fall to the courts to play an active role as creators and interpreters of more general excusatory defences. In so doing, according to the 'dynamic' version of common law values, judges should be seeking to secure reciprocity by applying to criminal statutes such defences (impossibility, reasonable ignorance of the law, due diligence, and so on), as will in the circumstances ensure that a regulatory scheme operates in a morally sound and fair way, as well efficiently and effectively. It is, hence, the courts that will—like it or not—in practice be the ones charged with

---

[102] See further, Andrew Ashworth, 'Is the Criminal Law a Lost Cause?'.

[103] See, for an analogous, if not identical, argument: George P. Fletcher, *Rethinking Criminal Law*, 792–798. Fletcher suggests that Ds should not be entitled to invoke defences unanticipated by the legislature when the rule under which they are being prosecuted has been the subject of detailed up-to-date legislative reflection.

[104] Lord Parker CJ's phrase, quoted in D. G. T. Williams, 'The Donoughmore Report in Retrospect' (1982) 60 *Public Administration* 273, 291.

upholding the plural view of the criminal law, if unnecessary or oppressive legislative encroachment on important values (and not only liberty) is to be avoided.[105] So, it is worth taking a small amount of space to explore the significance of one value that is particularly likely to fall to the courts to protect, in this context: freedom from the unjustified imposition of stigma upon conviction.

5. Excuses, Stigma, and Synchronic Order in a Legal System

The common good of reciprocity provides legislatures (in enacting) and judges (in interpreting) with a context-*independent* reason to insist on fault requirements in, or to provide for appropriate defences to, regulatory crimes. In other words, the demands of reciprocity provide a reason to favour fault requirements or defences irrespective of whatever considerations point in one direction or the other in the particular regulatory context, even though, clearly, the combined weight of context-specific reasons against providing some excuse or another could defeat the context-independent reasons in favour of the excuse. In deciding whether it is appropriate to create or interpret a regulatory offence in such a way as to permit excusatory pleas, the demands of reciprocity are not the only source of context-independent reasons in favour of taking such a course. I have said that openness to fault requirements and to excusatory defences (the essence of reciprocity) becomes morally important when the offence in question is serious, but seriousness can be measured in different ways. It can, of course, be measured by the possible penalty that may be imposed on conviction,[106] but it may also be measured by the degree (if any) of stigma attaching to conviction irrespective of the penalty that may be imposed. Unjustified moral stigma is, in general terms, one of a host of ills to be avoided, like prejudice, discrimination, poverty, and so forth; and freedom from unjustified stigma is one of the important liberties that can be protected by the inclusion of fault requirements in, or the application of defences to, regulatory offences.[107] The importance of the fact that stigma will

---

[105] It should be noted that my point is most definitely not meant to be an echo of the eighteenth-century suspicion of all independent, creative legislature activity. The point is, that, in seeking quite properly to regulate an area of activity, to enforce new kinds of duties in the public interest, and so forth, the Legislature may cast the net too widely, given the purposes it had in mind, and it can be one of the proper functions of the courts, *tolerated or even encouraged by the legislature itself*, to interpret the scope of crimes in such a way that unjust 'net-widening' is kept to a minimum. See further, Jeremy Horder, 'Criminal Law and Legal Positivism'.

[106] In Canada, if conviction for an offence may be followed by a sentence of imprisonment, the courts will as a matter of course apply a 'due diligence' defence to the offence: see *Re BC Motor Vehicle Act* [1985] 2 SCR 486.

[107] For a discussion of the kinds of liberty at stake—freedom 'from' and freedom 'to'—in regulatory offences, see Jeremy Horder, 'Strict Liability, Statutory Construction and the Spirit of Liberty', 468–470.

attach to conviction, in any given instance, is that this provides the legislature in enacting, or the judiciary in interpreting, with a *further*, context-independent reason to permit excusatory defences, beyond the reason provided by the demands of reciprocity. It is, though, particularly likely that it will fall to courts to use freedom from unjustified stigma as a reason to permit excusatory defences. This is because the courts bear a significant responsibility, as part of the 'mediating influence' (see chapter 1.7 above) they exercise as between the law-making officials and citizens, to maintain an adequate degree of 'synchronic' order within the legal system as a whole, and as between laws and the social practices they govern.[108]

For Finnis,[109] as for Raz,[110] the presumptive implication of fault requirements in statutory offences is one way in which the courts can express a preference for 'diachronic' order, for the maintenance of stability and continuity with the past. As Finnis puts it, the maxim *actus non facit reum nisi mens sit rea* is one of the 'second-order maxims favouring continuity in human affairs—i.e. favouring the good of diachronic order, as distinct from the good of a future end-state'.[111] This seems to be a relatively weak justification for a plural view of the criminal law, and hence for judicial efforts to ensure that regulatory offences operate in a fair and humane way as well as efficiently and effectively. It requires judges creatively to construct a past practice in the light of which they can view the interpretive obligations that they now regard themselves as being under, and many judges will construct that past practice in very different ways, making any given construction theoretically unstable. More significantly, in so far as excuses are to be regarded as a part of the diachronic order, Finnis's justification also seems to militate against the creation of (indeed, the tradition of creating) new defences alongside those long regarded as a part of the common law inheritance, such as duress, mistake, and so forth. His justification for the *actus non facit reum nisi mens sit rea* principle takes no account, in other words, of the 'dynamic' account of common law values, explained in section 4 above. A sounder justification for the plural view of criminal law, and hence for taking a robust and creative approach to defences to regulatory crime, emerges from Finnis's account of integral place of the criminal law within the broader, inter-connected ordering of human affairs through law, in the

---

[108] There is, of course, a responsibility on the legislature to ensure that an adequate degree of synchronic order within the legal system is maintained, but the legislature frequently fails to do this, for reasons perhaps best and most vividly explained by Bentham [from the Bentham MSS in the library of University College, London, cxl 92, cited by G. Postema, *Bentham and the Common Law Tradition* (Oxford: Clarendon Press, 1986), 264], 'The country squire who has his turnips stolen, goes to work and gets a bloody law against stealing turnips. It exceeds the utmost stretch of his comprehension to conceive that the next year the same catastrophe may happen to his potatoes. For the two general rules . . . in modern British legislation are: never to move a finger until your passions are inflamed, nor ever to look further than your nose'. [109] J. M. Finnis, *Natural Law and Natural Rights*, 287–289.
[110] Joseph Raz, *The Morality of Freedom*, 260.
[111] J. M. Finnis, *Natural Law and Natural Rights*, 288.

interests of the common good. This is, in effect, an account of the moral value of an adequate degree of synchronic order within a legal system.

For Finnis, criminal laws are not just 'bolts from the (legislative) blue', whose only function is to impose a sanction on conduct prescribed by law. They are, and should be seen as, just one part of a complex social–legal jigsaw puzzle, in which, for example:

[A]n unreasonable act, for example of killing, may be a crime . . . and/or a tort, and/or an act which effects automatic vacation or suspension of office or forfeiture of property, and/or an act which insurers and/or public officials may properly take into account in avoiding a contract or suspending a licence . . . etc.[112]

Shaping a criminal law to fit within the wider matrix of (civil and criminal) legal obligations and permissions, and ensuring not only that it governs conduct it is meant directly to affect in the right way, but also that it does not have an unintended negative impact on standing, desirable social practices, and so forth, governed by other norms, is what can be referred to as the maintenance of synchronic order within a legal system. It can be regarded as a significant part of the judicial role (although this role is obviously also one that must be taken seriously by those who draft and enact the law), to seek to maintain a degree of synchronic order as between inter-connected laws within the same system, and as between law and status, standing or social practice directly or indirectly affected by it.[113] The statute-based criminal law of theft and deception, for example, clearly plays an important part in the law's institutional commitment to the relative stability of property-holding, and to the integrity of property transfer.[114] It has frequently fallen to judges, however, within the limits of the freedom they have to exercise their interpretive obligations, to ensure that the law's definition of theft and deception keeps pace with the ever-evolving character of transactions in civil law, even when these have only a quasi-proprietary status, whilst remaining within the boundaries set for judicial activism by the principle *nulla poena sine lege*.[115]

---

[112] J. M. Finnis, *Natural Law and Natural Rights*, 283.

[113] The obligation is only to maintain a 'degree' of synchronic order, since the maintenance of such order may come into conflict with other legitimate goals pursued within judges' interpretive obligations. I should not be taken to be signing up to Dworkin's attempt to evaluate legal systems almost solely in terms of the degree of their diachronic and synchronic coherence. For criticism, see Joseph Raz, 'The Relevance of Coherence', in Joseph Raz, *Ethics in the Public Domain*, chapter 13.

[114] For further discussion of this point, see Jeremy Horder, 'Criminal Law and Legal Positivism', 232–233.

[115] In that regard, the European Court of Human Rights has said that domestic courts may use their interpretive discretion to meet the occasional need 'for the existing elements of an offence to be clarified or adapted to new circumstances or developments in society insofar as this can reasonably be brought under the original concept of the offence': *SW & CR v United Kingdom* (1995) 21 EHRR 363. On the point made in the text about the offence of theft and deception, see Stephen Shute, 'Appropriation and the Law of Theft' [2002] *Criminal Law Review* 445; Alan L. Bogg and John Stanton-Ife, 'Protecting the Vulnerable: Legality, Harm and Theft' (2003) 23 *Legal Studies* 402.

In the present context, the judicial obligation to maintain a degree of synchronic order entails not merely that there must be an appropriate degree of consistency in the application of excuses as between crimes (so, if applied to theft, the defence of duress should also be applied to obtaining by deception), but also that, *mutatis mutandis*, the consequences of *denying* an excuse must be considered in contexts both within and beyond that immediately connected with the offence in issue.

As we have seen,[116] the House of Lords has indicated that a flagrant breach on the part of the legislature of its obligation to maintain synchronic order, a persistent failure to create excuses (or elements of *mens rea*) for crimes that keep those crimes in touch with the social practices to which they relate, gives judges a moral and legal freedom to create or apply such excuses, a freedom they might not otherwise regard themselves as having. Similarly, a finding that stigma attaches to conviction for an offence may justify the courts in finding that an excuse (or a mental element) applies to an offence, even though that will impinge on the regulatory effectiveness of the offence, because the negative impact of that stigma may unfairly disadvantage D in a number of contexts going well beyond the area of conduct governed by the offence itself. Consider the case of *Barnfather v London Borough of Islington Education Authority*.[117] In this case, D, a mother of four children, was found strictly liable for failing to ensure that her child (a 13-year-old boy) attended regularly at school, contrary to section 444(1) of the Education Act 1996. Her appeal against conviction failed, on the ground that the imposition of strict liability did not fall foul of Article 6(2), the 'presumption of innocence' provision, of the European Convention on Human Rights. The judges in the Divisional Court differed, however, on whether—had Article 6(2) permitted review of the strict liability status of the offence—they would have gone on to imply a fault element or defence into section 444(1) of the 1996 Act. Maurice Kay J would not have done so, because although he accepted that there was a 'degree of social stigma' attached to conviction, procedural safeguards against conviction without prior fault were built into the pre-prosecution procedure under the Act, and 'the legitimate aim' of the Act (preventing truancy) in any event overshadowed in importance the significance of any such stigma.[118] He was much influenced, in that regard, by the evidence of a Department of Education and Skills witness to the effect that, 'This straightforward, easily provable offence, with limited penal consequences, is considered to be a useful tool within the local authority armoury to assist them in making parents face up to and discharge their responsibilities . . .'.[119] Like the departmental official, Maurice Kay J thus confines his assessment of the fault issue to the boundaries

---

[116] See the discussion of *R v K* [2002] 1 AC 462, in chapter 1.7 above.
[117] [2003] EWHC 418.   [118] Ibid., paragraph 31.
[119] Ibid., 418, paragraph 29 (evidence of Sheila Scales).

of the particular context in which the offence arises, without regard to any issue of synchronic ordering within the legal system as a whole.

By way of contrast, Elias J took the view that had Article 6(2) permitted review of the status of the offence under section 444(1) as one of strict liability, he would have found that the case for strict liability had not been met, and would (*scilicet*) have imposed a reverse onus on D to show that reasonable steps had been taken to ensure that the child in question attended regularly at school.[120] Amongst other reasons for so finding, he said this:

> I recognise that the penalties are small . . . and that is a factor which can properly be considered when determining whether an offence of strict liability is justified. However, in my opinion there is nonetheless a real stigma attached to being found guilty of a criminal offence of this nature. It suggests either an indifference to one's children, or incompetence at parenting, which in the case of the blameless parent will be unwarranted.[121]

Elias J is prepared to acknowledge, in a way Maurice Kay J is not, that the precise nature of the stigma involved in conviction for the offence under section 444(1) may have a negative impact going well beyond D's relations with the school and the local Education Authority. In the eyes of the relevant authorities or agencies, conviction might be thought to affect her suitability, for example, to qualify and practise in some aspect of child-care, to adopt or foster children, to work as a teacher herself, and so forth, as well as putting her at a disadvantage when applying for any job or benefit respecting which it is required that she answer 'no' to the question whether she has a criminal conviction. The making of a realistic assessment of these possible implications of conviction for D, as affecting her standing in a range of legal and quasi-legal contexts beyond that immediately connected with the offence, is what it means to take proper account of the moral dimension to the synchronic ordering of a legal system.

6. 'Due Diligence', Liberalism, Intrinsic Value, Individual Activity

The analysis of regulatory offences so far has unquestionably been skewed in favour of the view that the legislature—or failing the legislature, the courts—should make provision for excusatory defences to regulatory crimes. The analysis might thus be thought perversely to overlook the case for strict liability that is founded on the very real imbalance of power that may exist between, on the one hand, large, well-organized and highly profitable corporations that have the resources and manpower vigorously to contest prosecutions by making use of any available general excuses, and, on the

---

[120] *Barnfather v London Borough of Islington Education Authority* [2003] EWHC 418, paragraph 52.   [121] Ibid., 418, paragraph 57.

other hand, under-staffed and under-resourced regulatory agencies charged with securing the public good, in part through investigation and prosecution of the worst offenders.[122] The fact that liability is strict can be an important bargaining chip for such regulatory agencies, in seeking to secure compliance on the part of the recalcitrant in a (albeit grudgingly) consensual as well as in a cost-effective way; and prosecutions are in any event almost never undertaken except where there has been fault.[123] I have no particular quarrel with these arguments, insofar as they are confined to offences that are mainly aimed at, or predominantly concerned with, larger organizations that 'wield such power (in terms of economic resources and influence), that there is no social unfairness in holding them to higher standards than individuals',[124] organizations that are able to 'constitute the terrain upon which debates concerning legitimate and feasible forms of regulation are conducted'.[125] But the connection commonly made between the use of strict liability in criminal offences and the construction of a countervailing force, in the sphere of regulation, to oppose large corporations', 'attempt to exert as much control as possible over their operating environments',[126] overlooks two complexities about regulatory offences.

First, regulatory offences that employ strict liability have, of course, long been created as a means of exercising ever-greater state control over the relatively powerless, especially in the effort to maintain 'public order'. So, for example, offences connected with drunkenness in public places and with the possession of alcohol at or in connection with sporting events, have almost never required any—or any significant—mental element.[127] Secondly, at least some statutory offences (many being enacted in a regulatory context) are mainly aimed at, or have their principal effect on, individuals pursuing hobbies and interests, or 'one-man band' and small family businesses, such as

---

[122] See e.g. Celia Wells, *Corporations and Criminal Responsibility* (Oxford: Oxford University Press, 2001), 2nd edn., 67–70; Keith Hawkins, *Law as Last Resort* (Oxford: Oxford University Press, 2002), 244 and 420.

[123] See the discussion in A. P. Simester and G. R. Sullivan, *Criminal Law: Doctrine and Theory*, 1st edn., 159. See also, D. Cowan and A. Marsh, 'There's Regulatory Crime, and then there's Landlord Crime: from "Rachmanites" to "Partners" ' (2001) 64 *Modern Law Review* 831, 835–37; Keith Hawkins, *Law as Last Resort*, chapter 11 and part 5. The argument that prosecutions are not in practice undertaken unless there has been fault was regarded by Elias J as a weak argument in favour of permitting liability to remain strict, in *Barnfather v London Borough of Islington Education Authority* [2003] EWHC 418, paragraph 55.

[124] Andrew Ashworth, *Principles of Criminal Law*, 3rd edn., 169.

[125] F. Pearce and S. Tombs, 'Hazards, Law and Class: Contextualising the Regulation of Corporate Crime' (1997) 6 *Social and Legal Studies* 79, 81, cited by D. Cowan and A. Marsh, 'There's Regulatory Crime, and then there's Landlord Crime: from "Rachmanites" to "Partners" ', 836.

[126] F. Pearce and S. Tombs, 'Ideology, Hegemony and Empiricism' (1990) 30 *British Journal of Criminology* 423, 425, cited by D. Cowan and A. Marsh, 'There's Regulatory Crime, and then there's Landlord Crime: from "Rachmanites" to "Partners" ', 836.

[127] See e.g. section 91 of the Criminal Justice Act 1967; section 1(3) and section 2 of the Sporting Events (Control of Alcohol etc) Act 1985. For a brief history of these kinds of (formerly so-called 'police') offences, see Sir J. F. Stephen, *History of the English Criminal Law*, iii, chapter 32.

public houses and corner shops.[128] In such cases, the resources and manpower at D's disposal required to deliver the kind of corporate strategies that threaten the entire regulatory enterprise, and hence justify strict liability, are largely non-existent.[129] In such instances, the moral case against strict liability that is part and parcel of placing an emphasis on the context-independent reasons against it examined above (the common good of reciprocity and the need to avoid imposing unjustified stigma) gains particular force precisely *because* the D is an individual (albeit, in some instances, a corporate individual), rather than a large corporate body.[130] Yet, the courts have seen fit to treat with extraordinary harshness individuals pursuing hobbies, or 'one-man band' and family businesses, when it comes to the question whether such people should be found strictly liable if they fall foul of statutory offences in the pursuit of the hobby or business activity. So, to take the case of hobbies, when dog-owners,[131] antique gun collectors[132] or amateur radio broadcasters[133] have through no necessary fault on their part fallen foul of regulatory offences in the pursuit of their hobby, the courts have made criminal liability strict, even when the offence in question could be followed by a prison sentence.[134] Similarly, the courts have not been disposed to take a different, more generous, approach to the interpretation of statutory offences even when they are clearly aimed at, or will mainly have an effect on, the small business person rather than the larger-scale corporate operation. So, a corner shop owner has been found (vicariously) strictly liable for selling a lottery ticket to someone under 16 years of age, even though the seller reasonably believed that the buyer was old enough.[135] Similarly, chemists have been found liable for selling controlled medicines without prescription, even though they had no reason to suspect that the 'prescriptions' were in fact forgeries.[136] Likewise (although in a somewhat different context), a street performer[137]

---

[128] For an extended discussion of how this issue should affect the courts' approach to regulatory crime, see Jeremy Horder, 'Strict Liability, Statutory Construction and the Spirit of Liberty'.

[129] At the end of 1997–1998, of all UK firms, no less than 61 per cent were sole proprietorships. Of the 3.7 million businesses in the UK, over 2.3 million were 'size class zero', being sole traders of partners without employees: see the discussion in Judith Freedman, 'Limited Liability: Large Company Theory and Small Firms' (2000) 63 *Modern Law Review* 317, 320–321.

[130] Which is not to say that reciprocity and freedom from unjustified stigma have *no* moral relevance to the criminal liability of large corporations.

[131] *R v Bezzina* [1994] 1 WLR 1057.   [132] *R v Howells* [1977] QB 614.

[133] *R v Blake* [1977] 1 WLR 1167.   [134] As in *R v Howells* [1997] QB 614.

[135] *London Borough of Harrow v Shah* [1999] 3 All ER 302, where conviction could have been followed by a prison sentence. The Ds were described by the court as 'honest, decent and law-abiding shopkeepers', ibid., 307.

[136] *Pharmaceutical Society of Great Britain v Storkwain* [1986] 2 All ER 635. For a more sympathetic view of this decision, in context, see B. Jackson, '*Storkwain*: a Case-Study in Strict Liability and Self-Regulation' [1991] *Criminal Law Review* 892.

[137] *South Tyneside Borough Council v Jackson* (1998) EHLR 249 (DC), discussed in Andrew Ashworth, 'Testing Fidelity to Legal Values: Official Involvement and Law Enforcement', 303 n. 17, and at n. 171 and n. 177 below.

and a road-side trader[138] have been found strictly liable for breach of statutory crimes even though, prior to the alleged offence, they sought and obtained official or quasi-official advice to the effect that their conduct would be lawful. In other words, their claims of reasonable ignorance of the law (considered in detail in section 6.7 below) were rejected as legally irrelevant.

Whatever the rights and wrongs of using strict liability as a means of attacking corporate entities who see themselves as 'amoral calculators',[139] it is wrong to take the same approach to those who innocently fall foul of statutory offences when pursuing hobbies, or running businesses as individuals or as a small family unit. For a start, small business ethos may be very different, because ever-increasing profit margins are an irrelevance. As Freedman puts it, 'the small business sector . . . contains many firms which will never provide . . . much economic growth. [But] this is not a matter for criticism, since these firms have a real value for their owners and users'.[140] It may be, of course, that there is some risk of carelessness in relation to public welfare, where small businesses are concerned, stemming not from those small businesses' 'amoral' ethos but from the lack of time and resources that they are likely to put into compliance, simply in virtue of being so much less well staffed and professionally advised than larger enterprises.[141] Insofar as one believes, then, in the fairytale of significant deterrent effect brought about through the imposition of strict liability, over and above well-resourced and vigorous prosecution where D must prove absence of fault, perhaps such liability might be argued to have a role to play in promoting public welfare in a small business context. That just brings us, though, to the second objection to the imposition of strict liability on small businesses or similar activities, and on those pursuing hobbies. There may be a dimension of intrinsic value to the activities in which such individuals are engaged, lacking in larger-scale corporate activity, that is threatened by strict liability and that can only adequately be protected by a 'due diligence' defence.

For Raz, freedom, in the sense of autonomy, 'consists in the pursuit of valuable forms of life, and . . . its value derives from the value of that pursuit'.[142] To similar effect, Gardner claims that, 'our well-being consists in the wholehearted and successful pursuit of worthwhile activities . . . [and, further] the value which our virtues and skills bring to our worthwhile activities is *by its very nature intrinsic or constitutive value*'.[143] The key point

---

[138] *Cambridgeshire and Isle of Ely County Council v Rust* [1972] 1 QB 426.

[139] The phrase of F. Pearce and S. Tombs, 'Ideology, Hegemony and Empiricism', 425, cited by D. Cowan and A. Marsh, 'There's Regulatory Crime, and then there's Landlord Crime: from "Rachmanites" to "Partners" ', 836.

[140] Judith Freedman, 'Limited Liability: Large Company Theory and Small Firms', 320.

[141] That this is a factor accounted for in prosecution decision-making is argued by Hawkins: Keith Hawkins, *Law as Last Resort*, 365.   [142] Joseph Raz, *The Morality of Freedom*, 395.

[143] John Gardner, 'On the General Part of the Criminal Law', 220 (my emphasis). Something that has intrinsic or constitutive value has value for its own sake (i.e. other than purely instrumentally) even though what matters about the value that it has may be that it contributes to the well-being of people (beings with *ultimate* value): see Joseph Raz, 'Rights-Based Moralities', 188.

here is the link between the pursuit of intrinsic value and personal participation in certain kinds of activity (those that thrive on the exercise of virtues, skills, wisdom, and so forth). One will derive little or no value from freely choosing to be a teacher, unless one gives one's all in the teaching itself. One will derive little or no value from living in a thriving village community unless one identifies with and plays one's part in the life of the community. One will derive little or no value from having a pet dog unless one plays an enthusiastic part in the life one shares with the dog; and so forth. On this view, to be content in one's life as a whole to be a mere passive recipient of benefits of any kind, is not only to cut oneself off from much that is valuable because it depends on positive participation. It is also, almost inevitably, to tolerate some degradation of the benefit itself, through enjoyment of it only when it takes—or can be translated into—a passive form, such as sensory pleasure, the maintenance of idleness, and the like.[144] The realization of autonomy in an individual's life, then, depends in part on him or her being adequately motivated and guided by 'action-reasons', reasons to do things oneself, in a certain way and in a certain spirit, whatever the outcome.[145] In the present context, what is it that is important about Raz's and Gardner's 'active' account of well-being? The pursuit of a hobby, including the owning of pets, is a classic example of an attempt to give one's life intrinsic value through personal participation in a form of life (i.e. an activity that is to some extent 'socially defined and determined'[146]) recognized as yielding such value. By using the deterrent weapon of strict liability to convict those pursuing hobbies of a criminal offence when, by unforeseeable mischance or when they had done all they could to avert it, they fell into bad practice, the courts are riding roughshod over or simply ignoring the intrinsic value of the action-reasons by which Ds are guided when they

[144] A point that is meant to give no succour whatsoever to those who believe not merely that people can be criticized for long-term inactivity but also that they can legitimately be coerced into activity. For liberals, coerced activity is, in virtue of the coercion, stripped of its intrinsic value, because the activity will not be wholehearted. So, the coercion is self-defeating. I am not, of course, seeking to deny that sensory pleasure, and (a degree!) of idleness cannot form part of some intrinsically valuable *in*activity, such as passing one's holiday lying on a beach staring out to sea. It is only when it is in terms of such inactivity that one has come to see the value of one's life *as a whole*, that one has lost touch with what makes forms of life truly valuable, over a lifetime.

[145] This, 'active' account of well-being has come under attack from critics such as Roger Crisp, 'Raz on Well-Being' (1997) 17 *Oxford Journal of Legal Studies* 499. For Crisp, 'contentment', which can be achieved or reached through, for example, passively induced pleasurable experiences is (ibid., 502), 'a component of well-being . . . good or worth having in itself'. Without more, Crisp's suggestion fails to convince. It is strongly arguable that contentment achieved through passive receipt of benefits only gains value through the agent's experience of it *in contrast to* (perhaps, as a 'reward' he or she gives himself or herself for) valuable things that he or she seeks to achieve through active striving. A life that can consist of nothing but passively induced pleasurable experience is not (to use Crisp's words) 'good or worth having *in itself*' (ibid., 502, my emphasis) at all. Such a life is only 'good' when compared with something worse: for example, a life racked by constant and almost intolerable pain.

[146] Joseph Raz, *The Morality of Freedom*, 309.

engage in the activities in question. The same thing can be happening, *mutatis mutandis*, when the courts impose strict liability, irrespective of due diligence shown, on street performers, sole traders or small family businesses. For, in such cases, it can be the self-same intrinsic (personal, participatory) value of action-reasons that motivates those now being found liable to engage in such activities, activities that have—*ex hypothesi*, by unforeseeable bad luck—given rise to wrongdoing. The difference between such cases and larger scale corporate activity, is that in the former the business activity can be *identified with* the efforts of an individual, family or small partnership (being no mere passive shareholders or 'middle' managers) to sustain value in their lives through wholehearted participation in the role, perhaps tied to their local community, that they have created for themselves through their occupation.[147] By way of contrast, in organizations too large for their operation to be identified with the efforts of any individual or small group to achieve personal autonomy through their work, strict corporate criminal liability may be justified in part because it *saves* individual employees from the risk of personal criminal liability arising from their work-related activity.

The courts have persistently failed to appreciate this point, treating all business activity in much the same way as the judges' traditional left-wing critics, as devoted to nothing more than the calculating pursuit of (evergreater) profit. In *Hobbs v Winchester Corporation*,[148] the issue was not liability for a criminal offence, as such, but whether D, a butcher, was barred from claming compensation for the destruction of diseased meat in that he was 'in default'. Kennedy LJ held that D was barred irrespective of any element of guilty mind, because, 'the policy of the Act is this: that if a man *chooses for profit to engage in a business* which involves offering for sale that which may be deadly or injurious to health he must take that risk . . .'[149] In the highlighted words, Kennedy LJ presents the butcher as engaging in his business solely for an 'outcome-reason' (profit), as if he were a commodity broker trading in meat products because they offer the best profit margin.[150] On this—rational choice—model of commerce, people in business are assumed simply to be trading off the costs of taking the greatest possible care against the risks of detection and conviction, as if these were nothing more than factors bearing on the overall outcome reason: the profit-and-loss equation. This stereotypical image of business activity does scant

---

[147] See further, Jeremy Horder, 'Strict Liability, Statutory Construction and the Spirit of Liberty', 470–474. [148] [1910] 2 KB 471.

[149] Ibid., 483 (my emphasis). On the particular facts, the finding may not have been unjust: see the discussion in Celia Wells, *Corporations and Criminal Responsibility*, 2nd edn., 69–70.

[150] See, to the same effect, Lord Diplock's view in *Sweet v Parsley* [1970] AC 132, 163, that what matters is whether 'citizens have a choice whether they participate or not'; and also, Lord Reid's argument in *R v Warner* [1969] 2 AC 256, 271–272, that, 'a person [who] sets up as say a butcher, a publican, or a manufacturer . . . must take the risk and when it is found that the statutory prohibition or requirement has been infringed he must pay the penalty . . . it is a comparatively minor injustice.'

UNIVERSITY OF WINCHESTER LIBRARY

justice to the action-reasons, rather than outcome-reasons, for which millions of people engage in many kinds of small business, sole tradership, or other role or performance-orientated entrepreneurial activity (such as street performance or 'busking'[151]). In that regard, in this context, the obvious way in which to avert the risk posed by strict liability to the intrinsic value of action-reasons is by the application of a 'due diligence' defence to those who fall foul of regulations, whilst engaged in hobbies or small-scale business activity.

We have seen that Hart advocated a 'fair opportunity' basis for understanding defences which he thought might have an application to strict liability offences.[152] It seems clear, however, that what he had in mind embodied a traditional, classical view of how to deny fault or to excuse oneself.[153] This is a view focused on what D had reason to know, to be aware of, to remember, to have seen, to have understood, and so forth:[154] what we can call the 'cognitive' excusatory factors, which Hart placed alongside the 'emotive' excusatory factors (like provoked loss of self-control, and duress) and the—as he saw it—'disorder'-based excusatory factor of insanity. Such an account perhaps underpins the concentration, in *Proudman v Dayman*,[155] on 'honest and reasonable mistake'.[156] The excuse of 'due diligence' (understood as taking *all* reasonable steps to avert wrongdoing), as recognized in *R v City of Sault Ste Marie*,[157] cannot easily be accommodated within the traditional view of excusing conditions. That is because its focus is the effort D has put in to avoiding wrongdoing, rather than whether or not he or she realized or should have realized wrongdoing might result from his or her activities.[158] The excuse of due diligence, thus, fits much better with the 'active' account of well-being, with its emphasis on wholehearted endeavour, than with excuses that focus solely or mainly on cognitive excusatory factors. It fits better with an approach to ostensibly strict liability offences in which an emphasis is placed on the action-reasons D had, not merely to engage in the activity in question (hobby; small business; entrepreneurial performance) in the first place, but also positively to ensure that wrongdoing was not committed in the course of that activity. Unashamedly, then, moving the due diligence defence to centre-stage can be made part of

---

[151] See *South Tyneside Borough Council v Jackson* [1998] EHLR 249 (DC), where Mance J described D's act as '*bona fide* in a manner as attractive as it was ingenious'.

[152] See the end of chapter 1.6 above.

[153] H. L. A. Hart, *Punishment and Responsibility*, 28, 'the individual is not liable to punishment if at the time of his doing what would otherwise be a punishable act he was unconscious, mistaken about the physical consequences of his bodily movements or the nature or qualities of the thing or persons affected by them, or, in some cases, if he was subjected to threats or other gross forms of coercion or was the victim of certain types of mental disease.'

[154] For a more detailed examination, see A. P. Simester, 'Can Negligence Be Culpable?'.

[155] (1941) 67 DLR 536.　　　[156] Ibid., 540–541.

[157] (1978) 85 DLR (3rd) 161, 181–182.

[158] In terms of the analysis presented in chapter 2, 'due diligence' is a predominantly ascriptive, capacity-focused, adopted reason claim to excuse.

a liberal account of what it means to respect autonomy in the criminal law, through the forging of a link between liberalism, autonomy and the 'active' account of well-being.[159]

In that regard, Arden LJ has argued that strict liability, in the absence of a due diligence defence, may be contrary to Article 3 of the European Convention on Human Rights (banning 'inhuman and degrading treatment or punishment'), or may be a breach of Article 6(2) (guaranteeing the right to a presumption of innocence).[160] So, she argues, the courts should regard themselves as free[161] to create a defence of 'due diligence and all reasonable steps [taken] to rectify', to avoid a clash between the law and these provisions, in the regulatory context. She envisages an example in which a factory owner, through no fault on his or her part, accidentally pollutes the environment around the factory, and then pays a large sum of money to clear up the mess in order to limit the damage to his or her reputation that may occur in spite of the absence of fault. Arden LJ goes on to say:

> Suppose that he is then prosecuted for an environmental offence involving strict liability which carries an unlimited fine and he resists conviction on the ground that the accident had occurred accidentally and without fault. He contends that a conviction would cause him great loss of reputation. Can he successfully contend that for the law to impose strict liability, so that a person can show that the damage was not due to any negligence on his part, and that he has taken all the steps required to rectify the damage caused, has no defence, infringes his rights under Article 3?[162]

A number of points can be made about this passage, as they bear on the argument in this book. First, whilst the imposition of a duty to make every effort to rectify damage is obviously fully consistent with an emphasis on the due diligence excuse, and hence on the 'active' account of well-being, it is not, strictly speaking, an excusatory duty. More or less full rectification may mitigate a crime, but cannot excuse it, because it is not normatively related to the reasons why the offence came to be committed. A failure to rectify could, of course, itself be made an offence, or part thereof, but then the efforts D has made to rectify *are* translated into potentially excusatory ones, under the definition of the necessary conditions for excuse given in chapter 1.1 above. In terms of the 'active' account of well-being, Arden LJ would have done better to go beyond her reference to 'negligence' as the relevant fault element (a fault concept too frequently equated purely with cognitive issues), and to place emphasis on the excusatory need for D to have

[159] See, generally, John Gardner, 'On The General Part of the Criminal Law'.

[160] M. Arden, 'Criminal Law at the Crossroads: The Impact on Human Rights from the Law Commission's Perspective and the Need for a Code' [1999] *Criminal Law Review* 439.

[161] In virtue of section 3(1) of the Human Rights Act 1998, that obliges courts to interpret legislation, 'so far as possible . . . in a way which is compatible with the convention rights'.

[162] M. Arden, 'Criminal Law at the Crossroads: The Impact on Human Rights from the Law Commission's Perspective and the Need for a Code', 450, cited by A. P. Simester and G. R. Sullivan, *Criminal Law: Theory and Doctrine*, 1st edn., 651.

shown that he or she took all reasonable steps to avoid the offence in the first place, as well as placing emphasis on the 'mitigatory' need to have taken all reasonable steps to rectify the damage done. Secondly, whether or not the offence under which the factory owner is charged breaches Article 6(2)—which seems doubtful—the offence may breach the more general right under Article 6 to a fair trial, in virtue of denying D access to the common good of reciprocity and a chance, substantively, to answer the charges by way of defence.[163] This ties in with what Arden LJ says about Article 3. It is obviously true that the ban on inhuman and degrading treatment in criminal proceedings must be analysed separately from the ban on inhuman and degrading punishment; and that, perhaps, makes it easier to argue that, to deny D any defence at all in criminal proceedings, is to treat D in an inhuman or degrading way, whatever the punishment that may result from conviction. For, that is what a complete denial of access to the good of reciprocity amounts to.[164]

7. EXCUSING REASONABLE IGNORANCE OF THE LAW

In spite of the 'liberal' slant to the discussion in the last section, what I have been calling the plural view of the criminal law that inspires it does not—as is sometimes supposed—itself stand or fall depending on whether one wishes to defend a liberal account of excusing conditions. The plural view of criminal law can be clearly detached from a concern only with liberty, and *a fortiori* with liberalism. In this section, I hope to show how this can be done through a focus on a different value, 'respect for law', that may rightly be prized in any legal order, whether or not it is liberal. Before explaining what is meant by 'respect for law', though, something needs to be said about the context in which its value stands to be compromised in the modern bureaucratic and regulatory state. To this end, my focus will be Ashworth's innovative discussion of officially induced error of law.[165] In terms of the analysis given in chapter 1.1 above, a claim of officially induced error of law could be regarded as an excusatory claim (where D relies on a

---

[163] See section 4 above. This argument has particular force if D is an individual answering for his or her own conduct, or for that of his or her family.

[164] In spite of being a matter solely of mitigation, the fact that D has done all he or she can to rectify damage done also seems to have a bearing on whether, in all the circumstances, subjecting D to criminal proceedings amounts to inhuman and degrading treatment; but that point cannot be pursued here.

[165] Andrew Ashworth, 'Testing Fidelity to Legal Values: Official Involvement and Law Enforcement'. In this article, Ashworth is as much, if not more, concerned with entrapment as with officially induced mistake of law, but my focus is solely the latter. Ahead of his time, as ever, Ashworth has given much more detailed consideration to the kinds of excuses that are certain to arise following the emergence of the bureaucratic, regulatory state than almost any other theorist: see Andrew Ashworth, 'Excusable Mistake of Law' [1974] *Criminal Law Review* 652.

predominantly ascriptive, actively justificatory, adopted reason for the wrongdoing: see chapter 2 above); or it could be treated as claim for a stay of prosecution on the grounds of abuse of process.[166] In the discussion that follows, I shall not be especially concerned with the question when it would be appropriate to excuse *ex post facto*, rather than stay a prosecution *ex ante*. My main concern is with theoretical aspects of the claim of officially induced error of law, in so far as it is right to treat it as an excuse for committing a regulatory offence imposing ostensibly strict liability.[167]

Ashworth has explained how, in spite of the relatively diverse and heterogeneous nature of defences generally, the courts—influenced, no doubt, by the classical view of excuses, set out in section 1 above—have historically taken a narrow and unsympathetic view of excusatory claims arising out of the misconduct (whether or not blameworthy) of state officials.[168] This view was taken in spite of the fact that, as we saw in section 2 above, during the late nineteenth century the increasing scope and complexity of regulation through the criminal law meant that it was becoming ever harder to discover just what conduct one was—on pain of prosecution and conviction—obligated to refrain from or, crucially and increasingly, obliged positively to engage in (such as ensuring that one's children were vaccinated, and attended school).[169] Typical of the attitude English judges have taken towards such cases is *Cambridgeshire and Isle of Ely County Council v Rust*.[170] In this case, D was charged with obstruction of the highway, a charge relating to his stall that was pitched on the highway, and for which he had paid rates for three years. He pleaded 'lawful excuse' for the obstruction, on the grounds that before pitching the stall at the outset, he had made enquiries both of local and national authorities as to whether he could pitch the stall, and none of these authorities had suggested that his action might be unlawful. The Divisional Court held that, his enquiries notwithstanding, there could be no lawful excuse because 'everyone is supposed to know the law'. Ashworth contrasts this unnecessarily hard line with the approach taken in Canada, where there is a defence of 'officially induced error'.[171]

---

[166] There is a thoughtful discussion in Andrew Ashworth, 'Testing Fidelity to Legal Values: Official Involvement and Law Enforcement'.

[167] For obvious reasons, where D is accused of committing a crime that is a *malum in se*, the case for excuse, or for staying the prosecution, on the grounds of officially induced error of law is much weaker, and will not be considered further here.

[168] Andrew Ashworth, 'Testing Fidelity to Legal Values: Official Involvement and Law Enforcement'. It is only much more recently, in particular following the passing of the Human Rights Act 1998, that judicial attitudes have begun to change: see e.g. *R v Looseley* [2001] UKHL 53 on the issue of entrapment.

[169] The courts did stir themselves into action when the matter was whether a crime created by statutory instrument was actually unpublished or unavailable: see *Burns v Nowell* (1880) 5 QBD 444.

[170] [1972] 1 QB 426; but see, now, *Postermobile PLC v Brent London Borough Council*, *The Times*, 8 December 1997, both discussed in Andrew Ashworth, 'Testing Fidelity to Legal Values: Official Involvement and Law Enforcement', 302–303.   [171] See ibid., 303–305.

In *R v Cancoil Thermal Corporation*,[172] Lacourciere JA said, of this defence:

In order for the accused to successfully raise this defence, he must show that he relied on the erroneous legal opinion of the official and that his reliance was reasonable. The reasonableness will depend on several factors, including the efforts he made to ascertain the proper law, the complexity or the obscurity of the law, the position of the official who gave the advice, and the clarity, definitiveness and reasonableness of the advice given.[173]

Ashworth rightly believes the case for an excuse or stay of prosecution to be very much stronger in cases of reasonable reliance on an *officially* induced mistake of law than it is when the mistake stems from some other source,[174] but (in contrast to his views on entrapment by non-officials[175]) he is sympathetic to the view that reasonable reliance on statements of law by at least some non-officials should be an excuse or reason to stay the prosecution.[176] In that regard, as an example of the injustice wrought by taking the contrary, 'hard line' view, he cites the case of *South Tyneside Borough Council v Jackson*.[177] In this case D, a street performer, obtained and relied on police advice and counsel's opinion to the effect that he could be regarded as having taken 'all reasonable precautions' in relation to his 'act'; but the reliance on this advice was held by the Divisional Court to be irrelevant to the question of whether D in fact had taken such precautions.[178]

I shall assume that the case for some kind of excuse of officially induced error of law, broadly along the lines set out in *R v Cancoil Thermal Corporation*, needs no further argument to support it. My focus will be on whether the 'official' status of the person on whom reliance is placed by D for advice should be an absolutely crucial factor: perhaps a factor so important that if it is likely to prove impossible, in a particular legal system, to draw workable distinctions between kinds and grades of 'officials', for the purpose of saying when reliance by D on advice given was reasonable, the case for an excuse of 'officially' induced error of law may itself have to be abandoned. My argument will be that although the kind and degree of 'official' status possessed by the person who gave D advice is an important factor to be weighed,[179] in deciding whether D's reliance on the advice was reasonable, there will rarely if ever be a need to rule definitively on whether particular classes of adviser (say, barristers) can count as 'officials' for the purposes of the excuse. The view that 'official' status, in relation to the putative excuse of officially induced error of law, must by definition be crucial is

---

[172] *R v Cancoil Thermal Corporation* (1986) 52 CR (3rd) 188.   [173] Ibid., 188, 199.

[174] Andrew Ashworth, 'Testing Fidelity to Legal Values: Official Involvement and Law Enforcement', 304–309.   [175] Ibid., 320.

[176] Ibid., 304–309.

[177] [1998] EHLR 249 (DC), on which see n. 151 and n. 171 above.

[178] To similar effect, see *Surrey County Council v Battersby* (1965) 2 QB 194, where the misleading advice came from a Council official.

[179] As indicated in *R v Cancoil Thermal Corporation* (1986) 52 CR (3rd) 188, 199.

based on too parsimonious a set of jurisprudential principles. Too great an emphasis on the need for mistake of law to come about through official misconduct suggests (as Ashworth recognizes)[180] that the excusatory principles are solely part of the so-called 'internal' morality of law, the morality integral to the reciprocal relationship between those seeking to ensure governance through law, and those subject to that governance.[181] Whilst those principles may play an important role in setting the parameters for an excuse such as reasonable mistake of law, also significant is the partially 'external' or independent value of *respect for* law. As I shall define it, respect for law is a value that stands to be compromised almost as badly in at least some cases of inducement of wrongdoing by non-officials as it is by cases of official inducement of wrongdoing. So, what is 'respect for law'? In Ashworth's discussion of officially induced mistake of law, the notion of respect for law (he does not use that term, as such) is rightly tied to the idea that by seeking official guidance, D 'has behaved as a good citizen . . . [by] approaching the relevant authorities . . . This is behaviour that the State ought to value, and certainly ought not to punish . . . to recognise [the defence] would signal the value of citizens checking on the lawfulness of their proposed activities'.[182] I want to explore these ideas in more detail, drawing on Raz's discussion of respect for law, in the context of whether and in what circumstances there can be obligations to obey the law.[183]

For Raz, there is no general obligation to obey the law as such (i.e. irrespective of relevant merit-based criteria).[184] So, respect for law, in the broad sense, is not a value integral to the relationship between the governed and those charged with governance. Nonetheless, it is permissible—and sometimes entirely appropriate—to adopt an attitude of respect for law,[185] and if that is one's attitude then (other than in wicked legal systems) one is under a general obligation to obey the law. According to Raz, the attitude of respect for law is comprised of two elements, not normally distinguished in practice, a primarily cognitive dimension to respect, and a primarily practical dimension to it.[186] The primarily cognitive dimension to respect for law is concerned with beliefs, such as the belief that the law must be respected because it is endorsed by a democratically elected Parliament, because the law is respectful of human rights whilst contributing to social progress, and

---

[180] Andrew Ashworth, 'Testing Fidelity to Legal Values: Official Involvement and Law Enforcement', 329 n. 125.

[181] The classic discussion, from which Ashworth seeks to distance himself to some extent, is to be found in Lon Fuller, *The Morality of Law*, revised edn., chapter 2.

[182] Andrew Ashworth, 'Testing Fidelity to Legal Values: Official Involvement and Law Enforcement', 305. Obviously, D is not, strictly speaking, in fact being punished for his or her behaviour in making efforts to discover the law, but because the offence with which he or she is charged is one of strict liability, and does not indicate such efforts to be relevant to liability; but Ashworth's main point is clear enough.

[183] Joseph Raz, *The Authority of Law*, chapter 13.   [184] Ibid., chapter 12.

[185] There may be some officials, such as judges, of whom such an attitude can be required.

[186] Joseph Raz, *The Authority of Law*, 251.

so forth. In the wake of such beliefs may come affective states such as a feeling (not, obviously, inconsistent with a critical reflective attitude) of pride in one's legal system, or satisfaction at living under broadly reasonable laws and legal institutions free from widespread corruption. The primarily practical dimension to respect for law consists mainly in a disposition to obey the law because it is the law. In the wake of this practical disposition may come attitudes such as hostility to law-breakers, satisfaction when criminals are brought to justice, approval of and respect for people who remain law-abiding (perhaps especially in difficult circumstances), feelings of guilt and shame if one oneself breaks the law and so forth.[187] Raz separates the cognitive from the practical dimensions to respect for law, even though in practice they are intertwined, to emphasize that sometimes citizens may display one but not the other. Someone might adopt the practical attitude come what may, in the legal system. In other words, he or she might think that laws should always be obeyed however bad they are. Conversely, someone might have the cognitive attitude without the practical one. A British citizen might be a legal 'francophile', having the greatest admiration for the French legal system and for its laws, and yet also believe that tourists are under no special obligations towards the legal systems of the countries they visit (including France). Such a person would have the cognitive attitude of respect for law towards the French legal system, but not a corresponding practical attitude.[188]

In general (putting the cognitive and practical dimensions together), Raz says, the attitude of respect for law 'is a somewhat self-satisfied and complacent attitude',[189] in that the display of loyalty and commitment to the legal system it involves may be misplaced. Moreover, there are ways of displaying one's loyalty to a country other than through respect for law.[190] Even so, the important point for present purposes is that respect for law can have (as Ashworth impliedly asserts) genuine intrinsic value, in a just legal system. Raz puts it this way:

[R]espect is itself a reason for action. Those who respect the law have reasons which others do not. These are expressive reasons . . . Respect for law is an aspect of identification with society (the reverse of alienation) . . . A person identifying himself with his society, feeling that it is his and that he belongs to it, is loyal to his society. His loyalty may express itself, among other ways, in respect for the law of the community.[191]

It is the value of respect for law that is betrayed or threatened when the courts hold that D's efforts to establish the legal status of his or her conduct count for nothing, even when he or she is entirely reasonably led to believe

---

[187] All of these points are to be found in Joseph Raz, *The Authority of Law*, 251–252.
[188] Ibid., 252.   [189] Ibid., 261.
[190] In some instances, loyalty to one's country and to one's fellow citizens may require active opposition to particular laws: Joseph Raz, *The Authority of Law*, 261.   [191] Ibid., 259.

that his or her conduct complies with the law. As Hart said, a legal system is not, and should not be, shaped solely or mainly by the understanding that citizens are models of Holmes' 'bad man', who responds solely to the threat of sanctions. For Hart, much of the character of legal institutions is rightly shaped by a concern for what he calls the 'puzzled man', who wants to do as the law requires but needs guidance on how to do it.[192] When, as the court did in *Cambridgeshire and Isle of Ely County Council v Rust*,[193] courts deny D in a criminal case a defence of reasonable reliance on official advice, by invoking the maxim that *ignorantia juris neminem excusat*, or the presumption that everyone is presumed to know the law, they by implication adopt a 'bad man' view of the law as nothing but a sanction-based system of deterrence-cum-retribution. In so doing, they deny or undermine the expressive value of D's commitment to law-abidingness—as a model of Hart's 'puzzled man'—demonstrated by his or her efforts to discover the legal position, and by his or her reasonable reliance on what he or she took that position to be. D is, in effect, put in the same legal position (even if dealt with, following conviction, in a more lenient way) as the 'bad man' who does as he pleases, then just waits to see if prosecution follows, then if it does, denies guilt as a matter of course, and so on. Looked at in this way, i.e. from the perspective of Hart's 'puzzled man', we can see that, in principle, the value of respect for law can be undermined as much by cases in which D has relied on solicitors' or barristers' advice as when he or she has relied on the advice of a competent official in the department of government in question. It depends on the circumstances. So, a major corporation, with long experience of how counsel's opinion can turn out in the end to be misguided, may (other things being equal) be adjudged to have relied less reasonably on such advice than a street performer, like Jackson,[194] with perhaps little or no experience or appreciation of the status of legal advice.

There is nothing especially 'liberal' about a concern for the value of respect for law, whether that value is always reflected in the legislative definition of offences,[195] or whether it is always left to the courts to decide how best to defend it against unjust legislative encroachment (or something in between). Asking the question whether a legal system recognizes the value of respect for law, however, in the way that it has developed its criminal law excuses (or the grounds for stays of prosecution) is a good test of whether that legal system has got beyond the classical view of excuses, and the common law agenda set by that view, and has embraced the challenges set for a system of criminal law by the emergence of the bureaucratic, regulatory

---

[192] H. L. A. Hart, *The Concept of Law*, 40.

[193] [1972] 1 QB 426; but see, now, *Postermobile PLC v Brent London Borough Council*, *The Times*, 8 December 1997, both discussed in Andrew Ashworth, 'Testing Fidelity to Legal Values: Official Involvement and Law Enforcement', 302–303.

[194] *South Tyneside Borough Council v Jackson* [1998] EHLR 249.

[195] For a case where the court found that this was so, by implication, see the decision of the House of Lords in *Secretary of State for Trade and Industry v Hart* [1982] 1 WLR 481.

state. It is a good test of how thoroughgoing is a legal system's commitment to a 'plural' view of the criminal law. *Ignorantia juris neminem excusat* is a maxim perhaps appropriately regarded as exception-less in a system of criminal law comprised wholly or largely of *mala in se*.[196] But, a legal system that persists in a belief in the absolute character of that maxim in a world of ever more far-reaching, ever more technical and specialized, and ever more inaccessible regulatory criminal laws, is a legal system that has simply failed to adapt its moral thinking to modern circumstances.[197]

---

[196] See further, Douglas Husak and Andrew Von Hirsch, 'Culpability and Mistake of Law', in Stephen Shute, John Gardner, and Jeremy Horder (eds.), *Action and Value in Criminal Law* (Oxford: Clarendon Press, 1993), 157.

[197] The same criticism extends to legal systems, like those in (inevitably) England and Wales, that have no doctrine of '*de minimis*' providing grounds for an excuse or stay of prosecution. I will not pursue the point further here.

Bibliography

Ackrill, J. L., *Essays on Plato and Aristotle* (Oxford: Clarendon Press, 1997).

Akida, M., 'Criminal Law', in Bernard-Maugiron, N., and Dupret, B. (eds.), *Egypt and its Laws* (The Hague: Kluwer, 2002).

Alldridge, Peter, 'Rules for Courts and Rules for Citizens' (1990) 10 *Oxford Journal of Legal Studies* 487.

American Law Institute, 37th Annual Meeting, ALI Proceedings 1960 127 (1961).

Arden, M., 'Criminal Law at the Crossroads: The Impact on Human Rights from the Law Commission's Perspective and the Need for a Code' [1999] *Criminal Law Review* 439.

Aristotle, *Nichomachean Ethics*, (trans.) Thomson, J. A. K. (London: Penguin, 1955).

—— *De Anima*, in *The Complete Works of Aristotle*, (trans.) Barnes, Jonathan (New Jersey: Princeton University Press, 1995).

—— *Rhetoric*, in *The Complete Works of Aristotle*, (trans.) Barnes, Jonathan (New Jersey: Princeton University Press, 1995).

Ashworth, Andrew, 'Provocation in the Criminal Law' Ph.D. (University of Manchester, 1973).

—— 'Excusable Mistake of Law' [1974] *Criminal Law Review* 652.

—— 'Self-Defence and the Right to Life' (1975) 34 *Cambridge Law Journal* 272.

—— 'The Doctrine of Provocation' (1976) 35 *Cambridge Law Journal* 292.

—— 'Interpreting Criminal Statutes: A Crisis of Legality?' (1991) 107 *Law Quarterly Review* 419.

—— *Sentencing and Criminal Justice*, 2nd edn. (London: Butterworths, 1995).

—— *Principles of Criminal Law*, 3rd edn. (Oxford: Oxford University Press, 1999).

—— 'Is the Criminal Law a Lost Cause?' (2000) 116 *Law Quarterly Review* 225.

—— 'Testing Fidelity to Legal Values: Official Involvement and Criminal Justice', in Shute, Stephen, and Simester, A. P. (eds.), *Criminal Law Theory: Doctrines of the General Part* (Oxford: Oxford University Press, 2002).

Austin, J. L., 'A Plea for Excuses', reprinted in Corrado, M. L. (ed.), *Justification and Excuse in the Criminal Law* (New York: Garland, 1994).

Bacon, Sir Francis, *Maxims* (London: Benjamin Fisher, 1630).

Bainham, Andrew, *Children, Parents and the State* (London: Sweet and Maxwell, 1988).

Baroody, G. D., *Crime and Punishment under Islamic Law*, 2nd edn. (London: Regency Press, 1979).

Bayles, M., 'Character, Purpose and Criminal Responsibility' (1982) 1 *Law and Philosophy* 1.

—— 'Reconceptualising Necessity and Duress', in Corrado, M. L. (ed.), *Justification and Excuse in the Criminal Law* (New York: Garland, 1994).

Berger, Peter, 'On the Obsolescence of the Concept of Honour', in Sandel, Michael (ed.), *Liberalism and its Critics* (Oxford: Basil Blackwell, 1984).

—— and Kellner, Hansfried, *Sociology Reinterpreted* (Middlesex: Penguin, 1981).

Bernard-Maugiron, N., and Dupret, B. (eds.), *Egypt and its Laws* (The Hague: Kluwer, 2002).

Blackstone, Sir William, *Commentaries on the Laws of England*, 4 vols. (Oxford: Clarendon Press, 1765).

Bogg, Alan L., and Stanton-Ife, John, 'Protecting the Vulnerable: Legality, Harm and Theft' (2003) 23 *Legal Studies* 402.

Bond, E. J., *Reason and Value* (Cambridge: Cambridge University Press, 1983).

Bowling, Ben, and Foster, Janet, 'Policing and the Police', in Maguire, Mike, Morgan, Rod, and Reiner, Robert (eds.), *The Oxford Handbook of Criminology*, 3rd edn. (Oxford: Oxford University Press, 2002).

Brett, P., 'The Physiology of Provocation' [1970] *Criminal Law Review* 634.

Brudner, Alan, 'A Theory of Necessity' (1987) 7 *Oxford Journal of Legal Studies* 339.

—— 'Agency and Welfare in the Penal Law', in Shute, Stephen, Gardner, John, and Horder, Jeremy (eds.) *Action and Value in Criminal Law* (Oxford: Clarendon Press, 1993).

—— *The Unity of the Common Law* (Berkeley, California: University of California Press, 1995).

Buchanan, Alec, and Virgo, Graham, 'Duress and Mental Abnormality' [1999] *Criminal Law Review* 517.

Cameron, Deborah, and Fraser, Elizabeth, *The Lust to Kill* (Oxford: Basil Blackwell, 1987).

Cane, Peter, and Gardner, John, *Relating to Responsibility: Essays for Tony Honoré* (Oxford: Hart Publishing, 2001).

—— and Tushnet, Mark, *The Oxford Handbook of Criminal Law* (Oxford: Oxford University Press, 2003).

Clarke, D. C., and Feinerman, J. V., 'Criminal Law and Human Rights in China', in Lubman, S. C. (ed.), *China's Legal Reforms* (Oxford: Clarendon Press, 1996).

Clarkson, C. M. V., and Keating, H. M., *Criminal Law: Text and Materials* (London: Sweet & Maxwell, 1998).

Cohen, L. Jonathan, *An Essay on Belief and Acceptance* (Oxford: Clarendon Press, 1992).

Coleman, Jules, and Shapiro, Scott, *The Oxford Handbook of Jurisprudence and Philosophy of Law* (Oxford: Oxford University Press, 2002).

Colvin, Eric, 'Exculpatory Defences in Criminal Law' (1990) 10 *Oxford Journal of Legal Studies* 381.

Coombs, Mary, 'Outsider Jurisprudence: The Law Review Stories' (1992) 63 *University of Colorado Law Review* 683.

Coppel, Jason, *The Human Rights Act 1998* (Chichester: John Wiley, 1999).

Corrado, M. L. (ed.), Justification and Excuse in the Criminal Law (New York: Garland, 1994).

Cowan, D., and Marsh, A., 'There's Regulatory Crime, and then there's Landlord Crime: from "Rachmanites" to "Partners" ' (2001) 64 *Modern Law Review* 831.

Criminal Law Commissioners, Second Report, *Parliamentary Papers* XXXVI, (343), (1836), 36.

Criminal Law Revision Committee, *Offences Against the Person*, 14th Report, Cmnd 7844 (HMSO, 1980).

Crisp, Roger, 'Raz on Well-Being' (1997) 17 *Oxford Journal of Legal Studies* 499.

—— *Mill on Utilitarianism* (London: Routledge, 1997).

Crowther, M. A., *The Workhouse System 1834–1929: The History of an English Social Institution* (London: Batsford Academic and Educational, 1981).

Dan-Cohen, Meir, 'Decision Rules and Conduct Rules: On Acoustic Separation in Criminal Law' (1994) 97 *Harvard Law Review* 625.

Dell, Suzanne, 'Wanted: An Insanity Defence that can be Used' [1983] *Criminal Law Review* 431.

—— *Murder into Manslaughter: The Diminished Responsibility Defence in Practice* (London: Institute of Psychiatry, 1984).

Derbyshire, Penny, 'An Essay on the Importance and the Neglect of the Magistracy' [1997] *Criminal Law Review* 627.

DeSousa, R., *The Rationality of Emotion* (Cambridge, Mass.: MITR Press, 1987).

Devlin, Patrick, *Samples of Lawmaking* (Oxford: Oxford University Press, 1962).

Dressler, Joshua, 'Reflections on Excusing Wrongdoers: New Excuses and the Model Penal Code' (1988) 19 *Rutgers Law Journal* 671.

—— *Understanding Criminal Law*, 2nd edn. (New York: Matthew Bender, 1995).

—— *Understanding Criminal Law*, 3rd edn. (New York: Lexis, 2001).

Dubber, M., review of Norrie, A., *Punishment, Responsibility and Justice: A Relational Critique*, (2002) 65 *Modern Law Review* 311.

Duff, R. A., *Trials and Punishments* (Cambridge: Cambridge University Press, 1986).

—— *Intention, Agency and Criminal Liability* (Oxford: Basil Blackwell, 1990).

—— 'Choice, Character and Criminal Liability' (1993) 12 *Law and Philosophy* 361.

—— 'Law, Language and Community: Some Preconditions of Criminal Liability' (1998) 18 *Oxford Journal of Legal Studies* 189.

Dworkin, Ronald, *Taking Rights Seriously* (London: Duckworth, 1977).

—— *A Matter of Principle* (Cambridge, Mass.: Harvard University Press, 1985).

—— 'Civil Disobedience and Nuclear Protest', in Dworkin, Ronald (ed.), *A Matter of Principle* (Cambridge, Mass.: Harvard University Press, 1985).

—— *Law's Empire* (London: Fontana, 1986).

Dyzenhaus, David, 'The Politics of Deference: Judicial Review and Democracy', in Taggert, Michael (ed.), *The Province of Administrative Law* (Oxford: Hart Publishing, 1997).

Edwards, Susan S. M., *Sex and Gender in the Legal Process* (London: Blackstone Press, 1996).

Eekelaar, J. M., 'Corporal Punishment, Parents' Religion and Children's Rights' (2003) 119 *Law Quarterly Review* 370.

Emmerson, Ben, and Ashworth, Andrew, *Human Rights and Criminal Justice* (London: Sweet & Maxwell, 2001).

Emsley, Clive, 'The History of Crime and Crime Control Institutions', in Maguire, Mike, Morgan, Rod, and Reiner, Robert (eds.), *The Oxford Handbook of Criminology*, 3rd edn. (Oxford: Oxford University Press, 2002).

Ensor, Sir R., *England 1870–1914* (Oxford: Clarendon Press, 1936).

Farmer, Lindsay, reviewing Steven Shute and A. P. Simester (eds.), *Criminal Law Theory: Doctrines of the General Part* (Oxford: Oxford University Press, 2002), (2003) 23 *Legal Studies* 369.

Feinberg, Joel, *Doing and Deserving: Essays in the Theory of Responsibility* (New Jersey: Princeton University Press, 1974).

—— *Harm to Self* (New York: Oxford University Press, 1986).

Finkelstein, C., 'Duress: A Philosophical Account of the Defence in Law' (1995) *Arizona Law Review* 251.

Finnis, J. M., *Natural Law and Natural Rights* (Oxford: Clarendon Press, 1980).

——, Boyle, Joseph, and Grisez, Germain, *Nuclear Deterrence, Morality and Realism* (Oxford: Clarendon Press, 1987).

Fletcher, G. P., 'The Individualisation of Excusing Conditions' (1974) 47 *Southern California Law Review* 1269.

—— *Rethinking Criminal Law* (Boston, Mass.: Little Brown, 1978).

Forster, E. M., *Two Cheers for Democracy* (London: Edward Arnold & Co, 1951).

Frankfurt, Harry, *The Importance of What We Care About* (Cambridge: Cambridge University Press, 1988).

Freedman, Judith, 'Limited Liability: Large Company Theory and Small Firms' (2000) 63 *Modern Law Review* 317.

Frey, R. G., and Morris, C. W. (eds.) *Liability and Responsibility: Essays in Law and Morals* (Cambridge: Cambridge University Press, 1991).

Fuller, Lon, *The Morality of Law*, revised edn. (New Haven: Yale University Press, 1969).

Funk, Markus, 'Justifying Justifications' (1999) 19 *Oxford Journal of Legal Studies* 631.

Gardner, John, 'Justification and Reasons', in Simester, A. P., and Smith, A. T. H., *Harm and Culpability* (Oxford: Clarendon Press, 1996).

—— 'On the General Part of the Criminal Law', in Duff, R. A. (ed.), *Philosophy and the Criminal Law* (Cambridge: Cambridge University Press, 1998).

—— 'The Gist of Excuses' (1998) 1 *Buffalo Criminal Law Review* 575.

—— 'Punishment: In Proportion and In Perspective', in Ashworth, Andrew, and Wasik, Martin (eds.), *Fundamentals of Sentencing Theory* (Oxford: Clarendon Press, 1998).

—— 'In Defence of Defences', in Asp, P., Herlitz, C. E., and Holmqvist, L. (eds.), *Flores Juris et Legum: Festskrift till Nils Jareborg* (Uppsala: Iustus Forlag, 2002).

—— 'The Mark of Responsibility' (2003) 23 *Oxford Journal of Legal Studies* 157.

—— and Shute, Stephen, 'The Wrongness of Rape', in Horder, Jeremy (ed.), 4th Series, *Oxford Essays in Jurisprudence* (Oxford: Oxford University Press, 2000).

—— and Macklem, Timothy, 'Compassion without Respect: Nine Fallacies in *R v Smith*' [2001] *Criminal Law Review* 623.

—— and —— 'Provocation and Pluralism' (2001) 64 *Modern Law Review* 815.

—— and —— 'Reasons', in Coleman, Jules, and Shapiro, Scott, *The Oxford Handbook of Jurisprudence and Philosophy of Law* (Oxford: Oxford University Press, 2002).

Gardner, Simon, 'Necessity's Newest Inventions' (1991) 11 *Oxford Journal of Legal Studies* 125.

—— 'The Importance of *Majewski*' (1994) 14 *Oxford Journal of Legal Studies* 279.

Garland, David, *Punishment and Modern Society: A Study in Social Theory* (Oxford: Clarendon Press, 1990).

Gatrell, V. A. C., 'Crime, Authority and the Policeman-State, 1750–1950', in Thompson, F. M. L., *The Cambridge Social History of Britain 1750–1950* (Cambridge: Cambridge University Press, 1990).

Gavison, Ruth (ed.), *Issues in Contemporary Legal Philosophy* (Oxford: Clarendon Press, 1987).

Genders, Elaine, 'Reform of the Offences Against the Person Act: Lessons from the Law in Action' [1994] *Criminal Law Review* 689.

Goode, Matthew, 'The Abolition of Provocation', in Yeo, S. M. H., *Partial Excuses to Murder* (New South Wales: The Federation Press, 1991).

Gough, Stephen, 'Taking the Heat out of Provocation' (1999) 19 *Oxford Journal of Legal Studies* 481.

Green, Stuart, 'Why it's a Crime to Tear the Tag off a Mattress: Overcriminalisation and the Moral Content of Regulatory Offences', (1997) 46 *Emory Law Journal* 97.

Green, Thomas A., *Verdict According to Conscience* (Chicago: University of Chicago Press, 1985).

Griew, Edward, 'Reducing Murder to Manslaughter: Whose Job?' (1986) 12 *Journal of Medical Ethics* 18.

—— 'The Future of Diminished Responsibility' [1988] *Criminal Law Review* 75.

Griffin, James, *Value Judgement: Improving Our Ethical Beliefs* (Oxford: Oxford University Press, 1996).

Hale, Sir Matthew, *Pleas of the Crown*, 2 vols., 1736 (London: Professional Books, reprinted 1971).

Hampton, Jean, 'Mens Rea' (1990) 7 *Social Policy and Philosophy* 1.

Hansard, Parl. Deb., 1st series (41 vols). XIX, col. 647 (29 March 1811).

—— Parl. Deb. (1872), 212, 1701–1703 and 660–662.

Hardie, W. F. R., *Aristotle's Ethical Theory*, 2nd edn. (Oxford: Clarendon Press, 1980).

Harris, José, *Private Lives, Public Spirit. A Social History of Britain 1870–1914* (Oxford: Oxford University Press, 1993).

Hart, H. L. A., *The Concept of Law* (Oxford: Clarendon Press, 1961).

—— *Punishment and Responsibility* (Oxford: Clarendon Press, 1968).

—— 'Legal Responsibility and the Excuses', in Hart, H. L. A. (ed.), *Punishment and Responsibility* (Oxford: Clarendon Press, 1968).

—— and Honoré, A. M., *Causation in the Law*, 2nd edn. (Oxford: Clarendon Press, 1985).

Hawkins, Keith, *Law as Last Resort* (Oxford: Oxford University Press, 2002).

Horder, Jeremy, 'Mercy Killings: Some Reflections on Beecham's Case' (1988) 52 *Journal of Criminal Law* 309.

—— 'Sex, Violence, and Sentencing in Domestic Provocation Cases' [1989] *Criminal Law Review* 546.

—— 'Cognition, Emotion and Criminal Culpability' (1990) 106 *Law Quarterly Review* 469.

—— 'Autonomy, Provocation and Duress' [1992] *Criminal Law Review* 706.

—— 'The Duel and the English Law of Homicide' (1992) 12 *Oxford Journal of Legal Studies* 419.

—— 'Provocation and Loss of Self-Control' (1992) 108 *Law Quarterly Review* 191.

—— *Provocation and Responsibility* (Oxford: Clarendon Press, 1992).

—— 'Criminal Culpability: The Possibility of a General Theory' (1993) 12 *Law and Philosophy* 193.

—— 'Pleading Involuntary Lack of Capacity' (1993) *Cambridge Law Journal* 298.

—— 'Occupying the Moral High Ground? The Law Commission on Duress' [1994] *Criminal Law Review* 334.

—— 'Sobering Up? The Law Commission on Criminal Intoxication' (1995) 58 *Modern Law Review* 534.

Horder, Jeremy, 'Criminal Law: Between Determinism, Liberalism and Criminal Justice' (1996) 49 *Current Legal Problems* 159.

—— 'Two Histories and Four Hidden Principles of Mens Rea' (1997) 113 *Law Quarterly Review* 95.

—— 'Self-Defence, Necessity and Duress: Understanding the Relationship' (1998) 11 *Canadian Journal of Law and Jurisprudence* 143.

—— 'On the Irrelevance of Motive in Criminal Law', in Horder, Jeremy (ed.), *Oxford Essays in Jurisprudence*, 4th Series (Oxford: Oxford University Press, 2000).

—— 'How Culpability Can and Cannot be Denied in Under-Age Sex Crimes' [2001] *Criminal Law Review* 15.

—— 'Criminal Law and Legal Positivism' (2002) 8 *Legal Theory* 221.

—— 'Strict Liability, Statutory Construction and the Spirit of Liberty' (2002) 118 *Law Quarterly Review* 458.

—— 'Killing the Passive Abuser: A Theoretical Defence', in Shute, Stephen, and Simester, A. P. (eds.), *Criminal Law Theory: Doctrines of the General Part* (Oxford: Oxford University Press, 2002).

—— 'Criminal Law', in Cane, Peter, and Tushnet, Mark (eds.), *The Oxford Handbook of Criminal Law* (Oxford: Oxford University Press, 2003).

—— 'Reshaping the Factual Element in the Provocation Defence' (2005) 25 *Oxford Journal of Legal Studies* (forthcoming, issue 1).

Hornsby, Jennifer, 'On What's Intentionally Done', in Shute, Stephen, Gardner, John, and Horder, Jeremy (eds.), *Action and Value in Criminal Law* (Oxford: Clarendon Press, 1993).

Howard, M. N., 'The Neutral Expert: a Plausible Threat to Justice' [1991] *Criminal Law Review* 98.

Hume, David, *A Treatise of Human Nature* (1739–40), Selby-Bigge, L. A. (ed.), (Oxford: Clarendon Press, 1888).

Hurd, Heidi, 'Justification and Excuse, Wrongdoing and Culpability' (1999) 54 *Notre Dame Law Review* 1551.

Husak, Douglas, 'The Serial View of Criminal Law Defences' (1992) 3 *Criminal Law Forum* 369.

—— 'Partial Defenses' (1998) 11 *Canadian Journal of Law and Jurisprudence* 167.

—— and Von Hirsch, Andrew, 'Culpability and Mistake of Law', in Shute, Stephen, Gardner, John, and Horder, Jeremy (eds.), *Action and Value in Criminal Law* (Oxford: Clarendon Press, 1993).

Irwin, T. H., 'Reason and Responsibility in Aristotle', in Rorty, A. O. (ed.), *Essays on Aristotle's Ethics* (California: University of California Press, 1980).

Jackson, B., '*Storkwain*: a Case-Study in Strict Liability and Self-Regulation' [1991] *Criminal Law Review* 892.

Jackson, R. M., 'Absolute Prohibition in Statutory Offences', in Radzinowicz, Sir L., and Turner, J. W. C. (eds.), *The Modern Approach to Criminal Law* (London: McMillan & Co, 1945).

Kadish, Sanford H., 'Excusing Crime' (1987) 75 *California Law Review* 257.

Kant, I., *Metaphysics of Morals*, Gregor, Mary (trans.), (Cambridge: Cambridge University Press, 1991).

Kenny, A., 'Can Responsibility be Diminished?', in Frey, R. G., and Morris, C. W. (eds.) *Liability and Responsibility: Essays in Law and Morals* (Cambridge: Cambridge University Press, 1991).

Kenny, Sir C. S., *Outcomes of Criminal Law*, 14th edn. (Cambridge: Cambridge University Press, 1929).

Keown, J., *Abortion, Doctors and the Law* (Cambridge: Cambridge University Press, 1988).

King, P., 'Decision-Makers and Decision-Making in the English Criminal Law, 1750–1800' (1984) 27 *Historical Journal* 25.

Klimchuk, Dennis, 'Necessity, Deterrence and Standing' (2002) 8 *Legal Theory* 339.

Lacey, Nicola, *State Punishment: Political Principles and Community Values* (London: Routledge, 1988).

—— 'Partial Excuses to Homicide: Questions of Power and Principle in Imperfect and Less than Perfect Worlds . . .', in Ashworth, Andrew, and Mitchell, Barry (eds.), *Rethinking English Homicide Law* (Oxford: Oxford University Press, 2000).

—— Wells, Celia, and Quick, Oliver, *Reconstructing Criminal law: Text and Materials*, 3rd edn., (London: Butterworths, 2003).

Lambert, Roysten, 'A Victorian National Health Service: State Vaccination, 1855–71' (1962) 5 *Historical Journal* 1.

Lamond, Grant, 'Coercion, Threats, and the Puzzle of Blackmail', in Simester, A. P., and Smith, A. T. H. (eds.), *Harm and Culpability* (Oxford: Oxford University Press, 1996).

Law Commission for England and Wales, *A Criminal Code for England and Wales*, Law Com no. 177, (1989), clause 58.

—— *Legislating the Criminal Code, Offences Against the Person and General Principles*, Law Commission Consultation Paper No. 218, Cm 2370 (HMSO, 1993).

—— *Consent in the Criminal Law*, Law Commission Consultation Paper No. 139 (HMSO, 1995).

—— *Legislating the Criminal Code: Involuntary Manslaughter*, Law Commission Consultation Paper No. 237 (HMSO, 1996).

—— *Partial Defences to Murder*, Law Commission Consultation Paper No. 173 (HMSO, 2003).

—— *A New Homicide Act for England and Wales?*, Law Commission Consultation Paper No. 177 (2005).

—— *Murder, Manslaughter and Infanticide*, Lam Com no. 304 (2006).

LeDoux, Joseph, *The Emotional Brain: the Mysterious Underpinnings of Emotional Life* (New York: Simon and Schuster, 1996).

Leigh, L. H., 'A Philosophy of Provocation?' (1993) 56 *Modern Law Review* 600.

Mackay, R. D., 'Pleading Provocation and Diminished Responsibility Together' [1988] *Criminal Law Review* 411.

—— *Mental Condition Defences in the Criminal Law* (Oxford: Oxford University Press, 1995).

—— 'The Abnormality of Mind Factor in Diminished Responsibility' [1999] *Criminal Law Review* 117.

—— 'Diminished Responsibility and Mentally Disordered Killers', in Ashworth, Andrew and Mitchell, Barry (eds.), *Rethinking English Homicide Law* (Oxford: Oxford University Press, 2000).

—— 'Mentally Abnormal Offenders: Disposal and Criminal Responsibility Issues', in McConville, Mike, and Wilson, Geoffrey (eds.), *The Handbook of the Criminal Justice Process* (Oxford: Oxford University Press, 2002).

Mackay, R. D., and Mitchell, B. J., 'Provoking Diminished Responsibility: Two Pleas Merging into One?' [2003] *Criminal Law Review* 745.

Maguire, M., Morgan, R., and Reiner, R. (eds.), *The Oxford Handbook of Criminology*, 3rd edn. (Oxford: Oxford University Press, 2002).

McColgan, Aileen, 'In Defence of Battered Women Who Kill' (1993) 13 *Oxford Journal of Legal Studies* 508.

Miller, David, *Principles of Social Justice* (Cambridge, Mass.: Harvard University Press, 1999).

Montgomery, Jonathan, 'Healthcare Law for a Multi-Faith Society', in Murphy, J. (ed.), *Ethnic Minorities, their Families and the Law* (Oxford: Hart Publishing, 2000).

—— *Health Care Law*, 2nd edn. (Oxford: Oxford University Press, 2003).

Moore, Michael, S., *Law and Psychiatry: Rethinking the Relationship* (Cambridge: Cambridge University Press, 1984).

—— 'Choice, Character and Excuse' (1990) 7 *Social Policy and Philosophy* 29.

—— *Placing Blame* (Oxford: Clarendon Press, 1998).

Moran, Mayo, *Rethinking the Reasonable Person* (Oxford: Oxford University Press, 2003).

Morgan, J., 'Provocation Law and Facts: Dead Women Tell No Tales, Tales are Told About Them' (1997) 21 *Melbourne University Law Review* 237.

Morley, John, *Life of Gladstone* (London: Greenwood Press, 1971).

Morris, Norval, and Howard, Colin, *Studies in Criminal Law* (Oxford: Clarendon Press, 1964).

Morris, N., 'The Criminal Responsibility of the Mentally Ill' (1982) 33 *Syracuse Law Review* 477.

Morrison, W. D., *Juvenile Offenders* (New York: D. Appleton & Co, 1897).

Morse, Stephen J., 'Diminished Capacity', in Shute, Stephen, Gardner, John, and Horder, Jeremy (eds.), *Action and Value in Criminal Law* (Oxford: Clarendon Press, 1993).

—— 'Culpability and Control' (1994) 142 *University of Pennsylvania Law Review* 1587.

—— 'Excusing and the New Excuse Defences: A Legal and Conceptual Review' (1998) 23 *Crime and Justice* 329.

Murphy, J. (ed.), *Ethnic Minorities, their Families and the Law* (Oxford: Hart Publishing, 2000).

Nagel, Thomas, *The View From Nowhere* (Oxford: Oxford University Press, 1986).

Norrie, A., ' "Simulacra of Morality"? Beyond the Ideal/Actual Antimonies of Criminal Justice', in Duff, R. A. (ed.), *Philosophy and the Criminal Law: Principle and Critique* (Cambridge: Cambridge University Press, 1998).

—— *Punishment, Responsibility and Justice: A Relational Critique* (Oxford: Oxford University Press, 2000).

—— *Crime, Reason and History: A Critical Introduction to Criminal Law*, 2nd edn. (London: Butterworths, 2001).

—— 'From Criminal Law to Legal Theory: The Mysterious Case of the Reasonable Glue-Sniffer', (2002) 62 *Modern Law Review* 538.

Nozick, R., *Philosophical Explanations* (Cambridge, Mass.: Harvard University Press, 1981).

Nwabueze, B. O., *Constitutional Law of the Nigerian Republic* (London: Butterworths, 1964).

Parfit, Derek, *Reasons and Persons* (Oxford: Oxford University Press, 1984).

Pashukanis, E. B., *The General Theory of Law and Marxism*, Babb, Hugh W. (trans.), (Cambridge, Mass.: Harvard University Press, 1951).

Pearce, F., and Tombs, S., 'Ideology, Hegemony and Empiricism' (1990) 30 *British Journal of Criminology* 423.

—— and —— 'Hazards, Law and Class: Contextualising the Regulation of Corporate Crime' (1997) 6 *Social and Legal Studies* 79.

Peay, J., 'Mentally Disordered Offenders, Mental Health and Crime', in Maguire, Mike, Morgan, Rod, and Reiner, Robert (eds.), *The Oxford Handbook of Criminology*, 3rd edn. (Oxford: Oxford University Press, 2002).

Postema, Gerald, *Bentham and the Common Law Tradition* (Oxford: Clarendon Press, 1986).

—— 'Classical Common Law Jurisprudence (Part II)' (2003) 3 *Oxford Journal of Commonwealth Law* 1.

Poulter, S. M., *English Law and Ethnic Minority Customs* (London: Butterworths, 1986).

Power, Helen, 'Towards a Redefinition of the *Mens Rea* of Rape' (2003) 23 *Oxford Journal of Legal Studies* 379.

Radzinowicz, Sir L., *A History of the English Criminal Law: The Movement for Reform* (London: Stevens & Sons, 1948).

—— and Turner, J. W. C. (eds.), *The Modern Approach to Criminal Law* (London: McMillan & Co, 1945).

—— and Hood, Roger, *The Emergence of Penal Policy in Victorian and Edwardian England* (Oxford: Clarendon Press, 1990).

Raz, Joseph, *The Authority of Law* (Oxford: Clarendon Press, 1979).

—— 'Right-Based Moralities', in Waldron, Jeremy (ed.), *Theories of Rights* (Oxford: Oxford University Press, 1984).

—— 'Autonomy, Toleration and the Harm Principle', in Gavison, Ruth (ed.), *Issues in Contemporary Legal Philosophy* (Oxford: Clarendon Press, 1987).

—— *Practical Reason and Norms* (Oxford: Oxford University Press, 1990).

—— *Ethics in the Public Domain* (Oxford: Clarendon Press, 1994).

—— *Engaging Reason* (Oxford: Oxford University Press, 1999).

Restack, R., 'Rapid Response', *New York Times*, 5 November 1996.

Robinson, Paul, H., *Structure and Function in Criminal Law* (Oxford: Clarendon Press, 1997).

—— Cahill, M., and Mohammed, U., 'The Five Worst (and Five Best) American Criminal Codes' (2000) 94 *Northwestern University Law Review* 17.

Rogers, Jonathan, 'Justifying the Use of Firearms by Policemen and Soldiers: a Response to the Home Office's Review of the Law on the Use of Lethal Force' (1998) 18 *Legal Studies* 486.

—— 'Necessity, Private Defence and the Killing of Mary' [2001] *Criminal Law Review* 515.

Ruggiero, Vincenzo, *Crime and Markets: Essays in Anti-Criminology* (Oxford: Oxford University Press, 2000).

Saunders, T. J., *Plato's Penal Code* (Oxford: Clarendon Press, 1991).

Schneider, E., 'Equal Rights to Trial for Women: Sex Bias in the Law of Self-Defense' (1980) 15 *Harvard Civil Rights–Civil Liberties Law Review* 623.

Schofield, P., and Harris, J., ' "Legislator of the World": Writings on Codification, Law and Education', in Schofield, P., and Harris, J., *The Collected Works of Jeremy Bentham* (Oxford: Oxford University Press, 1998).

Schopp, Robert F., *Justification Defences and Just Convictions* (Cambridge: Cambridge University Press, 1998).

—— Sturgis, Barbara J., and Sullivan, Megan, 'Battered Women Syndrome, Expert Testimony and the Distinction Between Justification and Excuse' (1994) *University of Illinois Law Review* 45.

Sentencing Advisory Panel, 'Manslaughter by Reason of Provocation' (Consultation Paper, 2004), www.sentencing-advisory-panel.gov.uk.

Shute, Stephen, 'Something Old, Something New, Something Borrowed: Three Aspects of the Project' [1996] *Criminal Law Review* 684.

—— 'Appropriation and the Law of Theft' [2002] *Criminal Law Review* 445.

—— Gardner, John, and Horder, Jeremy (eds.) *Action and Value in Criminal Law* (Oxford: Clarendon Press, 1993).

Simester, A. P., 'Mistakes in Defence' (1992) 12 *Oxford Journal of Legal Studies* 295.

—— 'Can Negligence be Culpable?', in Horder, Jeremy (ed.), *Oxford Essays in Jurisprudence*, 4th Series. (Oxford: Oxford University Press, 2000).

—— and Sullivan, G. R., *Criminal Law: Theory and Doctrine*, 1st edn. (Oxford: Hart Publishing, 2000).

Simmonds, Nigel, 'Judgment and Mercy' (1993) *Oxford Journal of Legal Studies* 52.

Slater, A. J., 'In Defence of a Capacity-Based Theory of Criminal Culpability', Ph.D. (University of Birmingham, 2003).

Smith, A. T. H., 'Judicial Law-Making in the Criminal Law' (1984) 100 *Law Quarterly Review* 46.

Smith, David J., 'Crime and the Life Course', in Maguire, M., Morgan, R., and Reiner, R. (eds.), *The Oxford Handbook of Criminology*, 3rd edn. (Oxford: Oxford University Press, 2002).

Smith, Sir J. C., *Justification and Excuse in Criminal Law* (London: Sweet and Maxwell, 1989).

—— 'Individual Incapacities and Criminal Liability' (1998) *Medical Law Review* 138.

—— and Hogan, Brian, *Criminal Law*, 10th edn. (London: Butterworths, 2002).

Smith, K. J. M., 'Must Heroes Behave Heroically?' [1989] *Criminal Law Review* 622.

—— *Lawyers, Legislators and Theorists: Developments in English Criminal Jurisprudence 1800–1957* (Oxford: Clarendon Press, 1998).

—— 'Duress and Steadfastness: In Pursuit of the Unintelligible' [1999] *Criminal Law Review* 363.

—— and Wilson, William, 'Impaired Voluntariness and Criminal Responsibility: Reworking Hart's Theory of Excuses—The English Judicial Response' (1993) 13 *Oxford Journal of Legal Studies* 69.

Smith, Michael, 'Responsibility and Self-Control', in Cane, Peter, and Gardner, John (eds.), *Relating to Responsibility: Essays for Tony Honoré* (Oxford: Hart Publishing, 2001).

Sparks, R. F., 'Diminished Responsibility in Theory and Practice' (1964) 27 *Modern Law Review* 9.

Spencer, J. R., 'The Neutral Expert: an Implausible Bogey' [1991] *Criminal Law Review* 106.

Stallybrass, W. T. S., 'A Comparison of the General Principles of Criminal Law with the "Progetto Definitivo di un Nuovo Codice Penale" of Alfredo Rocco', in Radzinowicz, Sir L., and Turner, J. W. C. (eds.), *The Modern Approach to Criminal Law* (London: McMillan & Co, 1945).

Stephen, Sir J. F., *A History of the Criminal Law of England* (London: Macmillan & Co, 1883).

Strawson, Sir P. F., 'Freedom and Resentment', in Watson, Gary (ed.), *Free Will* (Oxford: Oxford University Press, 1982).

Stuart, Hamish, 'The Role of Reasonableness in Self-Defence' (2003) 16 *Canadian Journal of Law and Jurisprudence* 317.

Sullivan, G. R., 'Anger and Excuse: Reassessing Provocation' (1992) 12 *Oxford Journal of Legal Studies* 380.

—— 'Intoxicants and Diminished Responsibility' [1994] *Criminal Law Review* 156.

—— 'Making Excuses', in Simester, A. P. and Smith, A. T. H. (eds.), *Harm and Culpability* (Oxford: Oxford University Press, 1996).

Tadros, Victor, 'Practical Reasoning and Intentional Action' (2000) 20 *Legal Studies* 104.

—— 'The Characters of Excuses' (2001) 21 *Oxford Journal of Legal Studies* 495.

Tapper, Colin, *Cross and Tapper on Evidence*, 9th edn. (London: Butterworths, 1999).

Taylor, A. J. P., *England 1914–1945* (Oxford: Clarendon Press, 1965).

Thorne, S. E., and Baker, J. H., (eds.) *Readings and Moots at the Inns of Court in the Fifteenth Century* (London: Selden Society, 1990).

Tur, R. H. S., 'The Doctor's Defence and Professional Ethics' (2002) 13 *King's College Law Journal* 75.

Turner, J. W. C. (ed.), *Kenny's Outlines of Criminal Law*, 16th edn. (Cambridge: Cambridge University Press, 1952).

Uniacke, Suzanne, 'What are Partial Excuses to Murder?', in Yeo, S. M. H. (ed.), *Partial Excuses to Murder* (New South Wales: Federation Press, 1991).

—— *Permissible Killing: The Self-Defence Justification for Homicide* (Cambridge: Cambridge University Press, 1994).

Urmson, J. O., *Aristotle's Ethics* (Oxford: Basil Blackwell, 1988).

Victorian Law Reform Commission, *Defences to Homicide (Options Paper)* (Melbourne, Victoria: Victorian Law Commission, 2003).

Wasik, Martin, 'Partial Excuses in the Criminal Law' (1982) 45 *Modern Law Review* 516.

Weiner, M., *Reconstructing the Criminal: Culture, Law and Policy in England 1830–1914* (Cambridge: Cambridge University Press, 1990).

Wells, Celia, 'Provocation: The Case for Abolition' in Ashworth, Andrew, and Mitchell, Barry (eds.), *Rethinking English Homicide Law* (Oxford: Oxford University Press, 2000).

—— *Corporations and Criminal Responsibility*, 2nd edn. (Oxford: Oxford University Press, 2001).

Williams, D. G. T., 'The Donoughmore Report in Retrospect' (1982) 60 *Public Administration* 273.

Williams, Glanville, *The Sanctity of Life and the Criminal Law* (London: Faber & Faber, 1958).

—— *Criminal Law: The General Part* (London: Stevens, 1961).

—— *Textbook of Criminal Law*, 2nd edn. (London: Stevens, 1983).

Wilson, William, *Central Issues in Criminal Theory* (Oxford: Hart Publishing, 2002).

—— *Criminal Law: Doctrine and Theory*, 2nd edn. (Harlow: Longman, 2003).

Wright, Sidney, *The Law of Landed Estates* (London: Frank P. Wilson, 1897).

Yeo, S. M. H., 'Power and Self-Control in Provocation and Automatism' (1992) 14 *Sydney Law Review* 3.

—— *Unrestrained Killings and the Law* (Hong Kong: Oxford University Press, 1998).

Young, Jock, 'Crime and Social Exclusion', in Maguire, Mike, Morgan, Rod, and Reiner, Robert (eds.), *The Oxford Handbook of Criminology*, 3rd edn. (Oxford: Oxford University Press, 2002), 457.

Zillmann, Dolf, 'Our Unique Motives for Violence Sit Beside Archaic Animal Drives for Aggression', *Times Higher Educational Supplement* (no 1533), 12 April 2002.

Index of Authors

General Index

UNIVERSITY OF WINCHESTER
LIBRARY